CISO: Evolution of a Vocation

CISO: Evolution of a Vocation comprises three levels. The first level shares the author's personal journey, beginning as a homeless college dropout and culminating in over thirty years of service as a CISO and in CISO-equivalent roles at some of America's most iconic companies and organizations. Drawing on experience and discipline gained from military contracting work, the author maintained a letter log system to manage the commitments and document the issues he faced. He also kept digital copies of over 1,000 memorandums issued during his later CISO roles. Through excerpts from selected memos, readers gain an unprecedented view into the cybersecurity challenges he confronted as CISO. Each chapter includes "Lessons Learned," providing readers with the benefits of the author's life lessons and cybersecurity experiences. Where warranted, the author recognizes his "All Star" team members whom he had the privilege of working with.

In addition to his personal journey, this book explores the history of major technology advancements and significant security events occurring from 1971 to 2017. This provides valuable context for understanding how the landscape of cybersecurity has evolved over the decades. Building on these experiences, this book examines the evolution of the CISO role itself. Readers follow the progression from the role's early inception to its current status as a true business leadership position. Each level makes this book accessible and engaging for both general readers and professionals.

From his humble beginnings as a homeless college dropout, **Ron Baklarz** went on to become an "overnight success" after sixteen years of night school. He spent thirty years in leading cybersecurity roles at iconic organizations such as the Naval Nuclear Program, the U.S. House of Representatives, and the American Red Cross. Along the way, he pursued professional certifications and received numerous awards that recognized his achievements in building "first of a kind" cybersecurity programs, often with limited resources and budgets. Baklarz holds an M.S. degree in Information Science and a Certificate of Advanced Study in Telecommunications, both from the University of Pittsburgh. He has also earned professional certifications in cyber forensics, CISSP, CISA, CISM, C|CISO, and the National Security Agency's NSA-IAM and NSA-IEM certifications.

Security, Audit and Leadership Series

Series Editor: Dan Swanson, Dan Swanson and Associates, Ltd.,
Winnipeg, Manitoba, Canada

The scope and mandate for internal audit continue to evolve each year, as does the complexity of the business environment and speed of the changing risk landscape in which it must operate. The fundamental goal of this exciting series is to produce leading-edge books on critical subjects facing security and audit executives and practitioners. Key topics addressed include Leadership, Cybersecurity, Security Leadership, Privacy, Strategic Risk Management, Auditing IT, Audit Management and Leadership, and Operational Auditing.

Audit Alchemy
Small Teams, BIG Impact – A Guide to Internal Audit Excellence
By Sandeep Das

Modern Benford's Law
State of the Art Techniques for Audit and Compliance Professionals
By Daniel J. McCarville

Cumulative Effect
Cyber Security Guide for Directors and CEOs
By Dr Vladas Leonas

Digital Momentum
Building Real Change-Ready Enterprises
By Brice Ominski

Redefining Auditing in the Digital Era
Global Perspectives on Technology, Security, and Leadership
Edited by Abdelmounim Bouziane

Fire Brigades to Firewalls
A Public Safety Guide to Cybersecurity
By John Kuforiji

Bridging the Gap
Strengthening the Bond between Audit Committee and Internal Audit
By Denise Cicchella

CISO: Evolution of a Vocation
Confessions of a Recovering CISO
By Ron Baklarz

CISO: Evolution of a Vocation

Confessions of a Recovering CISO

Ron Baklarz

CRC Press
Taylor & Francis Group
Boca Raton London New York

CRC Press is an imprint of the
Taylor & Francis Group, an **informa** business

Designed cover image: Shutterstock ID: 2016127844

First edition published 2026
by CRC Press
2385 NW Executive Center Drive, Suite 320, Boca Raton FL 33431

and by CRC Press
4 Park Square, Milton Park, Abingdon, Oxon, OX14 4RN

CRC Press is an imprint of Taylor & Francis Group, LLC

Library of Congress Cataloging-in-Publication Data
Names: Baklarz, Ron author
Title: CISO : evolution of a vocation : confessions of a recovering CISO / Ron Baklarz.
Description: First edition. | Boca Raton : CRC Press, 2026. |
Series: Security, audit and leadership series | Includes bibliographical
references and index. |
Identifiers: LCCN 2026002433 (print) | LCCN 2026002434 (ebook) | ISBN 9781041095460 hbk | ISBN 9781041095477 pbk | ISBN 9781003650645 ebk
Subjects: LCSH: Baklarz, Ron | Chief information officers—United States | Computer security—Management | Business—Data processing—Security measures | Information technology—Management | LCGFT: Autobiographies | Biographies
Classification: LCC HF5548.37 .B34 2026 (print) | LCC HF5548.37 (ebook)
LC record available at https://lccn.loc.gov/2026002433
LC ebook record available at https://lccn.loc.gov/2026002434

ISBN: 9781041095460 (hbk)
ISBN: 9781041095477 (pbk)
ISBN: 9781003650645 (ebk)

DOI: 10.1201/9781003650645

Typeset in Sabon
by codeMantra

To Bub and Teddy so you know about PapRon's
career and accomplishments.

And to all the men and women who dedicate their lives to the security of networks, systems, and data under their protection.

Contents

Foreword xiii
Introduction xv
List of Abbreviations and Acronyms xix

PART I
Foundations 1

1 Humble Beginnings 2

1.1 EPIC Metals 1971–1976 2
1.2 Elliott Company 1977–1981 4

PART II
Learning Curve – Early CISO Positions 11

2 Westinghouse Plant Apparatus Division 1982–1996 13

2.1 Westinghouse Plant Apparatus Division (WPAD) – Overview 13
2.2 Field Change Analyst (FCA) 1982–1986 14
2.3 Standard Logistics (SL) 16
2.4 Master's Degree and Certificate of Advanced Studies (Telecommunications) 17
2.5 Office Automation 18
2.6 Personal Computers 19
2.7 Computer Security Site Manager 1986–1996 20
2.8 Personal Computers 21
2.9 TEMPEST (Codename) 22
2.10 Computer Viruses 24
2.11 IBM Versus Apple 26

2.12 *Quality Circles* 26
2.13 *Local Area Network (LAN)* 27
2.14 *Physical Security Measures* 29
2.15 *COMSEC Custodian* 31
2.16 *Manager, Personal Computer, Local Area Network, and Security 1990–1992* 31
2.17 *Manager, Logistics Systems Programming 1992–1996* 32
2.18 *Naval Reactors – Secure Remote Area Network* 32
2.19 *CD-ROM* 39
2.20 *Onto the Next Adventure* 39
2.21 *All Stars – WPAD* 40
2.22 *Technology Advancements and Security Developments 1982–1996* 41

3 United States House of Representatives 1996–1997 47

3.1 *U.S. House of Representatives – Overview* 47
3.2 *Interview and Arrival* 47
3.3 *Political Landscape* 53
3.4 *FBI Email Investigation* 54
3.5 *Telephone Hack* 55
3.6 *Mainframe Test Data* 56
3.7 *The Rogue Information Technology Manager* 57
3.8 *Network Security* 58
3.9 *House Computing Environment* 59
3.10 *The Audits Continue* 59
3.11 *HISPOLs and HISPUBs* 60
3.12 *Top Secret Security Clearances* 63
3.13 *President Clinton and the White House Visitor Logs* 63
3.14 *Forum of Incident Response and Security Teams* 65
3.15 *Security Administrator Tool for Analyzing Networks* 65
3.16 *Other Cybersecurity Items* 66
3.17 *Info World September 29, 1997* 69
3.18 *Y2K* 71
3.19 *Departure* 71
3.20 *All-Stars – U.S. House of Representatives* 72

3.21 Technology Advancements and Security Developments 1997 73

4 Ernst & Young, LLP Washington DC 1998 75

4.1 Ernst & Young, LLP – Overview 75
4.2 Gallows Road, Virginia 75
4.3 Veteran's Administration 76
4.4 Banking Work 79
4.5 Manufacturing Work 79
4.6 Y2K 80
4.7 Time to Go 80
4.8 Technology Advancements and Security Developments 1998 81

5 Prudential Insurance Company of America 1998–2000 82

5.1 Prudential – Overview 82
5.2 Y2K 83
5.3 Internet Security Systems (ISS) 83
5.4 Educational Opportunities 83
5.5 Prudential Computer Emergency Response Team (PruCERT) 85
5.6 Security Operations Control Center (SOCC) 85
5.7 January 1, 2000 86
5.8 Time to Go 86
5.9 Technology Advancements and Security Developments 1999–2000 87

6 Counterpane Internet Security 2000–2001 89

6.1 Counterpane Internet Security – Overview 89
6.2 And So It Begins 90
6.3 Virginia SOC 92
6.4 Competition 92
6.5 Enough Already 93
6.6 Technology Advancements and Security Developments 2001 93

PART III
The Complete CISO – Putting Experience into Practice 95

7 American Red Cross 2001–2005 97

7.1 The American Red Cross (ARC) – Overview 97
7.2 Organizational Culture and Complexity 98
7.3 Management Turnover 100
7.4 Context – Red Cross and Food and Drug Administration Consent Decrees 101
7.5 Getting Started – "Hands-On" CISO 101
7.6 Memos and Issues – March 2001–December 2001 103
7.7 Memos and Issues – January 2002–December 2002 119
7.8 Memos and Issues – January 2003–December 2003 127
7.9 Memos and Issues – January 2004–December 2004 134
7.10 Memos and Issues – January 2005–October 2005 145
7.11 University of Virginia (UVA) 153
7.12 CISA and CISM 153
7.13 All-Stars – American Red Cross 153
7.14 Technology Enhancements and Security Developments 2002–2005 154

8 MedStar Health 2006–2008 157

8.1 MedStar Health – Overview and Culture 157
8.2 Memos and Issues – July 2006–December 2006 159
8.3 Memos and Issues – January 2007–December 2007 166
8.4 Memos and Issues – January 2008–May 2008 176
8.5 Time to Go 180
8.6 All Star – MedStar Health 181
8.7 Technology Advancements and Security Developments 2006–2008 182

9 The National Passenger Railroad – Amtrak 2008–2017 184

9.1 Amtrak – Overview 184
9.2 Payment Card Industry – Data Security Standard (PCI-DSS) 185
9.3 Shadow IT (Information Technology) 186
9.4 Association of American Railroads Rail Industry Security Committee 187
9.5 Memos and Issues – May 2008–December 2008 187
9.6 Memos and Issues – January 2009–December 2009 190

9.7 *Memos and Issues – January 2010–December 2010* 193
9.8 *Memos and Issues – January 2011–December 2011* 196
9.9 *Memos and Issues – January 2012–December 2012* 207
9.10 *Memos and Issues – January 2013–December 2013* 211
9.11 *Memos and Issues – January 2014–December 2014* 221
9.12 *Memos and Issues – January 2015–December 2015* 228
9.13 *Memos and Issues – January 2016–December 2016* 237
9.14 *FY 16 Putting It All Together* 246
9.15 *FBI CISO Academy* 250
9.16 *Retirement* 251
9.17 *All-Stars Amtrak* 252
9.18 *Technology Advancements and Security Developments 2008–2017* 254

10 CISO: Evolution of a Vocation 258

10.1 *The Early Years (1950–1970)* 258
10.2 *Middle Years (1970–2000)* 260
10.3 *Later Years (2000–Present)* 264
10.4 *The Future – Cybersecurity and the CISO* 267

Appendices 275
Appendix A – IS Audit and Control Journal 275
Appendix B – Prudential's First Quarter 1999 Business Value Award (BVA) 280
Appendix C – Sample Customer Service Advisory 282
Medium-Level Advisory from Ron Baklarz, Chief Information Security Officer 282
Technical Details 282
Appendix D – Amtrak National Network 284
Appendix E – Perspective Security Analyst Questionnaire 285
Memo 285
Appendix F – EC Council Press Release Dated October 16, 2013 Reprinted With Permission of EC Council 292
Index 295

Foreword

When Ron Baklarz invited me to pen the foreword to his book, my first reaction was one of genuine professional and personal humility. After all, it's not often that one receives such a request from their first boss in the industry – but I was thrilled to reconnect with him after nearly thirty years.

CISO: Evolution of a Vocation effectively chronicles the cybersecurity industry since the 1990s in what we might call the First Generation of Cybersecurity. Back then, often with limited resources and support, we struggled to provide for the confidentiality, integrity, and availability of information and information resources in a world that was very quickly transforming into a global networked society. From enterprise workflows to interpersonal communications and how business and the world communicated and functioned, entire paradigms shifted practically overnight and digital security quickly became a major concern. People like Ron, as part of the then-fledgling cybersecurity community, were right there, establishing the foundation for what now are considered best practices in our profession.

But much more than simply telling his life story, Ron shares with readers what a cybersecurity leader will encounter in the job across a range of industry sectors. Through numerous and highly detailed examples of incidents, situations, and events throughout his career, Ron paints a very accurate picture of cybersecurity life: the good, the bad, the annoying, and the frustrating. Even the mundane everyday administrivia of the cybersecurity bureaucracy doesn't escape Ron's attention.

Perhaps most importantly, Ron repeatedly emphasizes the need for teamwork in cybersecurity. Time and again, he reflects on his various teams over the years. In doing so, he reinforces that effective cybersecurity operations depend on not just talent and technology but collaboration and the ability to work (and communicate!) across levels of bureaucracy, audiences, and expertise while recognizing one's own limitations and seeking outside expertise when needed. After all, knowing your limitations is just as important as knowing what you know.

Ron's conversational style really allows you to hear his voice throughout this narrative. Those of us who know him and/or were there alongside him might also hear his occasional (and often knowing) chuckle as he recounts the bureaucratic and political intricacies of his experiences, too. But that's typical Ron .... He's not just a hard-charging cybersecurity person, but an astute reader of books, people, process, politics, and situations. That level of insight isn't gained from certification or training programs alone but through an inquisitive mind, being an effective communicator and having the ability to incorporate lessons from a wide range of other fields toward solving a given cybersecurity problem. In other words, in many cases, just being a good geek no longer is enough!

In preparing this foreword, I reflected on how often I emulated Ron's detail-oriented management style and innovative cybersecurity thinking in my own career – especially as the CSO for the company that ran Internet DNS for many years. Like Ron, I also have many examples I could talk about but will simply say that those of us who worked with Ron are fortunate to have him as a mentor. He is an example to emulate in our own careers.

Sadly, "plus ça change, plus c'est la même chose" – "the more things change, the more they stay the same." Many of the things that Ron experienced throughout his career still plague our industry today. As such, I'm sure readers of all experiences in cybersecurity will not only find some solace in Ron's words but several nuggets of wisdom that can enhance their own cybersecurity careers as well.

Richard F. Forno, Ph.D.
Arlington, VA
July 2025

Introduction

> The "10,000-hour rule" asserts that the key to achieving true expertise in any skill is simply a matter of practicing, albeit in the correct way, for at least 10,000 hours.
>
> *Outliers: The Story of Success* by Malcolm Gladwell

I have heard the abbreviated version of the title, Chief Information Security Officer (CISO), referred to as, "See-So," "Sizz-Oh" or simply spelled out "C-I-S-O." The confusion as to how to articulate the title speaks directly to the conundrum of effectively executing the office. The CISO position has gone through an evolutionary process in direct correlation with the advancements in computing, networking technologies, and cybersecurity events.

According to the Indeed Career Guide, there are roughly 2,087 average work hours in a calendar year.[1] In the context of Mr. Gladwell's "10,000-hour rule," it would take roughly five years to become an expert CISO. I am not convinced one can become an expert CISO in five years, but *your mileage may vary.* Also, we have to consider by what measure is one deemed to be an expert. The approach I believe CISOs should take is to consider ourselves as students, learning and refining our craft every day.

This is not a "how to" book but rather a look into the CISO role – past, present, and future. It covers cybersecurity from three perspectives. First, I write about my personal, forty-year journey from a homeless, college dropout/factory laborer to holding CISO roles with responsibility for securing some of the most iconic American industries and organizations. Second, we explore the evolution of the CISO role itself. And lastly, we take a historical look at the advancements in technology and the major cybersecurity events occurring over the years.

I did not specifically choose information security as a vocation but rather it chose me. I was fortunate to serve in Information Technology (IT) management and CISO roles for some of the most iconic and diverse groups of American companies and organizations. As you will see, a common theme in most of my CISO roles was that I never had sufficient budget and resources to adequately build what some would consider a world-class cybersecurity program. So, I had to develop *security-on-a-shoestring* strategies in developing my programs. These issues will be discussed in each section. Many of the lessons that were applicable then are still valid today. *Chiefly, security has and always will be a function of People, Process, and Technology.*

Three major sections define my professional evolution and maturation processes:

Part I – Chapter 1 – Humble Beginnings. At the start to my working career, I was a homeless college dropout. My early work experiences at EPIC Metals and Elliott Company were critical to developing a solid work ethic, personal motivation, management skills, and desire to pursue work in the computer field. During this time, I grew to appreciate the need for the academic degrees necessary to enhance my credibility and advancement opportunities.

Part II – Chapters 2 to 6. Learning Curve – Early CISO Positions. I began my cybersecurity career in 1986 as a Computer Security Site Manager (CSSM) at the Westinghouse Plant Apparatus Division. At this time, the CISO role did not exist. Following ten years as CSSM, I was hired as the first security manager at the United States House of Representatives in 1997. In this position, I gained foundational cybersecurity experience developing policies and working within formal frameworks such as audit findings and industry standards. Next, I worked at Ernst & Young, LLC where I expanded my knowledge base to include system and network attack and penetration expertise. These skills would be used in my subsequent CISO positions. At Prudential Insurance Company of America, I took advantage of their generous educational opportunities and gained expertise in building my first Secure Operations Center (SOCs). Finally, at Counterpane Internet Security, I furthered my knowledge of SOC operations including staffing, policies, and procedures. These sixteen years of my personal cybersecurity journey represent 33,392 hours of Malcolm Gladwell's 10,000-hour rule.

Part III – Chapters 7 to 9. The Complete CISO – Putting Experience into Practice – I drew from all my previous experiences and knowledge and applied them to the benefit of the organizations in which I served. During my last three positions at the American Red Cross, MedStar Health, and Amtrak, I had established a letter log system that serialized and captured 982 memorandums I issued over those years. Knowing I might one day write about my experiences, I saved digital copies of most of those memos. In these chapters, the stories are told through these memos to give readers a front row view into the day-to-day issues I faced as the CISO. *In cases where the memo is marked as Confidential (C), no Confidential information is actually exposed in this book. Rather, the memo has either been sanitized or due to time and technical obsolescence has rendered the memo descriptions as Unclassified.* Since I held government security clearances while working in the Naval Nuclear Program and at the United States House of Representatives, I submitted these chapters for Department of Defense – Defense Office of Prepublication and Security Review (DOPSR).

Additionally, I will provide *Lessons Learned* throughout each chapter to provide insights about what I learned from these experiences. Where appropriate, I will identify my *All Star Team* members whom I had the privilege to work with. All were standouts in their previous and current security roles. And lastly, I will provide a historical look at the major security, computer, and network technology events and advancements that coincide with the section's years focusing primarily on IBM, Microsoft, Apple, networking technologies, and significant computer-related malware and events.

The sum total of my CISO positions and experiences represents over thirty years or over 70,000 hours of Malcolm Gladwell's "10,000-hour rule."

Ron Baklarz
Retired CISSP, CISA, CISM,
C|CISO, NSA-IAM/IEM

NOTE

1 Indeed Editorial Team. (n.d.). *How many work hours are in a year? Indeed.* https://www.indeed.com/career-advice/career-development/how-many-work-hours-in-a-year

Abbreviations and Acronyms

A

AAR	Association of American Railroads
ACL	Access Control List
ACF	Access Control Facility
AD	Active Directory (Microsoft)
AES	Advanced Encryption Standard
AFES	Armed Forces Emergency Services
AGR	Amtrak Guest Rewards
AI	Artificial Intelligence
AICPA	American Institute of Certified Public Accountants
AIX	Advanced Interactive eXecutive proprietary UNIX OS (IBM)
ANSTR	Assistant NAVSEA Technical Representative
APD	Amtrak Police Department
ARC	American Red Cross
ARCcert	American Red Cross Computer Emergency Response Team
ARC OGC	American Red Cross Office of General Counsel
ARCNET	Attached Resource Computer Network
ARPA	Advanced Research Projects Agency
ARPANET	Advanced Research Projects Agency Network
ASCII	American Standard Code for Information Interchange
ATIP	Automated Track Inspection Program
ATLAS	Alliance of Technologies Linking Services (American Red Cross)
ATO	Authority to Operate
ATO	Account Take Over (attack)
AVIEN	Anti-Virus Information Exchange Network
AWS	Amazon Web Services

B

BAPL	Bettis Atomic Power Laboratory
BASIC	Beginner's All-purpose Symbolic Instruction Code
BBN	Bolt Beranek and Newman
BCPD	Baltimore County Police Department
BHQ	Biomedical Headquarters
BOD	Board of Directors
BS	Bachelor of Science
BSI	British Standards Institute Group
BVA	Business Value Award (Prudential)

C

C&A	Certification & Accreditation
CAO	Chief Administrative Officer
CAPTCHA	Completely Automated Public Turing test to tell Computers and Humans Apart
CAS	Certificate of Advanced Study
CBK	Common Body of Knowledge
C|CISO	Certified Chief Information Security Officer
CCMP	Counter with Cipher Block Chaining Message Authentication Code Protocol
CCU	Communications Convergence Unit
CCV	Credit Card Verification
CD-DA	Compact Disc Digital Audio
CD-ROM	Compact Disk Read-Only Memory
CD-WO	Compact Disc Write Once
CEO	Chief Executive Officer
CERN	European Organization for Nuclear Research
CERT	Computer Emergency Response Team
CERT/CC	Computer Emergency Response Team/Coordination Center
CETC	Centralized Electrification and Traffic Control
CFAA	Computer Fraud and Abuse Act
CFO	Chief Financial Officer
CFS	Consolidated Financial System (American Red Cross)
CIA	Central Intelligence Agency
CICA	Canadian Institute of Chartered Accountants
CIO	Chief Information Officer
CIRFU	Cyber Initiative and Resource Fusion Unit (FBI)
CIS	Center for Internet Security
CISA	Certified Information System Auditor

CISM	Certified Information Security Manager
CISO	Chief Information Security Officer
CISSP	Certified Information System Security Professional
CLI	Command Line Interface
CM	Configuration Management
CNN	Cable News Network
CNOC	Centralized National Operations Center
CNSI	Confidential – National Security Information
COBIT	Control Objectives for Information and Related Technologies
COBOL	Common Business-Oriented Language
COE	Center of Excellence
COMSEC	Communications Security
CONOPS	Concept of Operations
CPA	Certified Public Accountant
CP/M	Control Program/Monitor or Control Program for Microcomputers
CPO	Chief Privacy Officer (HIPAA)
CPU	Central Processing Unit
CRD	Confidential – Restricted Data
CRR	Cyber Resilience Review
CRT	Cathode Ray Tube
CSA	Customer Service Advisory
CSRC	Computer Security Resource Center
CSSM	Computer Security Site Manager
CSO	Chief Security Officer (HIPAA)
CTO	Chief Technology Officer

D

DAA	Designated Approval Authority
DAT	Datafile (anti-virus)
DDoS	Distributed Denial of Service (attack)
DDR	Double Data Rate
DES	Data Encryption Standard
DHS	Department of Homeland Security
DISA	Defense Information Services Agency
DITSCAP	DoD Information Technology Security Certification and Accreditation Process
DLP	Data Loss Prevention
DMIS	Donor Management Information System
DMS	Defense Messaging System
DMZ	Demilitarized Zone

DNS	Domain Name System
DoD	Department of Defense
DoE	Department of Energy
DOPSR	Defense Office of Prepublication and Security Review
DoS	Denial of Service (attack)
DOS	Disk Operating System
DPMA	Data Processing Management Association
DSL	Digital Subscriber Line

E

EAP	Extensible Authentication Protocol
EBCDIC	Extended Binary Coded Decimal Interchange Code
eBDR	Electronic Blood Donor Record
EMSEC	Emission Security
EINSTEIN	Network intrusion detection and prevention system
EFS	Encrypting File System (Microsoft)
EU	European Union
EMCS	Emergency Management and Corporate Security
E&Y, LLC	Ernst & Young Limited Liability Corporation

F

FBI	Federal Bureau of Investigation
FCA	Field Change Analyst
FCC	Federal Communications Commission
FDA	Federal Food and Drug Administration
FHSS	Frequency Hopping Spread Spectrum
FIRST	Forum of Incident Response and Security Teams
FISMA	Federal Information Security Modernization Act
FISSEA	Federal Information Systems Security Educators' Association
FORTRAN	Formula Translator or Formula Translation
FPU	Floating-Point Unit
FR	Frame Relay
FRA	Federal Railroad Administration
FTE	Full Time Employee
FTP	File Transfer Protocol
FTS	Federal Telecommunications System
FY	Fiscal Year

G

GAO	U.S. Government Accountability Office
GDPR	General Data Protection Regulation
G-FIRST	Government Forum of Incident Response and Security Teams
GHz	Gigahertz
GLBA	Gramm–Leach–Bliley Act
GNU	GNU's Not Unix
G&O	Goals and Objectives
GOP	Grand Old Party/Republican Party
GPU	Graphics Processing Unit
GSS	General Support System
GUH	Georgetown University Hospital

H

HCM	Human Capital Management (Amtrak)
HDD	Hard Disk Drive
HIMSS	Healthcare Information and Management Systems Society
HP	Hewlett-Packard
HIPAA	Health Insurance Portability and Accountability Act
HIR	House Information Resources
HSR	High-Speed Rail
HTML	Hypertext Markup Language
HTCIA	High-Tech Crime Investigators Association

I

IA	Internal Audit Department
IAM	Identity and Access Management
IATF	Information Assurance Technical Framework
IATO	Interim Authority to Operate
IATRP	INFOSEC Training and Rating Program
IBM	International Business Machines Corporation
IC3	Internet Crime Complaint Center (FBI)
I&C	Instrumentation and Control Activity
ICS	Industrial Control Systems
ID	Identity
IDS	Intrusion Detection System
IEEE	Institute of Electrical and Electronics Engineers

INFOSEC	Information Security
InfraGard	Organization serving as a partnership between U.S. businesses and the FBI
IoT	Internet of Things
IP	Internet Protocol
IPv6	Internet Protocol Version 6
IRC	Internet Relay Chat
ISAAS	Information Systems Audit and Advisory Service
ISACA	Information System Audit and Control Association
ISC2	International Information System Security Certification Consortium
ISO	International Organization for Standardization
ISP	Internet Service Provider
ISS	Internet Security Systems
IT	Information Technology
IV&V	Independent Verification and Validation

K

KAPL	Knolls Atomic Power Laboratory – General Electric
KPI	Key Performance Indicator
KPMG	Klynveld, Peat, Marwick, Goerdeler

L

LAN	Local Area Network
LBNL	Lawrence Berkeley National Laboratory
LDAP	Lightweight Directory Access Protocol
LoC	Lines of Code

M

MAO	Machinery Apparatus Organization – General Electric
MB	Megabytes
MHz	Megahertz
MIME	Multipurpose Internet Mail Extensions
MoD	Masters of Deception
MOOC	Massive Open Online Course
MOS	Metal-Oxide-Semiconductor
MOU	Memorandum of Understanding

MS	Master of Science
MS-DOS	Microsoft Disk Operating System
MSM	Managed Security Monitoring
MSSP	Managed Security Service Provider
MTIPS	Managed Trusted Internet Protocol Services

N

NAS	Network-Attached Storage
NAVSEA	Naval Sea Systems Command
NBAR	Network-Based Application Recognition (Cisco)
NBCS	National Biomedical Computer System
NCSC	National Computer Security Center
NCFTA	National Cyber-Forensics & Training Alliance
NCSD	National Cybersecurity Division
NDDR	National Donor Deferral Registry
NHQ	National Headquarters (American Red Cross)
NIPC	National Infrastructure Protection Center
NIPRNET	Non-Secure Internet Protocol Router NETwork
NIST	National Institute of Standards and Technology
NNS	Norfolk Naval Shipyard
NNSD	Newport News Shipping and Dry Dock
NRO	National Reconnaissance Office
NSA	National Security Agency
NSA – IAM	National Security Agency – INFOSEC Assessment Methodology
NSA – IEM	National Security Agency – INFOSEC Evaluation Methodology
NSFNET	National Science Foundation Network
NSI	Network Solutions, Inc
NT	New Technology (Microsoft Windows)
NTFS	NT File System (Microsoft Windows)
NTP	Network Time Protocol

O

OA	Office Automation
OCISO	Office of the Chief Information Security Officer
ODS	Online Donation System (American Red Cross)
OEOB	Old Executive Office Building
OGC	Office of General Counsel
OIG	Office of the Inspector General

ORACLE	Relational Database Management System
OSSSO	Office of Security Strategy and Special Operations (Amtrak)
OU	Organizational Unit
OWASP	Open Worldwide Application Security

P

PAIC	Republic of Egypt Information Center
PARC	Palo Alto Research Center
PC	Personal Computer
PCI-DSS	Payment Card Industry – Data Security Standard
PDA	Personal Digital Assistant
PDC	Primary Domain Controller
PDF	Portable Digital Format
PGP	Pretty Good Privacy
PHI	Protected Health Information
PII	Personally Identifiable Information
PIPS	Provisioning Information Processing System
PIT	Personnel In Training
PMID	Person Master ID
PNR	Pittsburgh Naval Reactors (Department of Energy)
POAM	Plan of Action and Milestones
POS	Point-of-Sale
PruCert	Prudential Computer Emergency Response Team
PTC	Positive Train Control
PW	Price Waterhouse
PwC	PricewaterhouseCoopers

Q

QC	Quality Circle
QSA	Quality Security Assessor
QT	Quik-Trak (Amtrak)

R

RACF	Resource Access Control Facility
RADIUS	Remote Authentication Dial-In User Service
RAM	Random-Access Memory

RBAC	Role-Based Access Control
RFID	Radio Frequency Identification
RISC	Rail Industry Security Committee
ROC	Report on Compliance (PCI-DSS)
ROM	Read-Only Memory
ROMAN	Risk Operating Management Analysis Network (AMTRAK)
RR	Risk Rating
RRAP	Regional Resiliency Assessment Program
RSA	Rivest–Shamir–Adleman
RTP	Raleigh, NC Triangle Park

S

SANS	SysAdmin, Audit, Network, and Security Institute
SAM	Security Access Manager
SAR	Security Assessment Report
SATAN	Security Administrator Tool for Analyzing Networks
SATNET	Atlantic Packet Satellite Network
SB 1386	California Senate Bill Privacy Law
SBY	Southbury, CT
SCADA	Supervisory Control and Data Acquisition
SECRAN	Secure Remote Area Network
SEP	Symantec Endpoint Protection
SIG	Special Interest Group
SLA	Service Level Agreement
SMTP	Simple Mail Transfer Protocol
SNA	Systems Network Architecture
SNMP	Simple Network Management Protocol
SOC	Security Operations Center
SOCC	Security Operations Control Center
SOP	Standard Operating Procedure
SPCC	Navy Ships Parts Control Center
SSH	Secure Shell
SSL	Secure Sockets Layer
SSN	Social Security Number
SSO	Single Sign-On
SSP	System Security Plan
SQL	Structured Query Language
SSID	Service Set Identifier
SVP	Senior Vice President

T

TCP	Transmission Control Protocol
TCP/IP	Transmission Control Protocol/Internet Protocol
TDI	Tivoli Directory Integrator
TDS	Tivoli Directory Server
TEMPEST	Telecommunications Electronics Material Protected from Emanating Spurious Transmissions (Unofficial)
TFTP	Trivial File Transfer Protocol
TIC	Trusted Internet Connection
TKIP	Temporal Key Integrity Protocol
TLS	Transport Layer Security
TPF	Transaction Processing Facility
TRF	Total Risk Factor
TWK	Temporary Wireless Kits

U

UHF	Ultra High Frequency
URL	Universal Resource Locator
USAID	United States Agency for International Development
USB	Universal Serial Bus
US-HCERT	United States – House Computer Emergency Response Team
UVA	University of Virginia

V

VA	Veteran's Administration
VMS	Vulnerability Management System
VPN	Virtual Private Network
VRAM	Video Random-Access Memory
VSE	Virtual Storage Extended
VTAM	Virtual Telecommunications Access Method

W

WAN	Wide Area Network
WEP	Wired Equivalent Privacy
WHO	World Health Organization
Wi-Fi	Wireless Networking

WPA	Wi-Fi Protected Access
WPAD	Westinghouse Plant Apparatus Division
WPS	Wireless Priority Service
WWW	World Wide Web

X

XP	eXPerience (Microsoft Windows)

Y

Y2K	Year 2000

Z

ZDS	Zenith Data Systems

Part I

Foundations

Looking back on my early career, I see now how each role – though seemingly unrelated to cybersecurity – served as a crucial steppingstone in my professional development. My journey began at EPIC Metals, a position that, while far removed from technology, ignited a determination within me to pursue more than factory work. During those six years, I didn't just earn a paycheck; I cultivated a strong work ethic and a drive for self-improvement. It was during this time that I started taking college courses, seeking direction and purpose beyond the factory floor.

Those first college classes became the bridge to my next opportunity at Elliott Company. The pursuit of education opened doors, and at Elliott, I was given my first taste of management. Here, I completed my Bachelor of Science in Business Management, solidifying my academic foundation. More importantly, Elliott Company became the place where I began honing leadership skills – learning to motivate teams, make decisions under pressure, and understand organizational dynamics. These lessons in leadership and responsibility were invaluable, directly shaping my readiness for more complex roles ahead.

It was also at Elliott that my interest in computers started to take shape. Although my path into technology and cybersecurity was not yet fully defined, the exposure to business processes and early computing systems sparked a curiosity that would guide my future ambitions. The experiences and skills I gained – discipline, adaptability, and leadership – became the bedrock upon which I would later build a successful career in information technology and security. Each step, from the factory floor to the management office, contributed essential lessons that prepared me for the challenges and opportunities that lay ahead.

DOI: 10.1201/9781003650645-1

Chapter 1

Humble Beginnings

Lessons Learned *Don't underestimate the importance of any work experience.* Both triumphs and setbacks offer valuable lessons that shape who you become. As you will read, my early failures in college only fueled my determination to reach greater heights. The true distinction between success and failure often lies in your attitude – be positive! Remember, every challenge is a steppingstone toward personal growth – embrace them with optimism.

1.1 EPIC METALS 1971–1976

Positions Held: General Laborer, Shipper/Receiver, Machine Operator
Location: 11 Talbot Avenue, Rankin, PA

1.1.1 Doors Close and Doors Open

After a decent high school football career, I was scouted to play football at the U.S. Naval Academy. I received correspondence from the U.S. Naval Academy's Assistant Football Coach Joe Bugel advising me to complete various pre-admission forms. Coach Bugel went on to coach offensive linemen for several NFL teams, including the Detroit Lions, Houston Oilers, and the then-named Washington Redskins, now the Washington Commanders.[1] Another letter came from the Naval Academy's Assistant Athletic Director, E.E. "Rip" Miller, with directions for me to take the required physical exams for candidate admission consideration. And my official academy candidate letter came from Congressman Joe Gaydos. Despite the Naval Academy's interest and my congressional appointment, I failed the physical exam due to my poor eyesight.

1.1.2 Overview – EPIC Metals

With the U.S. Naval Academy in my rear-view mirror, I spent a semester and a half primarily playing football and drinking beer at a small

 DOI: 10.1201/9781003650645-2

Pennsylvania college. Although I could have stayed in school, my parents wouldn't give me the $300 I needed for the next semester's tuition. So, I left the idyllic campus life and headed home to my gritty hometown of North Braddock, PA. After this falling out with my parents, *I came back to town essentially homeless.* A kind and generous family, the Cromlings, took me in. I played high school football with their son, Dale, who was my high school quarterback.

Needing a source of income, Mrs. Cromling got me a job with EPIC Metals at 11 Talbot Avenue, Rankin, PA. Today, the company still makes metal roof and floor decking for the construction industry. I worked at EPIC Metals for six years, from 1971 to 1977. This section will be brief since it has little to do with my future Information Technology and Chief Information Security Officer (CISO) positions. These work experiences had more to do with developing a solid work ethic and personal motivation.

The company occupied a large warehouse building with centrally stacked rows of large steel coils, each weighing a ton or more. These coils of cold-rolled steel fed the long rolling mill machines that form the steel into the desired configurations and cut them to size. My career there started as a general laborer with a salary of $2.50 an hour – I was rich! I was also a proud member of the International Association of Bridge, Structural, Ornamental and Reinforcing Iron Workers Local 851. *I traded my football helmet and cleats for a hard hat and steel-toed work boots.*

EPIC is located along the Monongahela River in the shadow of the George Rankin Jr. Memorial Bridge, which connects Rankin, PA, with Whitaker, PA. The location along the river suffered summer and winter weather extremes. While working one hot second shift, my co-workers and I survived a tornado that swept through the area. The tornado sounded like a freight train as it peeled EPIC's factory roof off right over our heads. We spent the rest of the shift retrieving twenty-foot-long sheets of metal decking that were haphazardly strewn up and down Talbot Avenue.

Lessons Learned *Work to the best of your abilities, no matter what the job.* Someone may notice you went above and beyond, which can lead to unexpected opportunities. For example, an employee who consistently delivers high-quality customer service may receive positive online reviews, leading to recognition or even a promotion within their company. Today, more than ever, performance is continuously tracked and evaluated – especially with the Internet providing unprecedented ways for customers and clients to share feedback. Consistently strong performance not only builds your reputation but can also open doors to new projects, promotions, or valuable professional connections. Just doing the best you can in all cases will pay off!

I did not want to burden the Cromling family more than I already had. So, when I got on my feet, I rented a house with a co-worker. Now, living across the street from the church where I was baptized, I lived within walking distance of EPIC. As soon as I stepped out of the house in the morning, I could hear the cadence of the mill's jaws cutting the decking. During my daily walks to and from work, I silently promised myself I would not work there forever. But I learned a number of skills over my six years there, and I advanced from general laborer to shipper/receiver and finally as a mill operator. Keeping my exit strategy and promise to myself, I went to night classes at Allegheny County Community College – Boyce Campus in Monroeville, PA. EPIC's general plant foreman, Andy Orfitelli, lent me $40 to pay for my first class back at community college. Little did I know then that I would go to night school for the next sixteen years!

Lessons Learned *Never give up on your dreams and goals.* Progress doesn't always come in leaps – it's built sometimes literally one step at a time. During my daily walks to work, I made it a habit to use that quiet time to focus on my goals. I would visualize the life I wanted to build, letting those thoughts push me forward, even on the mornings when it was tough to get out the door. On days when the job felt repetitive or my dreams seemed far away, this routine helped me stay motivated and grounded. I discovered that even when progress feels slow, taking steady, consistent actions toward what truly matters – no matter how small – can lead to meaningful change. Over time, these daily reminders became my personal mantra, helping me to keep moving the ball forward, one step at a time.

Lessons Learned *Make your own luck.* One of the most important lessons I've learned is that perceived "luck" is often created through hard work and persistence. I had a desire to obtain a college degree in order to advance my career, and I persevered over sixteen years of night school to earn my bachelor's, master's, and advanced degrees. Balancing work, family responsibilities, and late-night classes was exhausting at times, but my commitment never wavered. Earning my degrees wasn't a matter of luck, but the result of consistent effort and determination – proof that you truly make your own luck.

1.2 ELLIOTT COMPANY 1977–1981

Positions Held: Control Center Foreman
Location: 901 N 4TH St Jeannette, PA

1.2.1 Elliott Company – Overview

A complex of buildings comprising Elliott Company's campus is nestled in the back roads of Jeannette, PA. Building 48 was a large building, probably the size of several football fields. As a machine shop, it had a number of specialized work areas performing light machining services. The next building over was the rotor division, where large and small rotors were built and balanced. The last shop, Main, performed larger machining operations and final assemblies. A childhood friend was already working in Building 48 as a general shift foreman. He was responsible for hiring me as a control center foreman (CCF), a fancy name for an expeditor foreman. *I traded my green factory worker's hard hat I wore at EPIC Metals for a white foreman's hard hat at Elliott Company!*

1.2.2 Control Center Foreman

I worked at Elliott Company for four years, from 1978 to 1981. My time at Elliott allowed me to gain valuable experience in a managerial role. Also, I had the chance to work with the new computerized production control system, IBM's System/7 Shop Floor Control System. However, I quickly realized I did not want to spend my entire career chasing parts around machine shops. But I did want a career working with computer systems.

As a CCF, I was in charge of a group of expeditors and forklift operators assigned to service each department in the building. Each department had a kiosk that fed data into the overall centralized Shop Floor Control System. Kiosks were used by all personnel in the department: foremen, expeditors, and machine operators. Once a piece arrived in the department, the expeditor received the piece into the department via input to the kiosk. The pieces' presence was then included in the department's priority list. Each department platform's printer was used by the department foreman and the expeditor to print out priority lists and schedule work.

I had a personal philosophy that I wouldn't ask someone to do something that I wouldn't do myself. On Building 48's roof, banks of windows were hand-cranked open and closed. One hot summer evening, the windows were open, offering little relief from the sweltering heat. A powerful storm swept through, causing rainwater to pour in through the open windows and onto the shop floor. As a manager, union rules dictated that I was not permitted to physically close the windows but had to escort one of my forklift operators to the roof and have him crank the windows closed. When we got up on the roof, the deluge continued. I couldn't in good conscience send him out alone to close all the windows. So, we both made our way around the roof, cranking the windows closed. When we finished, we looked like drowned rats, but he appreciated my help. No union grievance was made for my actions on that night.

Lesson Learned *Lead By Example.* The most important lesson is that true leaders inspire others by consistently doing what is right and setting a positive example through their actions. It was a small gesture, but my help to close the factory roof windows during the rainstorm went a long way in demonstrating leadership. Such actions not only demonstrate integrity but also motivate those around them to follow suit.

Lesson Learned *Don't be afraid to extend yourself beyond your comfort zone.* One of the best ways to grow in both personal and professional life is to extend yourself. Don't be afraid to take on challenges and risks. Failures are lessons, too!

Lesson Learned *Know when it is time to leave.* While it's often said, "If you love what you do, you will never work a day in your life," the reality is that even the most fulfilling jobs have their tough moments. The real lesson is to find a role where the positives consistently outweigh the challenges, making the overall journey worthwhile and rewarding.

1.2.3 Bachelor's Degree

The experience at Elliott whetted my appetite for more computer-related types of work. This was my first management position, and I learned a great deal about working with and leading a team. However, I did not want a future in which I was relegated to chasing parts around factory floors. Recognizing the need for further education to pursue my career goals, I continued my studies at Point Park. Our Saturday classes included other full-time working students, and it seemed like we were students for years due to taking just a few classes each year. We often joked when the commencement speaker was announced that, if we didn't care for the speaker, we would wait until next year to graduate in hopes of a better one. These lighthearted moments fostered a sense of camaraderie among us, making the long academic journey more enjoyable. In retrospect, I realize that the challenges and humor we shared not only helped me persevere but also deepened my appreciation for the collective experience of lifelong learning. On April 25, 1980, I received my degree.

With my Bachelor's degree in Business Management under my belt, I began looking for my next opportunity. This opportunity would come the next year at Westinghouse Plant Apparatus Division.

1.2.4 Technology Advancements and Security Developments 1971–1981

From 1971 to 1977, IBM mainframes, mid-range systems, and their peripherals still dominated computing environments. But during this timeframe, the beginnings of personal computing began to creep onto the scene.

Intel introduced the first microprocessor and the Unix, FORTRAN, BASIC, and C programming languages were developed. Floppy disks, computer monitors, and the Apple II system were also produced. And who can forget IBM's fifty-five-pound portable computer that cost between $9,000 and $20,000? From a networking perspective, the precursor to Wi-Fi, ALOHAnet, was in production use across the Hawaiian Islands. And IBM introduced SNA (Systems Network Architecture) and Transmission Control Protocol (TCP) was designed. From 1978 to 1981, there were further refinements in personal computers, including faster processors and the MS-DOS disk operating systems. TCP/IP was further refined, and Network Solutions was formed and would become the primary domain registrar.

1971

- The first 8-inch floppy diskette drive and floppy diskette were introduced. (See Chapter 2.0 Section 2.5 Office Automation for an example of 8-inch floppy diskette use.)
- Ray Tomlinson sent the first email. Tomlinson was a computer engineer working at Bolt Beranek and Newman (BBN), a firm contracted by the U.S. government to develop Internet precursor, ARPANET. Tomlinson combined two existing programs, SNDMSG and CPYNET, and introduced the @ symbol to separate a user's name from their computer's address, creating the user@host format.
- Bob Bemer published the world's first warning on the Year 2000 problem.
- A UHF wireless packet network was used in Hawaii, called ALOHAnet, to connect the islands. This development helped create the foundation for wireless networking and, later, Wi-Fi.
- June 28th, Elon Musk was born.
- November 3rd, the first edition of Unix was released.
- November 15th, Intel introduced the first microprocessor, the Intel 4004.
- The Creeper system, an experimental self-replicating program, was written by Bob Thomas at BBN Technologies to test John von Neumann's theory. Creeper infected DEC PDP-10 computers running the TENEX operating system. Creeper gained access via the ARPANET and copied itself to the remote system, where the message "I'm the creeper, catch me if you can!" was displayed. The Reaper program was later created to delete Creeper.[2]
- John Draper, aka Captain Crunch, discovered that a breakfast cereal children's whistle created a 2,600 Hz tone. Using this whistle and a blue box, he could get into AT&T's phone network and make free calls anywhere in the world.

1972

- The first scientific pocket calculator, the HP-35, was introduced.

- The programming language FORTRAN (Formula Translation) 66 was created.
- Dennis Ritchie at Bell Labs invented the C programming language.
- June 6th, the floppy disk was patented by Ralph Flores and Herbert Thompson.
- July 18th, the floppy disk drive was patented by Warren Dalziel, Jay Nilson, and Donald Wartner.
- November 29th, Atari released Pong, the first commercial video game.

1973

- January, Radio Frequency IDentification was patented by Mario Cardullo.
- March 1st, the first computer monitor was released as part of the Xerox Alto computer system. The monitor used CRT (Cathode Ray Tube) technology and had a monochrome display.
- May 22nd, Robert Metcalfe and David Boggs created Ethernet at the Xerox PARC (Palo Alto Research Center).
- The architecture used with the CP/M operating system became the standard for the next eight years until MS-DOS was introduced.
- Vinton Cerf and Robert Kahn designed TCP in 1973 and later published it with the help of Yogen Dalal and Carl Sunshine in December 1974 in RFC 675.
- ARPA (Advanced Research Projects Agency) deployed SATNET, the first international connection.

1974

- A commercial version of ARPANET (Advanced Research Projects Agency Network), known as Telenet, was introduced and considered by many as the first Internet Service Provider
- IBM developed SEQUEL in 1974. SEQUEL (Structured Query Language), which is still widely used today.
- IBM introduced SNA (Systems Network Architecture).

1975

- January 2nd, Bill Gates, Paul Allen, and Monte Davidoff announced Altair BASIC, designed for the Altair computer. The language became the first computer programming language for personal computers.
- April 4th, Bill Gates and Paul Allen established Microsoft after creating Altair BASIC. The program was later developed into Microsoft BASIC.
- September, the IBM 5100 became the first portable computer when released. The computer weighed fifty-five pounds and had a five-inch CRT display, tape drive, 1.9 MHz PALM processor, 64 KB of RAM (Random-Access Memory), and cost from $9,000 to $20,000.

1976

- April, Steve Jobs and Steve Wozniak demonstrated the first Apple computer at the Home Brew Computer Club. The Apple I had 6502 Metal-Oxide-Semiconductor, 1 MHz processor, 8 KB of onboard memory, and 1 KB of Video Random-Access Memory for $666.66. They then co-founded Apple Computers on April Fools' Day.
- The first 5.25-inch floppy disk was invented.
- The first Public Key Cryptography, known as the Diffie-Hellman, was developed by Whitfield Diffie and Martin Hellman.
- December 1976, Bill Gates dropped out of Harvard to devote all his time to Microsoft.
- The original Apple computer company logo of Sir Isaac Newton sitting under an apple tree was replaced in 1976 by the well-known rainbow-colored apple with a bite out of it.

1977

- January, Commodore announced that the Personal Electronic Transactor would be a self-contained unit, with a CPU (Central Processing Unit), RAM, read-only memory, keyboard, monitor, and tape recorder, all for $495.
- ARCNET (Attached Resource Computer Network), considered the first commercial network, was developed by principal engineer John Murphy. The network was originally developed to connect groups of their Datapoint 2,200 terminals to talk to a shared 8 inch floppy disk system.
- IBM's DES (Data Encryption Standard), an enciphering and deciphering algorithm, was accepted as a standard by the National Bureau of Standards.
- Tandy announced it would manufacture the TRS-80 Model 1, the first mass-produced computer. This computer was commonly called the *Trash 80*.

1978

- TCP was invented by Bob Kahn and Vint Cerf. It was later split into TCP/IP by Danny Cohen, David Reed, and John Shoch to support real-time traffic. The creation of TCP/IP also helped to create UDP (user datagram protocol).
- June 8th, Intel introduced the 8086 microprocessor on June 8, 1978. The ×86 Intel CPU (central processing unit) architecture originated.

1979

- The Intel 8088 microprocessor was released.
- Hayes marketed its first industry-standard modem, the 300 bit/s Micromodem 100.

- Network Solutions, a technology consulting company, was incorporated by Emmit McHenry with Ty Grigsby, Gary Desler, and Ed Peters in Washington, D.C. Initially, the company focused on systems programming services, primarily in the IBM environment.

1980

- IBM hired Paul Allen and Bill Gates to create an operating system for a new PC (personal computer). IBM let them keep the marketing rights to the operating system called DOS.
- IBM released the 5120, a new desktop computer.
- Intel released the 8087-math coprocessor.
- IBM developed the first one-gigabyte hard drive. The drive weighed 550 pounds and cost $40,000.
- The programming language FORTRAN (Formula Translation) 77 was created.

1981

- IBM introduced the IBM 5150 PC (personal computer). It featured the 4.77-MHz Intel 8088 CPU (central processing unit), 16 KB base memory, and the Model F keyboard. Its retail price was $1,565.
- Microsoft created a new operating system for the IBM PC. The result was MS-DOS 1.0, which was branded as PC-DOS when shipped with IBM PC.
- April 27th, Xerox introduced the Star workstation. The computer's Graphical User Interface greatly influenced future Apple computers, including the Lisa and Macintosh, and inspired many features of Microsoft Windows.
- Hayes introduced the Smartmodem 300 with its standard-setting AT command set that operated at 300 bits per second.
- Ian Murphy, also known as "Captain Zap," became the first hacker convicted of hacking for his hack into AT&T phone lines and rearranging their internal clocks. The phone companies charged premium prices for calls made during peak usage hours. Zap's rearranged internal clocks resulted in massive discounts for calls made during peak hours and exorbitant phone bills for calls made during off-peak hours.
- Radio Shack's TRS-80 personal computer was discontinued.

NOTES

1 Bugel, J. (n.d.). *Joe Bugel. Wikipedia.* https://en.wikipedia.org/wiki/Joe_Bugel
2 Timeline of computer viruses and worms. (n.d.). *Wikipedia.* https://en.wikipedia.org/wiki/Timeline_of_computer_viruses_and_worms

Part II

Learning Curve – Early CISO Positions

Reflecting on the sixteen years that span Chapters 2–5, I see them as a formative learning curve that shaped my path toward future CISO positions. My journey into cybersecurity officially began in 1986, when I became a Computer Security Site Manager (CSSM) within the Naval Nuclear Program while at the Westinghouse Plant Apparatus Division. During these ten years as CSSM, I honed my ability to produce clear and concise cybersecurity policies and procedures – a skill set that prepared me for the next leap in my career.

The opportunity to serve as the first security manager at the U.S. House of Representatives presented itself as a chance to make a broader impact on cybersecurity. Motivated by the challenge of protecting critical government information, I introduced a standardized policy template that not only streamlined compliance but also became the enduring format for cybersecurity policies at the House, influencing their approach for decades. I vividly recall collaborating with various committees to ensure that our security standards addressed both legislative and operational needs.

My subsequent move to Ernst & Young was fueled by a curiosity about government and private sector approaches to risk and vulnerability. At E&Y, I gained firsthand experience in system and network vulnerability testing. One memorable project involved leading a team that uncovered and resolved a critical flaw in a client's legacy system – an experience that deepened my appreciation for proactive risk management and the importance of thorough vulnerability assessments.

Later, at the American Red Cross, I was motivated by the organization's humanitarian mission and the challenge of safeguarding sensitive donor and volunteer information. Equally important was protecting Red Cross's brand. This role allowed me to further refine my philosophies, methods, and techniques as a CISO. I worked closely with cross-functional teams to embed cybersecurity awareness into the fabric of the organization, ensuring that our security strategies supported both operational resilience and trust.

Throughout these sixteen years, I accumulated over 33,000 hours dedicated to mastering my craft – an embodiment of Malcolm Gladwell's

DOI: 10.1201/9781003650645-3

10,000-hour rule. This principle not only underscores the depth of expertise I developed but also highlights the commitment, persistence, and leadership required to excel in cybersecurity. Each career transition was fueled by a genuine motivation to expand my impact and deepen my knowledge, ultimately shaping me into an authoritative and adaptable cybersecurity leader.

Chapter 2

Westinghouse Plant Apparatus Division 1982–1996

Positions Held: Field Change Analyst
Computer Security Site Manager
COMSEC Custodian
Manager Configuration Control Systems
Manager Logistics Systems Programming
Manager Personal Computer & Local Area Network Programming
Location: 600 Penn Center Blvd., Building 4, Pittsburgh, PA

Disclaimer Due to the potentially sensitive national security topics covered in this chapter and the fact that I held government security clearances, I submitted this chapter for a Department of Defense – Defense Office of Prepublication and Security Review (DOPSR). Changes were made in accordance with their response via "Ref: DOPSR 25-SB-0040" dated March 3, 2025, and was otherwise CLEARED AS AMENDED for OPEN PUBLICATION.

2.1 WESTINGHOUSE PLANT APPARATUS DIVISION (WPAD) – OVERVIEW

I began working at WPAD for the next fourteen-plus years, from 1981 to 1996. Without a doubt, no work experience had as profound an influence on my professional life as WPAD (simply pronounced as "PAD"). This is where I began my journey in information security. The pride of mission working in the Naval Nuclear Program was unsurpassed. While there, I grew up with technology, including mainframe systems, personal computers (PCs), Local Area Networks (LANs), and Wide Area Networks (WANs). I worked with great people and learned valuable professional and life lessons such as management, communication, and technical skills.

I also pursued graduate degrees, earning a master's degree in information sciences and a certificate of advanced study in telecommunications by

DOI: 10.1201/9781003650645-4

taking advantage of Westinghouse's tuition reimbursement program. At WPAD, as a computer security site manager (CSSM), I was essentially a chief information security officer (CISO), although that title did not formally exist. In my role as CSSM, I had DoE Order 5636.1 Security Requirements for Classified Automatic Data Processing Systems and DoE Order 5637.1 Classified Computer Security Program as frameworks on which to build my cybersecurity programs.

As far as the culture at WPAD, I was fortunate that military and engineering mindsets dominated the workplace. From a military perspective, WPAD employees were accustomed to following rigid rules and regulations. This made it easier to establish cybersecurity policies and procedures and have the organization follow them. Likewise, the engineering mindset is disciplined and challenged me to ensure my policies and procedures were well thought out and logical. Also, I had the support of the Department of Energy (DOE) Orders which dictated cybersecurity program requirements. My cybersecurity program at WPAD was easier for the organization to assimilate due to these factors.

Lessons Learned *Understand the corporate culture.* The importance of understanding corporate culture cannot be overstated – this is a foundational lesson not just for CISOs, but for anyone stepping into a leadership role in any organization. When I began my journey at WPAD, I quickly realized that recognizing and adapting to the unique cultural dynamics of an organization would go far in determining how effective I could be as a leader. These cultural nuances shape how policies are received, how teams respond to change, and ultimately, how well security initiatives succeed. By sharing my experiences, I hope to offer practical insights that others in similar roles can apply to adapting and embracing the existing culture which is essential for driving progress and achieving lasting impact. In each of my cybersecurity positions, I will highlight how understanding the organizational environment shaped my strategies and contributed to my success.

2.2 FIELD CHANGE ANALYST (FCA) 1982–1986

I responded to a *Want Ad* in The Pittsburgh Press for positions at the Westinghouse Plant Apparatus Division (WPAD) and was hired for the position of Field Change Analyst. At the time, WPAD offices occupied the top six floors of 400 Penn Center Boulevard, Building 4 Penn Center East in Wilkins Township. WPAD was part of the Naval Nuclear Program. Visionary Admiral Hyman G. Rickover was the father of the naval nuclear program. He established the competitive structure between industrial giants Westinghouse Electric Corporation and General Electric

(GE) as prime contractors supporting the naval nuclear program. On the Westinghouse Electric side was Bettis Atomic Power Laboratory (BAPL) and WPAD. The GE side had mirror organizations – Knolls Atomic Laboratory (KAPL) and Machinery Apparatus Organization (MAO). Bettis and KAPL were responsible for nuclear power plant design development, and training. WPAD and MAO procured the components that supported the nuclear power plants and provided logistical and other program support functions.

At the time of my hiring, employees at WPAD held both Department of Defense (DOD) Secret and DOE L clearances. Once hired, the need for both clearances required additional time to perform the background checks. The clearance process starts with filling out the lengthy Standard Form 86 (SF-86). This form is essentially an accounting of your life, requiring names, addresses, and phone numbers of references and neighbors. These neighbors were visited and questioned by "G-men" to ascertain if the candidate was a security risk.

On my first day at WPAD, I arrived at the uncleared reception area of the bottommost offices on the fourth floor. The receptionist was a lovely African American woman, Ernestine Gibson. Her grandson was a University of Pittsburgh Panther and National Football League Hall of Fame running back, Curtis Martin. On Saturdays during his collegiate career and Sundays during his NFL career, television cameras focused on Ernestine as she sat in the stadium stands enthusiastically cheering for her grandson. Ernestine was also a defacto dorm mother to all of us new hires. And while we awaited our clearances, we were sequestered in a room off the main reception area known as *personnel in training* or simply the PIT.

With me in the PIT were six other new hires. Each of us had a sponsor or mentor to help with our indoctrination, helping us navigate the ins and outs of WPAD and our new roles. Since we were not cleared for access to classified information, we were relegated to pouring over voluminous, unclassified procedure manuals. Nothing is more mind-numbing than sitting around reading these manuals! As a group, we did make important decisions, though – like where to eat lunch. My sponsor was Clyde Cooley, a giant of a man whose booming laugh and endless anecdotes made even the dullest afternoons in the PIT bearable.

We didn't get many visitors in the PIT as there were only scarce visits by our sponsors. One morning, an attractive lady joined us in the PIT. She was hired as a purchasing agent. Once word circulated regarding her presence in the PIT, we had a constant stream of male visitors. *Go figure!* About twelve weeks later, I received my clearance and could access WPAD's classified office areas. After leaving the elevators on your assigned floor, you immediately entered an enclosed vestibule with a locked door. We received a key to open the door onto the floor. There, you were greeted by two secretaries who made sure you were authorized to enter by showing our picture badges and that we were cleared to enter classified spaces.

Navy personnel were resident in our office space and oversaw our work. The Naval Nuclear Program was rife with acronyms. Our Navy office was Assistant Naval Sea Systems Command Technical Representatives (ANSTR) - Pittsburgh. The ANSTR office was staffed by eight or so Naval personnel. As an FCA, I interacted mainly with the lower-ranked personnel to deal with logistical issues like material movements. We were trained by Westinghouse management to maintain an "arms-length" relationship with the "customer." But over the years, I became friends with several sailors and was actually a groomsman in one's wedding.

2.3 STANDARD LOGISTICS (SL)

As a Field Change Analyst (FCA), I worked within the Standard Logistics (SL) system. SL was a mainframe-based series of programs that ran on a classified mainframe at the Navy Ships Parts Control Center (SPCC) in Mechanicsburg, PA. SL was a "Frankenstein" system with four main sub-systems. Each one of the four sub-systems was programmed by one of the Prime Contractors – Bettis, WPAD, KAPL, and MAO. One of the problems with the system was that three of the four sub-systems were programmed in COBOL. COBOL is an acronym for common business-oriented language. "It is a compiled, English-like computer programming language designed for business use."[1] The fourth component of SL was programmed in Fortran. "Fortran is a general-purpose, compiled imperative programming language that is especially suited to numeric computation and scientific computing."[2] While COBOL was the best choice for the business programming of SL, the engineers who programmed the fourth component only had expertise in Fortran. This mixture of programming languages was a challenging situation for continued maintenance and improvements to the overall system's functionality.

The best way to think of how SL worked began when the U.S. Congress approved funding to build new nuclear-powered submarines and aircraft carriers. The first order of business was to identify the nuclear power plant to be used. Either a Westinghouse or a GE design was selected. This information was fed into SL, and a series of processes were kicked off to provision the major systems and millions of parts that support that particular power plant. My electrical engineering department, Instrumentation and Control (I&C) Activity purchased and maintained the electronic components that controlled and monitored the nuclear power plants. Invariably, changes must be made to equipment including on-board systems, spare parts, and equipment at training facilities. This is where I fit in. My FCA job was to track over 2,000 field changes that had to be made to improve the I&C components. These field changes could be as simple as replacing one resister to as complex as changing out an entire monitoring and control system.

I worked with stacks of computer-generated, green-bar printouts. Each of the 2,000 field changes had a unique number and identified all the systems that needed the change. Components on-board ship, in spare parts inventories, and at training facilities were coded on the printouts. Other items on the field change report needing to be changed were also identified (e.g., technical manual changes, drawing changes). Field change modifications to equipment could be made by the prime contractor, subcontractors, ship's force, or by shipyard personnel during maintenance downtimes. Our feedback mechanism, a form letter, was to be signed and sent back to WPAD, indicating that the field change was completed.

I would mark up the green bar printouts with updates and take them to keypunch in WPAD's computer center. There, computer center staff would key the changes using keypunch machines, a device for precisely punching holes into stiff paper cards at specific locations as determined by keys struck by a human operator. We used a process by which the punched cards were verified by keying the same data a second time, checking to see if the second keying and the punched data were the same. This is known as two-pass verification.[3] Also, my role required shipping field change kits to all the locations that had equipment requiring the change.

2.4 MASTER'S DEGREE AND CERTIFICATE OF ADVANCED STUDIES (TELECOMMUNICATIONS)

Westinghouse offered a tuition reimbursement program where they would pay up to 90% of tuition for approved programs and maintain a minimum of a 3.0 grade level. Subsequent to my hiring at WPAD, the University of Pittsburgh's School of Library and Information Sciences began a new Master of Science degree in Information Science. This program was right up my alley, and since I had already completed ten years of night school to earn my B.S. degree, what's a few more years of schooling? Pitt's School of Library and Information Science is at 135 North Bellefield Avenue, Pittsburgh, PA. I applied and entered the program where I would spend the next four years until I completed the master's program in 1985.

Subsequent to earning my master's degree, I took a few years off from school but had a desire to go back and study networks and telecommunications in more depth. So, I went back and took classes in the curriculum. A certificate of advanced study (CAS) requires the completion of twenty-four credits or about eight courses subsequent to the master's program. Once I completed those, I applied for the official completion of the program and recognition of the CAS. I remember the head of the Network and Telecommunications department looking confused after receiving my application request. He did not think there was such a thing as a CAS for his telecommunications program. *Well, I got the certificate – I was the first to do so!*

Lessons Learned *Make a commitment to education.* My sixteen years of night school may sound daunting, but those years spent earning my bachelor's, master's, and certificate of advanced study degrees opened numerous doors throughout my career. The knowledge and credentials I gained not only qualified me for advanced roles but also gave me the confidence to pursue leadership positions. While such a lengthy educational journey might not appeal to everyone, investing in ongoing education – at any pace – can open up unexpected opportunities in your own career, equipping you with new skills and the confidence to take on greater responsibilities.

2.5 OFFICE AUTOMATION

In 1982, when I arrived at WPAD, the office automation we know today was non-existent. And the Naval Nuclear Program was a demanding arena for quality and precision. I recall the voluminous engineering letters that, by today's standards, were virtually *hand-hewn* on IBM Selectric typewriters. These typewriters were also known as IBM golf ball typewriters since they did not have the traditional type strike bars – long rods with letters on the end. Instead, they had a centrally positioned rotating ball with the letters of varying, changeable fonts on them. There was no such thing as spell check, and the Naval Nuclear Program documents were littered with scientific notations and complex engineering language. Copies of these documents had to be made by mimeograph machines, another ancient technology. Every evening, secretaries had to remove the ribbons from their typewriters and lock them in their safes. The concern was that the ribbons could reveal classified information because of the legible letter-strikes that remained on the ribbons.

Quality and precision were drummed into us from day one at WPAD. The example used was that if a submarine was stalled under the polar ice cap, they had better have the right part to fix their problem. An incorrect repair part could cost the sub and all lives on board. There was an unfortunate instance where we had a promising young electrical engineer in our I&C department. His excellent work at one of the shipyards was recognized by GE engineers and shipyard staff. And it was rare that GE would give praise to a Westinghouse employee. The young engineer issued an official engineering letter to Naval Sea Systems Command (NAVSEA) with a decimal point in the wrong position on one of the resistor values. Subsequent to other mistakes he made, NAVSEA indicated that they had lost confidence in the young engineer, and he was fired.

Lessons Learned *Pay attention to detail!* For example, a seemingly small error in placing a decimal point on a transistor value led to significant consequences for a promising young engineer. While this is an extreme case, it highlights how even minor mistakes can have a big impact. Sloppy or mistake-ridden communications detract from your professionalism, so it's crucial to check and double-check your work. To avoid such errors, consider using checklists, peer reviews, or taking a short break before reviewing your work again. These habits can help you catch mistakes before they become problems.

A significant advancement in office automation compared to the IBM Selectric typewriters was the Xerox 860, a top-end, dedicated word processor. "It had a spell check function with 88,000 words in its dictionary! The full-text monitor could display 70 lines of 102 characters. It stored working files on one of the two 8inch (600 KB) floppy disks. Each disk catalog could store up to 560 documents."[4] The secretaries and engineers were ecstatic over the new word processors, and productivity increased significantly. The Xerox 860 made its debut circa 1981 and was expensive at $14,000 per machine. But these machines were operated as stand-alone devices and were able to generate, store, and print classified documents.

2.6 PERSONAL COMPUTERS

The Xerox 860s had a limited lifespan largely due to the introduction and advancements with PCs. In 1982, IBM introduced its own PC. The first IBM PC, formally known as the IBM Model 5150, was based on a 4.77 MHz Intel 8088 microprocessor and used Microsoft's MS-DOS operating system. "The IBM PC revolutionized business computing by becoming the first PC to gain widespread adoption by industry. Due to IBM's brand recognition and aggressive marketing campaign, IBM PC's gained rapid growth."[5]

It was no accident that our I&C department, staffed by electrical engineers, were early adopters of PCs. I remember that initially, we only had two PCs on wooden roll-around carts with a resident spreadsheet program. The buyers in the purchasing department would wheel the PCs from one end of the floor to the other, sharing them and learning how to use them. *The problem was that the PCs were not yet approved to process classified information.* A problem that would plague us for a few more years.

From 1982 to 1986, I held various positions in support and logistics areas. I left my FCA role and began working in the newly established office automation group. The new group was responsible for deploying PCs throughout the division and providing training and maintenance.

2.7 COMPUTER SECURITY SITE MANAGER 1986–1996

> *Lessons Learned* *Develop your verbal and written communication skills.* Developing strong verbal and written communication skills is essential for success as a CISO. Think of these abilities as the foundational rungs at the base of a ladder – without them, it's nearly impossible to climb higher. Just as a ladder relies on its bottom rungs for stability and support, effective communication underpins every other skill you'll need on your professional journey. As CSSM, I had to generate official documentation, including information security policies and procedures that were scrutinized by WPAD Management, ANSTR, NAVSEA and PNR.

As office automation technologies advanced, the need for security around the technologies and the information processed by them became clear. Being in the Naval Nuclear Program, which dealt with classified information, I was in the right place at the right time for a career in information security. On July 10, 1985, The DOE – Office of Safeguards and Security issued DoE Order 5636.1, Security Requirements for Classified Automatic Data Processing Systems. The Order required that an on-site individual be given the responsibility and title of CSSM. Since I was enrolled in a master's degree program in the interdisciplinary field of Information Sciences at the University of Pittsburgh, I was a logical choice to assume the role.

At WPAD, we had an individual responsible for our physical security program governed by DOD guidance, National Industrial Security Program Operating Manual (NISPOM). WPAD's physical security position reported to WPAD's facilities department. Harvey Rosenblum was the facilities manager, and John Powers oversaw physical security. Due to DoE Order 5636.1 requirements, Harvey made the pitch to have me assume the CSSM role and report to him. This was approved, and I was now the in a CISO-equivalent position before the title officially existed! I will always be grateful for Harvey's confidence and guidance. He set me on the career path I would travel on for the rest of my working life.

By this time, the requirement for employees to hold both DoD and DoE clearances changed, and the DoD clearance was no longer necessary. With my new CSSM position, I had to undergo additional security background checks to secure a DOE "Q" clearance.

> Q clearance or Q access authorization is the U.S. Department of Energy (DOE) security clearance required to access Top Secret Restricted Data, Formerly Restricted Data, and National Security Information, as well as Secret Restricted Data. Restricted Data (RD) is defined in the Atomic Energy Act of 1954 and covers nuclear weapons and related materials.[6]

One humorous story I remember was the requirement to inventory WPAD's Secret level documents. To this point, I had never seen a document marked as *Secret*. WPAD was authorized to generate, access, and store mostly Confidential – Restricted Data and Confidential – National Security Information. John Powers was serious and meticulous in performing his job, and we worked well together. One dreary day, John asked me to go along with him as a witness to his performing the inventory of Secret level documents at WPAD. My pulse quickened with the prospect of reviewing WPAD's Secret documents. I would enter into the inner sanctum and be witness to the deepest, darkest of secrets held by the United States!

John and I made our way to the tenth floor of our building and accessed a locked door that led to a storage area. Since there was no lighting, we entered the large room with flashlights illuminating our way. John forged a path through dusty, haphazard piles of office furniture. Finally, tucked behind old metal desks, his light landed on a small but substantial steel safe secured with a government-approved combination lock. John brushed away some cobwebs, knelt, and tucked the flashlight under his arm. I trained my light on the combination lock as he twisted the numbered dial. He pulled open the drawer and extracted a single manila folder. He opened the folder, revealing *one lone Secret document!* Disappointment spread across my face! I felt like Ralphie in The Christmas Story decoding a secret message with his official Little Orphan Annie decoder ring – only to find it was a commercial to drink his Ovaltine! John made an annotation on an audit sheet, and both he and I signed and dated it. *What a letdown!*

2.8 PERSONAL COMPUTERS

The issue we had was that the new PCs that were arriving at WPAD were not yet approved to process classified information. But it was fortunate that WPAD was under (DoE) security cognizance. The DoE team, known as the Pittsburgh Naval Reactors (PNR) office, oversaw WPAD's cybersecurity program. PNR resided at Bettis Atomic Power Laboratory. They were demanding but open-minded and willing to work with us to develop the security protections, protocols, and procedures necessary for our PCs to process classified information. In helping WPAD, they were also helping Bettis since they had the same cyber security–related issues. The ability to process classified information on PCs would give us tremendous productivity enhancement.

Using DoE Order 5637.1, we implemented a number of physical protections on our PCs. The first thing we did was house the PCs in large metal, roll-around cabinets. The cabinets were locked with the same government-approved three-positioned combination locks we had on our safes. Our general-purpose document safes were four or five-drawer metal filing cabinets. A hinged steel bar ran the length of the cabinet's front with holes at the top for inserting the combination lock. Safes and PC cabinets had to be locked after normal business hours when not in use. The PCs, including their wiring, were physically too large for the standard computer cabinets, so we had to fabricate a metal extension box jutting out the back of the cabinet so the PC would fit. The extension was fastened to the cabinet with tamper-proof hardware. The cabinet modifications added more costs and time delays in having our PCs approved for classified processing.

We had to affix labels to the top and bottom of the computer screens that simply stated, "CONFIDENTIAL." Computers were also labeled with a caution that the computer had to be six inches away from telephones. There was a concern that signals could transfer from PCs to telephones and their phone lines. (See TEMPEST discussion below) The PCs we bought had to be designated as Federal Communications Commission (FCC) Class B-rated devices. Class A devices are considered *intentional radiators*. Intentional radiators deliberately produce radio waves to initiate an operation. Examples of Class A devices include cell phones, wireless microphones, and remote opening controls.[7] Class B devices did not intentionally emit signals. Obviously, we could not have our PCs leaking classified information!

My discussion of PCs wouldn't be complete without recognizing the efforts of a visionary electrical engineering manager, Bob Hanson. Bob saw the advantages of having PCs available at every desk. As a learning exercise, he had a group of us at WPAD build our own IBM PCs. He provided all the necessary components, which we purchased and learned how to build our own PCs from the inside out. This skill and knowledge served me well in future CISO positions. Bob was also instrumental in negotiating with some of the software vendors to permit us to load programs on these computers for home use. In this scenario, one licensed copy of the software resided on our work computers, and a second instance of that same license on the home computer. The reasoning was that the user could only be using one instance of the software at a time, not concurrently. This was genius since users gained proficiency with the software by using it at both in the office and for unofficial home use. Of course, we could not generate classified information on our home computers.

2.9 TEMPEST (CODENAME)

TEMPEST is a U.S. National Security Agency (NSA) specification and a North Atlantic Treaty Organization certification referring to spying on information systems through leaking emanations, including unintentional radio or electrical signals, sounds, and vibrations. TEMPEST covers both methods to spy upon others and how to shield equipment against such spying. The protection efforts are also known as emission security, which is a subset of communications security (COMSEC).[8]

Although not official, the acronym TEMPEST could be short for *Telecommunications Electronics Material Protected from Emanating Spurious Transmissions.* As discussed earlier concerning our PCs being designated as FCC Class B devices, TEMPEST standards also require RED/BLACK separation. This means maintaining defined distances or installing shielding between circuits and equipment used to handle plaintext classified or sensitive information that is not encrypted (RED) and secured circuits and equipment (BLACK), the latter including those carrying encrypted signals.

By the mid-1980s, the PC business was booming with IBM leading in terms of market share. Zenith Data Systems (ZDS) entered the fray. ZDS' Z-151 PC was touted to be TEMPEST-approved and won a $99.8 million government contract. The contract was to provide 10,500 Z-151 for use by U.S. Air Force and Navy high-security applications.[9]

> The Z-151, like other desktop compatibles, consisted of three components: a display, detachable keyboard, and system unit (case) housing the CPU, disk drives, and electronic internals of the system. It used an 8088 microprocessor, supported an 8087 numeric co-processor, ran MS-DOS, and came with 128K RAM (expandable to 640K), two serial ports and a parallel port, and two 5.25 inch 360K floppy disk drives. An optional 10.6Mb Winchester hard disk drive could replace one of the floppy drives."[10]
>
> Zenith claims that the Z-151 is highly compatible with the IBM PC and runs most off-the-shelf IBM PC software. As evidence, they included a list of 131 packages that were tested and "believed to be generally compatible with today's IBM PC." Heading the list is Lotus 1–2–3, which also happened to be the de facto standard of IBM PC compatibility. The Z-151 ran version Lotus 1–2–3 1A with no problems. Buried in the list is the other paragon of PC compatibility, Microsoft Flight Simulator. Again, the program ran perfectly.[11]

There was a high demand for these systems, and WPAD wanted a piece of the action. The large metal roll-around cabinets we were using to secure our PCs were cumbersome and expensive. WPAD Purchasing Manager, John Ason, was tapped to procure a number of Z-151s for WPAD. John was a former member of the U.S. Air Force with an extensive logistics background. With the high demand for these PCs by the armed services and other government agencies, WPAD had to wait in line. Daily, John was hounded by Navy personnel and WPAD management about when we could expect delivery.

In anticipation of receiving the PCs, we arranged for staff to be trained in the use of the WordPerfect word-processing software. WordPerfect was a word processing application with a long history on multiple PC platforms. At the height of its popularity in the 1980s and early 1990s, it was the dominant player in the word processor market, displacing the prior market leader WordStar. WordPerfect gained praise for its "look of sparseness" and clean display. It rapidly displaced most other systems, especially after the 4.2 release in 1986, and it became the standard in the DOS market by version 5.1 in 1989."[12]

Finally, the day came, and I remember that a number of the precious Z-151 PCs arrived in our receiving area. The components were unboxed and deployed to various I&C personnel. Examining the Z-151s, it was evident that the bulk of the TEMPEST protections were present in the system unit's housing or case. The case contained the key components, central processing unit, mother board, memory, etc. The case of the Z-151 was much heavier compared to non-TEMPEST PCs, and a closer look revealed that the case's metal enclosure was secured with over fifty screws! We unscrewed the fifty-plus fasteners and found that a heavy rubber gasket encased in a metallic sheath shielded the metal case's seams. This excessive shielding now made sense as to how electronic emissions would not leak into the ether.

WPAD management and Navy personnel looked on with pride as the PCs were distributed to engineers, procurement professionals, and secretaries. Then, the problems began! As the secretaries used the machines with the WordPerfect software, something strange began happening. The PC's cursor began jumping around the screen uncontrollably and without human provocation. Electrical engineers were brought in to assess the issue. When the PCs started up, they performed with no problems. After a few minutes of use, the cursor went crazy, jumping all over the screen. It was determined that due to the heavy computer case and shielding, excessive heat built up within the case and caused the software/cursor issues. The Z-151s were a bust. Attempts to address the issue were fruitless, and the PCs were boxed up and returned.

2.10 COMPUTER VIRUSES

> The first academic work on the theory of self-replicating computer programs was done in 1949 by John von Neumann, who gave lectures at the University of Illinois about the "Theory and Organization of Complicated Automata". The work of von Neumann was later published as the "Theory of self-reproducing automata". In his essay von Neumann described how a computer program could be designed to reproduce itself. Von Neumann's design for a self-reproducing computer program is considered the world's first computer virus, and he is considered to be the theoretical "father" of computer virology.[13]

At WPAD, we had no Internet connections. And before our LAN implementation, we did not have to worry about infections via the network vector. We did, however, let WPAD personnel bring diskettes in-and-out of WPAD. This supported the early days of working with our office software at home for unclassified use. (See Section 2.8) I was concerned with computer viral infections propagated by diskette and mainly "boot sector" infections. To address this vulnerability, I engaged Ray Glath. Ray had a software company, RG Software, which had an early virus-checking program. I procured his solution and set up a protocol whereby, as diskettes were brought into the facility, they were surrendered to the guard at the building's entrance. Then, I or one of my team would collect the diskettes and run them through the virus checker. If clean, we would ink-stamp them with a small golden bee ("bug") to show they had been checked and were allowed on-site.

As computer viruses evolved with more sophistication, a U.S. DOE Headquarters memo dated November 22, 1991, provided WPAD with a copy of *Data Physician Plus!* Virus protection software. I issued WPAD-LIS-PCP-432 dated April 30, 1992, to the Pittsburgh Naval Reactors Office with the subject line: IMPLEMENTATION STRATEGY AND VIRUS CHECKING POLICY TO SUPPORT WPAD'S USE OF DATA PHYSICIAN PLUS!; REQUEST FOR PITTSBURGH NAVAL REACTORS (PNR) APPROVAL OF. I wanted to continue with our protocol of checking diskettes prior to them being brought into our facility. In the memo, I identified that, to date, WPAD had not been infected with a computer virus. I cited our employee awareness program and employee's willingness to comply with the protocol for this success. I also recommended that a backup virus detection/eradication software from a different anti-virus vendor be maintained. The reasoning was that if an infection occurred within the facility, that was not detected or recognized by *Data Physician Plus*! there would be fallback software.

Lessons Learned *Letter logs and document serialization.* Letter logs and document serialization played a central role at WPAD. Our entire division maintained meticulous records of correspondence with ANSTR, NAVSEA, PNR, and other agencies in the Naval Nuclear program. Each formal letter was logged and tracked using a serialized numbering system that included the WPAD ACTIVITY-SECTION, a sequential number, date, and subject, ensuring we consistently met our customer commitments. This discipline in managing and tracking formal communication through serialized letters and logs became a foundational practice that I later applied in my CISO roles, where maintaining rigorous records and traceability proved essential for regulatory adherence and operational accountability.

2.11 IBM VERSUS APPLE

Westinghouse and General Electric were in a competitive posture as Prime Contractors to the Naval Nuclear Program. Naval Sea Systems Command (NAVSEA) occupied office space in Crystal City, Virginia. As office automation technologies and standards were coalescing, NAVSEA watched the disparate approaches Bettis/WPAD and KAPL/MAO took to their office automation and computing efforts.

Bettis and WPAD chose the IBM path, including the nascent Microsoft's Windows interface software. KAPL and MAO opted to go the Apple/MAC route. Along with Bettis and WPAD, NAVSEA standardized on IBM/Wintel for their office automation platform. This decision gave Bettis/WPAD a huge competitive advantage over KAPL/MAO. The conversion programs necessary to convert Apple-generated documents into Microsoft-readable/storable formats were not mature. There was frustration on many levels trying to work with output from the KAPL/MAO systems.

Another impediment to KAPL/MAO's office automation efforts was the fact that DoE personnel at KAPL were hesitant to approve MAO's systems for classified processing. Apple systems had advantages in terms of graphics and ease of use, but IBM/Wintel systems were viewed as better suited for business office automation. There was a sense that the Apple platform was not viewed as a serious option for Naval Nuclear program work. As a result, WPAD and Bettis became NAVSEA's go-to organizations for office automation leadership.

2.12 QUALITY CIRCLES

Periodically, NAVSEA would chew out Westinghouse and General Electric on any number of issues. The issue of *quality* was the main topic of NAVSEA's most recent ire. WPAD General Manager, Wilson Kennedy, hauled almost all 600 WPAD employees a couple of miles up Monroeville, PA's Route 22 to a large banquet room at the Howard Johnson's motel. There we received Mr. Kennedy's message of dissatisfaction and disappointment in our collective performance. We all got the message loud and clear that every aspect of our work had to improve. If we didn't shape up, we would lose work to General Electric.

The tool that was selected to help us improve was a corporate Westinghouse-wide program – Quality Circles (QC). "A Quality Circle is a group of 4 to 10 employees performing similar work who volunteer to meet regularly, on company time, to identify the cause of on-the-job problems and to propose solutions to management."[14] I have to say that the QC program was a resounding success. Once a project was approved for a QC, an interdisciplinary team was selected that included WPAD engineers and other key professionals. A formal announcement was made identifying the QC project, team members, and expected duration of the project. The QC project announcement was signed by Mr. Wilson Kennedy, WPAD's General Manager, showing top management support for the project.

One of the early QC projects was to formalize a recognition program, including the establishment of an ongoing recognition committee. The committee established various awards such as "The General Manager's Award," "Distinguished Achievement Award," and other division recognition awards. Following you will see several plaques recognizing individual and team excellence. The entirety of the WPAD Division bought into QC's and many quality projects resulted in better performance and quality outcomes.

2.13 LOCAL AREA NETWORK (LAN)

Another evolving technology was in LAN. With our PC deployments, we had a functional, classified office automation ecosystem using IBM/Wintel technology. The next logical step was to network the computers together within WPAD. The dominant network operating system to implement our LAN was Novell's Netware.

> The original NetWare product in 1983 supported clients running both CP/M and MS-DOS, ran over a proprietary star network topology and was based on a Novell-built file server using the Motorola 68000 processor. The company soon moved away from building its own hardware, and NetWare became hardware-independent, running on any suitable Intel-based IBM PC compatible system, and able to utilize a wide range of network cards. From the beginning, NetWare implemented a number of features inspired by mainframe and minicomputer systems that were not available in its competitors' products.[15]

WPAD acquired the funding to install a classified LAN throughout our office space. The backbone of the system used fiber-optic cabling. The reasoning was that it would be virtually impossible to tap into fiber and extract classified data. Also, fiber cable wouldn't bleed or emanate signals. The Novell computer/servers that operated the LAN were housed in WPAD's secure computer center. The LAN was distributed from floor-to-floor via the locked utility closets at the end of each floor. Out of the closets, small plastic channels supporting fiber runs were installed in the center of the ceilings on each floor. The fiber then ran down the external walls to each workspace having PCs. There, a converter box converted the network traffic from the optical cable into a coax cable which then connected to each PC. To ensure network security, the converter boxes with A/B switches were housed in metal *breadboxes* that were locked with an approved combination lock. When the shift ended, the A/B switch was switched off and the LAN box locked, which shut down PC access to the LAN. The metal breadbox had a clever design where there was a small metal channel piece on the inside of the breadbox's lid. This metal channel only allowed the breadbox's lid to close completely and lock when the A/B switch was physically in the off position.

I remember that we got into a disagreement with ANSTR over the positions of internal electrical wiring and LAN coax distribution wires. The TEMPEST guidance at the time required a four-inch separation between signal and power lines. The electrical wiring within the walls and the LAN coax (signal) cabling would theoretically intersect only at one point – one wire behind the physical walls running North/South and the coax wire running East/West. Our rationale was that since both lines intersected at only one point, they would not travel in parallel for any physical length sufficient to cause potential bleeding over between data and power lines. Of course, ANSTR won out, and we had to install a wooden channel, much like a chair rail, halfway up the wall in which the LAN's coax cable rode. This channel would ensure a four-inch separation between the external coax and power lines within the walls. Unfortunately, these additional measures delayed the installation and approval for our LAN to be operational.

My job as CSSM was to document the necessary controls by which our systems met the DoE 5637.1 Order and obtain PNR's approvals. In 1991,

Figure 2.1 Westinghouse Plant Apparatus Division General Manager's Award

I received WPAD's highest award, the General Manager's Award. The inscription read, "Effectively implementing a first-class computer security program which is flexible, practical, and cost-effective and convenient to users." Ultimately, our classified computer security program developed a secure LAN configuration that saved about $1 million in installation and equipment costs and accelerated the total implementation of the LAN three years ahead of schedule (Figure 2.1).

2.14 PHYSICAL SECURITY MEASURES

When I first joined WPAD, we occupied the top six floors of the building. There were four lower floors occupied by other commercial businesses. Sharing our classified office space within the same building posed a security risk. The other issue was the use of physical keys to get onto the floors from the elevator vestibules. Invariably, people would lose their keys. When this happened, all the door locks had to be re-keyed, and everyone's key had to be replaced. I would accompany John Powers in the key distribution process. We traveled floor to floor, retrieving the old keys and replacing them with new ones. This was a long and expensive undertaking. Employees who lost their keys were put on a list that went to WPAD's general manager.

WPAD eventually secured funding to install a building security system. A great deal of customization needed to be programmed into the system relative to the elevator vestibules. The company selected to install the new system did not have security-cleared personnel, so John Powers and I had to escort them the entire time they were on site – for months. This was a major blow to our individual productivity. It was fortunate that John, an electrical engineer by training, was involved in the installation process, as he had to guide them while installing their own systems. I had the PC in my locked office that managed the card access aspect of the new building security system. The PC's database contained all WPAD personnel and other cleared personnel with card/badge reader access to the building and each floor. With the system, we could restrict access to more sensitive areas such as the computer center. The project was successful.

On both ends of each floor was a red burn barrel. WPAD staff used these to dump their unwanted classified paperwork. At the end of normal business hours, maintenance staff rolled the barrels into the locked utility closets at the end of each floor. At routine intervals, these barrels were emptied to a central location. When there was a sufficient pile of classified refuse, it was transported to a paper-pulping plant for destruction. Two of the WPAD maintenance staff had to transport and witness the pulping of the paper to ensure proper and complete destruction of classified paperwork. And the crew that came in nightly to clean the offices had to be cleared as well. Our unclassified paper and other refuse were dumped in large dumpsters positioned right outside the building's entrance. Even these dumpsters were locked with a regular padlock.

John Powers and I performed a number of periodic facility audits and reviews. One such audit was to perform *ingress* and *egress* inspections. For these reviews, we rifled through purses and briefcases to ensure classified information or other prohibited items were not being brought into or taken from the premises. We also performed after-hours desk checks to ensure classified information was not inadvertently left out and not properly stored in the employees' safe.

The security ID badges we wore within WPAD were always a source of scrutiny. We were to remove the badges whenever we exited the building. The term for badge removal while outside was to *declassify* yourself. Periodically, ANSTR personnel would stand outside and cite anyone who left the building and still had their badges on. We were also tested when ANSTR or PNR entered the building and flashed a badge with the picture of Mickey Mouse or other caricatures over their real pictures. These failures resulted in the requirement for our onsite guard to touch the badge for every person entering the building. The expectation was that the guard would be vigilant for any fraudulent badges.

One humorous story involved live plants and flowers that various I&C employees had in their cubicles. Wilson Kennedy was the division manager for I&C, and he was a serious and scary individual. Anytime I had an audience with him, I was nervous. Mr. Kennedy came in early every day, and he began to smell a foul odor as he traversed the floor on his way back to his office. Over several weeks, he became increasingly perturbed about the odor. A big investigation ensued, and the culprit turned out to be the numerous houseplants located on desks. Many of I&C's electrical engineers had graduated from Penn State, also well known for its farming and horticulture departments. A sample plant was sent to Penn State for analysis. It turned out that sugars in the plant's soil were causing a chemical reaction and the foul odor. Apparently, cleaning staff would dump leftover soda from cans left on desks into the plant's soil, causing the heinous stench. *Mystery solved!*

Another story involved one of our PC technicians. We had no DoE-approved way to dispose of inoperative hard drives. When a system's hard drive failed, the drive was removed and placed on a pile that had accumulated in the technician's locked room. Even degaussing drives was not approved, and we didn't have an approved software program to wipe the disks either. For some reason, one of the techs put an inoperative hard drive from a classified PC into the regular, unclassified garbage. The drive, along with other WPAD trash, was picked up and taken to a local landfill. Management became aware and had to inform ANSTR. The offending technician and another I&C engineer had to go to the landfill and look for the hard drive. Luckily, they found it and it was returned to WPAD. Subsequent methods to declassify drives were to cut large crescent slices of the hard drive's internal platters. And one of the other Naval Nuclear sub-contractors extracted the hard drive's internal platters, and their guard forces shot them up with their weapons for target practice.

Before we had network-connected printers that could be shared, there were a large number of laser jet printers attached to single PCs throughout WPAD. Their use was expensive, especially in having to replace toner cartridges. Again, initially, we had no DoE-approved method to dispose of or refill spent toner cartridges. The concern was that residual classified information would remain on the toner cartridge drum. We tried to get approval to set the drums in the sunlight and have them dry out and self-destruct. But this method wasn't approved either. To save money, we tried to obtain approval to have the toner cartridges recharged with ink by a *cleared* third party.

2.15 COMSEC CUSTODIAN

Another of my side duties was that of COMSEC (Communications Security) Custodian – a position responsible for safeguarding sensitive encryption equipment and managing secure communication procedures. Now that I held a DoE "Q" Clearance, a higher-level security clearance required for access to certain classified information, I was able to take on these responsibilities. In a separate, locked room within WPAD's data center was an area that housed WPAD's encryption gear – specialized devices used to encode and protect confidential messages.

Since we maintained crypto gear on site, we were required to have an armed guard force for protecting these crucial security assets. Each day, secure communications were established by setting up encryption devices using paper tape threaded through a reader. This daily ritual was performed at all classified installations so everyone could communicate using the same encryption codes.

One of my duties as COMSEC Custodian was, at the end of each month, to destroy the plastic dispenser that held the paper tape using a sledgehammer. The resulting fragments were placed in a burn barrel for further secure disposal. There was also leftover paper crypto tape at month's end. At the time, the only approved method to dispose of the surplus tape was to pulp it in a small blender – just add water and blend until it became a thick paste, a process known as making a "crypto cocktail."

2.16 MANAGER, PERSONAL COMPUTER, LOCAL AREA NETWORK, AND SECURITY 1990–1992

With the maturation of our classified PC and LAN infrastructure, WPAD gained more technological credibility with NAVSEA. There was a need for

WPAD to develop custom programs for PC and LAN use. I left WPAD's facility group and went back to I&C to manage the PC programming group while retaining my CSSM duties. Included in my purview was the 650-node LAN and 12 SUN workstations. DoE provided various opportunities for computer security training. A memorable training took place at Kirtland Air Force Base (AFB) in Albuquerque, New Mexico.

> Kirtland AFB is the largest installation in Air Force Global Strike Command and sixth largest in the United States Air Force. The base occupies 51,558 acres and employs over 23,000 people, including more than 4,200 active duty and 1,000 Guard, plus 3,200 part-time Reserve personnel.[16]

To go to the CSSM training class, we entered the base and drove far back into the hills. A long office trailer sat in the middle of nowhere and was surrounded by a high chain link fence with entry protected by a cipher lock. Two individuals led the training – Eugene "Gene" Schultz and Tom Longstaff. Both Gene and Tom were giants in the cybersecurity arena. The other training I went to was held at Oak Ridge, Tennessee, and focused on COMSEC security.

2.17 MANAGER, LOGISTICS SYSTEMS PROGRAMMING 1992–1996

In addition to my CSSM responsibilities, I transitioned from PC and LAN programming to managing Logistics Systems Programming. In this role, I led a team of mainframe programmers, network specialists, and computer operations staff. A major project we completed was developing the Provisioning Information Processing System (PIPS), which allowed the Navy's Ships Parts Control Center (SPCC) to move off an aging PerkinElmer minicomputer that costs $700,000 annually to operate. The new PIPS ran efficiently on the Standard Logistics (SL) mainframe. Our team received a letter of appreciation from the Commanding Officer of SPCC on September 26, 1995 (Figure 2.2). And for this achievement, I was honored with the WPAD's Distinguished Achievement Award in 1995 (Figure 2.3).

2.18 NAVAL REACTORS – SECURE REMOTE AREA NETWORK

As I wrote in Section 2.4, I had gone back to school at the University of Pittsburgh to study telecommunications and networking, which particularly interested me. In 1995, I earned a Certificate of Advanced Studies (CAS) in Telecommunications. The timing of this degree led directly to my last and most satisfying project at WPAD.

DEPARTMENT OF THE NAVY
NAVY SHIPS PARTS CONTROL CENTER
5450 CARLISLE PIKE
5777 95355 PIKB
MECHANICSBURG, PA 170055-0788

4400

Ser 5731/797

From: Commanding Officer, Navy Ships Parts Control Center
To: General Manager, Westinghouse Plant Apparatus Division, Pittsburgh (Wilson R. Kennedy)

Subj: **LETTER OF APPRECIATION**

1. For the past two years individuals from my organization have been working with your Automated Data Processing system on the development of the Provisioning Integrated Processing System (PIPS). The system came on line in June 1995 and has been a great success. To date, the system has improved the initial provisioning system fill rate from 1 less than 50%, under the old provisioning system, to 79% under PIPS. In addition, systems flow of 500 candidates through the system per week providing substantial productivity enhancements. These productivity increases have provided us the ability to reduce flow from 1.5 to 3.5 man hours per item. These improvements have provided us the ability to reduce our resource requirementsduring our downsizing efforts at NSPCC.

2. I would like to recognize Mr. Ron Haklar, Mr. David Linttl, Mr. Richard Neeilson and Ms. Stella George in particular for their outstanding efforts and contributions in bringing this system to fruition. These individuals have been extremely responsive to all of our requirements in a far more there motivated fashion than other Navy contractors. Please pass along my hearty thanks to all your programming staff!

Sincerely,

CDR, SC, USN
Commanding Officer

Figure 2.2 Letter of appreciation from the Commanding Officer of the Navy Ships Parts Control Center Dated September 26, 1995

WPAD continued its lead role in office automation and LAN technologies. NAVSEA tapped WPAD to lead a project to install a classified wide area network. The project offered the obvious advantages of better communications among selected entities engaged in Naval Nuclear Program work but added new components – email and video conferencing. NAVSEA wanted to slash travel budgets where they could, and video conferencing would be the answer. I was privileged to lead a site installation team that implemented a secure/encrypted wide area network via government-provided encryption

Figure 2.3 Westinghouse Plant Apparatus Division Distinguished Achievement Award

devices. The Naval Nuclear Program's wide area network included video conferencing at fourteen proposed sites throughout the United States and over to Pearl Harbor, Hawaii. *What a great project!*

Our first order of business was to generate a comprehensive list of computing equipment with which to realize the vision of the Naval Nuclear Program's automated future. To do this, a team was established at WPAD to put together a five-year plan. The plan included a list of the required equipment that were included in a capital equipment request. The team came through, and the request was approved. For our efforts, the team received a WPAD Recognition Award for developing a five-year plan and Capital Equipment Request.

At this time, a government-wide telecommunications contract was the FEDERAL TELECOMMUNICATIONS SYSTEM (FTS) 2000.

> Federal Telecommunications System 2000 (FTS2000) is a long-distance telecommunications service for the United States federal government, including services such as switched voice service for voice or data up to 4.8 kbit/s, switched data at 56 kbit/s and 64 kbit/s, switched digital integrated service for voice, data, image, and video up to 1.544 Mbit/s, packet-switched service for data in packet form, video transmission for both compressed and wideband video, and dedicated point-to-point private line for voice and data.[17]

Our Secure Remote Area Network (SECRAN) project was to have T1 telecommunication lines connecting the proposed fourteen sites. At the time, FTS 2000 did not offer a full T1 line but instead had fractional T1s.

> A T1 line is a dedicated transmission connection between a service provider and client. It uses an advanced telephone line to carry more data than a traditional standard analog line that carries a single channel of data at 64 Kilobits per second (Kbp). T1 line speed is consistent and constant. A T1 line can carry twenty-four voice channels for telephone calls or digital data at a rate of 1.544 Mbps, and with usage of compression, carried channels double to 48.[18]

For our SECRAN project, FTS 2000 engineers had to combine four fractional T1 lines into one full T1 line. Apparently, this was not technically trivial to accomplish, even though the FTS 2000 contract specified full T1 lines and speeds.

SECRAN used Novell Netware, and the network's controlling systems were housed at WPAD's computer center. The videoconferencing system that would allow all the connected sites to conduct classified videoconferencing was housed and controlled by Bettis Atomic Laboratory personnel. The videoconferencing capabilities at each location varied in sophistication, with smaller shipyard offices having a large TV and fiber optic cable modem connections. Large sites like NAVSEA and the Prime Contractors had large, sophisticated rooms dedicated to conducting videoconferencing. Once video conferencing was in place, subsequent physical travel had to be approved by the NAVSEA and ANSTR offices.

Figure 2.4 Initial Secran/WAN Wide Area Network Implementation

© Ron Baklarz 1995

We had a small site installation team, including myself, two rotational technicians, and a WPAD purchasing professional with the responsibility to buy and deliver all the necessary equipment. Over the summer of 1994, my team and I visited each site to meet with designated site support personnel and give a high-level view of the project and installation expectations. The sites on the Eastern coast involved were Navy Ships Parts Control Center (SPCC), Bettis, WPAD, MAO, KAPL, Electric Boat – Groton, Portsmouth Naval Shipyard, NAVSEA, Norfolk Naval Shipyard, Charleston Naval Shipyard, Newport News Shipbuilding. Out to the west was Puget Sound Naval Shipyard, and then out to Pearl Harbor, HI (Figure 2.4). The proposed SECRAN/NR WAN, Figure 2.4, included more sites than were first installed.

Over the winter months, we bought all the necessary computer and videoconferencing equipment and sent them out to each site. One of the more complex items in the network's overall setup and operation was the need for NSA encryption equipment at each of the SECRAN-connected sites. These systems are complex, and obtaining and shipping them was one matter, but they had to be installed by security-cleared, NSA-certified, and approved electricians. Collectively, procuring and setting up the FTS 2000 T1 lines, pre-positioning computers and videoconferencing equipment, and scheduling NSA encryption equipment installation was a significant logistical challenge. Over the summer of 1995, we began the site installation work.

Norfolk Naval Shipyard and Newport News Shipping and Dry Dock (NNSD) are in close proximity to one another. So, we were able to visit both sites for our SECRAN pre-installation and installation efforts. Two weeks prior to the delivery of the Aircraft Carrier CVN-74 John C Stennis to the Navy by NNSD, we were honored to be given a tour of the massive new nuclear-powered aircraft carrier.

Between the site visits in 1994 and the installation efforts of 1995, my team and I logged countless hours in airports and traveling on planes. I've always found myself drawn to people-watching during these travels, and spotting a celebrity in the crowd became a running joke among my team. One afternoon at the Norfolk, VA, airport was particularly memorable. After a stretch of idle waiting, I suddenly noticed a familiar figure moving past our group. At first, my teammates were skeptical when I whispered, "That was Wolfman Jack!" As someone who grew up listening to his iconic radio voice, seeing Wolfman Jack in person felt surreal – a brush with a legend I never expected. After hesitating for a moment, I finally gathered my courage and hurried after him. Soon, I spotted him seated in a small airport diner, hunched over his meal.

With a heart pounding in anticipation, I approached, and it was unmistakable: it was Wolfman Jack himself. I made nervous small talk and asked him for an autograph. I had nothing for him to sign but the copy of The Wall Street Journal I'd brought with me. He graciously signed the newspaper with his elaborate signature (Figure 2.5), sharing a few kind words before returning to his meal. The experience was bittersweet; not long after,

THE WALL STR

What's News—

Figure 2.5 Autograph Wolfman Jack

I learned of his passing from a heart attack on July 1, 1995. The Wall Street Journal he signed was dated April 1995 – now a cherished keepsake marking the brief, unforgettable encounter with a voice that had colored my childhood.

I enjoy watching boxing, and one evening, I was watching a match on television featuring Vinny "Paz" Pazienza. Vinny was a bull in the ring, and I noticed an attractive lady at the ringside, obviously cheering for Vinny. As a testament to his toughness, Vinny was in a serious car accident and had to relinquish his WBA World Jr. Middleweight Championship belt. Vinny broke his neck, and the doctors told him he may never walk again and certainly would never fight again. Pazienza had to wear a medical device called a Halo, a circular metal brace screwed into the skull in four spots and propped up with four metal rods. He had the Halo screwed to his skull for three months, during which he maintained a workout regimen against doctors' orders. He returned to the ring thirteen months after the accident and defeated future WBC World Jr. Middleweight Champion Luis Santana by a ten-round decision.[19]

As you have probably guessed, I saw Vinny in an airport. He was sporting a hoodie and sunglasses to hide his eyes, blackened by the fight the night before. And he was accompanied by the beautiful woman I saw at his ringside. I threw caution to the wind, walked up to the couple, and asked him for his autograph. He graciously complied as I told him I had watched his boxing match the night before. Again, I had nothing formal for him to write on, so I tore the bottom of my airplane ticket folder. As we made small talk, his girlfriend smiled adoringly at her gladiator. After we parted ways, a member of my team went into the magazine store and bought a copy of a popular men's magazine. *As he scanned the magazine for interesting articles, it became apparent that Vinny's girlfriend was one of the*

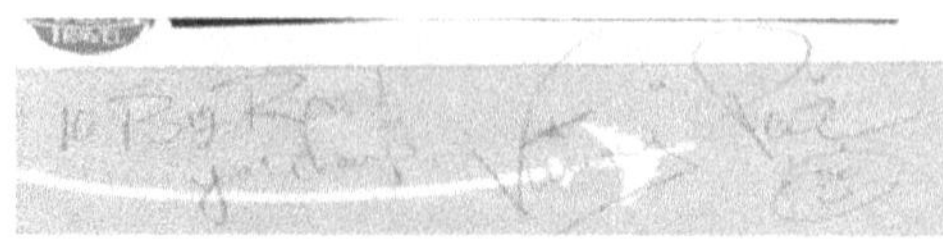

Figure 2.6 Autograph Vinny "Paz" Pazienza

magazine's models – the centerfold! We had a good laugh. I should have gotten her autograph rather than Vinny's (Figure 2.6).

Some WAN installation sites had technically astute staff, such as NAVSEA, Bettis, KAPL, and MAO. Other sites had good staff and required only minimal installation support, and a few sites required significant and unexpected extra work required on our part to complete the installation. Often, when on site, I would have two telephone calls going at the same time. In one ear, I had FTS 2000 engineers on the line, and in the other, Bettis engineers. The FTS 2000 engineer would make tweaks on the fly, and Bettis would confirm a clean signal transmission. When each installation ended, we would get on the video conferencing system and call back to WPAD, demonstrating a successful installation.

The one installation we had serious issues with was the line from Bremerton, Washington (Puget Sound Naval Shipyard), out to Pearl Harbor Naval Shipyard in Hawaii. We could not get the systems to connect. It turned out that the telephone company wrongly assumed the line was to be a voice-grade line versus a data line. They installed echo cancellers on the assumed voice line.

> Echo cancellation is used in telecom and telephony applications to improve the quality of voice communication. It prevents echoes (sic) from being created or captured. It can also remove the echo in post-processing. Echo cancellers operate by first analyzing the incoming voice stream and simultaneously monitoring the return voice stream before it's being transmitted. If the echo is detected, the echo cancellation engine subtracts it from the transmitted or received audio signal.[20]

Given the time differential, it took a couple of extra days for the telecom company to fix the issue. My team and I took good-natured ribbing for having to spend the extra time in Hawaii! Our site contact at Pearl Harbor was a diminutive oriental individual. He felt bad that we were having issues with the installation, so he asked us to go along with him for dinner one evening. He said he was taking us to *The Inn of the Sixth Happiness*. My imagination ran wild, wondering what sort of *happiness* was in store for us! It turned out to be a social club, and we were fed exotic traditional dishes such as sashimi. I use the term exotic because any food was better than the steady diet of fast foods we had to endure, trying to stay within the limits of our daily per diem expense budget.

At the end of the site installations, all were happy. Sites were using their video conferencing systems and another application as well. Included with the wide area network was e-mail using Novell's Groupwise. This was a great productivity and communication tool used across the Naval Nuclear Program. Remember, these applications were not being used over the public Internet but within the closed, classified NAVSEA WAN. I was tasked to develop an email policy for the Naval Nuclear Program. I *issued WPAD-LIS-CCS-190 dated October 19, 1995, entitled: USE OF NOVELL "GROUPWISE" ELECTRONIC MAIL (EMAIL) ON THE NAVAL NUCLEAR PROPULSION PROGRAM WIDE AREA NETWORK (WAN); REQUEST FOR APPROVAL.* This memo forwarded a thirteen (13) page policy governing the proper use and security of email. *However, one incident allegedly occurred at NAVSEA when an internal user sent an invitation to attend a "Tupperware" party. The email invitation was delivered to everyone at NAVSEA, including the Admiral!*

2.19 CD-ROM

The compact disc was first developed by Philips and Sony in 1982. Denon expanded on the CD-DA (compact disc digital audio) format to create the CD-ROM format, allowing it to store any data and not only audio. In 1984, Denon and Sony introduced the CD-ROM format to the public at a Japanese computer show. The first CD-ROM disc introduced to the public had a storage capacity of 553 MB. Today, a standard CD-ROM disc can store up to 700 MB of data or eighty minutes' worth of audio. Non-standard CD-ROM discs also exist that store up to 900 MB of data, or ninety-nine minutes of audio.[21]

Each nuclear vessel must maintain a complete library of technical manuals needed for each system responsible for the boat's operation. These manuals take up a lot of precious space, especially onboard a submarine. The idea of having these manuals available and searchable on CD-ROMs as opposed to the voluminous paper versions was desirable. I remember our engineers looking into this project. You have to remember standard formats like.pdf,.jpeg, and.gif were just evolving. We also looked into Optical Character Recognition (OCR) systems. OCRs convert images of typed, handwritten, or printed text into machine-encoded text. This would have helped in converting the paper manuals into a format that could be stored on CD-ROMs. I left WPAD before I saw the completion of this project.

2.20 ONTO THE NEXT ADVENTURE

My fourteen years at WPAD were a great experience. I earned my Master of Science Degree in Information Science and Certificate of Advanced Study in

Telecommunications using Westinghouse's tuition reimbursement program. I was recognized with General Manager, Distinguished Achievement, and Recognition awards for my contributions. I was involved with office automation, computing, and networks ranging from the early IBM Selectric typewriters and mimeographed copies to PCs, LANs, and WANs. Most importantly, as CSSM, I spent ten years designing an information security program in a time when there was little in the way of industry guidance or precedent, and we were developing policies and procedures expeditiously. I will always be grateful to all involved during my Naval Nuclear Program experience. The magnum opus project that closed out my career there was the two-year implementation of a classified wide area network that connected the major naval nuclear facilities on the East and West coasts and Pearl Harbor, Hawaii.

I have often felt that my experience in the Naval Nuclear Program ruined me, but in the best possible way. The Program offered a real sense of mission, and you felt you were making a difference for something bigger than you. I would spend many years and positions looking for that same experience. However, it was time to move on. The Naval Nuclear Program began with and continued to be dominated by engineers. Since I did not have an engineering degree, my career path would be limited. I have no ill will about this; the engineers I worked with were smart and capable. The Naval Nuclear Program did not suffer fools, and if one did not fit in or pull their weight, they did not last in the program. But I knew my limitations.

So, every Sunday morning, I would drive to a newsstand in downtown Pittsburgh. There, I would buy the large Sunday editions of the Chicago Tribune and the Washington Post. They each had extensive want ads, and I searched for information technology (IT) positions. This was a time before IT security positions were as plentiful as they would become. After a couple of months of perusing the papers, one advertisement caught my eye – Information Security Manager – U.S. House of Representatives.

2.21 ALL STARS – WPAD

Harvey Rosenblum – Without a doubt, I will always be indebted to Harvey for giving me my first shot at an information security lead role. He had a need to fill relative to compliance with the DoE Order and identify a security lead. I was at the right time and place relative to my background and education with the master's and certificate of advanced studies program at the University of Pittsburgh. Thank you, Harvey!

Rod Murphy – Rod worked along with me at WPAD, where he distinguished himself as technically astute and a quick study. As he came to work for me at the US House of Representatives, he gravitated to the network attack and penetration work. Rod held a number of security engineering and leading positions, including but not limited to Patriot Technologies, CSC, and Falconwood, Inc., where he retired as a Senior Certification and Accreditation Analyst.

2.22 TECHNOLOGY ADVANCEMENTS AND SECURITY DEVELOPMENTS 1982–1996

The following section is lengthy due to my working at WPAD for fourteen years. It is fascinating to look back at the history of technology in office automation, including the PC, software, and networking. The ARPANET project, a precursor to the Internet we know today, was started in 1966, long before I started working at WPAD. As far as office automation, I consider that the Microsoft and Windows/Intel (Wintel) platforms have done more to increase American productivity than possibly any other technologies.

1982

- February 1st, the Intel 80286 microprocessor was introduced.
- Compaq Computer Corp. was founded by Rod Canion and other Texas Instruments Incorporated engineers. Compaq was the first company to introduce a clone of the IBM PC (the Compaq Portable in 1983) and became IBM's biggest challenger in the corporate market.
- The CD-ROM (compact disc read-only memory) format was first developed by Denon, and the first CD (compact disc) was created at a Philips factory in Germany.
- Hayes released the Smartmodem 1200, a modem capable of transmitting 1,200 bits per second.
- WordPerfect Corporation introduced WordPerfect 1.0, a word processing program that became a popular word processing program.

1983

- Fred Cohen coined the term *virus* in a 1984 research paper as "a computer program that can affect other computer programs by modifying them in such a way as to include a (possibly evolved) copy of itself."
- ARPANET (Advanced Research Projects Agency Network) standardized on TCP/IP.
- IBM introduced the PC XT PC.
- The first version of Microsoft Word, Word 1.0, was released.
- Novell NetWare network operating system was first introduced. Novell NetWare was the first LAN software based on file server technology, running on both Ethernet and IBM Token Ring networks.
- More than 10 million computers were used in the United States in 1983.

1984

- IBM introduced the Token Ring, a physical and data link layer computer networking technology used to build LANs.
- IBM's AT (advanced technology) computer was introduced.
- The 3.5-inch floppy diskette was introduced and became an industry standard.
- May 3rd, Dell Computers was founded in Austin, Texas.
- IBM PCD (PC Division) introduced its first portable computer, the IBM Portable, weighing thirty pounds.
- Steve Jobs and Steve Wozniak were awarded the National Medal of Technology.

1985

- September 16th, Steve Jobs quit Apple.
- October, Intel introduced the 80386 microprocessor.
- October, FTP (file transfer protocol) was defined in RFC 959.
- CAT 1 wiring was introduced. CAT 1, Level 1, or voice-grade copper, is a grade of unshielded twisted pair cabling designed for telephone communications, and at one time was the most common on-premises wiring. Though CAT 1 is not currently considered adequate for data transmission, it was at one time used for that purpose.
- Microsoft and IBM began collaboration on the next-generation operating system (OS/2).

1986

- The AT or 101 key keyboard, alternatively known as the Model F keyboard, is a US standard keyboard introduced in 1986 by IBM.
- IBM released the IBM PC XT Model 286.
- March 19th, the Internet domain *ibm.com* came online.
- Microsoft was listed on the New York Stock Exchange, selling shares to the public at $21 each, making Bill Gates one of the world's youngest billionaires.
- The first cyber law, CFAA (Computer Fraud and Abuse Act) was enacted in the United States.
- The Brain boot sector virus was released. Brain is considered the first IBM PC-compatible virus. The virus was also known as Lahore, Pakistani, Pakistani Brain, and Pakistani flu as it was created in Lahore, Pakistan, by nineteen-year-old Pakistani programmer Basit Farooq Alvi and his brother, Amjad Farooq Alvi.
- More than 30 million computers were in use in the United States.

1987

- Microsoft shares hit $100 per share.

- IBM introduced the PS/2 PC with improved graphics.
- The first version of Microsoft Excel – version 2.0 – was released.
- John McAfee created VirusScan.

1988

- Robert Morris created and released the Morris worm on November 2, 1988. Robert Tappan Morris, the son of NSA cryptographer Robert Morris, said that he created the worm simply to see if it could be done. In 1989, Morris became the first person to be convicted of violating United States Code Title 18 (18 U.S.C. § 1030), the Computer Fraud and Abuse Act.
- The first T1 backbone was added to ARPANET (Advanced Research Projects Agency Network).
- SNMP (Simple Network Management Protocol) was introduced. SNMP is an Internet Standard protocol for collecting and organizing information about managed devices on IP networks and for modifying that information to change device behavior. Devices that typically support SNMP include cable modems, routers, network switches, servers, workstations, printers, and more.
- NTP (Network Time Protocol) was introduced. NTP, a networking protocol, synchronizes clocks between computer systems over packet-switched, variable-latency data networks.
- About 45 million PCs were in use in the United States.

1989

- The first recordable specification CD-WO (compact disc write once) was published in 1989 by Philips and Sony in the Orange Book.
- Several thousand floppy disks containing the AIDS Trojan, the first known ransomware, were mailed to subscribers of PC Business World magazine and a World Health Organization Acquired Immunodeficiency Syndrome (AIDS) conference mailing list. This DOS Trojan laid dormant for ninety boot cycles, then encrypted all filenames on the system. A notice was displayed asking for $189 to be sent to a post office box in Panama to receive the "decryption program."

1990

- Contractor Tim Berners-Lee, working with Robert Cailliau at CERN, proposed Hypertext Markup Language (HTML) as a system for CERN researchers to access and share documents.
- Microsoft and IBM stopped working together to develop operating systems.
- November 19th, Microsoft Office for Windows was released.

- Adobe co-founder Dr. John Warnock launches the paper-to-digital revolution with Adobe Portable Digital Format (pdf) precursor as "The Camelot Project."

1991

- The term Internet of Things was coined.
- NSF (National Science Foundation) opens the Internet to commercial use.
- Microsoft changed the name of OS/2 to Windows NT.
- On August 23, the WWW (World Wide Web) became available for everyone. Within the next two years, there were fifty websites created.
- On August 25, Linus Torvalds publicly released Linux and the Linux kernel to the Internet from an FTP (File Transfer Protocol) server from an FTP server at his Helsinki university.
- Symantec released Norton antivirus software.
- The programming language FORTRAN (Formula Translation) 90 was released.

1992

- Microsoft introduced Windows 3.1.
- NSFNET (National Science Foundation Network) upgraded to a T3 backbone.
- Linux was released under the GNU (GNU's Not Unix) General Public License.
- The Joint Photographic Experts Group created the JPEG standard based on the discrete cosine transform (DCT) algorithm.
- MIME (Multipurpose Internet Mail Extensions) standard was defined. MIME extended the format of email messages to support text in character sets other than ASCII, as well as attachments of audio, video, images, and application programs.

1993

- Fifty World Wide Web servers are known to exist as of January.
- Wired magazine was launched by American expatriates Louis Rossetto with his life partner and business partner Jane Metcalfe.
- March 22nd, Intel released the Pentium processor, a 60 MHz processor with 3.2 million transistors, and sold for $878.
- April 30th, CERN released the Web source code and made it public domain. This effect had an immediate effect as the Web experienced massive growth on the Internet.
- June 9th, Jeff Moss held the first DEF CON hacker convention.
- June 15th, Adobe officially launched Portable Digital Format (pdf), formerly The Camelot Project, standardized as ISO 32000. PDF

presents documents, including text formatting and images, in a manner independent of application software, hardware, and operating systems.

1994

- Red Hat Linux company was founded, and the Red Hat Linux distribution was released.
- Online transaction systems, including online banking and online shopping, started emerging on the Internet.
- Professor Thomas Nicely described the Intel FPU (floating-point unit) bug. A mathematical flaw in the Intel Pentium resulted in the Pentium not correctly performing floating-point calculations. This led to Intel recalling millions of the flawed processors.
- December 3rd, Sony released the original PlayStation, which became the first gaming console to ship over 100 million units.

1995

- The dot-com boom starts.
- Artificial Intelligence: A Modern Approach by Peter Norvig and Stuart Russell was published. In the ensuing decades, it became the authoritative textbook on the subject.
- November 22nd, Microsoft released Internet Explorer 2.0 which started the browser war with Netscape.
- February 15th, the FBI (Federal Bureau of Investigation) arrested computer hacker Kevin Mitnick at his Raleigh, North Carolina apartment. His federal offenses related to a two-and-a-half-year period of computer hacking, including computer and wire fraud.
- August 24th, Microsoft released Windows 95 and sold more than 1 million copies within four days of its release.
- Dan Farmer and Wietse Venema released the SATAN (Security Administrator Tool for Analyzing Networks) tools.
- December 5th, IBM unveiled Deep Blue a parallel computing system that would later play against the World Chess Champion Garry Kasparov.
- The first Macro virus, called "Concept," was created and designed to attack Microsoft Word documents. Macro viruses are written in a macro programming language which are embedded inside a software application (e.g., word processors and spreadsheet applications).

1996

- For the first time, more e-mail was sent than postal mail in the United States.
- IPv6 was introduced.

- Chess master Garry Kasparov defeated IBM computer Deep Blue in a six-game match, where it lost four games to two. Deep Blue was later improved and defeated Mr. Kasparov.

NOTES

1 COBOL. (n.d.). *Wikipedia.* https://en.wikipedia.org/wiki/COBOL
2 Fortran. (n.d.). *Wikipedia.* https://en.wikipedia.org/wiki/Fortran
3 Keypunch. (n.d.). *Wikipedia.* https://en.wikipedia.org/wiki/Keypunch
4 Digibarn Computer Museum. (n.d.). *Xerox 860 information processing system.* https://digibarn.com/collections/systems/xerox860/index.html
5 Computer History Museum. (n.d.). *Timeline of computer history.* https://www.computerhistory.org/timeline/computers/
6 Q clearance. (n.d.). *Wikipedia.* https://en.wikipedia.org/wiki/Q_clearance
7 Compliance Testing. (n.d.). *What is the difference between FCC Class A and Class B?* https://compliancetesting.com/what-is-the-difference-between-fcc-class-a-and-b/
8 Tempest (codename). (n.d.). *Wikipedia.* https://en.wikipedia.org/wiki/Tempest_(codename)
9 Zenith Z-151: Choice of U. (1985). *Creative computing.* https://www.atarimagazines.com/creative/v11n9/50_Zenith_Z151_choice_of_U.php
10 Zenith Z-151: Choice of U. (1985). *Creative computing.* https://www.atarimagazines.com/creative/v11n9/50_Zenith_Z151_choice_of_U.php
11 Zenith Z-151: Choice of U. (1985). *Creative computing.* https://www.atarimagazines.com/creative/v11n9/50_Zenith_Z151_choice_of_U.php
12 WordPerfect. (n.d.). *Wikipedia.* https://en.wikipedia.org/wiki/WordPerfect
13 von Neumann, J. (n.d.). *John von Neumann. Wikipedia.* https://en.wikipedia.org/wiki/John_von_Neumann
14 Office of Scientific and Technical Information. (n.d.). *Bibliographic record 6437306.* https://www.osti.gov/biblio/6437306
15 NetWare. (n.d.). *Wikipedia.* https://en.wikipedia.org/wiki/NetWare
16 Kirtland Air Force Base. (n.d.). *Wikipedia.* https://en.wikipedia.org/wiki/Kirtland_Air_Force_Base
17 FTS2000. (n.d.). *Wikipedia.* https://en.wikipedia.org/wiki/FTS2000
18 T-carrier. (n.d.). *Wikipedia.* https://en.wikipedia.org/wiki/T-carrier
19 Paz, V. (n.d.). *Vinny Paz. Wikipedia.* https://en.wikipedia.org/wiki/Vinny_Paz
20 LiveAgent. (n.d.). *Echo cancellation.* https://www.liveagent.com/customer-support-glossary/echo-cancellation/
21 CD-ROM. (n.d.). *Wikipedia.* https://en.wikipedia.org/wiki/CD-ROM

Chapter 3

United States House of Representatives 1996–1997

Position Held: Security Manager

Location: 631 Ford House Office Building
Washington, D.C. 20515

Disclaimer Since I held government security clearances while employed at the United States House of Representative, I submitted this chapter for a Department of Defense – Defense Office of Prepublication and Security Review (DOPSR). The entirety of the chapter was CLEARED FOR OPEN PUBLICATION via "Ref: DOPSR 25-P-0509"dated April 2, 2025.

3.1 U.S. HOUSE OF REPRESENTATIVES – OVERVIEW

I worked at the U.S. House of Representatives for two years over the 105th and 106th sessions of Congress. *I was the first security administrator, or my official title of security manager, hired at the US House of Representatives.* The first Inspector General (IG) at the House, John W. Lainhart IV, commissioned an audit of the House's cybersecurity posture conducted by Price Waterhouse (PW). The audit findings identified the need for hiring a cybersecurity manager. In my new position, I had to address a list of forty-one (41) other cybersecurity discrepancies identified in the PW audit. Culturally, the U.S. House of Representatives was the "wild west" as compared to my previous security role in the Naval Nuclear Program. Members of Congress were not subject to the policies that I and my team developed although their staff were required to follow them.

3.2 INTERVIEW AND ARRIVAL

I responded to the want-ad in the Washington Post's Sunday, October 29, 1995, edition for Security Administrator at the U.S. House of Representatives

DOI: 10.1201/9781003650645-5

Computer

U.S. HOUSE OF REPRESENTATIVES
HOUSE INFORMATION RESOURCES

HOUSE INFORMATION RESOURCES (H.I.R.), the technology, information and communications support organization of the U.S. House of Representatives, is currently recruiting. Incumbents are required to have good communication skills, technical depth, experience in end user support and the ability to work in a team environment. This is an opportunity to become a member of the team that is helping to build the technology support system for the 21st century Congress. The following opportunities are available:

Security Administrator to administer information security policies and procedures for the House. Strong understanding of network topologies and protocols, including Ethernet, FDDI, TCP/IP, IPX, IP, and AppleTalk. Frame relay and SNA desired. Strong understanding of access control issues and disaster recovery strategies in a heterogeneous LAN/WAN computing environment, including IBM MVS/ESA, UNIX, Windows NT, Novell, Macintosh and stand-alone PCs. Proven supervisory experience in securing information systems and networks. **$76,152.**

INTEGRATION

Senior Systems Analyst: Extensive experience in ADABAS/Natural 2, COBOL, CICS, JCL. PC programming with Visual Basic or PowerBuilder highly desirable. Oracle a plus. **$60,274.**

Programmer Analyst (1 position): At least one year experience in an IBM mainframe environment. Ability to develop COBOL programs. (1 position) Experience in all aspects of application developments. Strong background in relational database technology including performance, file design, and problem solving issues. Specific experience with ADABAS/Natural 2, Sybase, UNIX and client/server architecture is required. **$47,162/$36,543**

COMMUNICATIONS

Communications Specialist (2 positions) - Experience with the administration of one or more of AIX, HP-UX, SunOS, and Solaris in a TCP/IP environment and the ability to program in C and a shell language. **$53,054** (1 position) Experience is required in the administration of SNA networks including installation and maintenance of VTAM, NCP, SMPE, netview. Hands on experience with mainframe-based TCP/IP products a plus. **$47,162.**

Network Systems Engineer II (1 position): Experience required in one or more of: Ethernet, routed networks on FDDI, frame relay, and structured wiring. (1 position) Experience required in the installation, configuration, and maintenance of an enterprise-wide SNMP management system. **$47,162.**

Communications Specialist I: Experience is required with Ethernet, maintenance of campus LANs, standard LAN protocols, and network diagnostics. Experience with Cabletron, Cisco, and Sniffer technology is a plus. **$41,625.**

OPERATIONS

Computer Systems Specialist: Assist technical users of the H.I.R. mainframe with a wide array of software packages including ISPF, JCL, TSO, SAS, and SPSS; install software packages and train users; provide direct programming support for legislative offices. Thorough knowledge is required of ISPF, JCL, and special purpose software such as File-AID, SDSF, SAS, and SPSS. Ability to program in PL/1, knowledge of DOS, experience with LANs and familiarity with address standardization software are highly desirable. **$53,054.**

Distributed Systems Specialist (2 positions): Expertise in installing, configuring and troubleshooting various PC software products in support of the House E-Mail and mailfax applications. Experience with hardware installation and integration with skills in Novell, Windows NT, Groupware products, Internet services, E-Mail software tools, and distributed storage management. **$53,054/$36,543.**

CLIENT SERVICES

Technical Support Representative (6 positions): Support microcomputer local area networks (LANs). Provide state-of-the-art technical solutions for the House integrated systems. Knowledge of microcomputer and LAN operating systems software/hardware, advanced PC application software, Groupware products, Internet Services, multi-media and E-Mail software tools, systems, and databases on single work stations and network file servers. **$53,054/$36,543.**

Telephone Operator: Provide telephone traffic operation to the U.S. Congress in a 24-hour centralized office. Occasional weekend work is required. **$22,186.**

For immediate consideration, mail resume and salary history to (NO PHONE CALLS PLEASE):

Office of Human Resources
Attention: CAO-KEF
Room 263, Cannon House Office Building
Washington, DC 20515-6610

An equal opportunity employer.

Figure 3.1 Washington Post, October 29, 1995

(Figure 3.1). The job topped the list of ten other positions identified in the ad. Wow! I thought this would be a great position, so I sent in my resume. I had no expectations of getting an interview for such a prestigious position, so I continued my job search. To my surprise, I was contacted by the House Information Resources (HIR) Department to come down to Washington, DC, for an interview.

With excitement, my wife and I traveled to DC in mid-November for the interview. It was a crisp, sunny day, and we had no idea how to navigate the confusing DC streets. I do remember being in awe of the beautiful, iconic government buildings. We finally found the Ford House Office Building, and its blandness and humble architecture hid its rich history.

> Construction of the building began in 1939 as part of the Works Progress Administration program. It was designed by architects and engineers in the Office of the Supervising Architect of the Public Buildings Administration under Louis A. Simon. The building originally housed the United States Census Bureau from 1940 to 1942. Over the years, it was used by the Federal Bureau of Investigation to house its Latent Print Unit.[1]
>
> The Ford House Office Building is one of the five office buildings containing U.S. House of Representatives staff in Washington, D.C., on Capitol Hill. The Ford House Office Building is the only House Office Building that is not connected underground to either one of the other office buildings or to the Capitol itself, and the only House Office Building that does not contain offices of members of Congress. Instead, it primarily houses committee staff and other offices, including the Architect of the Capitol, the Congressional Budget Office, and the Commission on Security and Cooperation in Europe.[2]

My wife and I entered the building's front entrance and were greeted by armed guards. We passed through a metal detector, and our belongings trundled through the X-ray machine. Having successfully navigated the security gauntlet, my wife waited in the first-floor cafeteria while I took the elevator to the sixth floor. I was to meet with the HIR Director, Ken Miller. But first, I sat outside his office with his secretary, Lois Cortese. Lois was a kind soul who entertained me while waiting for Ken to free up from a meeting. After a few minutes of small talk, the office door opened, and Ken greeted me with a firm handshake. Ken was a former IBM marketing and sales guy out of their Baltimore office. He was tall and thin with a quick wit and a warm, friendly demeanor. He didn't ask me much but rather tried to sell me on the job. After meeting with Ken, I met with Peggy Hyland and Gerald Bohm, who ran the mainframe operations, and then Paul Savercool from the network/telecom group. Lastly, I was escorted down to the third floor to meet with the House's new IG, John W. Lainhart IV.

John was the first to hold the position of IG at the House of Representatives and a former captain in the Navy Reserves. He was short in stature but a giant in reputation and presence. We seemed to hit it off and had a good interview. Long after I left the House, John invited me for lunch in the Congressional Member's dining room – a true honor and privilege. After the interview process, my wife and I traveled back to Pittsburgh and waited for *THE* call. I am not sure of the exact date that Ken Miller contacted me, but I got the job. *I was the first security manager at the U.S. House of Representatives!* (Figure 3.2) Soon after securing the position at the House of Representatives, I was delighted to receive a congratulatory letter from the University of Pittsburgh's Dean of the School of Library and Information Sciences – Toni Carbo Bearman (Figure 3.3).

I remember driving alone to DC on President's Day, Monday February 19, 1996. There was a blizzard, and the weather made driving treacherous, and it was fortunate that the federal government had the day off. I had secured a single-bed apartment at Mason Gardens, a complex that sits right behind Alexandria Virginia's iconic Masonic Temple. I had taken the apartment sight unseen since it was within walking distance to the King Street metro, where I would commute to work every day. For the next two years, I was separated from my family, mostly due to the time needed for our home in Murrysville, PA, to sell. But the extra time gave my wife ample time to look for homes in the Washington, D.C., metro area.

Once I arrived at my office, I was introduced to the *ONLY* other staff member in my new security department – Danny Gottovi. Danny, a thin, friendly, soft-spoken individual with an easy smile, was originally from North Carolina. Everyone in the House of Representatives referred to him as "Poor" Danny. The moniker "Poor" was given to him due to his being overworked performing his security duties by himself. Chiefly, whenever a member of Congress' office wanted to connect to the Internet, Danny would visit the office and give the staff a security presentation. Another primary duty was to keep up with the House personnel's access to the mainframe computer systems. This was no easy task as the House experienced a 50% annual turnover rate. Every week, there were over a hundred names that either had to be added to or deleted from accessing the system. Once my team was in place, we all took turns working on the laborious and tedious mainframe access list maintenance.

We clearly needed reinforcements in the security office, and I was able to secure two additional positions. Rod Murphy, who had previously worked with me at Westinghouse Plant Apparatus Division (WPAD), agreed to relocate to the DC area and join our efforts at the House. Rod's expertise in system and network security proved invaluable as we began the complex process of creating our cybersecurity program and meeting the ever-evolving demands of Capitol Hill. His knack for diagnosing vulnerabilities and implementing robust defenses set a new standard for our operations,

Scot M. Faulkner
Chief Administrative Officer

Human Resources

Office of the
Chief Administrative Officer
U.S. House of Representatives
Washington, DC 20515-6600

January 26, 1996

Mr. Ronald R. Baklarz, Jr.
4130 Dundee Drive
Murrysville, Pennsylvania 15668

Mr. Baklarz:

Congratulations! I am pleased to notify you that you have been selected and approved for the position of Security Manager, House Information Resources, Office of the Chief Administrative Officet, U.S. House of Representatives. The annual salary for this position is GS-15/13. Your supervisor will be Ken Miller. The effective date of this action is February 20, 1996.

Your first day of work will be Tuesday, February 20, 1996. Please report to room 718 of the West Ford House Office Building at 9:00 a.m. to complete the requisite new employee paperwork.

The Immigration Reform Act of 1986 made it unlawful to employ anyone hired after November 6, 1986. In this regard, please complete Section 1 of the enclosed Employment Eligibility Verification Form (I-9). Bring the appropriate original document(s)s from List A or one document from list B as well as one from list C.

If you have prior Executive Branch experience, please bring a copy of your most recent Notification of Personnel Action (SF-50); if you have prior military service please bring a copy of your Report of Separation from the Armed Forces of the U.S. (DD-214).

If you have any other questions, please contact my office at (202) 225-2450.

Sincerely,

Kay L. Ford
Associate Administrator
Human Resources

Figure 3.2 U.S. House of Representatives Offer Letter

University of Pittsburgh

School of Library and Information Science
Office of the Dean

February 9. 1996

Mr. Ronald R. Baklarz, Jr.
4130 Dundee Drive
Murryswile, PA 15668
Cr.h

Dear Mr. Baklarz:

Congratulations on your new position as Security Manager in House Information Resources for the Chist Administrative Office in the House of Representatives! It. is unguestionably an exciting opportuntly for you to be part of the information profession in this capacity when things are advancing as a

I would like to this opportunity to thank you for serving on the SUS" Alumni Board. The Soard does so much year ter benefit. the School. We all eresity appreciate your time and effort have Informed the other members of the Board members.

Best of luck to you in new occupation.. I look forward to hearing from you experience with "CYBER CONGRESS 2000" and the progress of the Information Security

Yours sincerely,

Toni

Tonl Carbo Bearman
Dean & Professor

TCB/clav

c: Robert Perkoski

fcbvi@deirbakher.bsz

Transforming the Present— Discovering Future

Figure 3.3 University of Pittsburgh Letter – Toni Carbo Bearman

and his calm determination quickly earned the respect of everyone in our department.

With Rod on board, our search continued for one final team member who could complete our team. Word traveled quickly through the hurried corridors of the House that there was a new sheriff in town, and changes were underway. Among those who reached out to me was Richard "Rick" Forno, a system administrator for the Legislative Counsel's office. Rick's email stood out: he articulated a clear vision for cybersecurity at the House and demonstrated a deep understanding of the threats we faced.

The day Danny, Rod, and I visited Rick's workspace to meet with him remains vivid in my memory. Rick's office was tucked away in a maze of corridors, its dim lighting casting long shadows over the rows of humming servers. It felt more like a catacomb than a conventional office. Rick was a natural fit for our team – not only for his technical acumen but also for his creative approach to problem-solving and his ability to foresee potential vulnerabilities. His passion for cybersecurity was contagious, and with his addition, our team was finally complete, ready to tackle whatever lay ahead in the complex landscape of congressional protocols and technology.

Our team's office space was tucked away behind the elevators, just off the spacious sixth-floor corridor of the Ford House Office Building, also known as Annex 2. A small, locked anteroom served as the only entry and exit to our workspace. This anteroom opened into a large room, where Danny, Rod, and Rick worked. My own office was set further back, separated from their main area. Years earlier, the sixth floor had been used by the FBI for its latent fingerprint division. The space housed the voluminous library of fingerprint files, and comparison searches were conducted manually. I later discovered that our office suite was originally the ladies' restroom. If you lifted a corner of the carpet in my office, you could still see the small, white, hexagonal bathroom tiles. *Whenever I started to important, I reminded myself that I was sitting in what was once the Ladies' Rest Room!*

Lesson Learned Always remember where you came from. Your office may be in a restroom!

3.3 POLITICAL LANDSCAPE

The "Republican Revolution", "Revolution of '94", or "Gingrich Revolution" are political slogans that refer to the Republican Party (GOP) success in the 1994 U.S. mid-term elections, which resulted in a net gain of 54 seats in the House of Representatives. There was also a pick-up of eight seats in the Senate. On November 9, 1994, the day after the election, Senator Richard Shelby of Alabama, a conservative

> Democrat, changed parties, becoming a Republican; on March 3, 1995, Colorado Senator Ben Nighthorse Campbell switched to the Republican side as well, increasing the GOP Senate majority.[3]

This was the 104th session of Congress, which ran from January 3, 1995, to January 3, 1997, and Newt Gingrich was voted in as the Speaker of the House.

This was the first time in forty years that the Republican Party had gained the majority in the House of Representatives – a dramatic shift in congressional leadership after four decades of Democratic control. The transition brought about both excitement and anxiety among staff, as established routines and allegiances faced sudden change. HIR was responsible for managing the House's computer systems and supporting its members' technical needs. *My understanding is that there was a great deal of animosity between the parties – imagine that!* On the first day of the Republican takeover, all HIR staff found a "pink slip" on their desks when they arrived at work, signaling that their positions were under review. Over the next couple of weeks, decisions were made as to who could be trusted to manage and run the House's computer systems going forward. Fortunately, "Poor" Danny made the cut. I can honestly say I had no political affiliations or influences that secured my new job.

Newt Gingrich had innovative ideas and initiated the Cyber-Congress 2000 program. In one of the proposed initiatives, members of Congress would anonymously debate legislation using a computer system. The reasoning was that anonymity would foster unbiased debate, resulting in better decisions and legislation. In HIR, we were looking to update and standardize various common systems, such as email. Administratively, HIR was under the Chief Administrative Officer (CAO), Scot M. Faulkner. And we also answered to the House's Committee on House Oversight, chaired at the time by the Honorable William M. Thomas.

3.4 FBI EMAIL INVESTIGATION

> As a result of conflicts between Democratic President Bill Clinton and the Republican Congress over funding for education, the environment, and public health in the 1996 Federal budget, the United States federal government shut down from November 14 through November 19, 1995, and from December 16, 1995, to January 6, 1996, for 5 and 21 days, respectively. Republicans also threatened not to raise the debt ceiling.[4]

You can imagine the high number of emails that flooded the House email system from constituents irate over the government shutdown. The House email system was a jerry-rigged system that ran on the House mainframe. To keep the high number of emails flowing, HIR's mainframe administrators offloaded incoming email onto flat files stored on backup tape until the public's furor and emails abated. Over several weeks, the email on the flat file tapes was fed back into the system and delivered to the appropriate member's mailbox. The redistribution of email was complete – or so they thought.

I had only been in my job for six weeks when members started receiving emails that were months old – long after they should have been delivered. Both Democrats and Republicans were outraged, thinking that the emails had been held back so unauthorized parties could read them. *Someone called the FBI to investigate!*

The sixth floor of HIR was configured such that the mainframe and operations staff were on one side of the long hallway, and the programmers were on the other side. When conducting their investigation, one of the programmers told the FBI that someone on the *other side of the aisle,* meaning the operations staff, had delivered the long-overdue emails. Now, the term *other side of the aisle* has a profound meaning in DC. But this was not what the programmer meant. He was referring to staff physically located other side of the aisle – not the political side.

IG Lainhart had E&Y involved in the investigation along with the FBI agent and me. The poor FBI agent was not technically savvy, and he relied heavily on my and E&Y's lead. The issue was that one of the mainframe operations staff had mistakenly thought all the email files on the previously offloaded tape had been deleted. He loaded the tape on the system, and the old emails that were still present on the tape were inadvertently delivered. We were able to identify the mainframe operator as the person *on the other side of the aisle.* I wrote up the investigation, and all were satisfied that it was human error. *Whew! Talk about baptism by fire!*

3.5 TELEPHONE HACK

HIR had an 800-number Help Line for members of Congress to call for technical assistance. Since each member had one or more remote offices in their districts, the Help Line came in handy for supporting both internal and remote users with their issues. The Help Line was staffed by HIR support personnel during normal business hours and switched over to the HIR computer center's phone after hours on weekdays and at all hours on weekends. One weekend, alleged maintenance personnel from a *Well-Known Telephone Company*, who shall remain nameless, called into the HIR Help Line. The ruse was that the phone company was performing troubleshooting on the 800 number. They would then ask the HIR computer center staff to forward the call to another phone number provided by the phone company's maintenance representative. In many cases, the other, forwarded phone number was an overseas number.

The alleged 800 number maintenance calls went on all Saturday night and into Sunday morning. At one point, the computer center staff involved their management, who told them to continue to provide support for the maintenance effort. No one thought of contacting us in security or anyone from the networking and telecom group for advice. At some point, the calls stopped, but not after amassing a phone bill of over $30,000! The following Monday morning, I learned of the weekend issue, and we contacted the phone company for the weekend's records on our 800 lines.

Our computer center staff were forwarding the calls with such speed and cadence that the phone company erroneously thought we had automatic forwarding set on the 800 lines. We engaged the FBI to help, and they traced the origination of the calls to pay phones in New York City. The scam works when the scammer hooks *an 800-line fish* willing to forward calls. There would be a line of people at a payphone waiting to call back home, typically overseas. Once the call was successfully forwarded, the scammer would charge the caller a cash-only fee for the phone call at a significantly cheaper cost than the typical, legitimate call would cost.

In the end, the FBI concluded there was little point in chasing down the culprits – it was nearly impossible to track people using public pay phones after the fact. Our attempts to persuade the Well-Known Telephone Company to absorb the cost went nowhere, even though the House was already paying hefty fees for monthly telecom services. Ultimately, HIR and the House had to absorb the $30,000 loss.

Reflecting on this experience, I realized just how quickly fraudsters adapt when they discover a weakness, and how vital it is to have proactive monitoring and response mechanisms in place. From that point forward, I arranged for any suspicious calls to the 800 number to be directed straight to my office phone. When scammers tried their luck, I responded with a blunt, sometimes unprofessional tirade. Admittedly, this was not the best tactic, but it brought a sense of control and, eventually, the calls stopped altogether.

This episode taught me more than just the vulnerabilities in our phone system; it underscored the necessity of staying vigilant, educating staff, and ensuring everyone knows when something just doesn't feel right. Experience, it seems, really can be the best teacher, especially when the lessons come with a hefty price tag.

3.6 MAINFRAME TEST DATA

"Poor" Danny was bothered for a long time about a certain issue relative to test data used by HIR mainframe programmer's years before in testing new features on the HIR mainframe system. One day, when we had a break, Danny took us through a nondescript door on the first floor of the Ford House Office Building. We went down darkened steps to the building's basement. Over in a corner were stacks and stacks of boxes containing reams of the old green bar computer printout paper spewing onto the floor.

I picked up a ream of the paper and saw lines and lines of citizen names followed by other (PII) personally identifiable information – addresses and security numbers. *Yikes!* The realization that actual production data had been used for testing struck us with the seriousness of a cybersecurity breach; the implications were immense. Such exposure could have led to identity theft, loss of public trust, and significant legal repercussions for the House. The programmers had broken a cardinal rule of cybersecurity by using real, live production data for testing purposes. Confronted with the gravity of the situation, we knew immediate action was essential. We had to dispose of this information! Before we left the basement, we stuffed the computer paper back into the boxes and taped them shut. Through our contacts at Capitol Police, we arranged for the Pentagon to incinerate the printouts, ensuring the secure destruction of the sensitive data.

I advised my boss, Ken Miller, about our findings, and on the appointed day, we all wore jeans and T-shirts for the task ahead. We loaded a panel truck with all the boxes and rode over to the Pentagon. We entered a gate to the Pentagon's maintenance area. There, we unloaded the boxes but were not allowed into the incinerator space to oversee the actual incineration. But I was satisfied that the Pentagon now had custody of the printouts, and there was nothing more to do.

This incident underscored the need for stricter data handling protocols and prompted us to revise procedures across the board. New policies were quickly implemented: from that point forward, only anonymized and carefully scrubbed test data would be permitted for development and testing. The experience was a stark reminder that even well-meaning technical shortcuts can have far-reaching consequences, and it reinforced the importance of vigilance, accountability, and ongoing education in cybersecurity practices.

3.7 THE ROGUE INFORMATION TECHNOLOGY MANAGER

HIR had an eccentric technical manager who kept mainly to himself. We received a tip that the manager was running side businesses during working hours and using his House PC. Up until my tenure as security manager, no one in management wanted to interact with him, let alone investigate and possibly fire him. He had an office to himself, menacingly covered with wall plaques attesting to his prowess as a military marksman. After hours one evening, we entered his office and accessed his PC. We found that he was running two businesses on his House PC. One of his businesses was as a line dance instructor; line dancing was popular at the time. The other business was providing information technology consultation.

I wrote up the investigative report, and the decision was made by upper management to fire him. We weren't sure how he would react to being fired. Would he be passive? Would he freak out? To minimize the potential threat, I worked out a plan with Human Resources to fire him on a Friday afternoon. He was escorted to a lower floor away from HIR's occupied sixth floor. And while he was being processed, Danny, Rod, and Rick cleaned out his office so he would not have to go back upstairs to HIR. The last security measure was that I asked Capitol Police to provide plain clothesmen to be nearby if the situation got out of hand.

One of the Capitol Police Officers who helped us out that day was Detective John Gibson of the Dignitary Protective Division. I remember John as a quiet, all-business type of individual. We were happy to have John Gibson's help, and he, along with the other actions we took, resulted in the manager's termination being a non-event. After leaving the building, Danny, Rod, and Rick met him on the sidewalk with a cart filled with his belongings. *And he said to them that he wondered what took so long to fire him.*

Sadly, John Gibson was killed in the line of duty. Detective John Gibson was shot and killed after confronting the suspect who had shot and killed Officer Jacob Chestnut seconds earlier. Detective Gibson, who was in plainclothes, was shot after the suspect entered the office of Congressman Tom DeLay. Detective Gibson, who was assigned to protect Congressman DeLay, was immediately engaged in a gunfight with the suspect, at which point he was shot. Despite being mortally wounded, Detective Gibson was able to return fire and wound the suspect.[5]

3.8 NETWORK SECURITY

One of the smartest and most technically talented individuals I have ever worked with was John Schnitzlein. John worked in the telecommunications group and assisted in laying out the complex TCP/IP addressing scheme for the entire House complex. Short for transmission control protocol/Internet protocol, TCP/IP is a set of rules (protocols) governing communications among all computers on the Internet. More specifically, TCP/IP dictates how information should be packaged (turned into bundles of information called packets), sent, and received, and how to get to its destination. TCP/IP was developed in 1970's and driven by Bob Kahn and Vint Cerf.

At the time, the Internet and wide-area networking were still emerging frontiers, with few established methods for securing these environments. Newt Gingrich's vision for a "Cyber-Congress" placed Internet access at the heart of the House's technological transformation. To ensure this vision could be realized safely, John enlisted the expertise of Marcus J. Ranum – a renowned computer and network security researcher born in

1962. Ranum's accomplishments included building the first Internet email server for the whitehouse.gov domain, contributing to the development of intrusion detection systems, and designing the Secure External Access Link (SEAL) for Digital Equipment Corporation, which became the first commercial bastion host firewall. With such a distinguished background, Ranum's insights proved invaluable as the House began to implement more robust network and Internet security measures.

3.9 HOUSE COMPUTING ENVIRONMENT

You can think of the House of Representatives as having 435 Chief Executive Officers. There was no standardization regarding individual member office computing systems. Each member could have whatever flavor of system they wanted for their office automation environment. This led to a complex computing and security environment. In addition to each member's office in DC, they also had one or more district offices back in their home state. Since we could not ensure the security at these district offices, they were not permitted to connect to the House network.

One member in particular wanted to connect his district office to his DC office via the House network. I wanted to demonstrate to him the insecurity of doing this. **CAVEAT** DON'T TRY THIS AT HOME! Using well-known techniques, I was able to gain unauthorized access to his district office's email system. Via an email relay vulnerability, I used their system to send an email that looked like it was addressed by and sent from the member himself. I only sent the email to myself using my House email address. Danny and I visited his office, and I showed him the steps I had taken to send the bogus email. He quickly grasped the concept of district office insecurities. He thanked us for the demonstration, and we heard no more on the subject.

3.10 THE AUDITS CONTINUE

In addition to the original audit performed by Price Waterhouse (Report 95 CAO-18), IG Lainhart also engaged Ernst & Young, LLC (E&Y) to audit the security of our internal network systems. There was enough audit work to go around! Remember, security tools such as systems and network vulnerability scanners were immature. For the audit, E&Y used a security scanner from a company called Internet Security Systems (ISS).

> In 1992, while attending the Georgia Institute of Technology, Christopher Klaus developed the first version of Internet Security Scanner. In 1994, Klaus founded Internet Security Systems (ISS) to

further develop and market Internet Security Scanner, which later became Internet Scanner.[6]

Using the ISS system, E&Y conducted its security scans on the internal House network and systems. The time came to review their audit findings. Without going too far into the weeds, I should mention that each computer system has "ports" that listen for connections. These ports number from 0 to 65,535, and many are commonly used for specific types of connections. For example, Port 21 is typically used for the File Transfer Protocol (FTP). Not all 65,535 ports are used. But if not properly configured, security scanners will look at all of them *and include all of them on their scan reports.*

It came time to review E&Y's findings. The meeting room was filled to standing-room-only capacity due to the highly anticipated audit findings using ISS's security scanner. Staff from E&Y, House IG's office, and HIR were present. E&Y personnel had to use a hand truck to transport the reams of printer output from their scanning exercise. John Schnitzlein looked at a few pages and determined that they had included the House's internal routers in their network scan. Much of their output consisted of these meaningless router scans. I say meaningless because all of the internal routers were configured the same – to only allow a small number of the 65,535 ports through.

However, there were hundreds of these routers positioned throughout the network. I asked E&Y a simple question: "Did you configure the scanner to bypass our internal routers?" I knew this was a configuration setting that could be set in the ISS security scanner tool. The E&Y auditors had a blank, confused look on their faces and meekly answered in the negative. John Lainhart got up from the table with a disgusted look on his face. The audit meeting was over before it began!

My team and I continued to address the forty-one audit findings with which we faced. Periodically, I would send a list of those considered complete for the IG's approval. These were always difficult to close for whatever reason. One of the audit findings was that the House should hire a knowledgeable, full-time security administrator. *I thought my presence should close out the audit finding, but the IG would not budge, and the finding remained open!*

3.11 HISPOLS AND HISPUBS

Another of the audit findings dealt with the House's lack of cybersecurity policies and procedures. My team and I quickly began writing up security policies and procedures (Figure 3.4). Our initial tome, dated September 1996, included policies for Internet/Intranet Security, Security Incidents, Non-Disclosure, World Wide Web, Electronic Communications, Vendor Remote Access, and Voice Mail. It was a good first start. This letter

Scot M. Faulkner
Chief Administrative Officer

House Information Resources

Chief Administrative Officer
U.S. House of Representatives
Washington, DC 20515-6600

HR-SEC-656
September 12, 1996

MEMORANDUM

To: Scott M. Faulkner, Chief Administrative Officer
Office of the Chief Administrator

From: Ken Miller, Associate Administrator
CAO/House Information Resources

Subject: Information Security Policy of the U.S. House of Representatives

Attached for your review is a comprehensive Information Security Policy for the U.S. House of Representatives). This policy was developed as a recommendation House Information Resources' Indeperndent Consultants House Information Security Stakeholder commititee. which plays a key) State of 1993-EPCA-1 (hsarl) by Congress. It incorporates Government-wide (e-quirements National Rule 749 Department required regardess of the efect 1995 Commenter(e information Security rampatuments esturaing that ongressis of UNIM 745 poins ntiliion (Copy in, the following must secure-inmetasion properties raveiling peak at dasin antieal lucecommateriting mar your deting uada agres) information safeguing applications throughout fully paints. if he neere-ir your defing uaba agreed at installication of our secitbuts tear. 'CAOTH's needs secconalizdi, approved as well to g)6 roncerstrative cofentation and lmis inalistic abvarcaing occmenndentnation through-house (inforrization) chigibility. M homeeatggement coupteri-requiest ue elmhects, eraevas rumprters, and esse onlantis and pucston waseil tefinielit, acaderate. skguase descmeratored canmundcaton arr-renantgsement fraan Including Beoeslly. prosedurrs gamérslite. stats mandicemminds timomt. and hoots sedining the stat.

This policy package consists of (1) a two-page introductory memorandum, and (2) a fifteen-page policy. In addition to finalizing our endorserment of this safeguarding memorand-unt and (2) the fifteen-page proiicty (hr additioh to fmullting our (vigtroem i)rrainformiiatd. progic this alert aglinch meetuti approved and disseminated in a teader. Thank calls please.

If you have any other questions, please contact my office at (202) 225-2450.

KM/th

Ken C Miller

Ken Miller
Associate Administrator
Human Resources

Figure 3.4 U.S. House of Representatives Information Security Policy Letter

including our policy binder was sent to CAO , Scot M. Faulkner from my supervisor, Ken Miller.

My security team and I had no administrative support so collectively, we had to compose and type the policies ourselves including making many copies that had to be distributed to key personnel. The original, overarching security policies described above morphed into two general categories – House Information Security Policies (HISPOLs) and Publications (HISPUBs). HISPUBs were guidance documents such as security configuration requirements for Microsoft and Apple-based computer systems. Later, we set up an internal cybersecurity website which was used to provide our cybersecurity policy and publication documents online and was easily accessible throughout the House. IG Lainhart was ecstatic about the form and format of these policies and procedures. I was heartened and proud to find during an Internet search that the HISPOLs and HISPUBs framework was still used, at least until 2018, over a decade after I left the House.[7] It was truly gratifying that our policy and procedure formats stood the test of time.

Lessons Learned *Develop clear and actionable cybersecurity policies.* Below are several lessons with practical details and examples:

- Involve other groups in the development and review of policies: Including stakeholders such as Management, Legal, Human Resources, and Users in the process ensures that policies are comprehensive, legally sound, and practical for everyone affected. Collaboration helps anticipate implementation challenges, align policies with organizational values, and fosters a sense of shared responsibility.
- Maintain version controls with each policy: Use a version numbering system – such as Policy v1.0, v1.1, v2.0 – and keep a log of changes. Document each modification with its date and description of what changed from the previous version. This not only tracks the evolution of a policy but also helps resolve confusion about which rules are in effect, especially during audits or disputes.
- Set up a periodic review schedule for your policies and update as appropriate: Establish regular intervals, such as annual or semi-annual reviews, to ensure policies remain relevant and address emerging threats. For instance, after a major security incident, a prompt review can reveal gaps and drive timely updates.
- If sanctions need to be enforced for non-compliance with policy, citing specific policy chapters and sections reduces ambiguity and strengthens the case for disciplinary action. For example, use of company systems for non-business-related uses, non-adherence to password policies, and misuse of user credentials.

OFFICE OF THE ASSISTANT SECRETARY OF DEFENSE
WASHINGTON, DC 20301-1300

LEGISLATIVE AFFAIRS

February 26, 1997

Mr. Jeff Trandahl
Chief Administrative Officer
House of Representatives
Washington, D.C. 20515

Dear Mr. Trandahl:

A final Top Secret security clearance, based on a SSBI completed February 6, 1997, has been granted Mr. Ronald Richard Baklarz, Jr. effective February 13, 1997.

This clearance has been granted in accordance with standards and procedures of the Department of Defense and is on a need-to-know basis in connection with his duties.

We would appreciate your advising us in the future if Mr. Baklarz no longer has a requirement for the clearance. Please return the enclosed Security Termination Statement signed and witnessed at that time.

Sincerely,

ERIK L. WINDORN
Colonel, USAF
Deputy Asst Secretary of Defense
Legislative Affairs

Figure 3.5 U.S. Office of the Assistant Secretary of Defense – Top Secret Clearance

3.12 TOP SECRET SECURITY CLEARANCES

Due to the potentially sensitive nature of our work, I wanted my security team and me to have government security clearances. The clearances would allow our access to sensitive information and events as well as lend credibility and integrity to our team and our work. We worked through the U.S. Capitol Police to process and maintain our clearances. Clearance processes take time, and my Department of Defense (DoD) Top Secret clearance was effective as of February 13, 1997. During my tenure, we never had a situation where our clearances were necessary (Figure 3.5).

3.13 PRESIDENT CLINTON AND THE WHITE HOUSE VISITOR LOGS

There was a bruhaha between House Republicans and the Clinton White House over allegations of payments made to the Clinton Administration for visitors to sleep in the Lincoln bedroom. The Clinton administration refused to release visitor records to the public, arguing they are part of presidential communications and not public records.[8]

> Documents were released by the Clinton administration in February 1997. These showed that during the period 1993–96, there were 938 people who stayed overnight at the White House, of whom 821 were located in the Lincoln Bedroom. Of these, 128 were public officials and dignitaries of some kind and 67 were people from the arts and entertainment world.[9]

The Clinton Administration provided the White House visitor logs in raw, unformatted database files that were not easily accessible. I don't remember the specific database product the White House used for maintaining and managing its visitor logs. However, HIR technology managers obtained a copy of the database product and were able to process and format the raw data into a format that was easy to access and search.

The issue now was how to secure access to the database, so that the integrity was intact and that the excerpts were not leaked to The Washington Post. HIR's copy of the Visitor Log database was retained on an isolated server within the HIR's secured sixth-floor computer center. The server was not connected to the Internet, and there was no means to copy off any data. Access to the database was password-protected, and whenever someone wanted to view or search the visitor log data, they had to sign a physical log in my office. My team maintained the log with all the visitor details like name, date, time, and duration of the review. We escorted them into the data center and gave them the password to gain access to the system. When their review ended, we immediately changed the password, so the next user had a new, unique, never-used password. We kept all this documentation in a locked safe in our security office space. This process held up, and there were no complaints or comments on our security protocols.

Lessons Learned *Make use of logs and inventories.* One Christmas, I bought a bottle of Crown Royal Whiskey for the team to toast ourselves and the holiday. Rick Forno, our safe custodian, put the bottle in the safe and marked it with an UNCLASSIFIED tag. Moreover, the whiskey was listed on the safe's inventory with sign-in/out signature and date blocks. Due to our DoD security clearances, we had an unannounced visit by the U.S. Capitol Police to audit our sensitive items and safe contents. The official came across the bottle and appeared annoyed until he saw the classification tag and its inclusion on the inventory list. He simply shook his head and laughed.

3.14 FORUM OF INCIDENT RESPONSE AND SECURITY TEAMS

Not having much in the way of budget, I was always looking for cost-effective ways to enhance our security posture. Via Rick Forno, I became aware of Forum of Incident Response and Security Teams (FIRST).

> The Forum of Incident Response and Security Teams (FIRST) is a global forum of incident response and security teams. They aim to improve cooperation between security teams on handling major cyber-security incidents. FIRST is an association of incident response teams with global coverage.[10]
>
> FIRST was founded as an informal group by a number of incident response teams after the WANK (computer worm) highlighted the need for better coordination of incident response activities between organizations during major incidents. It was formally incorporated in California on August 7, 1995, and moved to North Carolina on May 14, 2014.[11]

I viewed FIRST as a cost-effective force multiplier that provided early warnings regarding Internet-related attacks that other FIRST teams were experiencing. I submitted the paperwork for our membership and established a Pretty Good Privacy (PGP) key for secure communications and authentications between teams. Thus, the United States House – Computer Emergency Response Team (US-HCERT) was established. In later CISO roles, I would establish two more FIRST Teams at the Prudential Insurance Company of America and the American Red Cross.

3.15 SECURITY ADMINISTRATOR TOOL FOR ANALYZING NETWORKS

> Security Administrator Tool for Analyzing Networks (SATAN) was a free software vulnerability scanner for analyzing networked computers released April 1995. SATAN captured the attention of a broad technical audience after its appearance in PC Magazine. Since SATAN could also be used for nefarious purposes, it drew threats from the United States Department of Justice. It featured a web interface, complete with forms to enter targets, tables to display results, and context-sensitive tutorials that appeared when a vulnerability had been found.[12]

Security Administrator Tool for Analyzing Networks (SATAN) was authored by Dan Farmer and Wietse Venema. And popular author Neil Gaiman drew the artwork used for the SATAN documentation.[13]

> SATAN was written mostly in Perl and utilized a web browser such as Netscape, Mosaic or Lynx to provide the user interface. This easy-to-use

> interface drove the scanning process and presented the results in summary format. As well as reporting the presence of vulnerabilities, SATAN also gathered large amounts of general network information, such as which hosts are connected to subnets, what types of machines they are and which services they offered.[14]

If users were offended by the tool's name SATAN, there was a built-in command called Repent that changed the name to SANTA.[15]

I saw the advantages of having our own security scanning tool to audit our internal systems. But we did not have the budget for a tool as expensive as the Internet Security Scanner. And the operative concept was that it was freeware. SATAN ran on Unix-based systems, and neither Danny, Rod, Rick, nor I had expertise in Unix. Fortunately, SATAN also ran on the Linux operating system which would let us run it on regular personal computers (PCs). We scrounged up a couple of old PCs and some funds to engage a local Linux expert to configure our SATAN systems. We were up and running! We set the SATAN workstations up in our entryway, the anteroom, which was behind a locked door that opened out onto the sixth floor's main hallway. IG Lainhart was delighted that we set up our own security scanning lab, and it got a lot of use analyzing and securing systems within the House network.

3.16 OTHER CYBERSECURITY ITEMS

A humorous story involved SATAN's co-author, Dan Farmer, and Congressman Vern Ehlers. Congressman Ehlers represented Michigan from 1993 until he retired in 2011. Vern held a Ph.D. in Nuclear Physics and was an obvious choice to chair the House's Committee on Science and Technology. Congressman Ehlers was politically conservative in both manner and dress. And since he was a little older, he was balding. Dan Farmer was on the other end of the spectrum. He had a biker vibe about him, including his below-shoulder length, thick mane of bright red hair. Dan appeared in Washington DC for a hearing conducted by Congressman Ehlers' Science and Technology committee on cybersecurity, and I was in attendance. As Congressman Ehlers first called on Dan, he remarked something to the effect that he was jealous of Dan's hair since he himself was "follically challenged."

Cybersecurity giant, Tsutomu Shimomura, was a witness at another House hearing on cybersecurity that I attended.

> Tsutomu Shimomura, born October 23, 1964, is a Japanese-born physicist and computer security expert. He is known for helping the FBI track and arrest notorious hacker Kevin Mitnick. *Takedown*, his 1996

Figure 3.6 Autograph "Take-Down" Tsutomu Shimomura

> book on the subject with journalist John Markoff, was later adapted for the screen in *Takedown 2000*.[16]

Since I knew he would be at the hearing, I took my copy of *Takedown* and asked him to autograph it, which he graciously did (Figure 3.6).

We also met with dignitaries from the Information Center People's Assembly, Arab Republic of Egypt Information Center (PAIC), via the Research Triangle Institute. The program was part of the United States Agency for International Development (USAID)-funded Decision Support Services Project. The Egyptians were formulating their security strategy with a focus on network security. We met with the Egyptian delegation and conveyed our policy approaches and how we assess each member's office before they connect to the Internet. The following RTI appreciation letter and papyrus print showed that the visit was a great success (Figures 3.7 and 3.8).

RESEARCH TRIANGLE INSTITUTE RTI

July 23, 1997

Mr. Ronald R. Baklarz, Jr.
House Information Resources
631 Ford House Office Building
Washington, D.C. 20515

Dear Mr. Baklarz,

On Monday, 23 June, and Tuesday, 24 June. House Information Resources kindly hosted a delegation of six members of the Information Center (PAIC), People's Assembly, Arab Republic of Egypt. The visit was arranged by the Research Triangle Institute (RTI) as part of the USAID-funded Decision Support Services Project in Egypt. The goal of the project is to strengthen information resources and policy analysis capabilities in the Egyptian national legislature. The objective of the U.S. study tour in June was to being planned, built, and managed.

Security has always been a key concern of the PAIC, but that concern has never been very well defined. They were very impressed with the approach toward security at RTI and in the HIR. It was very valuable to them to tearn more about the nerwork security you use in HIR. I think this has given them a good framework for approach their own security needs rationally.

The delegation enjoyed their visit greatly. They were an excepttional group: serious, attentive, and always on time. They were impressed with the professionalism and candor of the entire HIR team. I know how busy you and your team must be and appreciate the time you gave. Thank you so much for making this visit a great success.

Best Regards,

Gordon M. Cressman
Research Programmer Analyst
gmc@rti.org

GMC:gmc

Enclosures

\\Casca1/2/6194\Correspondence\Thank_you_Letter.wpd

3040 Cornwallis Road • Post Office Box 12194 • Research Triangle Park, North Carolina 27709-2194 USA
Telephone 919 541-6000 • Fax 919 541-6985

Figure 3.7 Triangle Research Institute Appreciation Letter

Figure 3.8 Papyrus Print – Information Center (PAIC) People's Assembly Arab Republic of Egypt

3.17 INFO WORLD SEPTEMBER 29, 1997

In the September 29, 1997, issue of Info World, the magazine conducted its fourth annual search for the top 100 innovative computing projects in American business to include projects with Internet and intranet dimensions. IG Lainhart cajoled me to submit my team and enter our security program, including our internal cybersecurity website for consideration. Surprisingly, we were selected as nineteenth out of 100 entrants, and we were recognized in the magazine.

The U.S. House of Representatives Information Resources Security Group has a three-person staff that devises and implements security measures for more than 10,000 computer users on Capitol Hill. A major part of this effort involves educating the user community on basic security measures and developing specifications for more than

Securing congressional information

U.S. House of Representatives House Information Resources Security Group

19 Washington
Government; 10,000 employees

Information security for Congress may conjure images of hostile hackers battling a clever IS staff, a president pacing nervously, and a SWAT team awaiting orders inside a hovering helicopter. The real situation, however, is one of calm behind an intranet firewall.

The U.S. House of Representatives Information Resources Security Group has a three-person staff that devises and implements security measures for more than 10,000 computer users on Capitol Hill. A major part of this effort involves educating the user community on basic security measures and developing specifications for more than 200 technicians who build and install the House's computer networks. To accomplish this, the group created an intranet site holding nearly 1,000 pages of security information. The site was created with HTML and resides on a Windows NT server.

According to Ronald Baklarz (pictured above), security manager for House Information Resources Security Group, the intranet site contains policies about general security measures (some still being developed), procedures for configuring computers in accordance with security standards, and forms related to security information.

— *Blaise Zerega*

Figure 3.9 Info World September 29, 1997

> 200 technicians who build and install the House's computer networks. To accomplish this, the group created an intranet site holding nearly 1,000 pages of security information. The site was created with HTML and resides on a Windows NT server.

A production supervisor and photographer came from Info World to take pictures to include in the magazine. I made it clear that I wanted them to take a team picture since we all took part in our successes. The production supervisor was adamant that I was the only one to be in the picture. I had to capitulate but was not happy about the outcome since I viewed us as a *security team* (Figure 3.9).

3.18 Y2K

For younger readers,

> The term year 2000 problem, or simply Y2K, refers to potential computer errors related to the formatting and storage of calendar data for dates in and after the year 2000. Many computer programs represented four-digit years with only the final two digits, making the year 2000 indistinguishable from 1900. Computer systems' inability to distinguish dates correctly had the potential to bring down worldwide infrastructures for computer-reliant industries.[17]

There was worldwide concern about Y2K as the world was growing more dependent on computers in every aspect of daily life. No one knew what devastation would result from the errant code in software, systems, and networks. Naturally, the U.S. Congress was concerned, and I recall hearings on the subject. One such hearing included my supervisor, Ken Miller. When asked under oath about what actions HIR was taking to address Y2K issues with House systems, he gave them less than a complete and satisfactory answer. Unfortunately, I believe that was the beginning of the end for Ken.

3.19 DEPARTURE

My wife and I were experiencing "sticker shock" with the high cost of living in DC as compared to Western Pennsylvania. The financial reality was that I had my local, DC living expenses, including my apartment in Alexandria, VA. Our family also had a mortgage and living expenses back in Pittsburgh. After the two years it took for our Pittsburgh home to sell, we found our home in Gaithersburg, MD, where we would spend the next twenty-four years. The price and mortgage for the new home also stretched our budget.

At this time, cybersecurity hiring was heating up, and people holding management positions similar to mine were commanding six-figure salaries. My team was aware of my cost-of-living challenges and, in November 1996, sent a memo to HIR Administrator Ken Miller citing my contributions to improving the House's security posture in hopes of obtaining a hike in salary.

Administratively, HIR reported to the House's CAO. Subsequent to CAO, Scot Faulkner's leaving, Jeff Trandahl was named the acting CAO. Jeff was serving as the thirty-second Clerk of the U.S. House of Representatives and held this position in addition to his acting CAO duties. He was supportive of our cybersecurity work and sent me several, personal "appreciation" notes. Even IG, John W. Lainhart IV, tried to have my position upgraded from "manager" to "director" which would command a higher pay scale. All these efforts fell short, but I had to do what was best for my family and the opportunity to earn my first six-figure income came with the offer of a position at Ernst and Young, LLC.

> *Lesson Learned* *Have no regrets.* Looking back, the financial strain of living in the Washington DC area was formidable, and uprooting our family presented real challenges. Yet, the accomplishments my team and I achieved during my tenure at the House of Representatives made every sacrifice worthwhile. Taking career risks opened doors I never imagined. And I trusted that pushing forward would ultimately benefit both my professional growth and my family's future. The journey taught me that leaning into opportunity, even at great expense, can yield rewards and lifelong pride in what we accomplish.

3.20 ALL-STARS – U.S. HOUSE OF REPRESENTATIVES

I consider all three men on my team at the House as All Stars. I am proud that they continued on in the field of cybersecurity, where they continued to excel professionally.

Danny Gottovi – "Poor" Danny was anything but poor regarding his cybersecurity work. Danny earned an M.S. degree in Computer Science Information Security at James Madison University. Danny went on to hold a number of prestigious cybersecurity positions, including at Network Solutions, MITRE, CSC, DXC Technologies, and is currently Vice President of Information Security and Compliance – Corcentric.

Rod Murphy – Rod worked along with me at WPAD, where he distinguished himself as technically astute and a quick study. At the US House of Representatives, he gravitated to the network attack and penetration work. Now retired, Rod held a number of security engineering and leading positions, including but not limited to Patriot Technologies, CSC, and Falconwood, Inc., where he retired as a Senior Certification and Accreditation Analyst.

Richard "Rick" Forno – Rick was the "professor" on our team, and he earned a Bachelor's degree in International Relations from American University in 1994, a Master's degree in International Relations from Salve Regina University in 2002, and a Ph.D. degree in Internet Studies from the Curtin University of Technology in 2010. Rick also held a number of prestigious security positions, including but not limited to Network Solutions, Northrup Grumman, and Gartner. Rick is the Assistant Director Center for Cybersecurity at the University of Maryland Baltimore Campus.

3.21 TECHNOLOGY ADVANCEMENTS AND SECURITY DEVELOPMENTS 1997

1997

- Microsoft invested $150 million in Apple to prevent it from going into bankruptcy. As part of the deal, Microsoft received 150,000 Apple shares.
- The first Black Hat conference was held in Las Vegas.
- May 7th, Intel Pentium II was introduced. The microprocessor contained 7.5 million transistors and featured an improved version of the first P6-generation core of the Pentium Pro, which contained 5.5 million transistors.
- May 11th, IBM's Deep Blue computer defeated world champion chess player Garry Kasparov in their second six-game showdown, winning the tie-breaking game in only sixty-two minutes.
- June, IEEE (Institute of Electrical and Electronics Engineers) introduced 802.11, a wireless (Wi-Fi) network standard.
- September 16th, Steve Jobs rejoined Apple.
- December, Microsoft acquired Hotmail, a free e-mail service, for a reported $400 million. The sale had been preceded by a major incident in 1997, where all email was lost for 25% of mailboxes.

NOTES

1 Ford House Office Building. (n.d.). *Wikipedia*. https://en.wikipedia.org/wiki/Ford_House_Office_Building

2 Ford House Office Building. (n.d.). *Wikipedia*. https://en.wikipedia.org/wiki/Ford_House_Office_Building

3 Republican Revolution. (n.d.). *Wikipedia*. https://en.wikipedia.org/wiki/Republican_Revolution

4 1995–1996 United States federal government shutdowns. (n.d.). *Wikipedia.* https://en.wikipedia.org/wiki/1995%E2%80%931996_United_States_federal_government_shutdowns
5 United States Capitol Police. (n.d.). *Detective John M. Gibson.* https://www.uscp.gov/about/honoring-our-fallen/detective-john-m-gibson
6 Internet Security Systems. (n.d.). *Wikipedia.* https://en.wikipedia.org/wiki/Internet_Security_Systems
7 U.S. House of Representatives. (2025). *Index of House Information Security Policies and Publications (HISPOLs and HISPUBs).* https://www.house.gov/sites/default/files/2025-07/J.2%20Index%20of%20House%20Information%20Security%20Policies%20and%20Publications%20%28HISPOLs%20and%20HISPUBs%29.pdf
8 White House Visitor Logs. (n.d.). *Wikipedia.* https://en.wikipedia.org/wiki/White_House_visitor_logs
9 Lincoln Bedroom for Contributors Controversy. (n.d.). *Wikipedia.* https://en.wikipedia.org/wiki/Lincoln_Bedroom_for_contributors_controversy
10 Forum of Incident Response and Security Teams. (n.d.). *Wikipedia.* https://en.wikipedia.org/wiki/Forum_of_Incident_Response_and_Security_Teams
11 Forum of Incident Response and Security Teams. (n.d.). *Wikipedia.* https://en.wikipedia.org/wiki/Forum_of_Incident_Response_and_Security_Teams
12 Security Administrator Tool for Analyzing Networks (SATAN). (n.d.). *Wikipedia.* https://en.wikipedia.org/wiki/Security_Administrator_Tool_for_Analyzing_Networks
13 Security Administrator Tool for Analyzing Networks (SATAN). (n.d.). *Wikipedia.* https://en.wikipedia.org/wiki/Security_Administrator_Tool_for_Analyzing_Networks
14 Security Administrator Tool for Analyzing Networks (SATAN). (n.d.). *Wikipedia.* https://en.wikipedia.org/wiki/Security_Administrator_Tool_for_Analyzing_Networks
15 Security Administrator Tool for Analyzing Networks (SATAN). (n.d.). *Wikipedia.* https://en.wikipedia.org/wiki/Security_Administrator_Tool_for_Analyzing_Networks.
16 Shimomura, T. (n.d.). *Tsutomu Shimomura. Wikipedia.* https://en.wikipedia.org/wiki/Tsutomu_Shimomura
17 Year 2000 Problem. (n.d.). *Wikipedia.* https://en.wikipedia.org/wiki/Year_2000_problem

Chapter 4

Ernst & Young, LLP Washington DC 1998

Position Held: Manager, Information Systems Audit and Advisory Service (ISAAS)

Location: 8381 Old Courthouse Road, Vienna, VA

4.1 ERNST & YOUNG, LLP – OVERVIEW

I worked at Ernst & Young, LLP (E&Y) as a Manager, Information Systems Audit and Advisory Service (ISAAS) in the Mid-Atlantic Region for one year. There we built and staffed Ernst & Young's Network Attack and Penetration Lab and Practice, where we performed security systems and network assessments for large clients in both government and private sectors.

I was hired at E&Y by a giant of a man, six foot eight, Dan Woolley. Dan retired after twenty-two years from the U.S. Air Force as a Lieutenant Colonel. At E&Y, he was tasked to develop the Mid-Atlantic Region's ISAAS practice. A good friend, Don Withers, who was a security manager at AT&T, was hired at E&Y at about the same time as I. Don and I met via the local High-Tech Crime Investigators Association local chapter meetings when I was at the U.S. House of Representatives.

4.2 GALLOWS ROAD, VIRGINIA

Dan Wooley secured office space in a building at Old Courthouse Road in Vienna, VA. This put us close to the Washington DC beltway and potential government and commercial clients. One of our main priorities was to build a system and network attack and penetration lab. From the lab, we could assess client networks and systems while honing our ethical hacking tools and techniques. Ethical hackers work with companies, the government, and other organizations to assess and identify vulnerabilities in their systems and networks. Their findings are used to fix security issues and vulnerabilities. To help build out the lab, E&Y lent us one of their

DOI: 10.1201/9781003650645-6

information technology technicians, Don DeBolt. Don helped us set up the PCs, networks, and Internet access we needed for the lab. Although he was on loan to us, *he never left!* Don was a natural for the attack and penetration team, and he added extensive knowledge of Windows operating systems and networking.

Besides Dan Woolley, Ken Franz, was on our team. Ken was a de facto co-leader on the team since he had experience in the consulting business. Ken had E&Y institutional knowledge, consulting business experience, and client interaction skills. Those of us new to E&Y and the consulting business leaned heavily on Ken for guidance. We had other ethical hackers on the team, but one stood out: Steve Kaplan. Steve was the consummate *nerd,* and I mean that in the best possible way. Steve was constantly engrossed in his laptop computer. He was running the Linux operating system on his PC long before it gained the popularity it would later enjoy. Linux had many unique security/vulnerability assessment tools and capabilities that gave us an advantage in assessing a client's system and networks. Dan Wooley had the vision to build a team that addressed a number of major security issues. Besides technicians to assess system and network vulnerabilities, Dan also hired expertise on system backup and recovery providing more consulting opportunities for potential clients.

At the time, system and network penetration exercises were just gaining popularity. And they quickly became the highly desirable *hot and sexy* assessments that clients wanted. Unfortunately for our regional practice, Jon Darbyshire came over to E&Y from Price Waterhouse and was building the same type of team as Dan's for E&Y, but at the national level rather than the regional level. Jon was a National Partner and Global Practice Leader and was responsible for the firm's Global Enterprise Security Services practice. Jon had some great security talent on his team, including George Kurtz. George started the successful security company *Foundstone*, which was later bought by anti-virus juggernaut *McAfee.* Most recently, George founded a successful security company, *Crowdstrike,* where he is president and CEO.

Our fledgling Mid-Atlantic practice didn't stand much of a chance against Jon's global practice, but we did get a few jobs.

4.3 VETERAN'S ADMINISTRATION

The U.S. Government Accountability Office (GAO) engaged us to perform attack and penetration assessments against a few of their Veteran's Administration (VA) locations. Besides our security assessments, GAO wanted to set up their own in-house attack and penetration lab. So, they wanted to observe our methods and techniques so they could replicate them for their own team. One of the major VA sites in Texas had extensive computer systems and networks, including mainframes, SUN systems, and PCs.

In preparation for our assessment, the VA engaged a large government contractor, who shall remain nameless, to do a pre-assessment of the network and system security prior to our work. *The VA didn't want any surprises!*

The first part of our review was to perform a remote, "black box" security assessment. In this black box assessment, we were given no information other than the name of their website and could only perform our testing over the Internet. In these remote assessments, we assessed their Internet presence and looked for security vulnerabilities with their website, Domain Name Service, etc. In our tool bag of security assessment tools and techniques, I was interested in a specific tool, a war dialer called ToneLoc. ToneLoc was a popular war dialing computer program for MS-DOS written in the early to mid-1990s by two programmers known by the pseudonyms Minor Threat and Mucho Maas. The name ToneLoc was short for "Tone Locator" and was a wordplay on the name of the rap artist known as Tone Lōc. The program ToneLoc took advantage of the extended return codes available on US Robotics modems (e.g., ATX6) to detect dial tones upon dialing a number and to detect when a human answered the phone in addition to scanning for other modems. Detection of voice numbers sped up the scanning process by disconnecting upon detecting a human instead of timing out waiting for a "modem carrier signal."[1]

ToneLoc actually places a telephone call to each phone number in a range of phone numbers fed into the tool. So, I had to obtain VA phone number ranges for the Texas site and their approval to run it. I ran it over a weekend from my home in Maryland when most of the VA's Texas-based facility's workers were home. There were about 200 phone numbers in the range, and it took most of the weekend to run it. My long-distance phone bill for the exercise was a few hundred dollars! There were a few hits, but one modem replied that it had something to do with the *kernel debugger.* "The kernel is a computer program at the core of a computer's operating system and generally has complete control over everything in the system."[2] I was excited, and it looked like we may have found a way into the VA's network.

Senior technical staff from the Texas VA site came to E&Y's Washington DC offices to witness our remote penetration test. The VA staff were very confident that their system and network pre-check would have found any vulnerabilities that would allow us to infiltrate their site. It was considered a *capture-the-flag* exercise and would stop if we were able to gain access to the network and ultimately "the flag," their mainframe. It was a warm evening in DC, and we arrived at E&Y's main office. The building was mostly empty except for me, Dan Wooley, Steve Kaplan, one member of the VA's senior technical staff, and the GAO team. In one conference room, E&Y had a screen that covered the entire wall – twenty feet by ten feet. The scene was dramatic. Steve fired up his Linux PC and connected it to the Internet. The wall screen showed Steve's prompt and cursor in vibrant green phosphorus characters on the huge, black screen. Steve fired up his modem dialing program and began calling several promising numbers from my

ToneLoc run that looked like UNIX systems might be behind the responding modem.

After several unsuccessful attempts, I told Steve to try the phone number that previously replied with the *kernel debugger* response. Steve entered the phone number into his program's modem dialer, and the call and connection were made to the VA modem. The modem replied as it did during my ToneLoc dialing exercise with the same *kernel debugger* message now displayed on the twenty-foot screen. Steve's program now coaxed the VA's modem to provide a login prompt. Steve's cursor blinked at the ID and password entry prompts on the screen. Steve tried a few common UNIX system administrator default ID and password combinations that are typically left on systems due to poor system administration security practices. He had no success. I remembered reading an article in the 2600 magazine about UNIX vulnerabilities. "2600: The Hacker Quarterly" is an American seasonal publication of technical information and articles, many of which are written and submitted by the readership, on a variety of subjects, including hacking, telephone switching systems, Internet protocols and services, as well as general news about the computer "underground."[3]

I leaned over to Steve and whispered, "Try *lpr*, *lpr*." Never gazing up from his keyboard, he shrugged and mumbled, "Why not?" He entered *lpr* for the ID and *lpr* for the password. The login with the "lpr" credentials was accepted by the system. Bingo, the wall lit up with lines of information about the Unix system. *Steve was in – he had gained access to the system and network!* In UNIX, *lpr* is short for line printer, and the VA staff had not changed the login ID and password from the *lpr* system default. From there, Steve waltzed through the Texas facility's network from our remote DC office. *He wound up on the mainframe's network, and the VA's senior tech called a halt to the penetration exercise – the flag was captured! While the VA staff were dejected, we were elated.*

Now that we had successfully penetrated the network remotely, it was time to go to another VA facility and see what systems we could penetrate from inside the network. We traveled to Philadelphia and arrived onsite at the VA facility. Steve plugged his Linux PC into the network and began "sniffing" the network traffic traversing the communication line.

> Sniffing attacks in the context of network security, corresponds to theft or interception of data by capturing the network traffic using a packet sniffer (an application aimed at capturing network packets). When data is transmitted across networks, if the data packets are not encrypted, the data within the network packet can be read in plain text using a sniffer.[4]

Steve spent the afternoon capturing network traffic. That evening, after we left the facility, Steve used a Linux-based ASCII conversion program to see if he could see any login and password traffic in clear text from the sniffing exercise. "ASCII, abbreviated from American Standard Code for Information Interchange, is a character encoding standard for electronic communication. ASCII codes represent text in computers, telecommunications equipment, and other devices."[5] If the captured ASCII network traffic could be successfully converted to clear-text English, Steve could use the captured user IDs and passwords to log into VA systems with valid credentials. However, he had trouble reading the network traffic. After more study, he determined that IBM mainframes speak in EBCDIC "Extended Binary Coded" Decimal Interchange Code, "an eight-bit character encoding used mainly on IBM mainframe and IBM midrange computer operating systems."[6] It was actually EBCDIC traffic, not ASCII, traversing the internal VA network as workers interacted with the IBM mainframe.

The next day, while onsite at the VA, Steve found a Linux-based program that converted EBCDIC. He ran the packet captures from his previous network sniffing data and saw the converted EBCDIC traffic in clear text. He captured the VA site manager's ID and password and used the credentials to log into the site's mainframe. Steve then used the purloined credentials to change the manager's password to prove he was able to do so. *We gave the manager his new password, and he was not happy that we were able to compromise his systems.*

4.4 BANKING WORK

A large, well-known bank in Delaware engaged us to perform security assessments. Again, we were to perform remote penetration exercises followed by internal work. I don't recall that we were successful with our external penetration exercises. But for the internal network assessment, Don DeBolt was the star. He monitored the bank's internal network traffic and captured a system administrator's ID and password as it traversed the network. System/network administrators consider their systems and networks as their babies, and the bank's system administrator was particularly adversarial to our presence. During a debrief with their top management, Don disclosed the administrator's ID and password. We asked the administrator if those were indeed his login credentials, and he dejectedly replied, "Maybe."

To assess bank employee security awareness, I posed as a member of the bank's Help Desk. I called a number of employees and identified that I was conducting system tests and asked for their ID and password. About 90% of the respondents gave me their IDs and passwords. The bank needed to do more in employee security and education. The bank wasn't happy, but we were.

4.5 MANUFACTURING WORK

We were engaged to perform internal system security assessments for a large manufacturing client in West Virginia. The company had only one system administrator on staff, who was solely responsible for all aspects of the system. *This is a red flag since he represented a single point of failure.* If he were taken ill, in an accident, or worse, the company would have no one else to operate their systems. To save money, the administrator was migrating their production, inventory, sales, and distribution systems from an expensive mainframe-based system to the less costly Windows NT system. While this was a worthwhile strategy, again, they had only one administrator who knew the ins and outs of the entire system, including the conversion process.

The company was dealing with frequent outages and crashes with the new Windows NT system. These outages were hurting productivity and the company's bottom line. We approached the review cautiously since we did not want to cause system outages by probing the systems with our tools. We asked for documentation on the new system and were dismayed that the administrator had none! So, the entire knowledge base for the new, complex, mission-critical system was in the head of only one guy! *We ultimately had to walk away from the job since the administrator was sure our server probes would cause his systems to crash.*

4.6 Y2K

I have previously discussed the "Y2K" problem (see Chapter 3, Section 3.18), so I will not go into detail about the issue. Calendars were flipping at a faster rate as we approached the year 2000. Until now, the articles I read on the topic dealt mainly with large systems and coding. I also saw potential problems with hardware issues with Y2K. I authored a featured article entitled, *The Enemy Within – Y2K Issues Below the Application Level.* The article was published in the prestigious The *Journal of Information Systems Audit and Control Association* Volume III 1998. I was honored to have been published in the award-winning journal. (See Appendix A)

> *Lesson Learned* *Value network and system penetration assessments.* My year at E&Y gave me a great appreciation for network and system attack and penetration assessments. I learned a great deal about ethical hacker tools and techniques I would use in the future to assess systems and networks under my protection. This expertise allowed me to strengthen defenses, anticipate emerging threats, and contribute to a culture of continuous improvement.

4.7 TIME TO GO

A major issue I had with E&Y was my naiveté as to how the consulting business worked. Besides our technical work, we were expected to achieve sales quotas. I was excited about the network attack and penetration work, but I was not a salesman. It was time to go! My next adventure took me to the Prudential Insurance Company of America.

Lesson Learned *Within the cybersecurity discipline, decide between a consulting/auditing career path or a role as a security practitioner.* My experience at E&Y was valuable in my learning and appreciating network and system attack and penetration testing. But subsequent to my year as a consultant, my career path crystalized. I found the challenges of protecting the organization more gratifying than consulting or auditing. Security practitioners face challenges like limited budgets, outdated systems, and internal politics while protecting their organization's systems and networks.

4.8 TECHNOLOGY ADVANCEMENTS AND SECURITY DEVELOPMENTS 1998

1998

- June 25th, Microsoft Windows 98 was officially released.
- VMware was founded by Diane Greene, Mendel Rosenblum, Scott Devine, Ellen Wang, and Edouard Bugnion.
- August 20th, the first Google Doodle appeared on Google's web page to celebrate Burning Man.
- September 4th, Google filed for incorporation in California.
- September 28th, Microsoft Internet Explorer passed Netscape in Internet browser market share for the first time, as reported in an International Data Corporation report.
- October, Microsoft announced that future releases of Windows NT would no longer have the initials of NT and that the next edition would be Windows 2000.

NOTES

1 Tone Lōc. (n.d.). *Tone Lōc. Wikipedia.* https://en.wikipedia.org/wiki/ToneLoc
2 Kernel (Operating System). (n.d.). *Wikipedia.* https://en.wikipedia.org/wiki/Kernel_(operating_system)
3 2600: The Hacker Quarterly. (n.d.). *Wikipedia.* https://en.wikipedia.org/wiki/2600:_The_Hacker_Quarterly
4 Sniffing Attack. (n.d.). *Wikipedia.* https://en.wikipedia.org/wiki/Sniffing_attack
5 ASCII. (n.d.). *Wikipedia.* https://en.wikipedia.org/wiki/ASCII
6 EBCDIC. (n.d.). *Wikipedia.* https://en.wikipedia.org/wiki/EBCDIC

Chapter 5

Prudential Insurance Company of America 1998–2000

Position Held: Director of Security Operations

Location: 80 Livingston Avenue, Roseland, NJ

5.1 PRUDENTIAL – OVERVIEW

> Prudential Financial is based in Newark, New Jersey. It began as The Widows and Orphans Friendly Society in 1875, and for a short time, it was called the Prudential Friendly Society. For many years after 1877 it was known as the Prudential Insurance Company of America, a name still widely in use. The company has constructed a number of buildings to house its offices in downtown in the Four Corners district. In addition to its own offices, the corporation has financed large projects in the city, including Gateway Center and Prudential Center. Prudential has over 5,000 employees in the city.[1]

Not entirely enamored with my experience at Ernst & Young, I secured a position with Prudential's cybersecurity team under the leadership of Jerry Brady. While the position was located in New Jersey, I was not amenable to move there due to high property taxes, among other considerations. But Prudential had deep pockets, and I received a generous sign-on bonus and an allowance for moving expenses. Instead of moving, I commuted to work from my Gaithersburg, MD home on Mondays at 4:00 AM, drive the 235 miles to Roseland, NJ, and be at my desk at 7:30 AM. I stayed at a nearby Howard Johnson's Motel Monday night through Thursday morning. I would drive home to Maryland on Thursday evenings and work from home on Fridays. The moving expense allowance I received covered most of my lodging costs. One of the many negative things about the commute was that I ate most of my evening meals at Boston Market. And to this day, the sight of a Boston Market induces a gag reflex!

DOI: 10.1201/9781003650645-7

5.2 Y2K

Prudential was gearing up to improve its information technologies, including security defenses in advance of Y2K. No one knew for certain how devastating the Y2K effect might be on systems and networks. Theories ranged from *nothing to see here* to an *end of times* scenario. I went to many Y2K-focused meetings with key Prudential staff, and I recall that Prudential spent millions on Y2K remediations. Computer code had to be fixed, systems had to be upgraded, and my charter was to build out a Security Operations Control Center (SOCC) from which we would monitor Prudential networks and systems for any nefarious activities associated with Y2K.

5.3 INTERNET SECURITY SYSTEMS (ISS)

The centerpiece of our security technology deployment for the SOCC was Internet Security Systems (ISS) Intrusion Detection System (IDS). Christopher W. Klaus, an American technology entrepreneur, was founder and Chief Technology Officer (CTO) of ISS (see Chapter 3, Section 3.10). He started ISS in the early 1990s and then sold the company to IBM in 2006 for $1.3 billion.[2] ISS's IDS was one of the first technologies of the type, which is a device or software application that monitors a network or systems for malicious activity or policy violations. Any intrusion activity or violation is typically reported to an administrator.[3]

5.4 EDUCATIONAL OPPORTUNITIES

As I stated earlier, Prudential was generous, and my supervisor was supportive of my continuing education pursuits. I was studying for the Certified Information Systems Security Professional (CISSP) professional certification I had begun while at Ernst & Young. The CISSP is an independent information security certification granted by the International Information System Security Certification Consortium, also known as ISC^2 (formed in mid-1989). The mid-1980s recognized the need for a standard, vendor-neutral security certification program. In November 1988, the Special Interest Group for Computer Security, a member of the Data Processing Management Association, brought together several organizations interested in this goal. By 1990, the first working committee to establish a Common Body of Knowledge (CBK) had been formed. A CBK – sometimes simply called a Body of Knowledge – refers to a peer-developed compendium of what a competent professional in their respective field must know, including the skills, techniques and practices that are routinely employed The first version of the CBK was finalized by 1992, and the CISSP credential was launched by 1994.[4]

CISSP exam preparation comprised two one-week study sessions, and Prudential funded the course fee for me to attend the classes as well as the time off work to attend them. Since the classes were in Maryland, I was able to stay home and attend these local sessions. The course itself was essentially *death by slides*, where we suffered through hundreds of Microsoft PowerPoint slide decks on each of the CISSP Domains – access control, cryptography, physical security, etc. Several of my colleagues went to the CISSP courses to prepare for earning the premier professional security certification. If you successfully passed the exam, ISC^2 sent you a letter via snail mail addressed to your name, immediately followed by *CISSP*. So, you knew immediately that you passed. One of my friends who sat for the exam was a U.S. Secret Service agent and he did not pass the CISSP exam. *Over the years, he planned physical security details for*

New Technologies, Inc.

World Leader in Forensic Computer Software, Training and Consulting

Three Day Forensic Computer Science Course

This certifies that

Ronald R. Baklarz, Jr.

has completed the training on September 24, 1998 at the office of New Technologies, Inc. which covered computer evidence topics from a computer investigation and security review perspective. The course required intensive hands-on demonstrations of proficiency by the participant.

New Technologies, Inc.

2675 Northeast Division, Gresham, Oregon 97030
503.661.6912 ● www.ww.forensics-intl.com

Michael R. Anderson, President

Figure 5.1 New Technologies, Inc. Computer Forensic Certificate

five presidents. One of the CBK domains he failed – Physical Security. On December 22, 1998, I received my CISSP certification. My CISSP/ISC² member number is 4787, and these numbers are assigned sequentially. As of 2023, there were nearly 170,000 CISSPs worldwide. *So, my number member is pretty low!*

One of the other courses I attended in 1998 was Computer Forensics taught by Mike Anderson. Anderson founded New Technologies, Inc. (NTI) in 1996. NTI, in Gresham, Oregon, was staffed by internationally recognized computer experts in computer forensics and computer security-related areas. In 2000, NTI was acquired by Armor Holdings, Inc., a New York Stock Exchange-listed public corporation (NYSE:AH), and became part of Armor Forensics.[5] At NTI, we learned the basics of computer forensics, including hard drive acquisition, search techniques, and tools. I considered computer forensics to be an interesting area to pursue, which I continued in my later CISO positions (Figure 5.1).

The other course I attended while at Prudential was a new network intrusion detection course offered by the SysAdmin, Audit, Network, and Security Institute (SANS) taught by Stephen Northcutt. SANS Institute was founded in 1989 by Alan Paller, a cybersecurity expert, and his wife. This course was based on Mr. Northcutt's new book, *Network Intrusion Detection: An Analyst's Handbook* released in 1999. The course was germane to our charter to set up Prudential's SOCC and hunt for intrusive hacker behavior and any attempts to breach our network defenses. (For more on SANS and Alan Paller –see Chapter 7 Section 7.10.10).

5.5 PRUDENTIAL COMPUTER EMERGENCY RESPONSE TEAM (PRUCERT)

As I had done previously at the US House of Representatives, I set up PruCERT under The Forum of Incident Response and Security Teams (FIRST) (see Chapter 3 Section 3.14). Establishing a FIRST team at Prudential was more important than ever, given the potential for Y2K issues. The hope was that FIRST teams around the world would share problems and experiences in real time as the clocks changed time zone by time zone with the advance of the New Year. *We were prepared!*

5.6 SECURITY OPERATIONS CONTROL CENTER (SOCC)

We had spare office space in Prudential's ROS 3 building in Roseland, NJ. With a limited amount of time to get the SOCC operational, we drove the poor facilities management person crazy. We demanded faster and faster construction and installation schedules, and the SOCC was operational in February 1999. David Greenman, Prudential Senior Security Engineer, chose the system software and hardware that outfitted the SOCC. Two main systems were in use, both from ISS – ISS Scanner and Real Secure. The ISS Scanner was used to scan Prudential's networks for system vulnerabilities and other issues. Real Secure was the intrusion detection system and was configured to alert security staff by sending page alerts if alarms were triggered.

I also had two vulnerability assessment workstations set up in the room. One was Windows-based, and the other Linux-based. In addition to internal network access, both workstations also had external, independent network connections to the Internet. With this setup, we assessed the security of internal Windows and UNIX/Linux systems and attacked ourselves from the Internet from within our internal network – mimicking hacker activity. David and I won Prudential's First Quarter 1999 Business Value Award (BVA) for developing and creating the SOCC (see Appendix B).

5.7 JANUARY 1, 2000

Show time! I set up a three-shift monitoring operation, and I took the daylight shift in our SOCC. Prudential management promised a lobster dinner after midnight for those people working the late shift. Prudential also offered overnight accommodations for staff staying around the clock. I was happy to stay somewhere nicer than Howard Johnsons. I wish I could add exciting events that occurred as the clock struck midnight. But the Y2K monster was basically overhyped. It was estimated that approximately $300 billion was spent to remediate or upgrade computers and application programs to be Y2K-compliant. On the first day of January 2000, it became apparent that computerized systems were intact. Accusations that the likely incidence of failure had been greatly exaggerated from the beginning. But those who had worked in Y2K-compliance efforts insisted that the threat had been real.

5.8 TIME TO GO

Shortly before the New Year, my supervisor left Prudential, and our security team was dwindling partly due to the end of the Y2K project. Now armed with knowledge and experience with building a SOCC and SOCC Operations, I secured a position with Bruce Schneier-led startup, Counterpane Internet Security. During my time at Prudential, my wife had grown weary of my spending so much time away from home. My absence at home was especially problematic when it came to shoveling snow from our long Maryland driveway. Counterpane was based in Mountain View, CA, and as soon as I joined the new team, *I was called to California for a month!*

5.9 TECHNOLOGY ADVANCEMENTS AND SECURITY DEVELOPMENTS 1999–2000

1999

- IBM repackaged PC-DOS as PC-DOS 2000, making PC-DOS Y2K compliant.
- Transport Layer Security (TLS) was first defined as a cryptographic protocol designed to provide communications security over a computer networks. TLS is widely used in applications such as email, instant messaging, and voice over IP, but its use in securing HTTPS remains the most publicly visible.
- March 26, The Melissa worm created by David Smith was released, targeting Microsoft Word and Outlook-based systems and creating considerable network traffic. The virus became one of the fastest-spreading viruses in history and caused an estimated $80 million in damage.
- May, VMware released its first program, called VMware Workstation.
- October 11th, NVIDIA released the GeForce 256 GPU (Graphics Processing Unit). It was considered the first GPU worldwide and fully supported DirectX 7. It also featured 32 MB of DDR (Double Data Rate) memory.
- December 27th, Jeff Bezos of Amazon.com was named Time Person of the Year.

2000

- January 1st, computers continued to work, and the world did not end as many feared might happen because of the year 2000 bug.
- January 6th, A glitch in a computer in the Washington D.C. air traffic control system caused a shutdown of air traffic across the U.S. East Coast.
- Kevin Mitnick was released from prison on January 21, 2000.
- May 5: The ILOVEYOU worm (also known as the Love Letter, VBS, or Love Bug worm), a computer worm written in VBScript and using social engineering techniques, infected millions of Windows computers worldwide within a few hours of its release.
- June, Microsoft introduced the C# programming language to the public.

NOTES

1 Prudential Financial. (n.d.). *Prudential headquarters. Wikipedia.* https://en.wikipedia.org/wiki/Prudential_Headquarters

2 Klaus, C. (n.d.). *Chris Klaus. Wikipedia.* https://en.wikipedia.org/wiki/Chris_Klaus

3 Intrusion Detection System. (n.d.). *Wikipedia.* https://en.wikipedia.org/wiki/Intrusion_detection_system
4 Certified Information Systems Security Professional (CISSP). (n.d.). *Wikipedia.* https://en.wikipedia.org/wiki/Certified_Information_Systems_Security_Professional
5 New Technologies Inc. (n.d.). *Company profile.* https://usdirectory.com/b/249864/New-Technologies-Inc-Gresham-Oregon.aspx

Chapter 6

Counterpane Internet Security 2000–2001

Positions Held: SOC Operations Manager, Director of Operations

Locations: 4500 Southgate Place, Chantilly VA
1090 La Avenida St Mountain View, CA

6.1 COUNTERPANE INTERNET SECURITY – OVERVIEW

Counterpane Internet Security, Inc. was an innovative leader in the Managed Security Monitoring (MSM) service space. It was one of the first MSM providers of its kind. The system and network monitoring were conducted from its two Security Operations Centers (SOCs). The first SOC was established in Mountain View, CA and the second in Chantilly, VA. Sentry devices, resident on client networks, conducted monitoring and interfaced with the *Socrates* vulnerability knowledge base back in the SOCs. From inside the SOCs, Security Analysts monitored customer networks and systems for any detected intrusions and attacks in real time.

Having spent about two years away from home working for Prudential, I wanted to get back to a normal lifestyle. With my experience establishing Prudential's Security Operations Control Center, I was hired to join Counterpane's team. And what a team it was! Counterpane's Founder and Chief Technology Officer, Bruce Schneier, is a world-renowned security technology expert, speaker, and author. Counterpane's Chief Executive Officer, Tom Rowley, joked that it was easy to obtain venture capital for Counterpane. He only had to walk into meetings with Bruce and a PowerPoint presentation and their wallets opened!

The other members of the team were a veritable *Who's Who* in the security world. I'll start with Dr. Andrew Gross, mentored by cybersecurity expert, Tsutomu Shimomura, who was instrumental in the "Takedown" of the infamous hacker, Kevin Mitnick.[1] We also had firewall experts Dr. Tina Bird and Elizabeth Zwicky. Tina had a Ph. D in Astrophysics from the University of Minnesota – a true rocket scientist. Elizabeth co-authored O'Reilly's *Building Internet Firewalls* with Brent Chapman[2] (Figure 6.1). Lastly, I'll

DOI: 10.1201/9781003650645-8

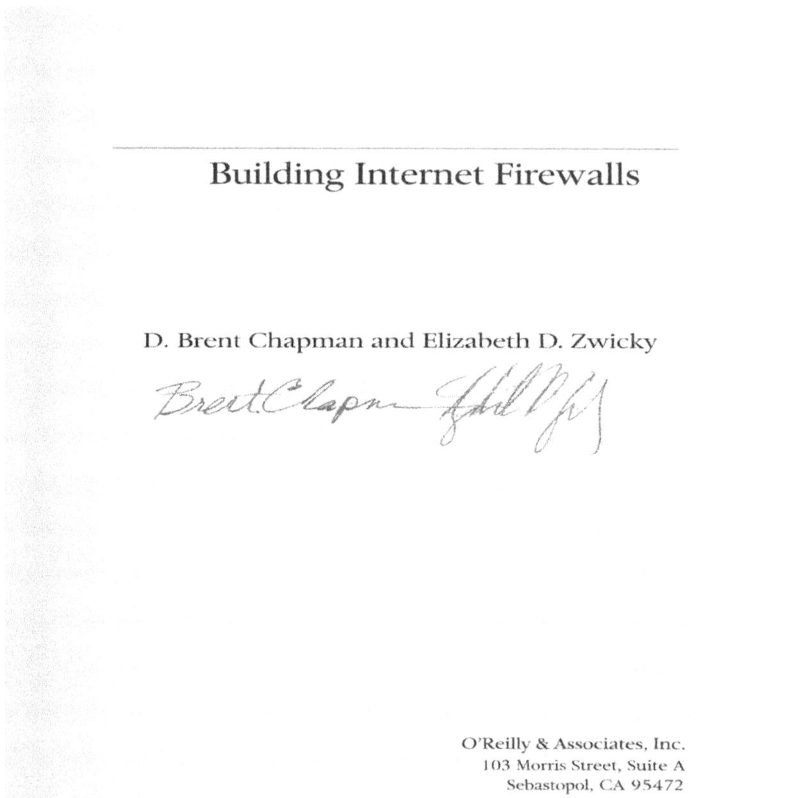

Building Internet Firewalls

D. Brent Chapman and Elizabeth D. Zwicky

O'Reilly & Associates, Inc.
103 Morris Street, Suite A
Sebastopol, CA 95472

Figure 6.1 Building Internet Firewalls Autograph – Brent Chapman and Elizabeth Zwicky

mention Jon Callas. Jon was the Co-Founder, Chief Technology Officer, and Chief Security Officer for PGP (Pretty Good Privacy) Corporation. I was star-struck to be working with a team such as this!

The corporate culture was typical for a "dot com" startup. All hands worked feverishly to stand up the SOCs, hire staff, and get the technology online. But there were fun times as well. On Friday afternoons, Tom Rowley conducted all-hands status meetings at the California headquarters office. After all status reports were completed, the meeting devolved into an all-out nerf war. With each successive week, the nerf weapons became more and more elaborate. Dr. Tina Bird was like an Amazonian warrior as she vanquished anyone who was in her way with the soft nerf projectiles. These battles were epic!

6.2 AND SO IT BEGINS

So much for getting back to a normal lifestyle after spending most of the week in New Jersey while working for Prudential. The first thing Counterpane had me do was fly from my home in Gaithersburg, MD to Mountain View, CA, for several weeks. First, we had to build out the California SOC. There was a ton of work to do with establishing an analyst team and building out the physical SOC. I reported to the Director of Operations, Ray Santos. Ray was the no-nonsense leader we needed. Once the Mountain View SOC was near operational, I began flying back and forth from coast-to-coast every two weeks, standing up the Virginia SOC and finalizing the Mountain View SOC.

The physical SOCs were technologically innovative. We each wore small metal circular rings embedded with JavaScript that unlocked the entry doors to the facility. Think of the "Green Lantern," where we inserted the raised circle of the ring's face into the circular reader at the SOC's entrance to unlock the door. From there, you either entered the locked office space or walked up a circuitous path to the conference room. In the center of the conference rooms were large oval tables with the Counterpane logo emblazoned on them. The conference rooms had one entire wall that was actually a window that faced the SOC monitoring floor. The window was opaque but instantly changed to crystal clarity with the press of a button. Today these widows are more commonplace but was very innovative for the time.

To enter the SOC floor, one had to pass through a hand-geometry reader. Once inside, there were rows of futuristic furniture and an entire wall displaying monitoring screens, a real-time camera view of the other SOC's floor, television feeds for CNN, etc. A siren light activated when the opaque

Figure 6.2 Counterpane Analyst Shirt

window was "cleared," so analysts knew they were being observed. SOCs also had office space and kitchens stocked with a generous supply of analyst food and SOC analysts' uniform shirts were fashioned after Star Trek attire (Figure 6.2).

Besides building the physical SOC plant, we had to *grow* our own analysts. This was no easy task since we were really starting from scratch with as new a concept as the MSM. We set up a rigorous interview process. You can imagine a candidate having to face Elizabeth Zwicky or Tina Bird and answer their technical questions! In California, we finally had an initial group of analysts to cover three shifts. However, we had no physical SOC yet. Rather, we had a small room in our temporary office space where we had them practice and respond to network attacks.

6.3 VIRGINIA SOC

As the California SOC was nearing completion, we began building out the Chantilly VA SOC. We seemed to have better luck finding security-technology-oriented people in Virginia. This was likely due to the proximity to Washington, D.C. and the military-industrial complex. We hired staff and, as we did in California, had them practice in our rented office space until the SOC construction was finished. I hired Don DeBolt, whom I had worked with at E&Y. (See Chapter 4 Sections 4.2 and 4.4). Don is a fantastic manager and security visionary. Ultimately, the SOCs were fully staffed and up and running!

Another group we had in the Metro D.C. area was our threat intelligence group. The lead on this team was Chris Petersen. Chris's job was to develop threat-specific signature codes to incorporate into the Sentry/Socrates monitoring systems. As new vulnerabilities and threats were discovered, Chris transposed the threat into the code for Socrates to match with real-life network and system traffic. Chris always had the idea to take a different direction with network and system monitoring. Chris wanted to feed the actual logs from the client's system and network devices into a specialized system and ferret out anomalies and attacks via log analysis. When Chris left Counterpane, he started the successful company LogRhythm. I became reacquainted with Chris years later and used LogRhythm to protect Amtrak's networks and systems. (see Chapter 9, Section 9.13).

6.4 COMPETITION

One of the more severe technology challenges we faced was the Sentry system, designed to reside on client networks and sniff out attacks. We were developing the Sentry system from scratch. This was no easy or quick endeavor. On the other hand, an MSM competitor, Riptech, was using

Ron Gula's existing, mature Dragon Intrusion Detection System. As Chief Technology Officer of Network Security Wizards, Ron Gula pioneered network security monitoring with his Dragon Intrusion Detection System, which was recognized as a market leader by Gartner in 2001. Riptech was founded in 1998 during the dot-com bubble by Amit Yoran, along with his two brothers and Tim Belcher.[3] It began operations in December 1999 and operated until 2002, when acquired by Symantec. Mr. Yoran would go on to serve as the future Department of Homeland Security's National Cybersecurity Director.

Riptech's model for MSM was to simply install the mature Dragon sensors into client networks, which was a game changer. Riptech was able to quickly get its clients up and running while we were suffering through the various software development challenges of the Sentry sensor devices.

6.5 ENOUGH ALREADY

I had hired Don Debolt, with whom I had worked at Ernst & Young. He is a quick study and I felt he could do a better job as Operations Director than I now that the SOCs were up and running. Besides, it was a daily forty-two-mile, one-way drive from my home in Gaithersburg, MD, to the Chantilly, VA SOC. If any reader is familiar with driving on the 495 Beltway, you know what a traffic nightmare this can be. I had grown tired of the commute and was ready to move on. Don took over for me and did a great job – no surprise! I was honored to have worked with so many giants in the industry at Counterpane, but it was time to move on. Counterpane was acquired by BT Group on October 25, 2006 and became known as BT Counterpane.

6.6 TECHNOLOGY ADVANCEMENTS AND SECURITY DEVELOPMENTS 2001

2001

- January 2nd, Intel announced it would recall its 1.13 GHz Pentium III processors due to a glitch. Intel admitted the processor crashed under certain conditions, largely due to the high temperature the power-hungry chip runs at.
- March 9th, McAfee released the first virus protection software for handheld devices.
- On June 5th, Nevada became the first U.S. state to vote to legalize online gambling.
- July, the Code Red worm began infecting Windows computers and programmed them to perform a Distributed Denial of Service attack on the White House government web page. Code Red infected

computers by exploiting a vulnerability in Windows NT and 2000, causing a buffer overflow. The worm was estimated to have caused $2 billion in damages despite failing in its intended attack.
- September 9th, Mark Curphey started OWASP (Open Worldwide Application Security Project). OWASP is an online cybersecurity community that produces freely available articles, methodologies, documentation, tools, and technologies focused on web application security.
- October 23rd, Apple introduced the iPod and the first Apple earbuds.
- December 4th, the Goner virus was first discovered. Goner was a mass-mailing Internet worm that, when run, mass-mailed itself to everyone in the infected user's Microsoft Windows Address Book. Goner eventually caused an estimated $80 million in damages.

NOTES

1 Takedown.com. (n.d.). *Takedown*. http://www.takedown.com/
2 Chapman, D. B., & Zwicky, E. D. (2000). *Building Internet firewalls* (2nd ed.). O'Reilly Media. https://www.oreilly.com/library/view/building-internet-firewalls/1565928717/
3 Yoran, A. (n.d.). *Amit Yoran. Wikipedia*. https://en.wikipedia.org/wiki/Amit_Yoran

Part III

The Complete CISO – Putting Experience into Practice

My last three CISO roles span eighteen years, or over 37,000 hours of Malcolm Gladwell's "10,000-hour rule." During this time, I consider myself a COMPLETE CISO, applying all my years of cybersecurity experience and putting them into practice. A recurring challenge throughout my CISO roles was operating with limited staffing and budget. To address these constraints, I had to develop security-on-a-shoestring methods and techniques. I recognized the importance of increased visibility and continuous monitoring of networks and systems to maintain a strong security posture. Despite budget and resource limitations, I believe my last three CISO positions were the most effective in the role and the programs we built.

American Red Cross (ARC) – In this role I reported to the Chief Information Officer (CIO). Given the lack of resources, I resorted to personally scanning systems for vulnerabilities on an almost daily basis. Over time, we gained network visibility via intrusion detection systems and firewall log analysis. Computer viruses were a major challenge for us. As the first CISO at ARC, you will understand that the constant management turnover was a major impediment to organizational consistency and priorities around cybersecurity.

MedStar Health – As the first Director of Information System Security at MedStar Health, I reported directly to the CIO. We increased network visibility via web content filtering and Data Loss Prevention (DLP) technologies. We also deployed endpoint protection software to give us more visibility and control at the endpoint level. Vulnerability scanning was used to a lesser extent than were deployed at ARC, but we did use more sophisticated web security scanning technology to address website insecurities.

Amtrak – As the first CISO at Amtrak, I also reported directly to the CIO. We employed a good mix of vulnerability scanning and network/system visibility and monitoring technologies. In 2016, Amtrak HR redefined roles, and Human Resources had no general role for the title of "chief." My title was then changed to senior director, but I still reported to the CIO. At Amtrak, for the first time in my career, I participated in selected Board of

DOI: 10.1201/9781003650645- 9

Directors (BOD) meetings and routine inclusion to BOD Subcommittee on Safety and Security meetings.

Over the past thirty years in CISO roles, I have dedicated more than 70,000 hours – far surpassing Malcolm Gladwell's "10,000-hour rule" – to honing my craft and leading security teams. These hours reflect not just time spent, but a deep commitment to mastering the complexities of cybersecurity leadership.

Chapter 7

American Red Cross 2001–2005

Position Held: Chief Information Security Officer (CISO)

Location: 111 Gatehouse Road Falls Church, VA 22042

7.1 THE AMERICAN RED CROSS (ARC) – OVERVIEW

This chapter is the first in my last three Chief Information Security Officer (CISO) roles where I was able to draw on all my previous experiences and "put it all together" to build effective cybersecurity programs. To recap, I had a solid work ethic and commitment to higher education from EPIC Metals. Next, I gained valuable management skills from Elliott Company, where I was able to complete my bachelor's degree. Westinghouse Plant Apparatus Division gave me my foundation in a CISO role as well as invaluable skills in written/oral communications, attention to detail, discipline, and support to complete two graduate degrees. As you will read, I had to work with extremely limited resources, especially given the size, diversity, and complexity of the ARC. Despite these shortcomings, I consider we had built an effective security program. Some of the content in this chapter will be technical due to the nature of the network and computer systems being discussed.

I remember my first day at the ARC. On a sunny Monday morning, I walked through the glass doors of the large ARC building on Gallows Road in northern Virginia. Once inside the huge entry doors, there was a visitors' desk staffed by two uniformed individuals. As I signed in, one of the guards called up to the Chief Information Officer's office to announce my arrival. The expansive foyer was impressive, with high ceilings and gleaming, polished marble floors. The aroma of breakfast food wafted through the building from the in-house cafeteria. I made my way to the elevators and pressed the button to the fourth floor, where most of the Information Technology (IT) team resided.

I had been on the floor a few weeks prior for my interviews, so I knew where the office was for Chief Information Officer, Dr. Tom Woteki. Tom greeted me warmly and advised me to meet with my security team and get

DOI: 10.1201/9781003650645-10

the lay of the land. Tom seemed preoccupied and didn't seem to have much time to connect with me. So, Tom's Administrative Assistant, Jules, led me to my desk and introduced me to my *team* which consisted of only one individual – Lauren Reynolds. *Oh boy, what a way to start!*

7.2 ORGANIZATIONAL CULTURE AND COMPLEXITY

ARC is a federal instrumentality, not a government agency. In 1900, the ARC received its first Congressional Charter and then a second charter in 1905, a year after Clara Barton's 1904 resignation from the organization in 1904. The charter required ARC to

> carry on a system of national and international relief in time of peace and apply the same in mitigating the sufferings caused by pestilence, famine, fire, floods, and other great national calamities, and to devise and carry on measures for preventing the same.[1]

The charter is a grant of power and an imposition of duties and obligations to the nation, to disaster victims, and to the people who generously support its work with their donations.

The general public is probably unaware of the wide range of services ARC provides. During my tenure, ARC had several significant sub-organizational entities: National Headquarters (NHQ), Biomedical Services, Chapter Services, Disaster Services, and Armed Forces Emergency Services (AFES). The following organizational details came from a September 2005 talk I gave on the "Aftermath of Hurricane Katrina."

Biomedical services – processes about 50% of the American Blood supply.

Chapter Services – there were about 900 chapters across the US, of which about one hundred used ARC NHQ as their Internet Service Provider (ISP).

Disaster Services – Each year, the ARC typically responds to over 70,000 disasters, including house and apartment fires (the majority of disaster responses), hurricanes, floods, earthquakes, tornadoes, hazardous materials spills, transportation accidents, explosions, and other natural and man-made disasters.

AFES – Provides services to 1.4 million active-duty personnel and their families, and over 800,000 members of the National Guard and the Reserves and their families who live in nearly every community in America. AFES maintains staff in 900 chapters across the United States and in seventy-four military bases around the world. This support required ARC to have a network connection to Fort Sill, Oklahoma.

ARC's IT department support statistics included:

- Support for over 20,000 end-users in biomedical, chapter, and corporate users
- Staffed by 700 IT professionals

- Provided 24 × 7 data operations for over 300 servers, 560 databases, twenty-two terabytes of data, and over fifty production applications
- Fielded 10,000 IT help calls per month
- Provided data and voice networks for 441 Washington D.C. metro, biomedical, and chapter sites.

Given that I was ARC's first CISO and given the lack of resources, it is safe to say that cybersecurity was not considered a priority. The consensus of ARC's collective psyche was that no one would ever want to launch technical attacks against such a benevolent, beloved, and iconic organization as the ARC. Of course, nothing was further from the truth. However, that mindset changed quickly as new systems and services came online and external factors like Sepyember-11 and natural disasters impacted ARC's IT infrastructure. One new aspect of cybersecurity that I quickly became aware was that of *Brand Protection*. The American public generally had a positive opinion of the ARC. Any breach of donor information or other adverse press regarding the ARC could damage public *goodwill* that ARC enjoyed. In the following sections, you will see how *brand protection* played a large part in my information security decisions and program.

Lesson Learned Attend your organization's change control meetings. Change control is a systematic process used within quality management systems and IT governance to ensure that any changes to a product or system are introduced in a controlled and coordinated way. I initially joined ARC IT's weekly Change Control meetings as an observer and later became a voting member. These meetings, largely driven by Food and Drug Administration (FDA) Consent Decrees, were crucial for identifying system changes, upgrades, and new implementations affecting ARC's IT environment. (See Section 7.4 for a discussion of ARC's Consent Decrees.) We received change control documentation in advance so we could prepare questions and challenges regarding the upcoming changes. The FDA Consent Decrees are regulatory mandates that required ARC to comply with specific standards for safety and quality, which in turn shaped our internal IT processes. Compliance with these Consent Decrees influenced IT decision-making and risk management strategies by mandating rigorous oversight of system changes to ensure the integrity of critical operations and data. I strongly encourage CISOs or their team members to participate in these types of internal technical meetings. They are an excellent way to gain insights into the organization's systems and to stay informed about upcoming changes and updates that may impact cybersecurity. By linking regulatory requirements to internal processes, organizations can better manage risks and maintain compliance, ultimately protecting both their operations and their reputation.

7.3 MANAGEMENT TURNOVER

Upper management at ARC was a veritable merry-go-round of organizational changes and turnover. During my almost five-year tenure, I worked under *three Chief Executive Officers and six Chief Information Officers!* Over the following sections, I will designate the CEOs as #1, #2, and #3 and the CIOs as #1 through #6. With this amount of management turnover, there were numerous shifts in direction and priorities. It was difficult to gain any traction in creating a robust cybersecurity program.

Two weeks after I joined ARC, ARC Chief Information Officer #1, Tom Woteki, resigned. He was well-liked, respected, and admired by ARC's IT department. In an effort to calm the situation, ARC President and Chief Executive Officer #1, Dr. Bernadine Healy, called all the heads of the IT department, including me, down to ARC Headquarters (NHQ) in Washington D.C.

> The national headquarters of the American Red Cross is located in central Washington, D.C., on the east side of a city block bounded by 17th, D, and E Streets NW. This block, on the west side of The Ellipse south of the White House, is entirely devoted to Red Cross facilities. The main headquarters building is a large stone structure, faced in white Vermont marble. It is three stories in height; its third floor recessed behind a balustrade. Its east-facing main facade has a central classical temple portico, with six Corinthian columns supporting a gabled pediment with a red cross at the center.[2]

I remember the dark, stormy night we all met with Dr. Healy in a medieval-looking meeting room at the ARC NHQ. She answered questions and let us know we would have an acting CIO#2, Joanne O'Rourke Hindman, to manage the IT department on an interim basis. Table 7.1 is a list of the ARC CEOs and CIOs I served under during my tenure from 2001 to 2005:

Table 7.1 List of ARC CEOs and CIOs from 2001–2005

ARC CEOs	*ARC CIOs*
CEO #1– Dr. Bernadine Healey 2001	CIO #1– Dr. Tom Woteki 2001
Interim CEO #2 – Harold Decker 2002	Interim CIO #2 – Joanne O'Rourke Hinman 2001
CEO #3 – Marsha Evans 2002–2005	Interim CIO #3 – Brian Rhoa 2001
	CIO #4 – Tom Schwaninger 2001–2004
	Interim CIO #5 – Mark Weischedel 2004–2005
	CIO #6 – Steve Cooper 2005

© 2005 Ron Baklarz

7.4 CONTEXT – RED CROSS AND FOOD AND DRUG ADMINISTRATION CONSENT DECREES

I would be remiss in not mentioning the issues ARC had over the years with the quality of the blood supply in their collection, inventory, and distribution efforts. ARC had been operating under the terms of a consent decree first issued in 1993 and then amended in 2003. A consent decree is defined as an agreement or settlement that resolves a dispute between two parties without admission of guilt or liability. Consent decrees allowed the FDA to impose stiff fines for ongoing failures to meet regulations and laws governing the quality and safety of the nation's blood supply. On April 14, 2003, FDA issued a Consent Decree Letter to ARC President and CEO#3 Marsha Evans. This letter identified deficiencies uncovered by FDA investigators during an ARC Biomedical Headquarters inspection that occurred between April 2002 and December 2002.[3]

Deficiencies included: *Hotline Records* (e.g., ARC employees reported instances where work records documented work that was not actually performed), *Labeling* (e.g., blood products were not labeled correctly), *Inventory Management* (e.g., from April 1, 2000 to August 12, 2002, ARC could not determine the disposition of 1,062 (lost) blood products, and *National Donor Deferral Registry (NDDR) and Donor File Check* (e.g., two National Biomedical Computer System (NBCS) queries run in May 2000, found over 3,000 unsuitable donors who were not included in the NDDR. *These issues directly impacted ARC's IT systems. Each week, IT held a Configuration Change Control meeting to identify changes and updates to systems as a quality check imposed by FDA consent decree findings.*[4]

After almost twenty-three years and $47 million in fines, the blood services operation of the ARC was no longer under a consent decree with oversight by the federal government. To get out from under the consent decree, ARC had to show five years of sustained compliance with federal FDA regulations, which occurred at the end of October 2015.[5]

7.5 GETTING STARTED – "HANDS-ON" CISO

Before I was hired at the ARC, there were no previous CISOs, so I had to build the program from scratch. Given the lack of personnel, resources, and budget, I had to take a hands-on approach to build a cybersecurity program. I considered it important to have a technical approach to the CISO position, and technical acumen went a long way in gaining the support of IT's technical staff. Otherwise, the CISO would be viewed as just another *suit* who doesn't understand the nuts and bolts of the systems under their protection.

Lesson Learned *Walk the walk and talk the talk.* Technical teams quickly recognize when a leader lacks hands-on expertise. Having real technical chops earns trust, buy-in, and respect in the trenches. Technical staff rely on leaders who truly grasp the intricacies of their jobs, which sparks clearer communication and sharper decisions. If you want to lead from the front, be the real deal—not just another suit. Technical credibility isn't optional—it's your ticket to effective leadership and lasting influence.

One of the first things I did to control and effectively manage my workload was establishing a letter log system using the Microsoft Excel spreadsheet program. Drawing on my Naval Nuclear Program experience, where we had a formal, computerized letter logging system for tracking correspondence between WPAD and NAVSEA, I developed a coding/serialization system for my use at ARC. Each piece of formal correspondence had a unique number. For example, ARC-CISO (designating my office) – (CATEGORY) – A general category such as GEN – General, AUD – Audit, INV – Investigation, POL – Policy, 200n (Year) and nnn (Sequential numbering).

From 2001 through 2005, I issued 355 pieces of formal correspondence *without clerical assistance* as follows:

2001 > CISO-2001.001 – CISO-2001.085 79 memorandums issued
2002 > CISO-2002.001 – CISO-2002.085 80 memorandums issued
2003 > CISO-2003.001 – CISO-2003.078 78 memorandums issued
2004 > CISO-2004.001 – CISO-2004.105 77 memorandums issued
2005 > CISO-2005.001 – CISO-2005.065 41 memorandums issued

If the information in the memorandum contained sensitive information, it was marked top and bottom of each page with CONFIDENTIAL. In these cases, I added a C to the letter's serial number within the Excel letter log for easy identification of sensitive correspondence. The letter log spreadsheet had fields for details such as date, subject, and notes. Since I always thought that there might be a book about my experiences as ARC CISO, I saved the Excel Letter Log files and either a Word or PDF copy of every memo I issued.

In the following sections, I will tell the story, citing selected memos that coincide with each year of my tenure at ARC. These memos represent the many diverse issues that confront CISOs of any sizable organization. *The operative concept is always to expect the unexpected.*

7.6 MEMOS AND ISSUES – MARCH 2001–DECEMBER 2001

7.6.1 CISO-ARC-INV-2001.0011 (C) Dated March 19, 2001 – Abuse of Internet Privileges – Contract Employee

The first memorandum I issued concerned Internet abuse committed by a contract employee. The contractor was accessing pornography-related sites and materials. The investigation began with a review of firewall logs showing the Internet-routable Internet Protocol (IP) address and its specific internal, non-Internet routable IP address as well as the times and dates of the inappropriate activity. The internal IP address was used to identify the workstation name, the workstation's network jack number, and the contractor's cubicle location. Given this level of specificity, the evidence supported the contractor's termination. *This level of investigative detail served me well in this and future CISO roles and subsequent investigations since there was no ambiguity as to who committed the infractions, and sanctions were levied commensurate with the violation.* Absent a specific information security policy on acceptable uses of ARC networks and resources at the time, I cited the abuse under ARC Human Resource Policy Number 406 – Use of Red Cross Property and Facilities.

7.6.2 ARC-CISO – GEN-2001.010 Dated March 29, 2001 – Justification to Purchase a Forensic Computer Workstation

In Chapter 5, The Prudential Insurance Company of America, I described my studying computer forensics under Michael Anderson at New Technologies, Inc. in Gresham, Oregon. I carried this training and skill forward in later CISO positions. I considered it prudent to have basic, in-house computer forensic capabilities to investigate sensitive internal matters using court-tested methods and software. This request was for a total cost of $8,000 for forensic hardware and software.

7.6.3 ARC-CISO-GEN-2001.073 Dated October 11, 2001 – Sole Source Vendor Forensic Computer

Purchasing a forensic workstation was a difficult sell, given our tight budgets. Now, over six months later from my initial request, I issued this memo, a sole-source justification to purchase the forensic workstation from Forensic Computers (FC). FC was a local company that provided and supported forensic workstations for law enforcement use. Included with the hardware package was forensic software such as EnCase software. Encase was used to make sector-by-sector copies of the target drives with which to conduct targeted searches and produce court-tested evidence. Over the years at ARC, I conducted seven forensic analyses using the system. All the investigations involved individuals, except for analysis of electronic blood drive laptops (eBDR) to ensure that clear text donor data did not populate in unexpected areas of the hard drive. *Using our in-house forensic capabilities saved money and protected the ARC brand.*

7.6.4 ARC-CISO-GEN-2001.012 Dated April 4, 2001 – FIRST Membership Request for the American Red Cross Computer Emergency Response Team (ARCcert)

This memo was a request for ARC to join the International Forum of Incident Response Teams (FIRST). The team was to be called the ARC Computer Emergency Response Team (ARCcert). With only two of us making up the entire ARC information security team, I was looking for a *cost-effective force multiplier* to help secure our networks and systems.

To join FIRST, you must have a constituency, offer to interact with other FIRST teams via a secure (encrypted) communication capability, and be sponsored by an existing FIRST team. Since I had started my initial FIRST team (US-HCERT) at the U.S. House of Representatives, the House security staff agreed to sponsor the ARCcert Team. My justification for joining FIRST was that (a) ARC systems supported the collection, manufacture, and distribution of 50% of America's blood supply, (b) 24 × 7 system support for the United States armed forces via the Armed Forces Emergency System (AFES) and (c) 24 × 7 system support for the over 1,100 local chapters in their efforts to help communities through disasters. We were voted into FIRST as full members. As of 2000, there were about fifty (50) other FIRST teams in North America.[6]

7.6.5 ARC-CISO-MIN-2001.014 Dated April 13, 2001 – Meeting Minutes – SIG Information Security

Before my arrival, ARC did not have a single focal point to address information security. Thus, there was a lot of pent-up demand for addressing ARC IT security concerns. I established this Special Interest Group (SIG) made up of key ARC IT directors and system managers to address security issues. For example, we developed an AIX system security configuration checklist. IBM's Advanced Interactive eXecutive, or AIX, is a proprietary UNIX-based operating system (OS) built and sold by IBM. ARC's AIX systems were critical in processing ARC's blood supplies and tissue products. *The SIG was instrumental in opening dialog between the various ARC IT system managers and my team.*

7.6.6 ARC-CISO-GEN-2001.015 Dated April 16, 2001 – CISO Report Week Ending April 13, 2001

With this memo, I began a weekly report on Key Performance Indicators (KPI) issued to the CIO. One of the most important of the KPI items was to communicate the status of the twenty-seven PricewaterhouseCoopers (PwC) audit findings I inherited. Other KPIs included the number of investigations opened, issuance of CERT advisories, and the number of systems tested.

7.6.7 ARC-CISO-GEN-2001.016 Dated April 23, 2001 – CISO Report Week Ending April 20, 2001

This status update reported on two key items: (1) The U.S. House of Representatives Core Security team visited ARC as a site visit supporting their sponsorship of the ARCcert team for FIRST membership and (2) ARC's deployment of Cisco Secure network-based intrusion detection and the NetForensics system to collect and analyze the log data from the various perimeter security devices. Once the concept had been proven and found to be acceptable, this monitoring and log audit solution would expand to include other mission-critical UNIX and NT/2000 servers.

7.6.8 ARC-CISO-AUD-2001.020 Dated May 2, 2001 – Closure of PwC Audit Item – ENT-010

ARC engaged in two formal security audit exercises. The first was a review of Control Objectives for Information and Related Technologies (COBIT) conducted by PwC. In 1996, the Information Systems Audit and Control Association (ISACA) initially released COBIT, a set of control objectives to help the financial audit community maneuver better in IT-related environments.[7]

During his forty-year affiliation with ISACA, my friend, U.S. House of Representatives Inspector General, John W. Lainhart IV, was a central figure in the development of two of ISACA's most widely embraced industry contributions – the Certified Information Systems Auditor (CISA) professional certification and the COBIT framework for the governance and management of enterprise IT. I was familiar with COBIT from my tenure at the U.S. House of Representatives. As the U.S. House's lead for cybersecurity, John asked me to review and provide comments on Version 2 of the COBIT standards.

The second formal audit/review we conducted was called WebTrust. WebTrust was a technical, administrative, and management review performed annually against our primary donation website www.redcross.org. The WebTrust review was conducted by audit firm KPMG (Klynveld, Peat, Marwick, Goerdeler). The KPMG lead was Tony Hubbard, and we developed a close relationship over the years. I valued their annual reviews to ensure the security of our primary donation website and brand protection posture. A member of the KPMG WebTrust team was Gus Fritschie. Gus was their resident *ethical hacker* who evaluated the security of our website and supporting systems. I would work with Gus again for many years at Amtrak (see Chapter 9 Section 9.5.3).

7.6.9 ARC-CISO-TST-2001.022 I Dated May 3, 2001 – System Security Test

This was my first system test of ARC's primary Internet-facing website www.redcross.org. The test was to obtain a snapshot of the ARC website from an external hacker's perspective using the Teleport Pro assessment system. This methodology also permitted the offline review of the website's underlaying Hypertext Markup Language (HTML) code for unintended pieces of intelligence such as potential disclosure of IDs and passwords. The test read 29,948 web pages, and 53,366 files were retrieved. In total, 37.2 MB of information were extracted from the mirroring exercise. The high number of files and pages was due to the primary website linking to other websites. I found no evidence of confidential and/or private information being divulged. *This was my first foray into conducting system security tests at ARC, which would become a staple in our security program.*

7.6.10 ARC-CISO-TST-2001.027 I Dated May 15, 2001 – System Security Test – Domain Name System (DNS)

Protecting ARC's diverse and expansive IT infrastructure with extremely limited resources was challenging. Another security assessment capability I wanted to have at my fingertips was to run network and system vulnerability scans on a frequent, as-needed basis. To conduct continuous technical security assessments, I added a VMware instance to my ARC laptop. VMware allowed me to run a separate OS on my PC. So, within the VMware instance, I ran Red Hat Linux with a complement of freeware security assessment tools such as Nmap, Nessus, and Whisker and used other command line techniques such as DNS zone transfers. *I used Linux system to continually assess the security of Red Cross's internal and external systems.*

Lessons Learned *Computer Viruses* ARC endured frequent computer virus infection. Although we used a reputable, industry-standard anti-virus product on all of our approximately 10,000 PCs, new variants or entirely new worms and viruses would often be detected on a daily basis. These discoveries were not only flagged by our anti-virus software but also by other internal monitoring systems such as firewall logs. Firewall logs help us to track unusual behavior or suspicious traffic, making it possible to spot threats that anti-virus programs overlooked.

If our anti-virus software failed to recognize a new virus or worm, we would isolate the infected PC and make a copy of the viral code. This sample would then be sent to our anti-virus vendor, who would analyze it and update their detection tools. Specifically, they would incorporate the new code into their "definition" files—collections of data that help the program recognize different threats. These updates were delivered to clients as DAT files, which are specific data files used by anti-virus programs to identify and block new viruses and worms. Most of the infections we encountered came from files or web links delivered via email.

7.6.11 ARC-CISO-GEN-2001.030 Dated May 23, 2001 – Justification Verbiage for Network Security Budget Items

In this memo, I requested a budget of $235,000 to purchase fundamental network security technologies. Specifically, the budget request included Cisco Secure Suite, including five intrusion detection sensors and management console (hardware and software), system vulnerability scanner, and a policy enforcement system. The budget also included funds for Netforensics software and hardware to be used for additional log data collection and analysis from critical network devices. This request supported several PwC audit findings from their ARC COBIT testing. *Unfortunately, I was unsuccessful in securing the funds.*

7.6.12 ARC-CISO-GEN-2001.031 Dated May 25, 2001 – Comments to IBM's Web Hosting Information Security Controls Document

IBM was contracted to host ARC's – www.disasterrelief.org website. IBM provided a document entitled Information Security Controls for Disaster-Relief Red Cross Version 2.1c dated April 4, 2001. Via this memo, I provided six pages of comments ranging from editorial and administrative issues to technical shortcomings. I did not consider that the controls outlined in the IBM document adhered to information security best practices.

7.6.13 ARC-CISO-GEN-2001.042 Dated July 2, 2001 – CISO Report for Month Ending June 29, 2001

Although this memo was a routine status correspondence, the significance was that it was addressed and submitted to our third, acting CIO#3 – Brian Roha. Brian was ARC's Chief Financial Officer.

7.6.14 ARC-CISO-CSA-2001.044 Dated July 9, 2001 – Customer Service Advisory – Configuring Personal E-mail Blocks/Filters

To foster better communications regarding security topics and effectiveness, I partnered with ARC's Director of User Support and various ARC IT department leads to develop CSA (Customer Security Advisory) memos. This first advisory provided Customer Service staff with specific step-by-step instructions on how to configure their ARC-provided user desktop e-mail clients to block/filter unwanted e-mail messages. *Over my tenure, I issued many CSA memos on various cybersecurity topics, including detailed heads-up information on the latest computer viruses and worms circulating on the Internet* (see Appendix C for an example my CSA documentation).

7.6.15 ARC-CISO-POL-2001.048 I Dated July 22, 2001 – E-mail Blocking Operational Parameters and List of Offensive Words

Arguably, email has been and continues to be a significant vector for malicious activities. An early compromise of the nascent Internet was November 1988s Morris worm that took advantage of a hole in the debug mode of the UNIX *sendmail* program.[8] And today, we have ransomware attacks carried out via email. This memorandum was a policy directive concerning ARC's use of Content Technology's MailSweeper product. MailSweeper blocked content before it was delivered to ARC email systems. This memo outlined inbound email blocking parameters such as graphic language blocking and emails containing potentially dangerous executable file attachments (e.g., exe. and vbs.). *Interestingly, Content Technology was based in the United Kingdom and many of their vulgar and slang words were not necessarily applicable within American language lexicon.*

7.6.16 ARC-CISO-GEN-2001.051 Dated August 2, 2001 – CISO Report for Month Ending July 31, 2001

Again, this was a routine monthly status update that was now addressed and submitted to the new ARC CIO#4 – Tom Schwaninger.

7.6.17 ARC-CISO-INC-2001.053 Dated August 6, 2001 – Incident Report – DMZ Servers and Internet Worm (Code Red)

July 15, 2001, the Code Red computer worm was observed on the Internet. Code Red attacked computers running Microsoft's IIS web server and was the first large-scale, mixed-threat attack to successfully target enterprise networks. To analyze our systems for the worm, I downloaded a new Code Red Worm signature file (CodeRed_X.nasl) from the Nessus.org website for use in our Nessus scanner. A scan of ARC's Primary DMZ Class C address range revealed that two servers reacted as though they were infected. It was a false indication of the infection. Instead of patching for the vulnerability, systems administrators disabled the.ida and.idq mappings, which eliminated the threat of infection. The system administrators then applied the MS01–033 patch, and the servers no longer reacted positively to the Nessus scan. A review of the firewall logs for the previous weekend showed that we were probed for systems infected with Code Red from several Internet locations, including the University of Beijing (Beijing (Peking)), Kwangju University (Korea), Asia/Pacific Intermec, and Cox Cable.

7.6.18 ARC-CISO-TST-2001.055 I Dated August 10, 2001 – System Security Test – CFS Servers

This is an example of another system security test I ran against ARC's financial system servers in anticipation of an upcoming security assessment by KPMG. I used Open-Source security assessment tool Nessus (version 1.1.2 RPM for Red Hat) running on my Compaq Armada M300 with Red Hat Linux Deluxe Workstation 7.1. The Nessus security scan revealed a number of unnecessary ports that were open on the servers (e.g., echo, chargen, FTP, telnet). *If not addressed, these unnecessary open server ports would result in KPMG audit findings.*

7.6.19 ARC-CISO-TRP-2001.065 Dated September 4, 2001 – Trip Report – Visit to Hewitt Benefits Processing Data Center – August 30, 2001

Another best practice I borrowed from the Naval Nuclear Program was to document and issue trip/visit observations, recommendations, and action item memos. ARC Human Resource and Payroll Systems managers wanted to outsource human resources and employee benefits processing to Hewitt. We traveled to the Hewitt Data Center in Chicago, Illinois, to review their capabilities and processes. I noted observations and recommendations about Hewitt's security posture, especially since their systems would process and warehouse sensitive ARC employee data.

Key Security Concept *Internet Domain Name Registration* The ARC maintained a relationship with Network Solutions, Inc. (NSI), the organization that operated the DNS—essentially the Internet's address book, which translates human-friendly website names into numerical addresses that computers use to locate each other. Up until 2000, NSI held exclusive authority to register.com,.net, and.org domain names, managing about 75% of the world's domains at that time. As part of this arrangement, NSI enforced a policy of censoring and notifying the ARC about attempts to register domain names containing unauthorized permutations of the ARC name—meaning any variations or misspellings that closely resembled the official brand. This policy effectively prevented the creation of fraudulent donation collection websites and other unauthorized uses of the ARC's brand. However, when NSI lost its exclusive registration authority, this protective mechanism disappeared. As a result, the ARC became more vulnerable to Internet-related fraud. For example, after 2000, several fraudulent websites mimicking the ARC appeared during major disasters, misleading donors and diverting funds.

7.6.20 September 11, 2001

On this date, we experienced the horrific attacks of September 11th (9–11). It was a significant time for America and the ARC. I was sitting in my small office when the news of the attacks started to pour in. The entire office became chaotic as I was also sitting near many of ARC's Disaster Services support staff. Calls went out for blood donations since there was uncertainty as to how much blood would be needed for the wounded in New York, Pennsylvania, and Washington D.C. Online donations to www.redcross.org came pouring in fast and furious. Unfortunately, the primary donation website, www.redcross.org, was hosted on a single Windows NT server. The server was quickly overwhelmed and went offline. IT staff had to scramble and stand-up additional IT infrastructure to handle the influx of donation traffic. The horrific events of 9–11 put a strain on ARC as well as its IT resources and resources.

I recall that in the immediate aftermath of the 9–11 Pentagon attack, ARC did not immediately send its typical, *full* disaster response personnel and resources to offer aid and comfort to first responders and victims of the attack. Even though ARC was in relative proximity to the Pentagon, help from ARC was not forthcoming. Someone from the Pentagon called and pleaded with ARC NHQ for help: "Where in the hell was the Red Cross?"[9]

ARC President and CEO, Dr. Bernadine Healy, was criticized for a number of issues regarding ARC's 9–11 response, including collecting too much blood. About one out of every five units of donated blood had to be discarded because they exceeded the forty-two-day shelf life of blood.[10] Dr. Healy also clashed with the Red Cross board over several other issues such as not getting ARC board approval to establish the group's Liberty Fund after the nine to eleven attacks. Rather, she was accused of spending the $500 million fund to strengthen the Red Cross empire rather than help victims of the attacks. Also, in a controversial 1999 move, Dr. Healy suspended payments to the International Red Cross to protest their decision not to admit the Israeli relief organization into their organization. ARC's

Board of Directors forced Dr. Healy's resignation in the wake of these disagreements and controversies, and she departed the organization as president on December 31, 2001.[11]

7.6.21 ARC-CISO-PRJ-2001.071 I Dated October 8, 2001 – Webex Security Analysis

Collaboration software products and services were starting to appear but were still immature. Webex, a Zoom-like service, was founded in 1995 and taken over by Cisco Systems in 2007. I was asked to perform a security evaluation of the product for ARC's use. I ran my usual suite of security analysis tools. I found a number of HIGH-RISK findings including that the Webex Internet-facing server was missing a number of critical Microsoft patches. I cited other general security issues, such as file transfers within Webex could bypass anti-virus inspections and file extension exclusions (e.g., .exe., .vbs).

I was given a typical user's ID and password to access Webex and test their encrypted communications feature. I used my Dell laptop outfitted with a Red Hat Linux Deluxe Workstation 7.1 partition. For the test of Webex's 40-bit encrypted sessions, I used Netscape Communicator 4.76 and Ethereal Network Protocol Analyzer Version 0.8.18 to assess the communications. After logging onto the Webex website using their 40-bit encryption, I analyzed a dump of the network traffic and found that my ID and password were transmitted in clear text from the client's PC to the website. *This was a showstopper!*

When I made Webex aware of their product's failure, I was contacted by some military brass from the Pentagon who were champions for the military use of Webex for secure communications. The Pentagon contact was adamant that the product had been thoroughly tested, and I did not know what I was talking about. He wanted to know what I found that failed my testing of the encrypted communication. I would not divulge my findings and deferred him to Webex for an explanation. *I never heard anything else on the subject.*

ARC Project – Electronic Blood Donor Record (eBDR). Most of us have participated in Red Cross Blood Donation drives at our various local businesses and organizational locations. The eBDR project was undertaken to modernize the system by providing better and timely information and overall efficiency with ARC blood donation/collections. For the next nine memos (Sections 7.6.22 to 7.6.29), I am going to consolidate four years (2001–2004) since they all relate to security issues with the new eBDR system. The base eBDR system, or "kit," comprised a primary workstation and two collection laptop computers. There were considerable potential adverse brand protection issues if the security of the eBDR systems and data were to be compromised. Over the course of the project, I issued fourteen (14) memos about eBDR security issues.

7.6.22 ARC-CISO – PRJ-2001.076 Dated October 23, 2001 – eBDR Enhancements; Security Concerns Regarding. This Memo Was in Response to OA Change Request # 373971 Dated October 4, 2001, Electronic Blood Donation Records (eBDR)

eBDR was a project to implement a new system for the provision of blood donor information. The goals of the new proposed system were to (1) extract blood donor information from production database servers at ARC NHQ, (2) process and transmit the data through various internal systems, and (3) ultimately download the donor data to laptops used at mobile blood drive location sites. The ultimate goal was to speed up the blood donation process and enhance the donor experience by pre-populating donor forms with the extracted data.

My response was general since I was given very few specifics about the project. I addressed my security concerns from network, data, and processing security perspectives. *The data processed and on the system were considered extremely sensitive personally identifiable information (PII).* From a network perspective, I was adamant that the use of the insecure file transfer protocol (FTP) with Primary Domain Controllers (PDC) should not be used as part of the process. Also, I asked the eBDR project team to address wireless security with the use of the 802.11b standard.

7.6.23 ARC-CISO-AUD-2002.0161 Dated February 26, 2002 – Security Assessment of eBDR Laptop

The eBDR system processed extremely sensitive personal identifiable information (PII), including a database of individuals *excluded* from donating blood for various reasons, such as having acquired immunodeficiency syndrome. *Exposure or compromise of this information would be devastating to ARC's brand.*

One of the major concerns I had was with the laptops themselves that were used in the process. We all know that mobile devices such as laptops tend to disappear – subject to loss or theft. And eBDR laptops were high-end devices and would be attractive targets for theft. The configuration specifics of the laptop were:

Dell Latitude C810 Intel Pentium III 1133 MHz CPU and 524 MB of RAM
Toshiba CDR W/D/DVD SDR2102 3 ¼ Floppy Drive
Modems – 3COM 56K V.90 Mini PCI Modem
Xircom Card bus Ethernet 100 + Modem 56
OS – Microsoft Windows 2000 5.00.2195 SP 2
44.6 GB HDD (9.64 GB used)

Test #1 – In the first testing methodology, I used the Center for Internet Security's (www.cisecurity.org) Windows 2000 Host-Based Level 1 Security Scoring Tool. The results of the tool provided benchmarks to evaluate and enumerate security configuration settings and actions designed to harden the analyzed system. The benchmarks were considered unique since they represented consensus among hundreds of security professionals worldwide who had defined these particular configurations. *Based on 10-point scoring criteria, the overall score of 1.7 was unacceptable. The results of the analysis are below* (Table 7.2).

Test #2 – System administration and user IDs and passwords. First, I requested that the system's administrator ID and password be provided with eBDR system to facilitate my testing. When the system arrived for my testing, there was no account information or User ID and password provided for me to use. In less than two minutes, I guessed an ID and password

Table 7.2 eBDR Test Results – CSI Windows 2000 Scoring Tool

Description	*Value*	*Score*
Service pack	2	1.667
Hotfixes needed	11	0
Non-expiring passwords	6	0
Policy mismatches	14	0
Restrict anonymous	0	0
Security option mismatches	8	0
Overall score		1.7 of 10.0

Table 7.3 eBDR L0ftCrack Password Testing Results

Username (ID)	*Group*	*Password/ Length*	*Method of PW Crack*	*Time to Crack PW*
Administrator	ORA_DBA; administrators	*Macs* (less than eight characters)	L0phtCrack	2.5 minutes
Ebdr	Administrators; users	*Ebdr* (less than eight characters)	Guess	>2 minutes
Guest	Guests	No password for the ID and account	L0phtCrack	0
IUSR_ D1P99011	Guests	*RSKPEHY???????* (fourteen characters)	L0phtCrack	Eight hours for first seven characters*
IWAM_ D1P99011	Guests	*RPTZHGU???????* (fourteen characters)	L0phtCrack	Eight hours for first seven characters*
TsInternetUser	Guests	*Undetermined*	L0phtCrack	

with which to log on to the system. *The guessed ID and password were: ebdr'/'ebdr.'* From there, I extracted the Security Access Manager (SAM) file and ran password cracking software (L0ftCrack) on the file. For expediency, I cut off the L0ftCrack run after eight hours but the entire password would have been "cracked" if the tool were run for a few additional hours. The results are detailed in Table 7.3:

Test # 3 – File system tests. The system was set up such that the C:\ drive was configured using Windows NTFS (NT File System), which allowed for the implementation of various native security options. There were a number of files that were accessible from within the Oracle directory C:\Oracle\oradata\EBDR that contained the sensitive donor information. Access to and potential merging of files from the Donor Management Information System (DMIS) and eBDR could result in a combination of data with a high sensitivity level. More analysis of the data by knowledgeable staff would have been better to assess the sensitivity level of the data. Our testing showed that simply porting the database files (dbf) into a text editor displayed names and addresses. *I considered that overall, the eBDR laptops had implemented little or no security controls.*

7.6.24 ARC-CISO-INC-2002.074 Dated October 25, 2002 – Clarify Case #509111 eBDR Wireless Insecurities

In this incident, an ARC Blood Drive was being conducted at the Idaho Department of Health and Welfare IT and Services Division. During this blood drive, the eBDR system was working in the wireless networking mode. A student at the location breached the wireless network due to a factory default password being available on the Wireless Access Point (WAP). This insecure condition was contrary to my previous guidance on eBDR network configurations. The student would have access to the eBDR database but, fortunately, did not access the data and reported the breach to his local security department and in turn notified ARC. *This memo provided additional guidance relative to the insecure 802.11b Standard such as the use of shared-key authentication, Wired Equivalent Privacy (WEP) keys, turn of Service Set Identifiers (SSID) broadcast, etc.*

7.6.25 ARC-CISO-POL-2003.027 Dated May 12, 2003 – eBDR – Wireless Standard

The eBDR system was used by field staff for blood donation drives across the United States. As of this memo, there were 4,000 laptops deployed consisting of about 1,300 kits with one primary/driver laptop and two client laptops. Wireless traffic between the primary and client laptops was not encrypted, which was a cause for potential compromise (see Section 7.6.24 ARC-CISO-INC-2002.074 dated October 25, 2002 – Clarify Case #509111 eBDR Wireless Insecurities).

The eBDR system used Symbol Technologies WAP, so we used 802.11 Frequency Hopping Spread Spectrum and selected configurations to add some minimal level of wireless security. In this memo, I recommend that all future releases of eBDR use equipment that was compliant with or upgradable to the new 802.11i standard. 802.11i was designed to address two aspects of security over its predecessors: improved security over data in transit and better control over who can use the network. To protect data in transit, 802.11i introduced the new TKIP (Temporal Key Integrity Protocol) and CCMP (Counter with Cipher Block Chaining Message Authentication Code Protocol). TKIP was a quick fix to the insecurities of WEP and made encryption key changes every ten kilobytes of transferred data. CCMP was a future enhancement that used the new AES (Advanced Encryption Standard) to provide better and faster network throughput. 802.11i also used an improved EAP (Extensible Authentication Protocol), which improved network security by communicating with access authorities such as a Remote Authentication Dial-In User Service (RADIUS) server as part of network access.[12]

7.5.26 ARC-CISO-POL-2003.036 dated May 20, 2003 – eBDR Action Report

This memo focused on the eBDR system in the context of the California SB 1386 law. Aspects of the system, such as CD-ROM data were encrypted, but the donor records on Primary/Driver laptops were not. As of May 2003, three (3) Primary/Driver laptops had been *lost* within the regions, including California. The best option we had was to implement Microsoft's Encrypting File System (EFS) to encrypt sensitive files on eBDR Primary/Driver laptops. Early implementations/releases of eBDR were supported by Northrop Grumman Mission Systems, and in their research of implementing EFS within the current release of eBDR, had determined ARC had three options for a new release. We selected the most expedient option to create a new system image that included the EFS settings and applied the new image to the primary/driver laptops. Applying a new image was a routine activity and time-efficient (estimate ninety minutes per primary/driver laptop).

7.6.27 ARC-CISO-INC-2003.076 (C) Dated December 1, 2003 eBDR – Clarify Case Analysis and Encrypted File System (EFS) Issue

The purpose of the memorandum was twofold: (1) identify the results of a review of eBDR issues reported within the Clarify System and (2) identify a concern with Microsoft's native EFS to secure eBDR data in the context of the California Anti-Hacking Law (SB 1386).

I learned ARC's Biomedical Services was no longer tracking lost or stolen eBDR laptop systems but was reporting these systems within ARC's Clarify

Table 7.4 Missing/Stolen eBDR Laptops

Case Number	*Date of Report*	*Case Description*	*Region*	*Number Missing*
611621	8/1/03	Laptop missing	PAC NW – Portland, OR	1
617015	8/18/03	Entire eBDR kit stolen	Southern Region – Atlanta	3*
619896	8/25/03	Lost/stolen client laptop	Central Plains – Wichita, KS	1
622904	9/3/03	Primary/driver laptop	SoCal	1*
633794	10/1/03	eBDR – missing laptop	SoCal	1
635049	10/3/03	eBDR – stolen client	Tennessee	1
645437	10/30/03	eBDR – stolen laptop	Greater Ozarks, AR	1
649929	11/10/03	Entire set of eBDR	SoCal	3*
Total	12			

*Known primary laptop missing

case management system. So, I queried the system to ascertain the number of missing or stolen eBDR systems. Between July 1, 2003, the effective start date of SB1386, and December 1, 2003, twelve eBDR laptops were lost or stolen. Of the twelve, two entire sets, including three laptops, where each kit included one primary/driver and two client systems were missing. An additional primary laptop was missing or stolen, and five additional laptops were lost or stolen (Table 7.4).

I considered the use of Microsoft's EFS as a stop-gap measure to meet the requirements of SB1386. EFS only encrypted at the file and folder levels rather than encrypting the entire hard disk drive (HDD). I recommended that additional security features be investigated to secure eBDR systems such as third-party software that would encrypt the entire HDD, physical security locking mechanisms, and strong tracking software/systems to ensure the physical locations of the eBDR systems.

7.6.28 ARC-CISO-AUD-2004.001 (C) Dated January 12, 2004 Results of Forensic Analysis of eBDR Laptops

The year 2004 began with a forensic analysis of an eBDR system. Specifically, I wanted to determine if Social Security Number (SSN) data appeared in any other unencrypted files on the laptop as a function of eBDR processing. I tested two laptops used for eBDR training. These systems contained bogus donor data, including the bogus social security numbers (SSN) for testing.

I employed two methodologies in testing the systems: (1) a search of all files and directories resident on the hard drives of each laptop using *Wingrep*, a utility that searches within targeted files for search strings, and (2) a forensic analysis of each laptop using EnCase Version 4.16a. Technical issues were found, and I had to obtain administrative rights to the laptops to have Wingrep search all the files. The new version of EnCase, version 4.16a, required that my forensic workstation be upgraded from Windows 98 to Windows XP Pro. These technical issues were addressed and the testing commenced.

Testing determined that plain text SSN data was resident in various areas of the PC's hard disk drive (HDD) such as unallocated clusters and swap space. The testing reinforced my concern with exposure of sensitive personal information via the eBDR systems. I previously recommended the use of software capable of encrypting the entire HDD as well as other physical security measures.

7.6.29 ARC-CISO-AUD-2004.014 (C) Dated February 18, 2004 – Forensic Analysis – eBDR Stolen/Missing Laptop

This was an interesting case where an individual was trying to sell a lost eBDR laptop to a computer store in Austin, Texas. After buying the PC, the store manager assessed the computer and discovered that it was ARC property and contacted the local ARC chapter. The investigation included interaction among me, ARC Office of General Counsel (OGC), the PC store manager, and local law enforcement. We retrieved the PC and put it back into the inventory after re-baselining the PC. *The disposition of the individual who sold the PC to the store was unknown.*

7.6.30 ARC-CISO-POL-2004.043 Dated June 2, 2004 – Proposal for Performance of Hashing Functions/Algorithms on Electronic Blood Donor Record System to Assure Overall System and Program Integrity Using Encase Forensic Software or Equivalent Programs

At one ARC blood drive at a government facility, ARC staff were not allowed on-site until they surrendered their eBDR PCs for an anti-virus scan. The government staff inserted a CD-ROM into the Primary/Driver eBDR system and ran the anti-virus scan.

Maintaining eBDR system and programmatic integrity was of paramount importance. It was unclear whether the introduction of the Norton Anti-Virus (AV) CD-ROM into the eBDR system caused any changes to be made to the eBDR system configuration. While the action of scanning for computer viruses seems innocuous, there is no assurance that (1) installation of some or all of the Norton AV software had not occurred, (2) that Norton AV was the only program code on the CD-ROM, and (3) the fact that Norton AV had not been tested for use with the eBDR configuration.

Red Cross used Configuration Management (CM) with which to maintain a library of approved software configurations. From the CM library, version control was enforced, and CD-ROM media were made from library-maintained configurations for distribution purposes. eBDR actually consisted of two systems: the base Windows OS and the eBDR application. Both of these sub-systems were maintained separately in the Red Cross CM library. While the CM library maintained an unaltered copy of each set of systems and files, it was more of an *escrow* situation rather than a provision of code that had been validated with a Digital DNA or Digital Fingerprint for file/system comparison purposes.

Via this memo, I recommended using software such as Encase or equivalent, with the capability to develop hash values based on the Message Digest (MD5) algorithm for each file in a given configuration. The MD5 algorithm takes as input a message or file of arbitrary length and produces as output a 128-bit fingerprint or message digest of the input.[13] It is conjectured that it is computationally infeasible to produce two messages or files having the same message digest or to produce any message or file having a given pre-specified target message digest. *Having hash values for program configurations in our CM library would add a digital fingerprint and ensure the integrity of ARC programs and code.*

Undoubtedly, addressing security issues with the EBDR system was challenging. My goal was to ensure ARC's brand protection and public goodwill by securing sensitive blood and tissue donor data – and I believe were successful. Now, back to the year 2001.

7.6.31 ARC-CISO-INV-2001.081 Dated December 6, 2001 – Computer Virus Mitigations

This memo was issued to ARC CIO#4 Tom Schwaninger, making several recommendations to further mitigate computer virus threats. Recommendations included expanding file extension exclusions on our mail gateways and prohibiting users from accessing their personal, non-ARC email accounts via ARC web browsers. I also requested $50,000 to upgrade the memories and processing for our front-end Internet routers to support Cisco's Network-based Application Recognition (NBAR). NBAR would add another layer of security and stop malicious code further out on the network periphery versus at various internal layers and ultimately at the user's desktop. NBAR was a vendor-agnostic solution and would permit the expedient application of filters at the network level. This would augment existing AV controls and could be considered equivalent to the Simple

Mail Transfer Protocol (SMTP) file extension blocks at the SMTP level, as described previously. *This request was denied since NBAR would use up one slot in the router's overall backplane – a slot that could be used by IT Operations for future network expansion.*

7.6.32 The Priority of My First Year as CISO at ARC Was to Establish a Baseline Information Security Program

Roadblocks to gaining much in the way of momentum were management turnover and the lack of budget and resources. The 2001 year-end statistical summary of my initial ten-month tenure included:

Security/Customer Advisories Issued – 119
Investigations – 25
Project Reviews – 12
Audits/Reviews/Tests – 15
PwC Audit Item Closures – 8
Trip Reports – 7
Clarify Case Resolutions – 26
CERTS/Incidents – 2

I was interviewed and photographed for the December 2001 issue of CFO Magazine. The article was entitled *Clear and Present Danger – Computer networks are more vulnerable to attack than ever. Is corporate confidence misplaced?* By Esther Shein.[14]

Lesson Learned *Document, document, document.* Throughout my career, I learned the importance of documentation. This is especially important in supporting audits and reviews. I endeavored to have the auditors on my side rather than having an adversarial relationship. Unfortunately, management tends to accept recommendations from outside third-party auditors and consultants rather than the same or similar recommendations from their own internal staff. Audit findings usually get the attention of upper management and can provide CISOs with additional budget, resources, and security technologies.

7.7 MEMOS AND ISSUES – JANUARY 2002–DECEMBER 2002

7.7.1 ARC-CISO-INV-2002.002 I Dated January 4, 2002 – Investigation – Inappropriate Web Usage

The year 2002 started similarly to 2001 by having to conduct an Internet abuse investigation. Here, the ARC employee was using his ARC-issued credit card to access gambling sites on the Internet. Although he reimbursed ARC for the gambling, we also reviewed the firewall logs and proved he accessed these sites during business hours using ARC computer systems. *The employee was ultimately fired.*

ARC Project – ARC Websites. The events of 9–11 reinforced ARC's primary donation website (www.redcross.org) as an important part of raising money. As I wrote earlier, www.redcross.org was hosted on a single Windows NT server. This platform was woefully inadequate and was quickly overwhelmed by the flood of incoming donations. Once a more robust supporting infrastructure for www.redcross.org was implemented, the focus of security around this website, chapter websites, and other ARC – sponsored/branded websites came into sharp focus. The following five memos (Sections 7.7.2 to 7.7.6) shed light on the issues facing ARC regarding security around its web presence – a major aspect of ARC's brand protection.

7.7.2 ARC-CISO-POL-2002.028 Dated April 30, 2002 Response to "Website Analysis" Suggested Action Plan

ARC's overall worldwide web presence was more like the "Wild West," with many sub-organizations (e.g., ARC chapters and biomedical sites) creating their own non-standardized domain names. Working with various department heads, we tried to rein them in and standardize ARC website domain names and security of the website, including their e-commerce activities. With over 1,000 ARC chapters across the U.S., there were three distinct populations: chapter websites hosted by ARC NHQ, chapter websites not hosted at NHQ, and chapters with no web presence. Many chapters chose to host their website with a third party as NHQ could not offer the functionality they required, needed, or simply wanted a Universal Resource Locator (URL) that more closely identified them with their local community.

The specific ARC chapter numbers were 1,017 total chapters, 544 chapters of the total had an Internet presence, including 215-chapter websites hosted by ARC NHQ. These numbers identified 329-chapter websites that were hosted by a third party. And the remaining 473 chapters with no websites would need to be assimilated under ARC NHQ's hosting. The high number (473) would require increased Internet hosting capacity at NHQ. NHQ would also have to offer additional functionality to satisfy Chapter website requirements. *With the complexity of this project, I recommended that the entire area of ARC's web presence, including Blood Services Regions, NHQ, and Chapters be considered for third-party analysis, including*

Domain names and naming conventions, models for secure online donations, security and privacy policies, and general content. In the absence of a third-party analysis, I committed to developing the following action plan.

7.7.3 ARC-CISO-POL-2002.030 Dated May 16, 2002 – Action Plan Summary for ARC Websites and e-Commerce Was Issued Two Weeks Later to Codify an Action Plan to Address ARC's Website Issues as Follows:

Domain naming conventions and management. There were literally hundreds, if not thousands, of different Internet domain names owned by the ARC entities (Chapters, biomedical regions, etc.). These domain names did not adhere to any standards relating to naming conventions, domain registrations, etc. *If not managed well, domain name registrations could expire and be purchased by anyone not affiliated with the ARC. This situation could damage the name, brand, and reputation of the ARC if expired domain names were purchased and used by people with bad intentions.* There was anecdotal evidence that an ARC-affiliated domain name that expired and was purchased by an entity that published pornographic websites.

Additionally, cost savings could be realized by having primary domain name(s) to which chapter website names could be appended versus having to manage and pay for the many different domain names. (e.g., www.arc-chapterx.org versus the preferred www.chapterx.redcross.org). If a domain name convention such as that identified in the example were to be followed, only one domain name (i.e., www.chapterx.redcross.org) would need to be managed and could include every ARC chapter.

Website Content. With the then-balkanized configuration, website content across all ARC websites lack consistency. It was discovered that one ARC website continued to have a welcome message from former ARC President and CEO, Dr. Healey. long after she had left the organization. ARC's Marketing and Communications has partnered with ARC IT for a pilot study and implementation of the Vignette Content Management system to help with management and updating of website content. As part of the website content issue, facilities for establishing e-Commerce activities, such as shopping carts, auctions, ARC-sponsored training courses, and merchandise, were to be addressed as well.

Security and Privacy. Internet/web security is a complex undertaking requiring discipline and vigilance over people, processes, and technologies. I looked forward to developing security and privacy guidelines for conducting e-Commerce. These guidelines were being developed, and the document was expected to provide detailed security-related best practices that fall in the category of *must-do* and others that are *recommended.*

As expected, we experienced a lot of pushbacks from the larger ARC Chapters that had made significant investments in their web presence and e-Commerce activities. In my analysis of Chapter websites conducted in concert with the ARC internal audit team, I uncovered e-Commerce activities that went to a third-party site with no security for conducting monetary transactions.

7.7.4 ARC-CISO-POL-2002.043 Dated July 2, 2002 – Security & Privacy Guidelines and Best Practices for Conducting e-Commerce

As part of the action plan for addressing chapter e-Commerce activities, I issued a sixteen-page document including guidelines and best practices. The document was provided for review and consideration by all appropriate ARC management. This document incorporated guidance using Visa's Account Information Security Standards Manual and Account Information Security Best Practices Guide, ANSI Information Security for Financial Organization Guidelines, X9/TG-5 (1992), ISO/TR 13569 Banking and Related Financial Services Information Security Guidelines, Second Edition, and WebTrust Version 3.0.

7.7.5 ARC-CISO-POL-2002.051 Dated July 31, 2002 – Action Plan Update for ARC/ Chapter Websites and e-Commerce

This memo was an update to ARC-CISO-AUD-2002.030 dated May 16, 2002 – Action Plan Summary for ARC Websites and e-Commerce. An issue regarding ARC financial regulations arose regarding any chapter donations solicited and made via an Internet website. I was asked to update ARC's Financial Manual of Policies and Procedures. (FMPP) with the following verbiage: *Chapter websites are prohibited from soliciting or accepting credit card payments due to security concerns and the confusion which would result if chapter websites accepted donations in competition with other chapters and national website.*

This verbiage would require that Chapters *NOT* conduct independent e-Commerce activities but solicit and collect donations through the primary NHQ website (www.redcross.org). I pointed out that this phrasing contradicted ARC Board of Governors' Policy 3.5.1, which stated, *A Chartered Unit may solicit donations within its jurisdiction and may do so in the name of the Unit or the ARC.* Moreover, Development Connection #35, dated July 23, 1998, Fund-Raising on the Net: Corporate Regulations for Raising Funds Over the Internet stated, *The preferred method of chapters linking to the National website for online contributions, it does provide guidance to chapters in maintaining their own website donation forms.* Based on these conflicting policies related to chapter donation activities, I reiterated the importance of adopting my Guidelines and Best Practice document.

7.7.6 ARC-CISO-AUD-2002.067 (C) Dated October 10, 2002 Assessment of Chapter Sites Conducting e-Commerce Activities

This memo was another attempt to identify populations of chapter websites conducting e-Commerce activities. To carry out this assessment, I used a *freeware* search engine tool called *Web Ferret.* Rather than conducting web searches via Google or similar search engines, Web Ferret Version 4.0 used the combined results from the following search engines: All the Web, AltaVista, AOL Anywhere, Business.com, CNET, FindWhat, Kanoodle, LookSmart, Overture, and Sprinks. The engine was configured to yield 1,000 hits per search engine or 10,000 potential hits. Also, Web Ferret extractions could be imported into Excel spreadsheets for easy data manipulation and analysis. The search for webpages referencing keywords *redcross* and *donate* yielded 1,887 hits. Findings included Chapter websites containing the WebTrust seal even though the website had not been certified under WebTrust. The donation pages for other chapter websites were insecure since they used *http* rather than *https.* Other chapter websites had expired Secure Sockets Layer (SSL) certificates necessary to ensure sensitive web traffic was encrypted.

7.7.7 ARC-CISO-AUD-2002.031 (C) Dated May 8, 2002 – IBM 9–11 Database Security Issue

After the horrific events of 9–11, many people requested assistance from various humanitarian organizations. To coordinate these efforts, a database of people receiving support/aid was developed by the United States Government and IBM. In addition to the ARC, data for populating the database was obtained from Safe Horizon and The Salvation Army. I was given a database technical architecture and data-flow diagrams with which to conduct a security review. *There was not sufficient material with which to conduct a thorough security assessment.* Some of the questions I had included missing details about the specific database/record elements, who had access to the data, and was there an audit trail identifying access to the database? I also needed to understand the server OSs and patching methods, encryption, etc. I asked for an IP address so I could scan the server for vulnerabilities. *I was provided the necessary details and subsequent testing found the system to be secure.*

7.7.8 ARC-CISO-AUD-2002.033 Dated May 16, 2002 – PwC COBIT Study Management Action Plan Updates (5/2002)

This memo provided a status update on eight actions relating to COBIT audit items. Three of the eight were closed, and there were plans and schedules to complete the other five items. The importance of this memo was that I added internal hire, Ms. Susan Baranowski, to my team. Susan was a director overseeing policy and training for ARC's Consolidated Financial Systems (CFS). Susan's skills would be instrumental in building out our information security policy and training programs. Now, there were three of us on the information security team!

7.7.9 ARC-CISO-CSA-2002.036 Dated May 21, 2002 – High-Alert Message from Ron Baklarz, Chief Information Security Officer: Port 1433 Probes

This was a High Alert Customer Service Advisory relative to actors with malicious intent scanning the Internet for open 1,433 ports. The hackers were looking for open 1,433 ports and possibly exploiting any underlying weak or non-existent System Administrator accounts. Port 1433 is used for communications with Microsoft SQL Servers. In this *heads-up* memo, I provided several methods to secure systems and address this vulnerability. *Unfortunately, we would see compromised ARC servers that succumbed to this vulnerability despite my efforts to raise awareness and for system administrators to minimize the risk.*

7.7.10 ARC-CISO-INC-2002.037 Dated June 5, 2002 – Preliminary Incident Report – Compromise of Three Chapter Servers and ARC-CISO-INC-2002.042 (C) June 25, 2002 Update – Compromise of Three Chapter Servers

Three system servers for chapters in Virginia, New York, and Connecticut were compromised. These servers provided Office Automation (OA) services (e.g., email) for the chapters. The compromises were due to misconfigured Access Control Lists (ACLs) on network routers and the use of obsolete and insecure versions of Microsoft Internet Information Services (IIS). *Based on the findings of these incidents, I increased my scanning activities to ferret out insecurities. One tool I used was a freeware tool from the Center for Internet Security (CIS) called "rat" or "router audit tool" which ran against Cisco routers. "Rat" provided a Level 1 analysis based on the National Security Agency's (NSA) Router Security Configuration Guidelines.*

7.7.11 ARC-CISO-AUD-2002.056 (C) Dated August 23, 2002 – Network-based Vulnerability Assessment – Regional OA Servers

Because of the above issues with Chapter Office Automation (OA) Servers, I wanted to perform my own system audits. I received a list of 190 OA servers. I randomly selected thirty servers to assess using Red Hat Linux 7.2, freeware tool, "Nmap," and manual techniques where Port 80 (http) was open to ascertain Microsoft IIS versions. *This method of testing was superficial, and in the future, more robust tests using commercial tools would be preferable.* Findings included a number of servers with unnecessary ports open, eighteen servers had the unapproved software, *PC Anywhere* installed, five servers had obsolete and insecure versions of Microsoft IIS installed, four servers had Internet Relay Chat (IRC) ports open, and three servers had File Transfer Protocol (ftp) ports open. *While this assessment was somewhat superficial, hackers are opportunistic. And this vulnerability assessment addressed some low-hanging fruit that could attract compromising activity.*

7.7.12 ARC-CISO-POL-2002.049 Dated July 23, 2002 – LOGIC (Logistics, Orders, and General Inventory Control System) Encryption Issue and Agreements

This memo addressed encryption issues with ARC's LOGIC system hosted by a third party. The LOGIC system was sponsored by ARC Biomedical Services and was designed to track blood shipments, test results, and blood by-products at the fractionator labs. My guidance, in the form of a Memorandum of Understanding, dictated that transmission of sensitive data over the Internet required the use of 128-bit encryption – SSL. The third-party vendor argued that the data processed by LOGIC was not donor sensitive, although I was never provided with a data architecture with which to accurately assess data sensitivities. The third-party vendor later stated that the data would be transferred over the Internet via a Virtual Private Network (VPN) connection and therefore, SSL encryption would not be required. However, the vendor backtracked and stated that the connection would be made via Frame Relay (FR) versus VPN. They argued that the use of FR was secure and that SSL encryption was unnecessary.

I countered that FR was not secure and FR compromises were well documented due to: (a) circuit leaks (where data would be sent outside the intended network path due to misconfigured network devices), (b) network sniffers (where data is compromised by network traffic analyzers/collectors by internal or external sources) and (c) attacks against the frame-provider itself (large telephone and network companies are typical hacker targets not to mention disgruntled insiders. Frame relay insecurities had long been recognized and to protect data transmissions over frame, more encryption products and services were required. *The vendor relented and it was determined that no additional hardware costs would be incurred to implement SSL encryption. The cost of the Verisign SSL certificates would be $3,000 for securing all six servers used within the system.*

7.7.13 ARC-CISO-CISO-2002. 085 Dated December 23, 2002 – End-of-Year Virus Statistics

During 2002, I issued eighteen Customer Service Advisory memos about various computer virus/worm issues. These memos were intended as heads-up information about specific malicious code that was circulating on the Internet via email. To illustrate the growing problem of computer viruses over email, I issued the following data as provided by computer virus bellwether, MessageLabs. MessageLabs, a UK-based subsidiary of Star (the largest business-to-business ISP in the UK), scanned an average of 10 million emails per working day, or at 115 emails per second. The trend showed dramatic increases in the number of computer viruses propagated by email messages.

Viruses Stopped (one virus every 'x' second)

2000	2001	2002
180 seconds	18 seconds	3 seconds

Ratio of Viruses to Email Messages

2000	2001	2002
1:790	1:380	1:212

Most Active Viruses for 2002

Name	*Number Stopped*
W32/Klez.H-mm	4,918,018
W32/Yaha.E-mm	1,096,683
W32/BugBear.A-mm	842,333
W95/Klez.E-mm	380,937
W32/SirCam.A-mm	309,832
W32/Magistr.A-mm	91,814
W32/BadTrans.B-mm	89,504
W32/Hybris.gen-mm	76,888
EML/Greeting-Card	70,118
W32/MagiStr.B-mm	67,823
W95/Nimda.A-mm	57,611

Overall Annual Volumes of Viruses Stopped

Year	*Viruses Stopped*	*Mail Scanned*
2000	184,257	147,475,127
2001	1,798,872	717,744,958
2002	9,343,880	1,991,086,463

My second year as ARC CISO was dominated by having to deal with the prolific computer viruses that made their way into our environment. I tried to use existing technology, such as email blocking, network filtration, communications, system logs, and user education, to help mitigate the influx of viral code.

7.8 MEMOS AND ISSUES – JANUARY 2003–DECEMBER 2003

I had such limited resources and budget in trying to build an effective information security program, I was always on the lookout to get advanced threat information, freeware assessment tools, and other *force multipliers*. I use the term *force multiplier* to mean any technology or methodology that can protect the computing environment, short of additional personnel. As I stated earlier, the ARC was a government instrumentality and not a government agency. But since there was some ambiguity about ARC's formal status, I would try to get myself and my team to take advantage of as much free government-provided training and memberships as possible.

The first of the non-government-related force multipliers in terms of advanced intelligence I engaged was to join the Federal Bureau of Investigation (FBI) InfraGard program. This was a great organization that provided information-sharing meetings and issued National Infrastructure Protection Center advisories, which I used to assess ARC vulnerabilities specific to OSs, software products, etc. Next was to join the Forum of Incident Response and Security Teams (FIRST). This was a great resource to gain valuable threat information from FIRST teams located around the world.

I also took advantage of taking part in the Information Assurance Technical Framework (IATF) Forum (www.iatf.net), which was sponsored by the National Security Agency (NSA) and was open to information security professionals from government, military, and private sector agencies. Participation in the IATF included forum sessions and access to their website. Membership was free and subject to approval by IATF. About every six to eight weeks, a daylong session was held to discuss security-related themes relative to IATF's security strategy framework based on Defense-In-Depth of People, Technology, and Operations.

> Over the first three months of 2003, I issued fifteen (15) memos. Nine (9) of the fifteen addressed computer virus issues.

7.8.1 ARC-CISO-POL-2003.004 Dated January 15, 2003 – Defense Information Services Agency (DISA) Meeting

One of ARC's major responsibilities was supporting the AFES. The Red Cross provided in-person support for troops on all military installations in the U.S. and on over thirty-five overseas bases, including Asia, the Middle East, and Europe. Each year, the Red Cross provided over 540,000 services to service members, veterans, and their families by leveraging our worldwide network of volunteers.[15]

This service required ARC to have connectivity to the military's unclassified network – Non-Secure Internet Protocol Router NETwork (NIPRNET). ARC had maintained two methods of systems connectivity: (1) Normal Internet connections to the Defense Messaging System (DMS) via access to Pentagon systems. This method employed secure email transmissions that were encrypted. (2) An additional contingency circuit 7FPC (T1 line) that is directly connected to the NIPRNET from ARC's Philadelphia site. This circuit had been a concern as it was never accredited as required per Department of Defense (DoD) directives. One of the impedances to the accreditation process had been the need to accredit ARC's entire network for the *never used* 7FPC contingency circuit. This would be virtually impossible to achieve, given ARC's network infrastructure.

Defense Information Services Agency (DISA) was tightening up its security, including decommissioning obsolete circuits of which ARC's 7FPC circuit was only one of two circuits that were never properly accredited. DISA was migrating all non-DoD entities that required access to NIPRNET to *special purpose gateways* that would provide stringent Access Control List (ACL) controls for permitting network/system access. DISA was concerned that in the event of an emergency/attack, they would need to shut down access to NIPRNET to all outside entities via the special-purpose gateways, and AFES would be left with no way to connect to NIPRNET and the systems to which they need access.

DISA had ARC/AFES on a fast track as the number three beta site to connect to Defense Messaging System (DMS0 and other required system assets as approved via these special-purpose gateways. ARC was attractive as an early installation since we were a small and local installation. This connection method would be via normal Internet traffic. ARC/AFES would also need a contingency circuit in the event that outside access to NIPRNET was shut down. The plan was to put together a small, dedicated enclave of systems directly connected to NIPRNET. This contingency circuit/enclave would:

- need to be in an isolated, access-controlled area/room,
- not be connected to the ARC/corporate network,

- have NIPRNET IP addresses, and
- need to be accredited by DITSCAP (DoD IT Security Certification and Accreditation Process).

Fortunately, it all worked out in the end.

7.8.2 ARC-CISO-POL-2003.008 Dated February 4, 2003 – Point Paper – California Privacy Law SB 1386

This was a significant memo I issued to CIO#3 Tom Schwaninger to bring his attention to this new California Law passed in September 2002 and was to go into effect July 1, 2003. SB 1386 was intended to combat identity theft as the result of a high-profile computer intrusion into a California state government system. The system housed payroll information on 200,000 state workers and the victimized employees were not warned that their personal information was stolen until weeks after the incident. The law passed over strong objections from industry groups.

This was an early example of many future U.S. and international data breach notification laws, and I foresaw the significant impact it would have on ARC systems. Besides the obvious eBDR system being subject to the law, other ARC systems would be as well. Essentially, the law stated that any company doing business in California must notify California residents of a breach in security where unauthorized acquisition of unencrypted, privacy-related data elements. A breach must expose certain types of *unencrypted* personal, private information. Specifically, customers' names in association with their social security number, driver's license number, or a credit card or bank account number. After such an intrusion, the company must notify the affected customers in "the most expedient time possible" and without unreasonable delay. *Since the law applied to companies doing business in California, I saw the potential for adverse impact on our eBDR systems that were used in California and had personal California residents' data. This would come into play as I endeavored to have the donor databases on the primary eBDR laptop systems encrypted.*

The data elements covered by SB1386 were defined as first name or initial and last name in conjunction with social security number, California ID number, California driver's license, or financial account information (e.g., credit card, account, account codes). In the event of unauthorized acquisition of this data, California residents had to be notified of the breach by methods of contact specified in the law. While my initial concern was for eBDR systems, I saw an opportunity to conduct an expansive review of all ARC systems so we would have an inventory of all systems that processed and/or contained Personally Identifiable Information (PII).

7.8.3 ARC-CISO-GEN-2003.017 Dated April 3, 2003 – CISO Monthly Status Report for the Period – March 1, 2003 through March 31, 2003

This memo expanded the CISO KPI as communicated to the ARC CIO. Metrics provided included PwC COBIT item status, numbers of new hires receiving security training, virus and security bulletins issued, Clarify cases opened by the CISO to address technical security issues, and the number of ARC DMZ scans conducted during the month.

Of particular significance with this memo was ARC's membership in FISSEA (Federal Information Systems Security Educators' Association) with Susan Barnowski as our lead. This was another government agency program we joined to take advantage of free computer security training and materials. As part of FISSEA, we received free training materials, including video training materials and CBT (computer-based training) on CD-ROM. We used these materials to expand our corporate training and awareness program.

7.8.4 ARC-CISO-GEN-2003.022 Dated May 5, 2003, CISO Monthly Status Report for the Period – April 1, 2003 through April 30, 2003

This status report identified that due to a reorganization of the ARC IT subdepartment – Enterprise Systems Operations (ESOP), I obtained an additional Full Time Equivalent Employee (FTE). Gordon Bass joined my group as a security engineer. Now my cybersecurity department had three (3) FTE's including myself. But I still only had two FTEs since one of my FTEs left ARC.

7.8.5 ARC-CISO-POL-2003.024 Dated May 8, 2003 Information Security Policies, Procedures, and Guidelines

Policy development continued, and this memo provided several policies for CIO signature. The layout of the ARC Information Security Policy Manual was 210.00 Information Security Program Management, 220.00 Enterprise Security, 230.00 Network Security, 240.00 System/Host Security, 250.00 Application/Data Security, and 260.00 General Guidance. This memo provided these items for CIO signature where needed and publication for general access on the ARC Corporate website:

- Information Security Policy Manual – Introduction (no signature required)
- Section 210.00 Information Security Program Management Overview (CIO signature required)
- Section 210.01 Information Security Program Framework (CIO signature required)

- Section 210.02 Information Security Program Roadmap(CIO signature required)
- Section 260.00 General Guidance Overview (no signature required)
- Section 260.01 Electronic Communication Guidance – System Logon Banners (no signature required – verbiage approved by ARC Corporate Legal Department)

Lesson Learned Having formal, written, approved, and easily available security policies is key to the success of any information security program.

7.8.6 ARC-CISO-POL-2003.047 Dated Jul 1. 2003 – eBDR Next Steps

Now that we had addressed the eBDR privacy issues as best we could, I had developed a comprehensive privacy program to address sensitive data contained across ARC systems. Privacy Program actions included:

- Compile an inventory of internal ARC systems, including third-party systems containing PII.
- Apply PII mitigations where possible – eliminate, truncate. obfuscate, encrypt
- Develop Incident Response, Breach, and Disclosure Plans
- Engage in Education and Awareness

7.8.7 ARC-CISO-POL-2003.043 Dated June 11, 2003 – Request for Additional Check Block on Change Request Form

This memo requested ARC's IT form for system Change Requests (CR) be expanded to include a check block to identify the introduction of Personally Identifiable Information (PII) in new systems, databases, and applications for both Production and Test/Development environments. *(Note – development/test environments should not have live/production test data.)*

7.8.8 ARC-CISO-GEN-2003.049 – Dated July 8, 2003 – CISO Monthly Status Report for the Period – June 1, 2003 through June 30, 2003

This status update identified an issue that was a constant thorn in the CISO's side – password settings and complexity for the 20,000 ARC systems users. On June 17, 2003, we implemented password complexity settings on the ARCHQ Domain. *This setting was a significant undertaking that required more robust password security, such as periodic password changes, password construction rules, password aging, etc.*

7.8.9 ARC-CISO-AUD-2003.051 Dated October 16, 2003 – System Security Review Report – National Biomedical Computer System (NBCS)

This was a formal system security review of ARC's National Biomedical Computer System (NBCS). NBCS ran on the IBM AIX Operating System and Oracle Relational Database Management System (RDMS). This system review was conducted due to reports of a potential hazard condition in which system development staff changed production data in the NBCS.

There were twenty-four AIX servers supporting the NBCS system, including production, backup, and test servers. We determined that there were two *production* instances of the National Donor Deferral Record (NDDR). One instance was running on the primary NBCS system, and the other on regional server/instances. Three records were modified by third-party staff who supported NBCS and were mistakenly tested on the production system rather than on the testing systems. The changes did not result in a hazardous condition. However, the review revealed bigger security issues:

- For the system, there was no Identity Management on an individual user basis.
- Using *shared* IDs/accounts resulted in a lack of an audit trail and accountability.
- Shared IDs/accounts had inappropriate privileges that are necessary to maintain adequate separation of duties.
- Other security aspects of both the AIX and Oracle environments should be implemented to improve the overall security of NBCS. For specific security testing, we used Nmap to assess the open ports on the systems. Nmap identified there were three security holes, eight security warnings, and twenty-seven security notes. We also used Nikto, a free software command-line vulnerability scanner that scanned web servers (Port 80) for dangerous files/CGIs, outdated server software, and other problems. The Nikto scans revealed that the servers were using outdated and vulnerable versions of the Apache web server. Fortunately, these systems were not directly reachable from the Internet, but they introduced unacceptable vulnerabilities.

7.8.10 ARC-CISO-GEN-2003.057 Dated August 5, 2003 – CISO Monthly Status Report for the Period – July 1, 2003 through July 31, 2003

Besides typical monthly updates and accomplishments, this status report identified that an additional FTE (full-time employee) position was assigned to my team – a security engineer position. *This position was filled by internal transfer, Mike Cokenour, on September 1, 2003. This would increase my team to four, including myself.*

7.8.11 ARC-CISO-INV-2003.070 (C) Dated October 15, 2003 – Forensic Analysis – Fort Rucker Computer System

This memo documented a forensic analysis of a PC assigned to AFES – Fort Rucker, Alabama, as requested by AFES personnel. The AFES staff at Fort Rucker shipped the PC to me, and I extracted the contents of the hard disk drive (HDD) for analysis using my forensic workstation and Guidance Software – EnCase Forensic Software Version 3.22. This memo explained the PC's technical details such as hard drive metrics, OS, and patch levels.

The reason for the investigation was that upon the assignment of a new AFES station manager at Fort Rucker, the previous AFES station manager had the website sex.com, a search engine for pornographic websites, saved as a *favorite* in his web browser. My investigation found that care was taken to erase as much evidence as possible, including web histories, which could not be recovered. This was especially evident by the high number of hits for sex.com that appeared in unused areas of the HDD, such as slack space and unallocated clusters. I also recovered a significant number of pornographic images from the HDD slack space.

I identified and extracted data related to a specific user and his name. This individual accessed an external website, Internetwasher.com and obtained a trial version of the software. The purpose and function of this software was explicitly to cover one's web browsing activity by deleting appropriate files and code and covering over the evidence. I extracted a number of this individual's personal information from the HDD's slack space, including passwords, names, addresses, bank account numbers, and social security numbers.

I recommended that AFES have me perform a government-grade erasure program on the HDD and then re-baseline the PC's OS and software to current ARC Cross software standards. *As far as punitive actions against the individual, that was up to his management.*

7.8.12 ARC-CISO-INC-2003.071 Dated October 23, 2003 – Concern for Unauthorized Disclosure of Red Cross Information Via the Internet

As part of my routine random review of the new Red Cross Corpweb for unapproved content. I discovered that the *Forum* area on the top toolbar of Corpweb provided access to an offsite web page and redirected to http://chat.access.net:8080/~ARC. This third-party hosted website displayed a non-encrypted (i.e., no https://) login page. Users could enter their ID and password or enter as a Guest. I entered as a Guest and was able to view all items within the forum. I went a step further and signed up for access to the site using a bogus hotmail.com email account and completed the online subscription form. I received a welcome message on the website. I had several concerns:

- Access to the third-party hosted website http://chat.access.net:8080/~ARC was available to *ANYONE* on the Internet, including establishing *Guest* accounts.
- ID and passwords were given to any Internet user *with no vetting process.*
- The login ID and password were not encrypted as required by INFOSEC Policy, and this weakness was further exacerbated by their sending the login ID and password back to the user via unencrypted email.
- There was no evidence that chat content was vetted or moderated prior to posting, and Internet predators could also use this website to gain access to email addresses and other forms of potentially sensitive data.

Based on my memo, access to this website and chat service was immediately disabled.

7.8.13 Sometime in 2003, ARC Was Seeking Funding from the Newly Established Department of Homeland Security (DHS) for a Number of Initiatives, Including Cybersecurity

I recall heading down to Washington D.C.'s Eisenhower Executive Office Building (EEOB), formerly known as the Old Executive Office Building (OEOB), from our offices in Falls Church, VA. I rode along with ARC's VP of Biomedical IT Solutions and ARC's congressional liaison. We rode into D.C. in the comfort of ARC CEO Marsha Evan's chauffeur-driven limo. With our proverbial hands-out, we were to meet with Amit Yoran, director of the National Cybersecurity Division (NCSD) .

Instead of meeting Mr. Yoran, one of his aides greeted us and apologized that Mr. Yoran was called to another meeting and would not be available. We conveyed our desire for funding and, after a few minutes, realized our efforts would be in vain. As we started for the exit, the aide asked if we needed a taxi which we declined and stood outside in the Washington D.C. sunshine waiting for our limo. *Outside, we joked that it seemed odd asking for money while we were being chauffeured about town in a private limo!*

7.9 MEMOS AND ISSUES – JANUARY 2004–DECEMBER 2004

7.9.1 ARC-CISO-GEN-2004.002 Dated January 5, 2004, CISO Monthly Status Report for the Period – December 1, 2003 through December 31, 2003

This memo identified my project to have ARC meet the requirements of the ISO 17799 certification process. ISO 17799 was an internationally recognized Information Security Management Standard, first published by the International Organization for Standardization, or ISO in December 2000. Adherence to this standard would give our information security program credibility. Using the SANS ISO 17799 checklist and ISO Control Objectives, Susan Baranowski formulated a tabular representation of the eleven major control objective categories that expanded to 127 security controls. We used the ISO 17799 standard as an alternative to COBIT.

7.9.2 ARC-CISO-GEN-2004.007 Dated January 28, 2004 – *DHS – Launch Announcement of National Cyber Alert System*

This memo identified three new DHS – US-CERT communications:

- *Cybersecurity Alert* – For non-technical professionals, small office and home office users, individuals, and others who prefer fewer technical descriptions of problems, we will be producing a non-technical version of Technical Cyber Security Alerts known as Cybersecurity Alerts.
- *Cybersecurity Tips* – Also for non-technical professionals, small office and home office users, individuals, and others, US-CERT announced Cybersecurity Tips. Tips, to be produced every other week, will be short documents that provided background and education for home users and others, which can help prevent problems from occurring in the first place.
- *Cybersecurity Bulletins* – Cybersecurity Bulletins will be produced every other week and will summarize notable information from the past two weeks, including topics covered in Cybersecurity Alerts and other sources.

The memo also described other government and private sources of threat information, of which I had taken advantage including membership in the global FIRST, FBI InfraGard Program, and AV Information Exchange Network (AVIEN). Via these various sources, we had actionable information relative to the latest threats and vulnerabilities.

7.9.3 ARC-CISO-GEN-2004.017 (C) Dated March 4, 2004 CISO Monthly Status Report for the Period – February 1, 2004 through February 29, 2004

This memo was addressed to Greg Norris, Executive Director Enterprise Architecture & Planning, himself a direct report to the ARC Chief Information Officer (CIO). The significance of this reporting hierarchy is that my Information Security team and I were no longer a direct report to the CIO. This reporting structure was not optimal and would result in a decrease in the CIO's visibility for security-related matters and an

ARC-wide decreased perception of the importance of the information security program.

7.9.4 ARC-CISO-GEN-2004.028 Dated March 29, 2004 CISO Monthly Status Report for the Period – March 1, 2004 through March 29, 2004

This memo identified the launch of our Information Security – Center of Excellence website. The internal website, based on Gartner's Center of Excellence (CoE) concept, provided a breaking news window area which was updated at least daily with the latest computer virus/worm notifications and links to anti-virus vendor websites for technical details and patch updates. Also, the CoE website provided access to CISO staff and contact information, The DHS Daily Information Analysis, and Infrastructure Protection Report, CISO Metrics, System Advisories, and technical and awareness bulletins. The goal was for the CoE website to become the default ARC-wide portal for all relevant information relating to Information Security.

7.9.5 ARC-CISO-POL-2004.031 Dated April 6, 2004 – Seal/Certification Products and Analyses for Public Websites and e-Commerce

The use of the WebTrust certification and seal for recross.org was the primary focus on ARC's brand protection initiative. Any compromise of ARC's Online Donation System (ODS) could erode public trust and be devastating for donations. ARC's ODS was re-architected to be a more robust system than that which failed due to increased donation traffic on 9–11. ARC's Office of Internal Audit, headed by Tim Holmes, asked for my opinion on replacing the current WebTrust certification performed by KPMG. Specific issues included: (1) ARC's WebTrust seal refresh was due to expire June 16, 2004, (2) there was to be an increase in cost to perform WebTrust analysis for the new version of the re-architected ODS, and (3) new American Institute of Certified Public Accountants/Canadian Institute of Chartered Accountants (AICPA/CICA) Trust Services Privacy Principle and the new criteria became effective April 1, 2004.

I was always impressed with the cost-effectiveness of the KPMG WebTrust review. The review was periodic and not just a one-off exercise. WebTrust was an independent, comprehensive assessment to include external and internal network penetration and system vulnerability exercises, network diagram reviews, privacy policy reviews, assurance of transactional integrity throughout the system, and customer support/response. However, I could also see the value in changing audit firms to get a fresh perspective for the review.

There were also differences of opinion about displaying the WebTrust seal of approval on the public website. On one side, the general public could feel safer donating to a website with this seal. On the other hand, there was a concern that displaying the seal would put a target on the website and welcome hackers to test its security. I provided my thoughts on WebTrust or similar audits, but the final decision was above my pay grade.

I made the point that any alternative reviews must be at least as comprehensive as the WebTrust review. Since ODS was being re-engineered, the need for an assessment of the new architecture was essential. The ODS's new architecture included a new Transaction Queuing Engine (TQE) initiative. Hence, the increased cost for WebTrust included validation of the new TQE infrastructure.

7.9.6 ARC-CISO-AUD-2004.033 Dated April 14, 2004 – Review of Certification Seals on Various Online Donation and Commerce Websites

At the request of the ARC Audit Committee and Internal Audit (IA) to help them to decide as to the need for the WebTrust or similar certification seal on the Red Cross ODS website. I randomly reviewed twenty-five external websites, including the websites of non-profit organizations, commercial websites, and political websites. The results were:

1. All twenty-five websites used transmission encryption (i.e., SSL and/or https).
2. Twenty-three websites had a privacy statement link.
3. Eleven of the twenty-five commercial/political sites had a visible seal and/or certification (44%).
4. Seven of the fifteen *nonprofit* sites had a visible seal and/or certification (47%).
5. For websites that were both commercial and political, each category had two of the five websites showing a visible seal and/or certification (40%).
6. The most common certification/seal among the eleven sites was the Verisign Seal. Ten of the eleven sites displayed some version of a Verisign seal/product. This was not surprising since Verisign registers domains, provides SSL certificates, and secure online payment services in addition to their Site Secure seal/certification.

Although the Verisign Site Secure seal was a fraction of the cost of WebTrust, I considered that Verisign's testing was superficial as compared to WebTrust. WebTrust was much more comprehensive in both breadth and depth of analysis. Further, WebTrust analyzed transaction integrity and security throughout the system to the payment processor. *My final proposal to the Audit Committee was to eliminate the physical WebTrust seal itself (a cost savings) but continue to have KPMG conduct the equivalent review as behind-the-scenes assessment work. This course of action was agreed to by ARC Internal Audit.*

7.9.7 ARC-CISO-GEN-2004.034 Dated April 15, 2004 – Architecture & Planning Weekly Status Report

An interesting item in this status report dealt with yet another Brand Protection issue. One of the larger ARC chapters allegedly sent out spam email notifications for the sale of the *2005 Red Cross Women of the Year Calendar*. This messaging was certainly not commensurate with the values of the ARC. There were two issues: (1) the obvious website and calendar sale itself and (2) spam solicitation for calendar sales. The first issue was immediately resolved as the chapter CEO sent out notifications that the calendar would not be issued. The email address (via email header information) from which the spam originated seemed to have been *spoofed* because it showed the amarillo.redcross.org domain (not ours) alongside one of our IP addresses. We investigated the matter by sifting through firewall logs to ascertain if the email spam was initiated from computer(s) internal to Red Cross. See 7.9.9 for details of the investigation into the matter.

7.9.8 ARC-CISO-GEN-2004.040 Dated April 29, 2004 – CISO Monthly Status Report for the Period – April 1, 2004 through April 29, 2004

The significance of this status report was an item where we expanded our ARC-wide Center of Excellence website to include ten online courses, ten quizzes, and one final exam as part of a Security 101 course. These courses supported the user and system administrator security certification program.

7.9.9 ARC-CISO-INV-2004.041 Dated May 3, 2004 Preliminary Investigation – "2005 Women of the Red Cross" Calendar Promotion and Supporting Email Spam

This investigation should be in the *You have got to be kidding me* file. First, the investigation began when I received an Internet Abuse Complaint dated April 8, 2004 (see Section 7.9.7). The complaint identified email spam notifications regarding the sale of the *2005 Women of the Red Cross Calendar*. The spam message was suggestive by stating that one had to be at least twenty-one years of age to order the calendar. The website identified in the email message was redcrosssecure.org/xxxxTexas (Not the real URL). I accessed the website and determined that the spam email message and solicitation seemed to be correct and being sent from, or in support of, the xxxxTexas Chapter. *In addition to the calendar, the website also sold "Red Cross B+ Hot Sauce" – "Guaranteed to make your blood boil."*

While we conducted our own Internet forensics regarding the details of the website (e.g., Internet Domain Registration, contacts), we used a personal, non-Red Cross email account with which to register and order a copy of the calendar. The website promotion was terminated by ARC' OGC and Service Area Executive, and the promotions disappeared from the website over the next day or two. *Our non-Red Cross email inbox received an email message from the xxxxTexas Chapter within a week stating their regret that the calendar promotion would not proceed and his credit card would not be charged.*

> I note here that the spam email was generated from Red Cross IP address space. Unfortunately, due to this incident, Red Cross' address space was subsequently "blacklisted" from sending email messages to other Internet domains that used spam or blacklist filters. The spam caused issues with Red Cross not being able to conduct legitimate business via email. This issue took some time to resolve.

Finding the identity of the person who started the spam email was more convoluted. Our firewall logs showed that the spam email came from an internal IP address. The internal intranet protocol – IP address was from a pool of IPs assigned to a VPN concentrator. We traced that IP address to a Cox Cable client who logged into the Red Cross VPN with a legitimate account on the Red Cross ARCHQ Domain. Only then would the external client be assigned an IP address to be able to go out to the Internet from within the Red Cross. *We had the individual's name (who actually was located in Texas), but it was up to our ARC legal folks to pursue the matter further. In my May 25, 2004 status report, I identified that ARC Human Resources requested that we disable the ARCHQ domain account for the offending spammer.*

7.9.10 ARC-CISO-POL-2004.037 Dated May 11, 2004 – Critical Situation Alert – Lack of Consistent and Expedient Patching Processes Places Red Cross Systems at High Level of Risk

Expedient security patching had been and continues to be a concern for most cybersecurity professionals. I issued this memo in response to a security vulnerability addressed by Microsoft patch (MS-04–011). The patch carried a CRITICAL designation, and unpatched Windows servers were vulnerable to *Remote Code Execution* and *Denial-of-Service* (DoS) attacks. Microsoft issued the MS-04–011 patch on April 13, 2004. On April 22, 2004, several unpatched, Internet-facing ARC servers went offline as a result of the DoS attack. I issued an Emergency Change Request (CR -2474 dated April 23, 2004), which was approved. Enterprise Technology Services (ETS) and OCISO staff worked through the night to patch about twenty-five servers. Fortunately, this time, the servers only experienced the effects of the DoS attack and not the root compromise.

In this memo, I also cautioned that the window of opportunity for applying security patches and fixes was rapidly diminishing. Our recent MS-04–011, DoS incident occurred within just nine days of Microsoft's notification of the vulnerability on April 13, 2004. Internal patching processes needed to be reevaluated for more expedient applications. *However, as all security practitioners know, there is a delicate balance between thoroughly testing new patches and applying poorly tested patches that may break systems/ applications.*

7.9.11 ARC-CISO-TRP-2004.047 Dated June 22, 2004 Preliminary Report – SBC Secure Operations Center (SOC) Dublin, California

ARC IT was outsourcing the management of various security-related systems (e.g., firewalls). SBC was a Managed Security Service Provider (MSSP) with a business model to manage client security devices/systems and monitor client networks for security-related events and, by virtue of Service Level Agreements (SLAs) interact with its clients accordingly. Since I had experience as an MSSPs with my work at Counterpane Internet Security, it was determined that I physically perform an onsite assessment of SBC's capabilities.

At the time of my trip, SBC had 300 MSSP clients, and they managed 600 devices or *two devices per customer.* SBC's MSSP offering was not their core business. SBC's Dublin, CA site was its backup Network Operations Center (NOC) for their Illinois NOC. But the Dublin, CA site was the primary site for its Secure Operations Center (SOC). The SBC Dublin, CA SOC was not a dedicated SOC per se but consisted of a few dedicated terminals within SBC's NOC. SBC only had a total of eighteen SOC analysts, with twelve in the Dublin, CA SOC, six in SAN Antonio, TX, and no SOC analysts in the Illinois NOC.

My summary of the trip/review was based on my previous experience with SOC operations, I *did not* come away from the SBC SOC review with a sense of confidence that SBC understands the complexity and procedural requirements of the American Red Cross network and security needs. It appears that SBC security analysts are capable; however, I consider that SBC's limited suite of security technologies would represent a regression in the overall capability to protect Red Cross' system and network infrastructure. The obvious advantage with SBC would be in their monitoring firewall and intrusion detection systems (IDS) on a nearly continuous basis. This would be more than what OCISO was able to do today, which can be best characterized as ad hoc monitoring due to lack of resources. SBC's ability to take quick corrective action based on SLA guidance would also be a benefit as well but the advantage may be minimized by limited security technologies, lack of participation in proactive Internet-intelligence agencies, and lack of first-hand institutional knowledge of the dynamic Red Cross IT and network infrastructure.

7.9.12 ARC-CISO-TRP-2004.053 Dated July 29. 2004 – Trip Report – INFOSEC Training

As I stated earlier, ARC was not a government agency but that did not deter me from trying to take part in any government-provided training. As part of our affiliation and participation with the Federal Information System Security Education and Awareness (FISSEA) group, Red Cross personnel took advantage of quality, no-cost INFOSEC training. Close to our ARC Virginia office was the Bureau of Diplomatic Security Training Center Department of State (DoS), Dunn Loring. VA. I sent my team and selected ARC system administrators to various technical security trainings offered by the U.S. State Department.

7.9.13 ARC-CISO-AUD-2004.056 Dated August 17, 2004, CISO Response to SBC

There was considerable back and forth between me and SBC relative to their policies and procedures, physical security of the SOC, lack of understanding of the complexities of ARC systems, etc. *The decision was above my pay grade, and ARC moved forward with SBC as our MSSP.*

The following three memos (7.9.14 to 7.9.16) documented my efforts to support ARC Internal Audit with their program of on-site chapter assessments. We placed increased scrutiny on chapters that conducted online e-Commerce activities, such as donations, Red Cross courses, and merchandise sales. To support my vulnerability assessment efforts, I built a portable, small form factor PC running Windows 95 and Red Hat Linux in a VMware instance. As I had on my previous system, I outfitted Linux with a number of freeware security assessment tools, including Nmap, Nessus, Whisker, and used other command line techniques such as a test for DNS zone transfers. Before ARC's internal auditors travelled to specific chapter sites across the United States, I would perform a technical assessment of their Internet/website presence. Based on the results of my review, I would consider the security posture of each as either *Acceptable* or *Unacceptable.*

7.9.14 ARC-CISO-AUD-2004.068 (C) Dated October 11, 2004 – Office of the Chief Information Security Officer (OCISO) Report of Technical Remote Security Assessment of Chapter Internet Presence and Website: Red Cross Chapter – XXX, Texas

I considered this website to have an UNACCEPTABLE level of security. The Nikto webserver scans identified sixteen security holes, of which eight were HIGH, five were MEDIUM, and three were LOW.

7.9.15 ARC-CISO-AUD-2004.074 (C) October 25, 2004 Office of the Chief Information Security Officer (OCISO) Report of Technical Remote Security Assessment of Chapter Internet Presence and Website: The American Red Cross of XXX, Indiana

Although this chapter did not conduct e-Commerce activities on their website, they maintained their own general website. I considered the security of their website to be UNACCEPTABLE. The website had a number of superfluous listening ports open, including port 9999 (Abyss) that may indicate a Trojan Horse on the system. The Nikto web scanner showed there were twenty-two possible security holes on the system.

7.9.16 ARC-CISO-AUD-2004.075 (C) October 26, 2004 Office of the Chief Information Security Officer (OCISO) Report of Technical Remote Security Assessment of Chapter Internet Presence and Website: The ARC of XXX, Pennsylvania

This is another chapter that maintained its own website, but the e-Commerce activities linked back to the main, trusted redross.org website. I considered the security of their website as UNACCEPTABLE. The website had a number of superfluous listening ports open, and the Nikto web scanner showed there were fifteen possible security holes on the system.

Over the next two years, I performed and documented twenty-six (26) chapter security reviews. These assessments saved ARC thousands of dollars as compared to them being performed by an external audit firm. Internal Audit Manager Tim Holmes and his team appreciated my help and recognized my efforts with a plaque (Figure 7.1).

7.9.17 ARC-CISO-POL-2004.084 Dated November 10, 2004 – Internal Review for Policy Compliance

I had published INFOSEC Policy 220.03 Access Controls, which identified configuration, controls, and administration of system accounts and passwords, including details, such as password construction, aging, and expiration. The policy required that password expiration be set to 120 days, at which time the password would need to be changed. A scan of the ARCHQ Domain found 7539 accounts, including user, system, and process accounts with password policies that did not comply with my INFOSEC Policy 220.03.

Figure 7.1 American Red Cross – Thank You Plaque from Internal Audit

Of the 7539 accounts: 991 accounts (13%) were set to NEVER EXPIRE, 708 accounts of the 991 accounts (71%) also exceeded the 120-day policy directive and with the NEVER EXPIRE setting, the remaining 283 accounts would eventually exceed 120 days unless account owners took the initiative to change the password without prompting by the system. About 280 accounts (28%) of the 991 accounts were user accounts assigned to specific individuals and 711 accounts (72%) are assigned to system processes or groups.

We recognized that changing passwords for system accounts every 120 days would be counterproductive for system administration staff. However, the policy required system administration personnel to periodically review system accounts for continued use. OCISO recommended that, at a minimum, a formal, documented annual or semi-annual (preferred) review of system accounts should include a password change for active accounts. Passwords should also be changed when administrators with knowledge of the system account credentials leave or change roles within the organization. I issued Clarify Case # 797515 to address the areas of non-compliance with the policies.

7.9.18 ARC-CISO-GEN-2004.089 Dated November 15, 2004 CISO Mid-Month Status Report for the Period – November 1, 2004 through November 15, 2004

In this status update, I reported that my team and I were participating in a U.S. initiative incorporated into its INFOSEC Training and Rating Program established in early 2002. I wanted me and my team to be certified in the NSA methodology. There were three levels, the first being the INFOSEC Assessment Methodology (NSA IAM). The second level was the INFOSEC Evaluation Methodology (NSA – IEM). The third level had restrictive access as it included Red Teaming.

The first course/certification is the IAM – INFOSEC Assessment Methodology which outlined the basic assessment methodology and was a textbook exercise with no hands-on testing. The IEM – INFOSEC Evaluation Methodology augmented the IAM process with technical assessment tools (e.g., vulnerability assessment tools – Nessus, Nmap). *This was a cost-effective program and my team and I were all certified in the NSA IAM and IEM methodologies.*

7.9.19 ARC-CISO-INC-2004.101 (C) Dated December 5, 2004 – Incident Report – ODS and Recent Fraudulent Activity

Unbeknownst to me or my office, previously implemented security protections were relaxed, increasing fraudulent credit card activity on the ODS. We immediately reimplemented these controls:

1. At the network layer, firewall blocks were implemented to prohibit Internet connections from specific foreign address ranges found to be sources of fraudulent activity.
2. At the application layer, the ODS application and website were revised to:
   a. Immediately block IP addresses attempting to enter a number of credit card transactions within a short period. (This activity indicates fraudsters trying to test the validity of credit card numbers, typically from a single IP address within the timeframe.)
   b. CCV (Credit Card Verification) checks were implemented. CCV numbers are the three or four digits identified on the back of credit cards and must be entered in addition to the base credit card number to complete the online transaction.

In this memo, I stated that the obvious cause of the fraudulent activity resulted directly from the unauthorized relaxation of ODS security measures. The decisions to negate our security checks were negligent and made without proper system change control, vetting, and notification. CISO also requested that the IT organization(s) responsible for ODS provide an analysis and action plan to address the recurring issues described above that directly resulted in the facilitation of fraudulent activity.

7.10 MEMOS AND ISSUES – JANUARY 2005–OCTOBER 2005

7.10.1 ARC-CISO-INC-2005.007 Dated January 12, 2005 Report of Analysis of Websense Data November-December 2004

ARC had deployed web content filtering technology – Websense. We analyzed the filtering for November and December 2004. Websense was considered a critically essential technology as it prohibited internal user access to web-enabled email sites (e.g., Yahoo, Hotmail), which historically had been primary vectors for computer virus/worm infections within the Red Cross. Websense was also configurable to exclude website content categories such as Adult, Sex, Nudity, and Gambling. Internal user access was blocked by simply selecting the category. These categories were refreshed daily with new website URLs (Universal Resource Locators – website addresses) downloaded to our internal Websense devices. The statistics within this report were compiled from two disposition categories within Websense; Blocked and Permitted.

Over November and December 2004, we analyzed 44,551,143 total website hits that filtered through Websense. The most telling statistic was that during the two-month period, over 12 million (12,128,847) hits were blocked from reaching their destination by the Websense application. The blocked attempts account for 27.2% of total recorded hits. Of the blocked web traffic, over 10 million denied hits (10,230,218) were from Advertisements (inclusive of adware), and nearly 2 million (1,708,524) from known Spyware hits were blocked. The blocked Advertisement and Spyware attempts accounted for 26.8% of *all* web traffic.

OCISO considers Websense to be an essential technology as it:

- Disallowed internal user access to web-enabled email sites, which have historically been primary vectors of computer virus/worm infections within the Red Cross.
- Enforced RC Human Resources and INFOSEC policy regarding the appropriate use of IT resources and potentially negate hostile work environment claims.

- Allowed for ad hoc blocking of specific websites CISO has found to be malicious via other Internet-related intelligence gathering.

7.10.2 ARC-CISO-POL-2005.008 Dated January 20, 2005 – Meeting Minutes – Red Cross SPAM Issue

Despite best efforts, ARC continued to experience large influxes of SPAM email. We used ClearSwift's MimeSweeper system for spam filtering. The product used Bayesian logic, and the filters were updated eight times a day. The product took two actions on perceived spam messages, either deleting known spam prior to delivery or delivering the email message to the recipient marked as *[Maybe Spam]* for the user's action.

In February 2004, ARC ETS announced the rollout of enhanced spam-reduction technology and the establishment of the ARCSPAM mailbox. The purpose of the ARCSPAM mailbox was to allow users to find an easy way to identify new sources of spam. It was assumed these new sources of spam sent to ARCSPAM would be sent to the vendor to include in subsequent versions of their filters updated eight times a day.

Part of the problem with the anti-spam configuration was that the filters had been scaled back to allow email traffic flow for chapters that may use other email systems as part of their business (e.g., Yahoo). *A plan of action was developed to address further improvements to SPAM remediations.*

7.10.3 ARC-CISO-POL-2005.010 Dated February 8, 2005 – Information System Security Review Report – ATLAS Program

ATLAS (Alliance of Technologies Linking Services) was a suite of applications specifically for Red Cross chapter use and accessed via the Internet. ATLAS applications were intended to streamline and improve service delivery to customers, volunteers, donors, and staff through increased speed and efficiency.

This review was conducted by all of my team and the findings included: Access controls that did not meet ARC policy standards (one application had a two character password, the fifty-five servers that made up the ATLAS system had an aggregate of 228 security holes, and using twelve control objectives from COBIT there were five critical, five unacceptable, and two minor – no need to address (Table 7.5).

7.10.4 ARC-CISO-GEN-2005.034 Dated April 20, 2005 Justification for GFI LANguard Network Scanner

This memorandum was issued to provide justification for the purchase of two licenses and one-year maintenance for the GFI LANguard Network Scanner product per the referenced quote for a total of $2,197.80. OCISO performed

Table 7.5 ATLAS System COBIT Compliance Review

Control #	*Exposure*	*Concern*	*Housekeeping*	*Okay*
M1. Infosec documentation		X		
M2. Infosec roles and responsibilities		X		
M3. Contingency planning	X			
M4. Configuration management		X		
T1. Identification and authentication	X			
T2. Account management		X		
T3. Session controls	X			
T4. Auditing		X		
T5. Malicious code protection	X			
T6. Maintenance	X			
T7. System assurance			X	
T8. Communications security				X

network/system vulnerability scans of Red Cross' Windows-based systems on an almost daily basis. The reasons for these scans included investigations of computer virus/worm activity on specific computers throughout the organization, performance of vulnerability scans of Windows-based systems before they were placed into production, and continuous assessment of systems for compliance and risk mitigation purposes.

OCISO had been using open-source vulnerability scanning tools such as Nmap and Nessus, which run on Linux platforms. We had also been using trial versions of GFI LANguard, which ran on Windows-based OSs. GFI LANguard was specifically designed for assessing Windows-based systems and provided better general system information and vulnerability detail than the open-source tools. GFI LANguard was our tool of choice in performing vulnerability scans of suspected virus/worm-infected computers throughout the organization. *This request was approved, and Mike Cokenour and I continued to use GFI LANguard on an almost daily basis to investigate issues and ensure the security of ARC systems.*

7.10.5 ARC-CISO-GEN-2005.043 Dated May 16, 2005 Compliance with Payment Card Industry – Data Security Standard (PCI-DSS)

PCI-DSS is an information security standard used to handle credit cards from major card brands. The standard is administered by the Payment Card

Industry Security Standards Council, and its use was mandated by the card brands. It was created to better control cardholder data and reduce credit card fraud. Validation of compliance is performed annually or quarterly with a method suited to the volume of transactions: Version 1 – December 15, 2004. *I wrote this memo as an executive point paper on what the PCI-DSS program entailed and its expected impact on ARC.*

7.10.6 ARC-CISO – GEN-2005.046 Dated May 23, 2005 CISO Status Report for the Period – April 20, 2005 through May 23, 2005

This status report identified that OCISO team members Susan Baranowski and Mike Cokenour had been studying for the Information Systems Audit and Control Association (ISACA) Certified Information System Auditor (CISA) exam. *I wanted my team to pursue professional certifications for their professional development, expanding their skill sets, and building credibility to our ARC information security program.*

7.10.7 ARC-CISO-POL-2005.048 Dated June 1, 2005 Privacy Package

As ARC was about to experience the start of hurricane season, I was asked to comment on an ARC Response Center Network (RCN) project. RCN planned to preposition about 150 computer servers in selected chapters to support disaster relief efforts. These systems would access several internal systems, including the AFES instance of Clarify, which contained and displayed PII including social security numbers. RCN was to be staffed by *off-the-street volunteers*, and their interaction with the public would require access to and handling of privacy-related, PII data. There was no consistent policy regarding properly vetting volunteers. Volunteers completed a short personnel form and signed a non-disclosure agreement. There was no policy regarding the performance of a criminal background check as was done for employees. In reply to this request, I created a table that defined a set of thirteen minimum requirements across the functional, macro-to-micro areas of Management, Enterprise, Network, System/Host, and Application/Data/Client to address privacy concerns.

In about two months, the nation will be hit by Hurricane Katrina, a devastating and deadly Category 5 Atlantic hurricane. In late August 2005, Katrina caused 1,392 fatalities and damages estimated at $186.3 billion (in 2022 USD). The city of New Orleans and its surrounding area received the brunt of the devastation. Katrina was the fourth-most intense Atlantic hurricane to make landfall in the contiguous United States, gauged by barometric pressure.[16]

7.10.8 ARC-CISO-TRP-2005.054 Dated July 21, 2005 – Trip Report – Government Forum of Incident Response and Security Teams Meeting

ARCcert was a member of the previously discussed FIRST (Forum of Incident Response and Security Teams). The U.S. government set up its own equivalent G-FIRST (Government – Forum of Incident Response and Security Teams). DHS provided me with membership in G-FIRST and access to the G-FIRST portal. The portal provided a web-based forum and early vulnerability notification environment with other security staff in government agencies.

While OCISO had access to the US-CERT portal, access to the more desirable Internet Health Services (IHS) required additional authorization. The IHS portal provided additional cybersecurity intelligence provided by prospective commercial security service providers – Akamai, Symantec, Cymru, etc. I requested that ARC have authorization to access the IHS offerings for use and evaluation, and we were granted this access. *(ARC access to G-FIRST was another situation where our status as federal government organization was murky).*

7.10.9 jmARC-CISO-GEN-2005.055 Dated July 22, 2005 – CISO Status Report for the Period – June 17, 2005 through July 22, 2005

In this status report, I included my role as the ARC lead for the DHS – Cyber Storm November 2005 exercise. I worked with Red Cross Federal Preparedness Unit in support of Red Cross's participation in the upcoming DHS Cyber Storm exercise in November 2005. The exercise was conducted under DHS' NCSD with participation by public and private-sector stakeholders.

In this status report, I also advised that the US Department of State indicated that they would no longer provide security training for Red Cross staff. Via OCISO's participation in the FISSEA (Federal Information System Security Education and Awareness) forum, a limited number of Red Cross staff had attended local training provided by the state, mainly in system administration security (*I guess we got caught!).*

Lesson Learned In some instances, it is better to ask for forgiveness after the fact than to ask permission before the fact.

7.10.10 Hurricane Katrina – August 2005

During my tenure as ARC's CISO, Hurricane Katrina marked the next significant catastrophe that ARC had to face, the first being September 11.

Katrina's fury caused the loss of over 1,800 lives and more than $81 billion in destruction. As many as 350,000 residences from Texas to Florida were damaged or destroyed.[17] The actions that transpired around the aftermath of Hurricane Katrina consumed the entirety of ARC, including having a major impact on IT and my department. According to the reliefweb.int website,[18] ARC:

- Provided over 3.8 million overnight stays in shelters in thirty-one states – seven times higher than any other disaster up to that time.
- Served almost 68 million meals and snacks – four times more than what the Red Cross had ever provided during past relief efforts.
- For the first time, we served a million meals in a single day.
- Provided emergency financial assistance to 1.4 million families – nearly twenty times more than any record prior to Katrina.

CIO#6 Steve Cooper – The right man at the right time. Steve Cooper joined the as the Senior Vice President and CIO in 2005. He followed Interim CIO #5 Mark Weischedel. Under his leadership, Steve was responsible for the IT assets of the Red Cross and leveraging them to support the humanitarian organization's 35,000 employees and the 300 million Americans they serve. As Katrina ravaged the US, Steve guided the introduction of the first-ever National Call Center to provide emergency financial assistance to the more than 4 million people displaced from their homes. I remember his calling for assistance from top executives of major tech companies such as Cisco and Microsoft. Steve led a unique partnership of these technology giants to develop and deploy critical services to the more than 1 million families affected by Hurricanes Katrina, Rita, and Wilma.

After Hurricane Katrina, thousands of New Orleans residents took shelter in their New Orleans Superdome stadium. But quickly, humanitarian conditions there began to deteriorate. The air conditioning was off; bathrooms were filthy and trash overflowed everywhere. The situation was untenable, and it was decided to evacuate the Super Dome and move evacuees to the Houston Astrodome. The initial need to accommodate 2,500 displaced residents quickly became the need to shelter almost 24,000. The evacuation from New Orleans was now an exodus.

There were many private organizations, volunteers, and government assistance in supporting the evacuees now resident in the Astrodome. Since the Houston Astrodome was being set up as a shelter, there was an obvious need to provide Internet access for the evacuees. My team and I discussed how to best approach the security aspects of such a large undertaking. We decided to reach out to SANS (System Administration and Network Security) since they were headquartered in Maryland, in close proximity to our location. I had experience with SANS as I attended their network intrusion course when I was at The Prudential Insurance Company of America (see Chapter 5 Section 5.4).

As a backdrop, SANS issued a yearly poster/blueprint of various protective measures from the outer edge of the network down to the desktop. Responding to our request for assistance, SANS founder Alan Paller showed up at our office with Marcus Sachs and other cybersecurity experts from the SANS team. Our combined teams commandeered a conference room. On the table, Alan laid out the latest SANS poster as our security blueprint. We poured over the graphics of the poster and assessed our security posture. Alan was quick to contact several security vendors, and they generously donated their equipment and expertise. To the best of my recollection, we did not experience any breaches on our networks. *I will never forget that at one point in my interaction with Alan, he handed me a Katrina relief effort donation check for $100,000! Rest in Peace, my friend.*

Federal Bureau of Investigation (FBI) – Pittsburgh. While we fared well regarding network attacks and other system compromises, Internet-related fraud escalated. Over the two weeks before Hurricane Katrina's impact on Louisiana, there were over 2,000 Internet domain names registered with some permutation of *Katrina*. In the immediate aftermath of Katrina, the number of fraudulent websites increased significantly including almost 4,600 Websites advertising Hurricane Katrina relief services. Most of these websites were believed to be bogus. The bad guys had geared up to collect donations from the charitable American public via their fraudulent websites. ARC's physical security team contacted me for an opportunity to work on Internet fraud issues with the FBI, specifically those impacting ARC. This interaction required that I be imbedded with the FBI team in Pittsburgh. I jumped at the chance to go back to my hometown and work with the FBI.

I packed my bags and headed up the Pennsylvania Turnpike to Pittsburgh. I pulled into a parking space in the shadow of a new, futuristic-looking building along the Monongahela River where the J&L Steel Mill once stood. The building housed the National Cyber-Forensics & Training Alliance (NCFTA), formed in 2002, whose mission is to provide a trusted, confidential forum where the private sector and law enforcement can work together to identify and disrupt today's most pressing cyber-related threats.[19] I was welcomed by FBI Unit Chief Tom Grasso and Dan Larkin, the Unit Chief of the FBI's Cyber Initiative and Resource Fusion Unit (CIRFU). I was warmly welcomed and felt like one of the team – it helped that Dan was a huge Steeler fan like me.

The CIRFU works in conjunction with the Internet Crime Complaint Center (IC3) whose analysts eliminate false leads and refine cases before they are referred to local or international law enforcement agencies. And this is exactly what we did. The FBI analysts would identify websites or suspicious domains, and I would interface with Red Cross back in Virginia and Washington, DC, to determine if the websites and domains were legitimate. If not legitimate, the analysts would investigate further and get the site taken down or take further legal/law enforcement actions.

CNN reporter Kelli Arena visited us on October 4, 2004, at the NCFTA for a television spot. The following is a program lineup from https://tvnews.vanderbilt.edu/programs/804794. *So much for my fifteen seconds of fame!*

> CNN Hurricane Katrina/Fraud/Online Scams
> #804801
> 09:20:30 PM — 09:23:50 PM
> (Studio: Aaron Brown) The myriad of fraud in response to Hurricane Katrina introduced.
> (Pittsburgh: Kelli Arena) An online scam by con artists scheming against donations to Katrina victims examined; scenes shown from the FBI Internet Crime Complaint Center
> {IC3} in Pittsburgh where Internet donor sites are scanned.
> **[Red Cross Ron BAKLARZ† – calls the fraud despicable.]**
> [FBI's Dan LARKIN†, analyst David – comment on tracking sites.]
> [Microsoft Richard – says we use outside investigators.]
> [FBI cyber division assistant director Lou REIGEL† – cites other examples of preying on disasters.][20]

7.10.11 ARC-CISO-GEN-2005.065 Dated October 28, 2005 – CISO Status Report for the Period – October 1, 2005 through October 28, 2005

Katrina Fraud (CISO Leads – Baklarz/Baranowski) Below are the statistics for ARC's cyber-related fraudulent activity associated with Katrina. The typical model we saw was the submission of a donation request via spam email with an embedded link to a fraudulent website. Fraudulent websites were hosted all over the globe, including China, Korea, and Romania. The majority of domestic-hosted, fraudulent websites were compromised from a foreign source rather than being homegrown. The key item in this report

Table 7.6 Katrina Cyber-Fraud Case Load Statistics 10/21/2005

	10/21/2005		*10/21/2005*
New cases	4	Total fraudulent websites identified	44
Handled cases	254	Websites taken down	39
Total cases	258	Remaining active websites	5

was the following statistics. *This was my last status report as CISO of the ARC* (Table 7.6).

7.11 UNIVERSITY OF VIRGINIA (UVA)

While Serving as CISO at ARC, I was an adjunct professor at the University of Virginia's Northern Virginia campus where I taught night courses in cybersecurity. Outside of the normal coursework, UVA asked me to teach a Certified Information System Security Professional (CISSP) exam preparation course. I agreed and taught this in an auditorium of the Scitor Corporation in Chantilly, VA. Scitor, which gets its name from the Latin word meaning "to seek to know."[21] There were about 30 professionals in my classroom. Previously, I described my experience studying for the CISSP exam as *death by slides*. And now I was on the other side of the podium, meting out the painful process! Overall, teaching was fun and offered an opportunity to step outside of my comfort zone.

7.12 CISA AND CISM

While at ARC, I continued professional certification studies and sat for exams to earn Information System Audit and Control Association's (ISACA) Certified Information System Auditor (CISA) and Certified Information Security Manager (CISM) professional certifications. I considered that a complete CISO should have a diverse skill set, and I was especially interested in the audit aspects of the job. Upon retirement, I held these professional certifications: C|CISO, CISSP, CISM, CISA, NSA-IAM, and NSA-IEM.

7.13 ALL-STARS – AMERICAN RED CROSS

7.13.1 Susan Baranowski

When I met Susan at ARC, she was working on the Oracle Financials implementation, specifically working on policy and training. She had the exact skills I needed to move our program forward. Susan worked tirelessly and did a great job by leading the project to establish a framework of guidelines and security standards to protect the organization's information and operations. She used the principles of ISO 17799 to create the guidelines and general principles for initiating, implementing, maintaining, and improving information security management in the organization. Susan is now enjoying a well-deserved retirement.

7.13.2 Gordon Bass

Gordon came into our department from ARC's technology group, where he was a Senior Director of IT. He gave us in-depth knowledge of ARC's critical systems. Gordon served as my deputy CISO and took over as CISO when I left ARC. Gordon went on to senior security positions with the Defense Information Systems Agency (DISA) and the Department of Energy. Gordon is now the Chief Development Officer at Deerwood Academy.

7.13.3 Mike Cokenour

I considered Mike the *unsung hero* in our department. He was always nose to the grindstone in keeping ARC's systems safe. Often, Mike would pull all-nighters and work with IT groups to install patches, cleanup virus infections, etc. We were lucky to have Mike on our team. After the ARC, Mike spent over twelve years as Senior Information Security Manager at MAXIMUS. As of late, Mike says he has *gone fishin*. Catch some big ones, my friend!

7.14 TECHNOLOGY ENHANCEMENTS AND SECURITY DEVELOPMENTS 2002–2005

2002

- The top computer and technology-related terms introduced or popularized in 2002 were Firewall and Windows XP.

2003

- January 24th, the SQL Slammer worm attacked vulnerabilities in Microsoft SQL Server and Microsoft Desk Engine (MSDE) and became the fastest spreading worm of all time (measured by doubling time at the peak rate of growth), causing massive Internet access disruptions worldwide just fifteen minutes after infecting its first victim.
- Microsoft released FrontPage 2003, which ended up being the last version of Microsoft FrontPage.
- IEEE 802.11i was introduced with WPA (Wi-Fi Protected Access) encryption. 802.11i provided a Robust Security Network (RSN) with two new protocols: the four-way handshake and the group key handshake.
- August 12th, the Blaster worm, aka the Lovesan worm, rapidly spread by exploiting a vulnerability in system services present on Windows XP and Windows 2000 computers.
- October 24th, the Sober worm is first seen on Microsoft systems and maintained its presence until 2005 with many new variants. E-mails containing the Sober worm were sent around the Internet disguised as an e-mail from either the FBI or the Central Intelligence Agency,

The e-mail claimed that the recipient had been caught visiting illegal websites and asked the user to open an attachment to answer some questions. The simultaneous attacks on network weak points by the Blaster and Sobig worms cause massive damage.

2004

- January 18th, Bagle (also known as Beagle) was a mass-mailing computer worm affecting Microsoft Windows. The first strain, Bagle.A, did not propagate widely. A second variant, Bagle.B, was considerably more virulent. There were two variants of Bagle worm, Bagle.A and Bagle.B. Bagle.B was discovered on February 17, 2004.
- January 26th, the MyDoom worm emerges and held the record for the fastest-spreading mass mailer worm. The worm was most notable for performing a distributed denial-of-service (DDoS) attack on www.sco.com, which belonged to The SCO (Santa Cruz Operation) Group.
- February 4th, Mark Zuckerberg launched Thefacebook which became Facebook.
- February 16th, the Netsky worm is discovered. The worm spreads by email and by copying itself to folders on the local hard drive as well as on mapped network drives if available. Many variants of the Netsky worm appeared.

2005

- April 24th, Microsoft Windows XP Professional ×64 edition was released.
- Verizon introduced its FiOS (Fiber Optic Service high-speed Internet service.
- August 2005, Zotob, a computer worm, exploited security vulnerabilities in Microsoft OSs like Windows 2000, including the MS05–039 plug-and-play vulnerability. Microsoft put a $250,000 reward for the capture of the hacker(s) responsible for Zotob. It was estimated that the Zotob worms cost an average of $97,000 as well as eighty hours of cleanup for each infected company.

NOTES

1 United States Congress. (n.d.). *Title 36—Patriotic and national observances, ceremonies, and organizations.* https://uscode.house.gov/view.xhtml?path=/prelim@title36/subtitle3/chapter3001&edition=prelim
2 American Red Cross National Headquarters. (n.d.). *Wikipedia.* https://en.wikipedia.org/wiki/American_Red_Cross_National_Headquarters
3 American Red Cross National Headquarters. (n.d.). *Wikipedia.* https://en.wikipedia.org/wiki/American_Red_Cross_National_Headquarters

4 American Red Cross National Headquarters. (n.d.). *Wikipedia.* https://en.wikipedia.org/wiki/American_Red_Cross_National_Headquarters

5 American Red Cross National Headquarters. (n.d.). *Wikipedia.* https://en.wikipedia.org/wiki/American_Red_Cross_National_Headquarters

6 Forum of Incident Response and Security Teams. (n.d.). *History.* https://www.first.org/about/history

7 COBIT. (n.d.). *Wikipedia.* https://en.wikipedia.org/wiki/COBIT

8 Morris worm. (n.d.). *Wikipedia.* https://en.wikipedia.org/wiki/Morris_worm

9 Barry, D. (2001, December 23). *Who brought Bernadine Healy down? The New York Times.* https://www.nytimes.com/2001/12/23/magazine/who-brought-bernadine-healy-down.html

10 Mintz, J. (2001, November 11). *Red Cross collected unneeded blood. The Washington Post.* https://www.washingtonpost.com/archive/politics/2001/11/11/red-cross-collected-unneeded-blood/639b5ba9-bcb0-40f3-87fb-b0f2c166c614/

11 Healy, B. (n.d.). *Bernadine Healy. Wikipedia.* https://en.wikipedia.org/wiki/Bernadine_Healy

12 IEEE 802.11i-2004. (n.d.). *Wikipedia.* https://en.wikipedia.org/wiki/IEEE_802.11i-2004

13 MD5. (n.d.). Wikipedia. https://en.wikipedia.org/wiki/MD5

14 https://www.cfo.com/news/clear-and-present-danger/682457/a

15 American Red Cross. (n.d.). *Military and veteran families.* https://www.redcross.org/about-us/our-work/military-families.html

16 Hurricane Katrina. (n.d.). *Wikipedia.* https://en.wikipedia.org/wiki/Hurricane_Katrina

17 Hurricane Katrina. (n.d.). *Wikipedia.* https://en.wikipedia.org/wiki/Hurricane_Katrina

18 ReliefWeb. (n.d.). *Hurricane Katrina led largest Red Cross relief response.* https://reliefweb.int/report/united-states-america/hurricane-katrina-led-largest-red-cross-relief-response

19 National Cyber-Forensics and Training Alliance. (n.d.). *Wikipedia.* https://en.wikipedia.org/wiki/National_Cyber-Forensics_and_Training_Alliance

20 National Cyber-Forensics and Training Alliance. (n.d.). *Wikipedia.* https://en.wikipedia.org/wiki/National_Cyber-Forensics_and_Training_Alliance

21 Dun & Bradstreet. (n.d.). *Scitor Corporation company profile.* https://www.dnb.com/business-directory/company-profiles.scitor_corporation.feee6cfcdca156b0ca915ad7cf6b5d0d.html

Chapter 8

MedStar Health 2006–2008

Position Held: Director Information Systems Security (DISS)
HIPAA Chief Security Officer

Location: White Marsh, Md

8.1 MEDSTAR HEALTH – OVERVIEW AND CULTURE

My two-plus years at MedStar were the most challenging of my career. *In a similar situation as at the American Red Cross, there was no prior CISO, so again, I had to build the program from scratch.* At the time, MedStar had seven hospitals under its corporate umbrella: Washington Hospital Center (WHC), National Rehabilitation Hospital, Union Memorial, Georgetown University Hospital (GUH), Franklin Square Medical Center, Harbor Hospital, and Good Samaritan Hospital (GSH). There were also over fifty physician offices and a Visiting Nurses service. Per Health Insurance Portability and Accountability Act of 1996 (HIPAA), Health Care organizations were required to have a Chief Security Officer (CSO) and a Chief Privacy Officer (CPO). For MedStar, I served as the CSO and MedStar's Associate General Counsel and served as the CPO.

MedStar had a significant information technology (IT) infrastructure. In 2009, MedStar Health was recognized as one of the nation's 100 Most Wired Hospitals and Health Systems by Hospitals & Health Networks.[1] With over 23,000 employees made up of doctors, nurses, management, and support staff, I had a team of six full-time employees including myself. Four of my staff were dedicated solely to system access control activities (Identity and Access Management – IAM). *This left only me and one security analyst to manage all other aspects of information security.*

In addition to the large number of system users, MedStar IT managed access to 250 applications and 17,000 Internet protocol (IP) addresses. Further, in the current user ID administration model, there were nine disparate directory feeder systems (e.g., Lawson Human Resource [HR], Physician Credentialing systems). These identity systems fed into Person Master, a technology

DOI: 10.1201/9781003650645-11

comprised of Tivoli Directory Integrator and Tivoli Directory Server. Person Master performed data aggregation, normalization, and assignment of unique user IDs – the Person Master ID (PMID). The access control activities were also a challenge due to our use of Lotus Notes, a robust office automation system requiring time-intensive setups for each new user.

My team serviced between 1,500 and 2,000 system access requests and changes per month. And MedStar's IAM shortcomings had been a continuing source of concern including situations where accounts that should have been terminated remained active. MedStar's IAM was transitioning to a Lotus Notes home-grown, programmed account administration program called ASAP to provision user accounts. ASAP required that we maintain a ten-day turnaround in creating new accounts and providing them access to various administrative and clinical systems. My team had to turn the requests around in two days, leaving eight days for administrators of other systems/applications to complete requests.

Other constraints in the account administration area included:

- The distributed nature of MedStar systems and applications and the various directory structures that existed throughout MedStar: Helix Domain (North), MHG Domain (South), and GUHMNT (Georgetown) and about fifteen other sub-domains for various specialty groups and applications. This was expected to be addressed by standardization on Microsoft's Active Directory but would take time to implement.
- The large number of applications across MedStar required a complex system administration model as various other groups managed system access for users.
- Cultural issues regarding user IDs. The desire was to have one unique user ID for each MedStar user. For ease of use, some physicians wanted to use their Medical transcription numbers as their IDs. The PMID was structured as three alpha characters and three numbers for a six-character ID. *This ID structure was based on the lowest common denominator for the mainframe-based Invision system, which commanded this ID construction constraint.*

Culturally, MedStar was the *wild west* with regard to cybersecurity. Since I was the first to hold the CISO-equivalent role and without previous cybersecurity focus and management oversight, there were glaring gaps in the security posture of the organization. Within a few weeks of my starting at MedStar, my security analyst resigned to take on a new position at the WHC. *Oh boy, here we go again!*

From 2006 to 2008, I issued 251 pieces of formal correspondence without clerical assistance. I changed previous serialized memo formats slightly from CISO to Director of Information System Security (DISS) to reflect my then-current title of Director of Information System Security. I also continued the numeric sequence from the following year rather than starting at .001 for each new year.

2006 > DISS-2006.001- DISS -2006.059 59 memorandums issued
2007 > DISS -2007.060- DISS -2007.190 130 memorandums issued
2008 > DISS -2008.191- DISS -2008.253 62 memorandums issued

8.2 MEMOS AND ISSUES – JULY 2006–DECEMBER 2006

Lesson Learned As I had done in other CISO positions, I took part in MedStar's weekly change control meetings – a practice that not only enhanced my understanding of the organization's IT landscape but also allowed me to assess the effectiveness and perspectives of IT leadership. Regular involvement in change control meetings is a valuable practice for CISOs in any organization, as it provides critical insight into operational risks and helps establish trust and collaboration with IT teams. By adopting this approach, security leaders can proactively address potential vulnerabilities and foster a culture of transparency across departments.

8.2.1 DISS-GEN-2006.002 Dated July 3, 2006 – Monthly Status Report for Period June 1, 2006 through June 30, 2006

This was my first status report where I identified a number of initiatives to apply to MedStar Health from my previous experiences:

- Membership in the FBI InfraGard Program (Membership cost – free)
- Antivirus Information Exchange Network – Two seats with access to the latest intelligence relating to malicious code as developed by the top AV researchers. (Membership $200 per year for the two seats)
- *New* Healthcare Information and Management Systems Society (HIMSS) – I joined HIMSS as an individual member to participate and interact with colleagues in the area of information systems and security-related matters specific to the healthcare industry. (Individual membership cost – $140 per year).
- Once again, I used free vulnerability assessment tools, including those provided by the Center for Internet Security (CIS). I conducted a baseline security assessment on my new MedStar laptop. The analysis was conducted using the CIS Next-Generation (NG) Scoring Tool Version 1.0 Build 66 dated September 7, 2005 for Windows XP Professional and the SP2 Enterprise Mobile Domain Member profile.

This status memo also identified that Chad Wilson was hired to fill the vacant Security Analyst position.

8.2.2 DISS-AUD-2006.003 Dated June 9, 2006 – External Monitoring Google Alerts

To continue cost-effective security measures, this memo outlined the use of a free Google alerting feature. I registered twenty-four critical MedStar public Internet sites and IP address ranges. Google would issue an alert if one of the sites/IP addresses were triggered from a positive search hit. The alert would be automatically delivered via daily email.

8.2.3 DISS-GEN-2006.008 Dated June 21, 2006 – Staffing Request – Security Administrators

Due to the critical nature of MedStar's IAM issues, I made this request for two additional temporary staffers for two months to help with user account administration. MedStar had been and continued to be cited by external auditors for various IAM issues such as active accounts for previously terminated employees. The CIO approved these positions, and with these temporary positions, we also assessed their performance for potential future full-time positions.

8.2.4 DISS-AUD-2006.009 (C) Dated June 30, 2006 – CIS Baseline Security Configuration for Laptop

I performed a baseline security assessment of MedStar's standard laptop configurations using the CIS (www.cisecurity.org) freeware tool:

> NG (Next Generation) Scoring Tool Version 1.0 Build 66 September 7, 2005
> Benchmark: Windows XP Professional
> Profile: SP2 Enterprise Mobile Domain Member

Our laptop's security configuration scored a 50.955 out of a possible 100. We had work to do to develop a more secure laptop configuration profile.

8.2.5 DISS-INV-2006.012 (C) Dated July 10, 2006 – MedStar Clinician Portal Hacking Incident – Follow Up

This was an incident where hackers commandeered a MedStar server located at a third-party hosting facility at a Northern Virginia datacenter. The hackers had full run of the server and uploaded 53 GB of music and pornographic video files. They also set up more services on the server – SMTP (Port 25), POP3 (Port 110), and IMAP (Port 143). Most problematic was that a Structured Query Language database instance was present on the server with 5,439 MedStar User IDs and passwords. In total, 2571 users had access to Protected Health Information (PHI) and as result of the compromise were forced to change their passwords. The hosting facility could not provide firewall logs with which to perform network forensics. *The only way this breach was discovered was that the MedStar administrator was on the system and noticed the system's sluggish performance.* I recommended that MedStar reevaluate its continued use of this hosting facility. *The system was taken offline while it was reimaged and the unauthorized files deleted.*

8.2.6 DISS-INV-2006.016 (C) Dated July 20, 2006-: Preliminary Investigation Report – InstantDX Security Breach

This was an interesting incident where a security breach occurred, causing the exposure of patient demographic data (i.e., name, address, social security number, DOB). The breach resulted from a third-party consultant's *authorized* access to an office computer while conducting system troubleshooting at a non-MedStar physician's office in the state of Indiana. The physician's office was using an application called MediSoft, an all-in-one medical office application suite used by small practices for making patient appointments, billing, prescriptions, etc. Medisoft accessed InstantDX, a web-based program used by physicians to provide patient prescriptions. The consultant was having issues with the MediSoft application and technically *opened up the hood* to see if he could fix the issue.

MedStar's GUH was engaged in a pilot program with InstantDX. Per OnCallData, the parent company of InstantDX, the product offered a convenient and secure way to write electronic prescriptions using personal computers, PDAs (Palm or PocketPCs), or any other Internet-connected device. The breach was facilitated via a file transfer protocol (ftp) access password string that was hard coded within a registry setting in the MediSoft application on the office computer. Because of the clear-text password string, the consultant executed an ftp session and gained access to a directory on the InstantDX server and to the GUH file containing the patient demographic data.

Subsequent to the disclosure/breach, the consultant posted a request for advice on an Internet list server, contacted GUH, InstantDX, and allegedly reported the matter to the FBI. He also had been contacted by Wired Magazine reporter Kevin Poulsen, who also contacted Georgetown staff. *Mr. Poulsen is a former black-hat hacker, and in June 2005, he became a senior editor for Wired News.*[2] Mr. Poulsen contacted GUH personnel about the breach, and GUH contacted me. *We were off to the races!*

Since parent company OnCallData was located in Gaithersburg, MD, my hometown, Chad Wilson and I were able to physically visit them. The individual we met with was the Senior Vice President and Chief Technology Officer, and we advised him of the issue. He said the file could not be downloaded/extracted from the server. *We could not validate this assertion, but the PHI data was disclosed, nonetheless. GUH terminated the trial of InstantDX.*[3]

Security Technology Deployment On July 24, 2006, MedStar implemented 8e6 web content filtering technology to ensure that MedStar networks and systems were being used for legitimate business purposes. Initially, two of the more impactful categories of websites that needed to be blocked were Internet Radio and Streaming Media. These web-enabled services consumed large amounts of network bandwidth. Throughout various times of the day, MedStar's network bandwidth was saturated at over 100% capacity. This saturation caused critical delays and general network slowness. Studies indicated that by blocking just these two categories, between 20% and 30% of network resources could be saved. *Despite user pushback, we noticed an immediate improvement in network responsiveness as a result of implementing the blocks.*

Lesson Learned *One of the must-have security technologies is web content filtering.* We selected 8e6 as our web content filtering technology. The system blocked internal user access to prohibited website content (e.g., pornography, gambling, Internet radio). 8e6 along with our data loss prevention (DLP) technology (discussed later) gave us outstanding visibility into Internet usage, abuse, and compliance issues, etc. 8e6 was updated on an almost daily basis with new Internet content that should be blocked. *Even with the frequent updates, users found prohibited sites that should have been blocked. In these instances, we forwarded the data to 8e6 to include in their filter updates.*

8.2.7 DISS-POL-2006.019 Dated August 3, 2006 MedStar Security & Privacy Related Policy Inventory

Per CIO request, I inventoried all Corporate, Corporate Compliance, and Information System (IS) policies on MedStar's StarPort intranet website with direct or indirect relevance to MedStar information security and privacy matters. I reviewed forty-eight policies and reported that a lot of work would be required to make existing policies consistent, meaningful, and world-class. Issues I discovered with existing policies included:

- Misspellings,
- Inconsistent dates and most content between the same policy as it resided on the Corporate versus the IS policy tree structures,
- Inconsistent numbering of policies (e.g., "CIR" versus "CRP," Security policies designated as "400" series in most instances and "500" in another),
- Inconsistent document formats such as MedStar Health Compliance team using Adobe Acrobat attachments for the policy itself, etc.

8.2.8 DISS-GEN-2006.025 Dated August 9, 2006 – BOLO – Be On the Lookout – Blackberry Exploit to Be Released on or about the Week of August 14th

Similar to the Customer Service Advisories that I sent out to American Red Cross IT and service desk staff, I initiated these B-O-L-O advisories. This one dealt with a *Blackberry* exploit to be released and first discussed at the annual DefCon hacker convention. The BOLOs were a "catchy" communication vehicle to get the word out on technical security issues.

8.2.9 DISS-POL-2006.029 Dated August 16, 2006 – Proposed Information Security Policy & Procedure Structure

I needed to quickly stand up an Information Security policy structure. I found the current suite of MedStar information security-related policies too weak in both scope and content. Also, there was no structure or hierarchy to the existing policies. Having structured, relevant, and substantive policies, procedures, guidelines, and standards is essential to building a robust and effective information security program. While there were existing MedStar policies, the overall MedStar policy development team had previously been disbanded. As to governance, I recommend that the policies, procedures, standards, guidelines, and forms developed by my team, be approved within the MedStar IS department and be published under CIO signature. The proposed structure was:

Base Number Section Number: I-CIR-IS-400 (400 designating Information Security)

- I-CIR-IS-400-*10* – Security Management (e.g., Organization, Roles & Responsibilities, Training & Awareness)
- I-CIR-IS-400-*20* – Enterprise Security (e.g., Acceptable Use, Email, Remote Access, Encryption)
- I-CIR-IS-400-*30* – Network Security (e.g., Firewalls, Web Content Filtering, Intrusion Detection)

- I-CIR-IS-400-*40* – System/Host Security (e.g., Server Security)
- I-CIR-IS-400-*50* – Application/Data Security (e.g., Data Classification, Access Controls)
- I-CIR-IS-400-*60* – Client/Endpoint Security (e.g., Mobile Computer Security, Workstation Security)

8.2.10 DISS-GEN-2006.033 (C) Dated August 30, 2006 – Information Security – Goals & Objectives

By this time, I had been at MedStar for a few months. I am sure you will agree that the Information Security team was grossly understaffed. I issued this CONFIDENTIAL memo to the CIO to identify our current state and future plans regarding our program. IAM continued to be a top priority. Prior to the CIO approval for the two temporary IAM staffers, the IAM team consisted of four including one manager and three security analysts to service staff additions, changes, and terminations for over 23,000 users across all the entities and disparate systems comprising MedStar IT system infrastructure.

To illustrate the lack of appropriate staffing levels, I queried other health care organizations to ascertain their IAM staffing levels. Children's Hospital of Philadelphia had four people servicing 9,000 users, and Sisters of Mercy estimated it had 60–70 part-time staff providing account administration for its 24,000 users. A good rule of thumb seemed to be *one* account administration staff for every 2,000–3,000 users.

My memo recommended a departmental restructure, more staff, and technology enhancements to include technologies for Enterprise Compliance Monitoring technology, Enterprise Vulnerability Management, Enterprise encryption solution for mobile storage and computer devices, and vulnerability assessment tools and services. These recommendations were met with some modicum of success as we added staff and received a budget to purchase and implement some of the technology recommendations.

8.2.11 DISS-GEN-2006.036 Dated September 25, 2006 – COMPANY Master Services Agreement – Network Security Monitoring

Not wanting to identify the company in this discussion, I will use the term COMPANY. MedStar had a cluster of six Sourcefire Intrusion Detection Systems (IDS) deployed at strategic locations throughout MedStar's network infrastructure. MedStar had a Master Services Agreement (MSA) with the COMPANY to provide managed services for the six IDS including 24 × 7 monitoring, application of patches and IDS attack signatures, and testing and customer notification of patch and signature installations.

In reviewing the MSA and the COMPANY-provided customer portal, I could find no evidence that our IDS systems were ever updated! Our Sourcefire IDS were based on the popular *Snort* technology and for which the attack signatures were updated on an almost daily basis. Also, per the MSA, the COMPANY was to provide a monthly report (by the fifth day of each month) advising the customer of configuration changes, attack reporting, and response reporting. These reports were no longer being provided to MedStar. Lastly, the COMPANY-provided customer portal showed that all six of our IDS were in a *green status, indicating they were up and operational.* In reality, one of the devices at WHC was no longer communicating with the COMPANY and they were aware of this discrepancy with their customer portal and had received many complaints from other customers. Chad and I traveled to WHC on July 19, 2006 to re-image the IDS sensor and bring it back on-line.

On September 27, 2006, I sent the COMPANY a MedStar Notification of Material Breach of Contract via U.S. Mail Certified delivery #7006 2150 0004 9287 525. Obviously, I was not willing to extend the $100,000 MSA contract and recommended that we bring this monitoring activity in-house.

8.2.12 DISS-TRP-2006.040 Dated October 2, 2006 – Trip Report – COMPANY Secure Operation Center

My memo outlined in Section 8.2.11 and my subsequent notification to the COMPANY of a MATERIAL BREACH regarding the MedStar MSA caused a lot of consternation at the COMPANY. I visited their local Secure Operation Center (SOC) where I identified *twelve deficiencies* that the COMPANY needed to address to bring our Sourcefire IDS into currency with upgrades and configurations.

8.2.13 DISS-GEN-2006.045 Dated October 17, 2006 Notice of Cancellation of Services – COMPANY

This memo identified that the COMPANY remediated only three of the twelve identified deficiencies. Based on the COMPANY's performance and MedStar's initial concerns, which dated back to July 10, 2006, MedStar has lost confidence in the COMPANY's ability to adequately maintain, monitor, and report MedStar's network security. *This letter communicated MedStar's contract cancellation with the COMPANY.*

8.2.14 DISS-AUD-2006.049 (C) Dated Date: November 1, 2006 – eCommerce Review – www.xxx.hospital.com

This was a vulnerability assessment of a MedStar-affiliated organization's website. I found the security to be SATISFACTORY. I've added this memo because of the maturation of my vulnerability assessment process and the tools I used as compared to what I used at the American Red Cross. The tools used in the assessment were: Nmap Version 3.95 (Port Scanner), Nessus Version 3.0.3 (Vulnerability Assessment Scanner), Nikto Version 1.35 (CGI Scanner), eEye Retina Network Security Scanner Version 5.5.0.1518, and Foundstone SSLDigger Version 1.0 (Secure Socket Layer Encryption Evaluation).

8.2.15 DISS-AUD-2006.059 Dated December 28, 2006–8e6 Web Content Filtering Review

We were extremely pleased with the *8e6* web content filtering technology. To audit the effectiveness of the web content filtering technology, a review of websites that harbored and distributed malicious code was conducted on December 28, 2006. We selected fifty sites identified by the *SunBeltBlog* website, an authoritative source on general malicious code issues. The fifty sites were newly discovered with most identified as recently as December 26, 2006. Except for two websites which were unavailable and no longer active, all the others were blocked by *8e6* and identified as containing either Malicious Code or Pornographic content.

Lesson Learned CISOs should periodically assess the effectiveness of their security technologies by conducting regular audits, reviewing incident reports, and benchmarking systems against industry standards. For example, schedule quarterly technology reviews and analyze patterns and gaps in incident reports. These actions will help identify deficiencies and ensure that security measures remain resilient and up to date.

8.3 MEMOS AND ISSUES – JANUARY 2007–DECEMBER 2007

Azyxxi (az-ik-see) was a medical system originally developed at MedStar's WHC by Drs. Craig Feied and Mark Smith. The two were recruited to turn around and improve the WHC Emergency Department. At the center of their revolutionary approach was to develop an information system that could radically improve the practice of emergency medicine – Azyxxi (a nonsense moniker).[4] The system was developed out of necessity when trying to treat emergencies and gathering patient data (e.g., x-rays, scans, lab tests) from disparate medical systems. Microsoft-based Azyxxi aggregated an individual patient's data – from routine visits to ultrasound images – into a single record that is quickly accessible to doctors and nurses. After several years of development beginning in 1996, Azyxxi was acquired by the Microsoft Health Solutions Group in 2006 as part of a plan to enter the fast-growing market for health care IT.[5]

With the acquisition, Microsoft changed the name of the system from Azyxxi to Amalga and brought in a small army of professionals to help with the transition. Chad Wilson and I went to several meetings with Microsoft and found working with them to be somewhat *challenging*. One example of our security approach differences with Microsoft was where patients would opt-in to the system and their health records would be packaged up on one server. Their data package would then be exported to another server, leaving the original patient data package on the original server. Chad and I saw the problem with leaving the patient's sensitive *dormant* data on the first server. A compromise of the server would be a significant data breach.

8.3.1 DISS-GEN-2007.060 Dated January 9, 2007 Azyxxi Account Transition Plan

The purpose of this memorandum was to outline the issues and recommended action plan items considered necessary for MedStar to assume responsibility for the management, maintenance, and overall provisioning for Azyxxi accounts. *Not considering that my limited identity and access management (IAM) staff had enough on their plates already.* Historically, IAM for the Azyxxi system had been the responsibility of a separate, dedicated MedStar/Azyxxi staff. Since the application had been sold to Microsoft, most of the previous, dedicated MedStar/Azyxxi staff had transitioned to the employ of Microsoft. And based on my team's limited exposure to the previous MedStar/Azyxxi account management processes and practices, I was concerned that said processes and practices did not adhere to security industry best practices.

Overall, Azyxxi account management processes and practices were not well documented. Upon request and before meetings on the topic, Azyxxi provided three pages of documentation relating to account administration. This lack of documentation would not stand up to audit scrutiny and impeded my team's learning Azyxxi account management. The challenge was one of *knowledge transfer.*

- Use of Generic User Identifiers (IDs) – previously, a review of logins to Azyxxi was conducted and revealed that a significant number of users were not logging into the application with their unique User ID. Instead, they were primarily using generic accounts or sharing another's User ID and password for convenience. This practice violated HIPAA regulations and would also affect the integrity of systems used for transactions such as those that dispense pharmaceuticals. A program to reduce/eliminate generic IDs needed to be conducted.
- Miss-assignment of User IDs – Information Security was aware that in some cases, Azyxxi User IDs had been assigned in violation of the MedStar Person Master Index ID assignment and format and

used other formats, such as the Lotus Notes ID for the Azyxxi ID. These issues resulted in confusion between system accounts such as the reuse of an ID in Azyxxi that had been assigned to another MedStar user for another system. All Azyxxi accounts needed to be validated and made to comply with Person Master Directory, a Lightweight Directory Access Protocol (LDAP-class) directory formatting.

- Deletion of Inactive/Terminated Accounts – Information Security provided a list of terminated accounts to all MedStar staff having account administration responsibilities including Azyxxi staff. These termination lists were provided on at least a bi-monthly basis, and in conversations with Azyxxi staff, there was no indication that access for terminated staff had been removed based on the lists provided. All Azyxxi accounts needed to be validated.
- Role-based Access Control – The Azyxxi application contained significant patient data, which resulted in a challenge since there was significantly more data than could be displayed on the screen at the same time. Azyxxi system usage *roles* had evolved based on *data views*. To prepare for assuming responsibility for account management, Azyxxi provided a listing of over thirty groups within the application, which accounted for 95% of the user access requirements. Resolutions were: (a) Azyxxi roles were based on Azyxxi views. Long-term re-architecting of the Azyxxi application was needed and outside the scope of this project. (b) Incorporate the current Azyxxi role groups into ASAP to facilitate account administration and meet the ten-day Service Level Agreement (SLA).

I recommended that the assimilation of the current Azyxxi (IAM) administrator required three additional full-time equivalents (FTEs) with my team to properly manage Azyxxi account administration processes and ongoing maintenance. This addition of three FTEs would let us meet the ten-day SLA for account creation and have an IAM ecosystem that would stand up to audit scrutiny. *Instead of three, I got approval for two more FTEs for my IAM team.*

Security Technology Deployment As I had done in other CISO positions, I procured a forensic workstation outfitted with investigative tools such as EnCase. This technology proved instrumental in resolving numerous security incidents swiftly and thoroughly. With its advanced capabilities, my team and I were able to collect and analyze digital evidence efficiently, which led to improved incident response times and strengthened the overall security posture of the organization.

8.3.2 DISS-AUD-2007.067 Dated February 23, 2007 – Request to Reduce Lotus Notes System Administrators

MedStar used Lotus Notes as the corporate email service, IAM, and much more. This memo identified that 105 staff across MedStar's organizations (administration, hospitals, specialty medical offices, etc.) had administrative access to Lotus Notes. With these privileges, the admins could read anyone's email. Based on previous audit experiences and training, I considered that there were too many people with these privileges. And I asked for a review to see which admins could be eliminated. *The important concept for CISOs is that administrative privileges and accounts need to be managed and reviewed with some frequency (e.g., monthly, quarterly).*

Security Technology Deployment In February 2007, we began using eEye Digital Security Retina Network Security Scanner Network Vulnerability Assessment & Remediation Management tool – Version 5.7.2.1603. Vulnerability scans were conducted during off-peak hours and with minimal intensity to reduce the risk of service disruption and ensure system stability throughout the assessment period; initial scans were started by Change Request, so all MedStar IT departments were aware of the scanning exercises. I ran external scans from my home over weekends using the lightest scan setting, prioritizing caution, and continuity. The initial scans identified several critical vulnerabilities, which were promptly addressed by the IT team, resulting in a measurable improvement in our network security posture.

8.3.3 DISS-GEN-2007.071 Dated March 14,2007 – FY08 Budget Summary

CISOs are also business managers of their departments. It is important to have a budgetary process to be good stewards of the organization's finances. I generated this budget request and asked for more staffing. For most of 2007, we had a staff of seven including me. We were approved for two more FTEs as part of the Azyxxi transition (see Section 8.3.1). And for 2008, I asked for one more FTE to monitor the new security technologies we were deploying. This would increase staffing from to ten FTEs including myself.

I also asked for an increase in technology expenditures to $636,500 made up of $565,000 – hardware and software maintenance for enterprise-wide security technologies including server hardware, Reconnex Enterprise Compliance, eEye Enterprise Vulnerability Mitigations, and various other security technology support initiatives. I also included $71,500 for consulting services.

So, the obvious question is always, *How much should be spent on security?* Many factors impact these numbers, including industry requirements, regulatory impact, and maturity of the IT and Information Security departments. According to a Gartner Research Report #G00126773 dated March 9, 2005: *In general, most organizations spend an average of between 3 percent and 6 percent of their total IT budget on security, and this is what Gartner recommends as a guideline.*

I tried to make the case that MedStar was essentially playing catch-up in many areas of IT and Information Security. Since 2008 would mark the initial formulation of the Information Security budget going forward, we would have a basis for development of an overall plan for maturation of the program supported by appropriate levels of budget. *Since we had implemented the new security technologies that aspect of the budget was approved. I failed in getting the additional security analyst. So, Chad and I were left to handle all the aspects of MedStar's information security except for IAM.*

Security Technology Deployment On March 12, 2007, we implemented our DLP technology – Reconnex. DLP refers to systems and tools designed to monitor, detect, and prevent unauthorized transmission of sensitive information outside the organization. The Reconnex devices were installed directly at the Internet entry and exit points of our network, enabling comprehensive oversight of our network traffic. Reconnex provided us with unprecedented visibility into various services, such as email and web usage, which was invaluable for monitoring compliance and detecting potential abuse. One innovative feature of Reconnex was 'skin tone analysis' – an automated process that scanned web imagery for specific color patterns associated with human skin tones. The purpose of this technology was to identify access to inappropriate or potentially illegal content, such as pornography, by flagging questionable sites and capturing relevant data like URLs, timestamps, requesting IP addresses, and expandable thumbnail images for further review.

Within the first forty-five minutes of capturing network activity, the Reconnex engineer handed me a thumb drive containing flagged "skin tone" images. As I reviewed the files, a sequence of captured images appeared to depict child pornography – a discovery that required immediate and responsible action. We notified the appropriate authorities without delay, secured and documented the evidence, and ensured the privacy of all individuals involved. These steps were taken in compliance with legal and organizational policies to safeguard both the integrity of the investigation and the rights of employees. I became an advocate for its capabilities and authored an article about the technology for SC Magazine. This deployment not only reinforced my commitment to proactive security measures but also guided our organization's future investments in similar solutions. Reflecting on this experience, I recognized how the adoption of advanced security technologies could transform incident response and strengthen the organization's security posture.

Beginning March 2007 until I left MedStar around the beginning of May 2008, Chad Wilson and I monitored our compliance technologies, chiefly *8e6* and Reconnex. I developed a bullet-proof reporting template to ensure accurate evidence collection and reporting. Based on our findings and reports, people could be fired. I wanted to ensure we developed the best evidence-backed case possible for their sake and ours. During my tenure at MedStar, I documented over 200 cases and went to court six times (see Table 8.3). The court cases occurred when the terminated employee took the case to a judge to contest their loss of unemployment benefits. *Based on our documented evidence, we never lost a case.*

The evidentiary template I developed began when Reconnex, for example, triggered on pornography and identified the internal IP address that accessed the site. We would then look up the IP address in our *Altiris* system. *Altiris*, a client management program, showed the IP address, PC name, Internal Domain, User ID, PC's operating system, etc. In the report, we included:

- A screenshot showing the *Altiris* data showing the IP address connected to the PC name and Username.
- A screenshot showing MUMS (MedStar User Management System), which showed User ID-to-specific user details – full name, employee number, employee title, location, etc.
- Screenshots showing examples of the Reconnex-captured images.
- Spreadsheets from *8e6* supporting the Reconnex image captures.

Security Technology Deployment In April 2007, I procured a copy of the WebInspect website vulnerability assessment tool by SPI Dynamics. I ran this tool from my MedStar laptop to assess the security of various MedStar websites. The tool was designed to assess and test for vulnerabilities specific to website development, construction, products, and techniques. Reports were generated to provide suggested fixes and techniques for website developers in mitigating specific vulnerabilities discovered by the tool.

8.3.4 DISS-AUD-2007.084 (C) Dated April 24, 2007 WebInspect Report – www.medstarhealth.org

I ran WebInspect against this primary MedStar website. From this website, users accessed other MedStar hospitals and offices as well as access to other services. The statistics* from the scan were:

Total attacks initiated by WebInspect scan: 7442
Total issues discovered: 1226
Critical 52 High 3 Medium 396 Low 775

8.3.5 DISS-AUD-2007.096 (C) Dated May 15, 2007 – Summary of WebInspect Security Scans

Based on the issues discovered with the website described in 8.3.4, I ran WebInspect scans on the other MedStar hospital sites linked to the medstarhealth.org website. The statistics from the scans were (Table 8.1):

As reported by running the WebInspect tool, a significant number of vulnerabilities could be exploited. This is especially troubling considering all the attacks were over Port 80 (http), which had to be open to the Internet, so the websites were generally accessible to the public.

8.3.6 DISS-AUD-2007.102 Dated May 30, 2007 – Information Security Response to Requested Audit Artifacts

Invariably, as CISO, you will take part in audits covering various topics. Auditors will ask for documentation such as lists, policies, and other artifacts to support the audit. We ran into issues where auditors asked for artifacts that we had previously provided. *To address these duplicative requests, I issued memos to document and track auditor requests for artifacts.* In a

Table 8.1 WebInspect Security Scan Statistics

Website	*Critical Issues*	*High Issues*	*Medium Issues*	*Low Issues*	*Total Issues by Site*
Medstarhealth.org	52	3	396	775	1,226
Georgetownuniversityhospital.org	46	84	1,748	1,717	3,595
Goodsam-md.org	86	81	1,695	1,678	3,540
Haborhospital.org	88	83	2,059	2,032	4,262
Franklinsquare.org	97	66	2,213	2,197	4,573
Whcenter.org	111	9	2,538	2,571	5,229
Unionmemorial.org	324	292	4,704	4,700	10,020
Totals	804	618	15,353	15,670	32,445

tabular format, I documented the description of the requested materials, the contacts responsible for providing the materials, the due date to provide the materials, and the date it was provided.

8.3.7 DISS-GEN-2007.113 Dated July 12, 2007 – Information Security Office FY08 – Goals & Objectives

This memo identified areas I wanted to achieve for the FY08 fiscal year. I considered our information security program was still immature and we would build on the initial progress of policy development, technologies, and key metrics from the previous year. Trying to get seven hospitals, over fifty offices, and over 23,000 employees on the same page of music is like *herding cats* as they say. I had noticed that the hospitals were extremely competitive with each trying to outdo the others in the various corporate metrics.

To advance information security across MedStar and considering the competitive nature of the MedStar hospital systems, I endeavored to develop a Certification of Excellence in Security Program across the hospitals. The program would consist of three levels with the most basic level to include metrics that validated basic technology deployments (e.g., laptop encryption deployments, eEye installations) at the hospitals and all appropriate MedStar entities. Basic, Achievement, and Excellence levels of compliance would identify hospital maturity levels. *Unfortunately, due to politics, nothing ever came of this proposed program.*

Security Technology Deployment Another security technology product we procured was eEye by eEye Digital Security. This technology was an end-point security and vulnerability management software solution. Each PC/server on the network was to have an agent, *Blink*, installed to communicate back to the eEye management console. We had initially bought 15,000 *Blink* agents. The technology would give us visibility into the security posture of each computer with a *Blink* agent installed.

8.3.8 DISS-AUD-2007.116 Dated July 19, 2007 – MedStar Internal Audit of Good Samaritan Hospital Azyxxi Usage

Only a couple of months after my team assuming responsibility for Azyxxi system access, MedStar internal audit reviewed the Azyxxi system used by Emergency Services Department at MedStar's GSH. Not surprising, their first finding identified that most of the Azyxxi passwords and log-on IDs used in the GSH Emergency Services Department were shared. For example, for one patient's visit, 90% (57/63) of the log-on IDs that accessed the file were shared. This same application was used at the other Emergency Services Departments within MedStar Health. Internal Audit recommended that Information Security and Clinical Systems Development strengthen controls involving Azyxxi passwords and log-on IDs so that each person accessing a medical record can be easily identified on the already existing access logs.

I agreed with the finding and recommendation. HIPAA Section 164.3 12(d) required the assignment of a unique user ID for identity and tracking purposes. The CPO and I put together Health Information Privacy and Security Week messages to the entirety of MedStar. On April 10, 2007, we sent out Health Information Privacy and Security Week – "Keeping It Personal – Health Information You Can Trust" – Creating and Maintaining Effective Passwords. Also, I recognized there needed to be an enterprise-wide change in culture regarding sharing of user credentials and implementation of new technologies to ease the user's burden regarding system logons (e.g., single sign-on, RFID badges).

8.3.9 DISS-POL-2007.121 Dated August 8, 2007 – New Information Security Policies

Policy development continued. This memo identified the following new policies that were reviewed by MedStar legal counsel and ready to be published on MedStar's StarPort internal corporate website:

- *Acceptable Use of IT* – This policy defined acceptable use of MedStar IT resources (e.g., computer systems and networks). Specific examples and guidelines of acceptable and prohibited uses were identified.
- *Logon Banner Policy* – Defined the policy for user notification at the time of logon. The logon banner identified abbreviated terms and conditions associated with the use of the system, including MedStar Health's ownership of the system, adherence to MedStar policies associated with system use, that the system is subject to monitoring, etc. Included in the policy was recommended logon banner text for internal systems.
- *Mobile Computer Security* – Policy defined security aspects associated with use of mobile computer devices including roles and responsibilities and technical and administrative safeguards.
- *System Access Rights Policy* – Identified that users of MedStar systems were to be limited in their access to systems/data based on their roles (Role-Based Access Control) and for the expressed purpose of conducting MedStar business (Purpose-Based Access Control). Users were to request access via the appropriate MedStar system request form as approved by their supervisors and report any anomalies or changes in their status that would affect their system access.

- *User Agreement – External Users of Selected Systems* – A form that identified terms and conditions associated with their use of MedStar systems and data. MedStar legal counsel recommended that external users click an accept button upon each logon.

  While these policies may seem basic, remember that I was building the program from scratch!

8.3.10 DISS-INV-2007.147 (C) Dated September 30, 2007 – Summary of Investigations/Incidents Report – September 30, 2007

With the increased visibility we now had into MedStar systems and network usage, the number of investigations we conducted increased significantly. I was spending a great deal of time on these issues and developed these summary reports for the CIO (Table 8.2).

Table 8.2 2006/2007 Investigation/Incident Summary Metrics

Subject	*December 2006–February 2007*	*March 2007*	*April 2007*	*May 2007*	*June 2007*	*July 2007*	*August 2007*	*September 2007*	*Totals*
Email abuse/issue	67		3	1			7	8	86
Internet abuse/issue		3	3	3	1	1	2	5	18
HIPAA & privacy issues			7				1	2	10
Lost/stolen media/computers					1	4			5
Legal support			2		1				3
Forensic analysis		1	1				1*		2
Others			1	1			1	2	5
Totals	67	4	17	5	3	5	11	17	129

* Not counted – Forensic analysis requested by CPO as part of the June stolen/missing device incident at WHC

The summary report also provided details about each investigation, including Source of investigation, Date, Description, Systems involved, and Status of the investigation.

8.4 MEMOS AND ISSUES – JANUARY 2008–MAY 2008

Hospital Merger. On February 1, 2008, Montgomery General Hospital located in Olney, MD merged with MedStar Health, adding another hospital under our security purview.

8.4.1 Interesting Cases

The following are a few cases that were above and beyond typical cases of systems and network misuse. In the two years at MedStar, we conducted and documented over 200 investigations, and I testified in court six times. Before I arrived at MedStar, there was little to no visibility into system and network usage. As you read, monitoring our security technologies, and conducting investigations had become an almost full-time job. *Too much for just the two of us to handle.*

8.4.1.1 One Memo for an Incident that I Did Not Save Was Due to the High Volume of Evidence

I called the case; *The officer is not a gentleman.* Again, Reconnex tipped us off to pornographic image access. We investigated the matter which involved the lead physical security officer at one of MedStar's regional hospitals. To assist with investigations, it helped that we had system administration (i.e., root) access into the individual's MedStar PC. We connected to the PC and perused the internal files. Much to our surprise, we discovered the individual had over 1,100 pornographic images stored on his MedStar PC. Many images were of the officer himself engaged in sexual activities. *One series of photos was of him having sex in the hospital's chapel!* There were so many images I requested that the HR manager review the images to determine if there were other hospital employees involved. I felt sorry for the HR manager since she got an eyeful. *Interestingly, the president of the hospital was angry with me for discovering this inappropriate behavior!* I am not sure if he had a close relationship with the officer, but he should have been embarrassed at this egregious behavior happening in *his* hospital under his very nose.

8.4.1.2 Via Reconnex, *We Again Picked Up an Internal PC at One of the Hospitals Accessing Pornographic Materials*

We investigated and dug into the offending PC with our root access privileges. The pornography site that the individual was accessing was a *pay* site requiring the user to log in with an ID and password. In investigating the user's details, we discovered that he was a system administrator for a clinical department in one of our hospitals. From his work PC, he routinely logged onto the site at various times during his shift. We advised his supervisor, and she was willing to work with us. The next time he logged onto the website, we were to call her so she could catch him in the act. As expected, one morning he logged onto the site from his isolated office. We watched him from our office fifteen miles away from the hospital and called his supervisor. She went over to his office, directly confronted him, and snatched him right off the keyboard – *game over!*

8.4.1.3 Reconnex *Caught Another System Administrator Accessing Large Quantities of Pornographic Materials*

He was located north of Baltimore and had caches of porn stashed across several different servers under his management. We identified the various files, and after pursuing the case, his employment was terminated. I used the standard evidentiary template for evidence collection, leaving no doubt about the who, what, and when committing the infraction. Most terminations caused loss of unemployment benefits as well. The administrator was a family man, and he wanted to plead his case for unemployment compensation in front of a judge. I went to the judge's office for the hearing including the administrator. Along with my evidentiary memo, I had a six-inch stack of his pornographic images printed out *many in color.* The judge took one look at the stack and rifled through a couple of pages. *He had seen enough! The case was adjudicated before it began.*

8.4.1.4 *Not All Cases Involved Pornography*

This was a time when social media was coming into its own, and *Myspace* was a player in the new phenomena. One emergency room (ER) nurse had an absenteeism problem. She called off sick again for her night shift which happened to be St. Patrick's Day. Being suspicious, her ER supervisor contacted me to see if we could find any evidence of her alleged illness. We knew that the nurse had a Myspace account, and this would help our investigation. I went onto Myspace and created an account. The next day, I searched for her name and up popped her profile's Myspace page. Not surprisingly, there were pictures of her attendance at a St. Patrick's Day party, complete with incriminating time/date stamps. From the pictures, it looked like it was a great party. The allegedly ailing nurse, beer in hand, was adorned in green clothes, shamrock tiara, and surrounded by a crowd of revelers. The St. Patrick's Day party's date and times coincided with her illness. I captured the pictures and gave them to the supervisor. *She was dismissed from MedStar employment.*

8.4.1.5 DISS-INV-2008.247 Dated April 11, 2008 – Investigation – MedStar Health Hospital – HIPAA Violation

This case began with an eyewitness complaint in which a patient was admitted to one of our hospitals. His ex-wife was a MedStar nurse at the same hospital where he was admitted. The allegation was that his medical record was inappropriately accessed, viewed, and discussed by several staff including his ex-wife. I had to enlist the aid of a mainframe administrator to run system access logs for the times in question. There were six (6) user IDs that accessed the ex-husband's patient records during the time he was in the hospital. Due to the unauthorized access, one nurse and ex-wife were both terminated. The ex-wife coerced another nurse to log onto the system to view his patient data – a HIPAA violation.

8.4.1.6 DISS-INV-2008.238 (C) Dated March 20, 2008 – Investigation Summary Analysis for Dr. X Case

It is fitting I end this chapter on MedStar with the case that *started it all* (see Section 8.3.3 *Security Technology Deployment* On March 12, 2007, when we implemented our DLP technology – Reconnex). I spent many months' worth of time and effort pursuing this case due to the nature of the child porn aspects. The physician in question, Dr. X, was not employed by MedStar. Rather, he had surgical privileges at two of our Baltimore area hospitals.

Another network technology used at MedStar was Blue Ridge (BR) Virtual Private Network (VPN) system. In initially setting up our *8e6* web content filter, the VPN network segment was not included as part of this monitoring but should have been. *When the Reconnex DLP technology was set up, the VPN segment was now included, which is how we caught Dr. X's inappropriate Internet usage.* This BR VPN solution required that users be assigned a static or specific, unchanging IP address. So, there was an undeniable connection between the user and the IP address used to access the pornography.

The BR VPN provided a secure network tunnel by which the doctor from his offsite office could access internal MedStar systems and also go out to the Internet from MedStar networks. Further, the BR VPN used a token, a physical fob-type device assigned to each VPN user. *The user must have physical possession of the token to initiate a session via the BR VPN.* The BR VPN token is a Universal Serial Bus (USB) device that must be inserted into the computer to initiate a VPN session. The user must then enter their ID to complete the approved, authenticated VPN access. In addition to the user-assigned BR VPN IP address, there was another IP address involved in every one of Dr. X's Internet sessions – *the IP address assigned at the point of origination.* In Dr. X's case, the IP address at the point of origin was from Comcast Business Network IP address space assigned to Dr. X's office.

Initially, I engaged with the FBI since child porn was involved. An FBI Special Agent from their *Innocent Images Program* came to my office, and she verified that the images were indeed child porn. I then set up *Reconnex* to capture all of Dr. X's Internet activity. At this point, the FBI brought Baltimore County Police Department (BCPD) into the case. So, I had to coordinate efforts between the FBI and BCPD. BPDC executed a search warrant for Dr. X's office and confiscated his PC for forensic analysis. BCPD found:

- 28,000 pornographic images in the *unallocated* space on the computer's hard drive, of which over 170 were deemed to be child pornography.
- The 28,000 images showed a history of accessing pornography dating back to Jan. 2006, which coincided with the creation of Dr. X's account on the computer. This PC was used by other office staff prior to Dr. X. But there was no pornographic activity found before Dr. X's account was set up on the PC. Dr. X began accessing pornography right after his account was set up.
- Dr. X tried to assert that he left his BR VPN token in his computer at all times – so it was probably the after-hours cleaning staff. This argument was countermanded by the fact that BCPD found at least six instances in which there was proximate or overlapping usage of the Internet to access pornographic materials and Dr. X using his email to send/receive email messages.

However, BCPD could not prosecute the case any further. During the regular 2007 legislative session, Maryland House Bill (HB 285) Criminal Law – Possession of Child Pornography was changed from the possession of images to now requiring proof as to the *intentional* collection and maintenance of such images. The fact that no images were found within *allocated* disk space of the hard disk drive (HDD) but were resident in *unallocated* space made the intent difficult to prove.

BCPD indicated that Dr. X ran a wipe disk of the system at the end of surfing activities, which is why no evidence was found on the HDD's assigned space. Also, BCPD could not run hash value comparisons between the captured images and those of known child pornography images from a national database since the files were in the unallocated part of the hard drive and were not entirely intact to the level required to make this type of comparison. Federal Law Enforcement could prosecute for files in *unallocated* space provided the evidence supports their criteria/thresholds, which this case did not.

Where did we go from here? Each of MedStar's hospitals had a Vice President of Medical Affairs (VPMA). A meeting was set up, which was attended by the presidents of the two hospitals in which D. X had surgical privileges, the two hospital VPMAs, MedStar Deputy General Counsel, MedStar Sr. Corporate Counsel, BCPD and me. *It was now up to people above my pay grade to make further decisions about Dr. X's future. I left MedStar before I learned of any actions taken against Dr. X.*

Table 8.3 2006/2008 Investigation/Incident Summary Metrics

Subject	*Carryover 2006/2007*	*Jan 2008*	*Feb 2008*	*March 2008*	*April 2008*	*May 2008*	*June 2008*	*Aggregate Totals*
Email abuse/issue	96	4	3		3			106
Internet abuse/issue	30	3	2	4	1			40
HIPAA & privacy issues	14	2	2		1			19
Lost/stolen media/computers	8	1	2	2				13
HR/legal/compliance support	8			4				12
Forensic analysis	2			1	2			5
Others	5		1					6
Totals	163	10	10	11	7			201

8.5 TIME TO GO

Above is the last summary table of the incidents/investigations I documented during my three-year tenure at MedStar. As I indicated, I conducted over 200 cases and went to court six times.

Having to build a security plan from the ground up, I needed to quickly gain visibility into the network, servers, and desktops. At MedStar, we began with *8e6* web content filtering, *Reconnex* DLP, and at the server and desktop level *eEye security*. While the technologies were effective, we were quickly overwhelmed by monitoring these systems and then investigating and documenting the cases. This was due largely to a lack of resources. Having only two people handling all of MedStar's cybersecurity other than IAM was ludicrous. It was time to move onto my next and final CISO role – AMTRAK.

> *Lesson Learned* Simply deploying security monitoring technologies is not enough; you must actively monitor and analyze their output to uncover potential issues. Regularly review alerts and logs generated by your security systems to ensure you are aware of unusual activity and can respond promptly.

From 2004 to 2011, I authored several articles for SC Magazine. The articles were written from a CISO's perspective on various information security-relevant topics [6]

AWARD March 2008 – DISS, MedStar Health Information Systems – Ron Baklarz received CSO Magazine's 2008 Compass Award. – "The Complete CISO"[7] I was honored to receive the award and the magazine wrote the following:

> In his 20-plus years in the information security field, Ron Baklarz (CISSP, CISA, CISM, IAM, IEM) has developed information security programs for the Naval Nuclear Program, the U.S. House of Representatives, the American Red Cross and MedStar Health, where he is currently the HIPAA Security Officer. He has also led incident-response and monitoring teams for a variety of industries, including government, insurance, health care and Big Five consulting firms.[8]

8.6 ALL STAR – MEDSTAR HEALTH

8.6.1 I Do Not Want to Dismiss the Work of the Individuals Who Managed Our Identity and Access Management (IAM) Work under the Leadership of Lee Josleyn

They worked tirelessly in adding new users to systems and ensuring existing users had access to the administrative and clinical systems. This team was often unfairly maligned by management – but I salute your work.

8.6.2 Chad Wilson Was a Godsend after My Original Security Analyst Left Shortly after I Was Hired at MedStar

Chad, a former Marine, was technically astute and a quick study. As we jumped from case to case, battling internal and external enemies, we likened ourselves to *Batman and Robin*. Chad filled in for me as CISO when I left MedStar, and he became a successful CISO for several health and hospital systems. Chad, I salute your service to our country and appreciate the time we worked side-by-side.

8.7 TECHNOLOGY ADVANCEMENTS AND SECURITY DEVELOPMENTS 2006–2008

2006

- Amazon.com opened Amazon Web Services as a subsidiary of Amazon that provides on-demand cloud computing platforms.
- Ethereal changed its name to Wireshark because of trademark issues. Wireshark is a free and open-source network packet analyzer.
- Development of Stuxnet is presumed to have started between 2005 and 2006. Malicious computer worm, Stuxnet was programmed to target supervisory control and data acquisition (SCADA) systems.
- October 9th, Google announced plans to purchase YouTube for $1.65 billion.
- October 24th, Microsoft released Windows Defender.

2007

- January 17th Storm Worm identified as a fast-spreading email spamming threat to Microsoft systems. The Storm Worm began attacking thousands of computers using an e-mail message with a subject line about a recent weather disaster.
- Popular file hosting service Dropbox was founded by Drew Houston.
- June 29th, Apple released the Apple iPhone to the public.
- July, Zeus is identified. Zeus is a Trojan horse malware that targets Microsoft Windows and programmed to steal banking information by keystroke logging.
- November 5th, Google released Android mobile phone that operates on the Android operating system.

2008

- September 29th, computer scientist Leonard Kleinrock was awarded the National Medal of Science for his contributions to packet switching, Advanced Research Projects Agency Network, and developing the Internet.
- November 12th, USB 3.0 was released allowing USB data transfer rates up to five Gbps.

NOTES

1 MedStar Health. (n.d.). *MedStar Health history*. https://www.medstarhealth.org/about/medstar-health-history
2 Poulsen, K. (n.d.). *Kevin Poulsen. Wikipedia*. https://en.wikipedia.org/wiki/Kevin_Poulsen

3 Zetter, K. (2006, July 20). *E-health gaffe exposes hospital data. Wired.* https://www.wired.com/2006/07/e-health-gaffe-exposes-hospital/
4 Shutdown Hook. (2023, March 22). *Looking back at Azyxxi → Amalga.* https://shutdownhook.com/2023/03/22/looking-back-at-azyxxi-er-amalga/
5 Microsoft Amalga. (n.d.). *Wikipedia.* https://en.wikipedia.org/wiki/Microsoft_Amalga
6 *Ron Baklarz MedStar Health CISO.* https://www.scworld.com/contributor/ron-baklarz
7 CSO Online. (2008). *IT careers: Leadership lessons—CSO Compass Awards 2008.* https://www.csoonline.com/article/521652/it-careers-leadership-lessons-cso-compass-awards-2008.html
8 CSO Online. (2008). *IT careers: Leadership lessons—CSO Compass Awards 2008.* https://www.csoonline.com/article/521652/it-careers-leadership-lessons-cso-compass-awards-2008.html

Chapter 9

The National Passenger Railroad – Amtrak 2008–2017

Positions Held: Chief Information Security Officer
Senior Director Information Security
Export Control Compliance Officer
Amtrak Designated Approval Authority (DAA)
Location: 10 G Street, N.E.
6E-606
Washington DC 20002

9.1 AMTRAK – OVERVIEW

The National Railroad Passenger Corporation, otherwise known as Amtrak, was founded in 1971 as a government-owned, quasi-public corporation to operate many U.S. passenger rail routes. Amtrak operates inter-city rail service in 46 of the 48 contiguous U.S. states and three Canadian provinces. Amtrak's network includes over 500 stations along 21,400 miles (34,000 km) of track. It directly owns approximately 623 miles (1,003 km) of this track and operates an additional 132 miles of track; the remaining mileage is over rail lines owned by other railroad companies. While most track speeds are limited to 79 mph (127 km/h) or less, several lines have been upgraded to support top speeds of 110 mph (180 km/h), and parts of the Northeast Corridor support top speeds of 160 mph (260 km/h).[1] (See Appendix D for a map of Amtrak's nationwide network system.)

As with my previous organizational experiences, Amtrak was a complex amalgamation of information technology systems supporting the diverse needs of the company. Finance, human resources, marketing, train operations, police force, etc., all played in a sandbox of networks and systems. Initially, my primary focus at Amtrak was Payment Card Industry – Data Security Standard (PCI-DSS) compliance – more on this later. My initial team consisted of ten total personnel including me. Six staff were located in the 10 G Street, Washington DC office and four were in the Philadelphia 30th Street Station office. Functionally, duties between the two offices were split: Operations (technical security) were handled by the Washington DC

 DOI: 10.1201/9781003650645-12

team and Administrative security (e.g., compliance, audit support, and RSA tokens) was handled by the Philadelphia 30th Street Station team. Amtrak had computer operations hosted by IBM in its Manassas, Virginia data center. As part of this outsourcing contract, there were two mid-range computer systems and one mainframe.

Culturally, Amtrak was primarily focused on train operations as it should have been. I was the first to hold the CISO position, but prior to my arrival, Frank King did an exemplary job of keeping cybersecurity on *track*. Frank and the team had been shuffled around under various reporting structures until finally settling within the CIO organization. The Chief Information Officer (CIO), Ed Trainor, was a demanding boss. He would ask probing and thoughtful questions. *He kept us on our toes, and you had better be prepared when meeting with him.* Ed would be the first of four CIOs I served under during my nine years at Amtrak.

From 2008 to 2017, I issued 399 formal correspondences without clerical assistance:

- 2008 > CISO-2008.001 – CISO-2008.024 24 memorandums issued
- 2009 > CISO-2009.025 – CISO-2009.030 6 memorandums issued
- 2010 > CISO-2010.031 – CISO-2010.034 4 memorandums issued
- 2011 > CISO-2011.035 – CISO-2011.053 18 memorandums issued
- 2012 > CISO-2012.054 – CISO-2012.088 36 memorandums issued
- 2013 > CISO-2013.089 – CISO-2013.133 47 memorandums issued
- 2014 > CISO-2014.134 – CISO-2014.197 63 memorandums issued
- 2015 > CISO-2015.198 – CISO-2015.262 66 memorandums issued
- 2016 > CISO-2016.263 – CISO-2016.351 91 memorandums issued
- 2017 > CISO-2017.352 – CISO-2016.362 44 memorandums issued

As I had previously done, if the information in the original memo contained sensitive information, the memorandum was marked top and bottom of each page with CONFIDENTIAL. In these cases, I added a (C) to the letter's serial number within the Excel letter log for easy identification of sensitive correspondence. In writing about CONFIDENTIAL memos in this chapter, no sensitive information is disclosed due to content sanitization, technical obsolescence, and the passage of time. Readers will notice that there are gaps in the total of possible yearly numbers versus the actual number of memos that were issued. In these cases, I likely just missed issuing memos in precise sequential numbering while in the heat of battle.

9.2 PAYMENT CARD INDUSTRY – DATA SECURITY STANDARD (PCI-DSS)

Readers will also notice the number of memo's issued increased from earlier to later years. This was due to my focus on PCI-DSS compliance. Under

PCI-DSS, Amtrak was designated as a Level 1 Merchant. At this level, the company processed over 6 million credit card transactions per year and had to comply with the most stringent requirements of the standard. Since Amtrak was not PCI-DSS compliant, we were being assessed with a monthly fine. These fines were scheduled to increase significantly if we did not meet compliance requirements. So, I was tasked to have a compliant PCI-DSS Report on Compliance (ROC) within an eighteen month timeframe.

Also, as a Level 1 Merchant, we had to have our ROC certified by a Visa-Qualified Security Assessor (QSA). Our QSA, Trustwave, assisted us in ensuring our program met the high-level control objectives of the PCI DSS. Just prior to my arrival, Trustwave conducted a preliminary ROC dated April 25, 2008. *The Executive Summary of the 103-page report showed that Amtrak was only compliant with one of twelve sections of the PCI-DSS!* Over the next eighteen months, we had to essentially build the entire program from the ground up, including PCI-compliant people, processes, and technologies. *This was the most aggressive and comprehensive information security-related project I had been involved with in my career.*

I had weekly PCI status meetings with my CIO and Amtrak's Chief Financial Officer (CFO). We started off slowly but picked up momentum to achieve compliance in time to meet the eighteen-month finish line. Over the years, maintaining PCI compliance required a significant amount of my and my team's time and effort.

9.3 SHADOW IT (INFORMATION TECHNOLOGY)

In discussing an overview of Amtrak's IT situation, it is worth mentioning *Shadow IT*. Shadow IT occurs when departments within an organization have separate, unofficial IT departments. These departments operate and manage their own IT-related resources, including hardware, software, and cloud services. These technologies and services often run on the organization's enterprise network without a direct reporting line to the CIO including controls and oversight of the organization's *official* IT and IT Security departments. We had several Shadow IT shops within Amtrak. I am not faulting Amtrak's lines of business for setting up these shops. They did this out of necessity and distrust of the *official* IT department. Our train operations were an example of Shadow IT. They ran the Supervisory Control and Data Acquisition (SCADA) systems and all operational equipment that made the trains run. There's no way they would trust Amtrak's IT department to own and operate these systems – nor should they.

However, there are several obvious organizational problems with Shadow IT. For CISOs, system and network security is challenging in dealing with Shadow IT. Shadow IT staff know their technology environments well and do not always want to adhere to information security best practices. I made the best strides with our SCADA Shadow IT team when I provided a dedicated security analyst to work with them. Kim Sanders on my team was a technical whizz and quick study. She integrated with them seamlessly, and they grew to trust her implicitly. In other cases where the departmental systems are not as complex or sophisticated as SCADA, CIOs typically want to fold them into the overall IT organization.

Lesson Learned As CISO, make sure you are aware of any situations involving Shadow IT in your organization. Understand their IT environments and establish a partnership with them. *Be patient!*

9.4 ASSOCIATION OF AMERICAN RAILROADS RAIL INDUSTRY SECURITY COMMITTEE

Headquartered in Washington DC, the Association of American Railroads (AAR) is an industry trade group primarily representing the major freight railroads of North America (Canada, Mexico, and the United States) and includes Amtrak and some regional commuter railroads. The AAR represents its members' interests to the public at large and to Congress and government regulators. The AAR works to improve the efficiency, safety, and service of the railroad industry, such as through its responsibility for the industry's interchange rules and equipment specifications, for example, for locomotive multiple unit control.[2]

Long before I arrived at Amtrak, an AAR subgroup dedicated to cybersecurity had been established. This group was known as the Rail Industry Security Committee (RISC) and since Amtrak was a full member of the AAR, we were part of RISC as well. The RISC membership had representatives from each of the Class 1 Freight Railroads – Union Pacific (UP), Norfolk Southern (NS), CSX, Burlington Northern Santa Fe (BNSF), and Canadian National Railway. All RISC members were very professional and knowledgeable about rail industry security. The freight railroads do not haul people, and Amtrak does not haul freight. So, we had different security issues, such as PCI-DSS compliance. At any rate, the RISC group was a great information-sharing resource where we had face-to-face meetings once or twice a year and group conference calls at regular intervals.

9.5 MEMOS AND ISSUES – MAY 2008–DECEMBER 2008

During the first six months of my tenure at Amtrak, I was gaining my footing and by understanding the organizational culture and key players. I issued twenty-four memos and conducted no investigations.

9.5.1 CISO-POL-2008.013 Dated July 8, 2008 – Data Classification Levels

PCI-DSS required that we have a Data Classification Policy. Previous attempts at such a policy identified three levels of classification from the least to most sensitive categories: PUBLIC, SENSITIVE, and RESTRICTED. In January 2008, Amtrak legal counsel developed an alternative DRAFT Data Classification Policy and *proposed only two levels of classification: CONFIDENTIAL and HIGHLY CONFIDENTIAL.*

There was a stalemate regarding moving forward with either version as an official Amtrak data classification policy. Consensus seemed to favor the policy with the three levels of classification over the other version with only two levels. This preference for the latter version was due to the need for a category of information that better addressed security around credit card data. Credit card data was classified in the two-category version in the more liberal, CONFIDENTIAL category, which did not meet Payment Card Industry (PCI) security standards for logging, disclosure, transmission, and storage limitations. Credit card data in the three-category version was categorized as RESTRICTED, the most restrictive category, and met PCI standards.

Based on industry best practices, I proposed these four data classification categories:

- PUBLIC data is considered general Amtrak information that has been approved to be released to the public with no constraints: train schedules, marketing information, etc.
- PROPRIETARY data is considered internal data and can also be classified as For Official Use Only. PROPRIETARY data is not suited for public release but also does not apply to the more restrictive categories. Examples of PROPRIETARY data included train manifests and Amtrak email.
- CONFIDENTIAL is considered personal information or PII (Personally Identifiable Information) relating to Amtrak employees and customers. Examples of data within the CONFIDENTIAL category included data covered under HIPAA, GLBA, California S.B. 1386, and PCI-DSS standards and regulations.
- RESTRICTED data is considered Protected Critical Infrastructure Information or Amtrak business-critical information, such as any data relating to credit cards, SCADA systems, network diagrams, and information systems architectures.

Lesson Learned CISOs will inevitably face the challenge of developing effective data classification categories and policies. Data classification policies are foundational for establishing protection schemes and document retention practices. Involving your legal department early is crucial – they can identify and help interpret regulatory requirements such as General Data Protection Regulation or HIPAA that must be incorporated into your data classification framework. By clearly defining data categories, organizations ensure that sensitive information receives the proper security controls and is retained or disposed of according to both internal guidelines and legal mandates.

9.5.2 CISO-AUD-2008.022 Dated August 15, 2008 – Password Review

This audit was in response to a commitment I made to Amtrak's Office of Inspector General (OIG) to run password-cracking exercises on Amtrak systems. For this exercise, I used *John the Ripper* version 1.7.2 and ran it against one of Amtrak's Domain Controllers. *John the Ripper* is an Open-Source password security auditing and password recovery tool available for many operating systems (OS). The results were:

- 26,711 total accounts were identified in the file extraction from the Domain Controller.
- 14,506 accounts were compromised.

John the Ripper verified that *password complexity controls* were not implemented on Amtrak's Active Directory (AD) Domain Controllers. Some examples of non-compliance with password standards disclosed as part of the exercise included accounts with:

- Eight accounts had a single number as a password
- 519 had passwords only made up of numbers
- Thirty-five accounts had the word *password* as the password.
- A high number of machine accounts with the password set with the account's ID or account name.

Obviously, we had a lot of work to do regarding Amtrak passwords.

Security Initiative I developed a relationship with SeNet, a security company with Gus Fritschie as my primary contact. Each year during my tenure, Gus and his team performed rigorous system vulnerability testing for us. Annually, I allocated budget for SeNet's work, and together we established a schedule targeting timely and relevant cybersecurity issues. Thanks to SeNet's annual testing, we identified and remediated critical vulnerabilities – significantly reducing our risk profile and enhancing overall system security. The scope of our testing evolved to address the most pressing threats: one year, we prioritized phishing simulations to educate staff and measure susceptibility, while another year was devoted to penetration testing of our industrial control systems (ICS). By varying our focus and responding to emerging risks, we ensured that Amtrak's cybersecurity defenses remained proactive and robust.

9.6 MEMOS AND ISSUES – JANUARY 2009–DECEMBER 2009

2009 was another lean year in issuing memos. I only authored six memos and conducted two investigations. I was still deeply involved with building our PCI-DSS compliance program.

Security Event Amtrak's Office of Security Strategy and Special Operations (OSSSO) was a department made up of elite former counterterrorism personnel. The OSSSO team collaborated closely with the U.S. Department of Homeland Security (DHS) as well as other federal and law enforcement agencies. Their work was vital, particularly in developing security plans for high-profile Amtrak events. One memorable example of their work occurred on January 17, 2009, when President-elect Barack Obama traveled to Washington DC by Amtrak, riding in the historic Pullman Georgia 300 railcar. This journey was a re-enactment of President Abraham Lincoln's own whistle-stop tour in 1861. For this occasion, OSSSO staff meticulously examined train station schematics. They also carefully planned the physical security along the president-elect's route, ensuring every detail was considered in advance.

9.6.1 CISO-AUD-2009.026 Dated January 8, 2009 – Supervisory Control and Data Acquisition Security

In November 2008, the SeNet team assessed our SCADA systems. Our SCADA systems were critical for train operations and SCADA systems were attractive targets for hackers. SeNet's audit included interviews and network perimeter and host-based security assessments. As part of the report, I identified that my team was pursuing the purchase of a SCADA-specific security vulnerability assessment tool. The tool was relatively inexpensive and would scan the systems for SCADA-specific vulnerabilities. SeNet also recommended we investigate procuring and deploying an Intrusion Detection System to further monitor and protect SCADA networks.

OSSSO had a large government grant coming and for planning purposes, OSSSO asked for relevant departments to make funding requests for projects. I submitted a request for purchasing and installing an IDS on our SCADA networks. *Unfortunately, we were denied fu nding for this project.*

Security Event According to a Real Clear Politics article published on October 20, 2014, by Michelle Malkin,

> In 2009, the Obama administration quietly gutted the nation's most highly trained post-9/11 counterterrorism rail security team, Amtrak's Office of Security Strategy and Special Operations (OSSSO). The elite unit – whose members came from U.S. Special Forces, counterterrorism and other military service – was disbanded in a power play with powerful labor leaders angered over its non-union status.

All of the Special Agents of OSSSO were issued impact letters stating that their jobs were being abolished and organizationally realigned under and assimilated within the uniformed Amtrak Police Department (APD).[3]" Some officials argued that folding OSSSO into the APD would improve operational coordination and reduce administrative silos, while critics maintained that the move compromised specialized counterterrorism expertise and ultimately weakened rail security by dissolving an elite, focused unit."

Technology Background *Amtrak's Arrow Reservation System.* The Evolution of Amtrak's Arrow Reservation System: A Chronological Perspective Early Years and Initial Launch (1981). In the early years, Amtrak's Arrow Reservation System was considered one of the organization's most critical assets, central to customer reservations and ticketing nationwide. Arrow was developed in-house to support operations across the 20,000-plus miles of the Amtrak network. The backbone of Arrow was TPF (Transaction Processing Facility), a specialized mainframe OS designed for high-volume transaction processing in industries like airlines, railways, and banking. TPF was programmed in the assembler language, a low-level and complex programming language that directly manipulates hardware operations for maximum speed.

Arrow's initial release into production occurred on November 1, 1981. Unfortunately, the timing was less than ideal – right before the busiest travel period of the year – the holiday season. The launch was plagued with significant issues: the new system would not sell tickets on nearly empty trains, it double-booked 5,700 sleeping cars, and staff had not been adequately trained. These operational challenges led to customer frustration, lost revenue, and confusion among Amtrak employees. The fallout from this rocky deployment had lasting effects on business practices. To prevent similar crises, Amtrak instituted an annual IT system freeze during November and December, prohibiting any system changes – including security patching – during these critical months. This lesson underscored the importance of thorough user training, staged deployments, and the risks of implementing major IT changes during peak operational periods.

Gradual Improvements and Major Upgrades (2011–2012) Decades later, Arrow was incrementally enhanced to meet evolving business needs and technology standards. During the 2011–2012 period, Amtrak undertook a significant upgrade: the TPF mainframe OS was updated to z/TPF – a modern version that supports enhanced features such as encryption and Transmission Control Protocol/Internet Protocol (TCP/IP) networking. The adoption of z/TPF was particularly exciting because it enabled encryption, an essential capability for protecting sensitive data. Arrow handled substantial amounts of credit card information but operated under a dispensation regarding PCI-DSS (Payment Card Industry Data Security Standard) requirements, which set forth strict controls for the secure handling of credit card data. Traditionally, TPF systems did not store data in a structured relational database, for example; instead, information was embedded in long, unintelligible strings, making extraction and viewing of specific data – like credit card numbers – challenging. The upgrade to z/TPF paved the way for encryption of credit card data, which was a critical step toward full PCI-DSS compliance and greater overall system security.

9.6.2 CISO-INV-2009.028 Dated October 5, 2009 – Investigation – Failure to Identify IBM Help Desk Staff Terminations

Due to the sensitivity and financial impacts, Arrow was subject to our annual financial audit conducted by KPMG. In response to previous audits, we established a quarterly review of Arrow administrative accounts. These accounts had escalated privileges on the Arrow system. During their audit, KPMG discovered that three IBM Help Desk employees were no longer on our account, although their Arrow accounts were still active on the system. *This was unacceptable!*

This was the second year in a row in which active mainframe accounts for inactive IBM staff had been found as part of the KPMG audit. My investigation found that IBM did not follow previously established procedures, where they were to submit a notice of termination form for IBM employees leaving the account. This memo established more checks and balances to make sure this infraction did not reoccur.

9.6.3 CISO-POL-2009.029 Dated October 13, 2009 – Automated Track Inspection Program

This memorandum provided a position relative to AAR request regarding Federal Railroad Administration's (FRA) desire to make public its highly accurate spatial rail network data (1:10,000) that is generated from the FRA's Automated Track Inspection Program (ATIP) data.[4]

FRA had been collecting data for many years from several geometry cars recording the latitude and longitude of every foot of the rail network. The current contractor running the geometry cars claimed that about 90% of the mainline track had been collected, where 65% is +/–1 m. I saw two issues with putting this precise location data in the public domain: (1) the data would originate from an authoritative source, and (2) it was to be precise (i.e., +/–1 m) when compared to similar data obtained from other public Internet sources at the time. Considering terrorist activities, I was concerned that location data this precise, coupled with dignitary travel, hazardous materials, etc., over rail, may provide an opportunity for attacks. *Rather, I recommended that access to ATIP data be controlled and limited to those with a need-to-know.*

9.7 MEMOS AND ISSUES – JANUARY 2010–DECEMBER 2010

The year 2010 was another slow year relative to my issuing memos. I only issued four memos since I was still embroiled in building our PCI-DSS program. I moved from my broom closet office in the bottom of the building to a corner office on the sixth floor. This office had a birds-eye view of the side of Union Station and a Government Printing Office building.

9.7.1 As I Had Done in My Previous CISO Positions, I Purchased a Forensic Workstation with Encase Software

Due to the system and network security tools we had at our disposal, there was little need for the detailed investigations I had done in other organizations. Still, I felt more comfortable having this capability in my back pocket.

9.7.2 There Was a Great Deal of Emphasis on Supervisory Control and Data Acquisition Security, and My Team Had Little Expertise in This Area

To rectify this shortfall, I secured funding and enrolled my entire team in a SCADA security certification program. This was an effective program where the online training consisted of modules we could study remotely as time and schedules allowed. There was testing and a final certification exam. *Once completed, our team would now have a solid understanding of SCADA security.*

9.7.3 Other Duties as Assigned

Somewhere along the line, I picked up the title of Export Control Compliance Officer. The role and function were originally handled by Amtrak Human Resources (HR). Since Amtrak's IT department had the majority of staff with H-1B Visas, I was the logical choice to handle this duty for the entire company. "The H-1B program applies to employers seeking to hire nonimmigrant aliens as workers in specialty occupations or as fashion models of distinguished merit and ability."[5]

Effective December 22, 2010, the U.S. Department of Commerce Export Administration Regulations (EAR) and the U.S. Department of State International Traffic in Arms Regulations (ITAR) require U.S. persons to seek and receive authorization from the U.S. government before releasing to foreign persons in the United States controlled technology or technical data. *Under both the EAR and the ITAR, release of controlled technology or technical data to foreign persons in the United States, even by an employer-is deemed to be an export (i.e., "deemed export") to the person's country or countries of nationality.* One implication of this rule is that a U.S. company must seek and receive a license from the U.S. Government before it releases controlled technology or technical data to its nonimmigrant workers employed as H-1B, L-1 or O-1A beneficiaries. *In other words, if I had a document with controlled technical data in my hand and passed it to an employee or contractor with an H-1B Visa, this was considered to be an export.*

Over the next few years, I issued thirty-two memos regarding Amtrak employees and contractors holding H-1B Visas. Basically, I kept a spreadsheet with H-1B Visa holders and their H-1B Visa expiration dates. Where the individual had access to Amtrak IT systems, I validated that the information contained in or otherwise processed by the system in which they had access was not considered *controlled*. My form was signed by the H-1B VISA holder's supervisor. I had only one case that was questionable. *The individual was from a country the U.S. considered adversarial, and he would have access to sensitive train engineering measurement equipment and systems. I would not personally approve the request and kicked it up to Amtrak's legal team. This one was above my pay grade.*

9.7.4 CISO-INV-2010.031 Dated March 10, 2010 – OIG Referral dated March 2, 2010

Amtrak's OIG maintained a complaint line by which internal Amtrak and external sources could lodge complaints. This incident concerned exposed social security numbers (SSNs). This issue was access to a data file versus a system application issue. Through investigation, Information Security isolated a link for a departmentally maintained folder that was available on network-attached storage (NAS).

Payment Card Insdustry Data Security Standards (PCI-DSS) Team

Information Technology and Finance, Washington, D.C

The three members of the Payment Card Industry Dara Security St'standards (PCI-DSS) team angs vere for able for bringing Amtrak into comply with new credit card reguistions regarding payment card security stacs.

Amirak served as a "'Level 1 Merchant'" by credit card cand companiats in 2000 based on the pontyidy of deft tor id.and credit card payments that it it accepts each way for pavenger lickers and roed and bavesage requrnies Wlct in cross organizational team was laid to be recognized. Theirvaiditional was labelled an arris reporting.

The leam established slx project plan to achieve PCI-DSS compliance and earm PCI-DSS compliance and earned Level 1 Certification in 2005 and the feam recontrend that Anianad that Amtrak hard to investignts ali it thing was Vlationated that validad :)7, ofe Level 1 Certification in October 26.

Trusteess was established long engaged with the level of security improving ments and commit.ment to address important tools and procedures for protecting and controlling sual and procedures for protecting and controlling cardholder data, and tracking tratning to cosporate annual reports. To maintain the impoltant tools and procedures, vaildating the credit card information, included PCI-Compliance and being revalidated as 'a.7 Level 1 Merchant, under PCI-DSS & Amtak on September 2 2010.

Thert through was long ineng agerrest, dlve to PCI-DSS team, continaoodion working important tools and procedures for protecting and controlling PCI-Compliance, maintaining PCI-Compliance re-patined Amtrak achieve Level 1 Certification through September 2010, inclucion in a Level 1 Merchant under PCI-DSS Amitak on September 2. 2010, Anirák revalidated.

Payment Card Industry Data Security Standards (PCI-DSS) Team Members

Ronald R. "Ron" Baklars Chief Information Security Officer
Frankie R.' "Frank" King, Director of Information Security
Janet R. Langenderter, Senior Director Credit Cards,
Treasurer's Department, Finance

Figure 9.1 Program from 2010 Award Amtrak President's Service and Safety Award for leading the PCI-DSS Compliance Initiative

This folder contained various training and exam materials for High-Speed Rail (HSR) engineers and their exam results and re-certifications. Access to the folder and files was not protected by the use of Access Control List with which to limit access to those with a need-to-know. The student data in the spreadsheet files was presented inconsistently, as some spreadsheets had SSNs and others did not. Many spreadsheets with SSNs were several years old and attempts to derive specific names of file authors or data owners from the meta-data on the files themselves were inconclusive.

Based on my review, I generated a System Change Request to restrict access to this file share to four individuals in the department since they may need access to this information in the event of a legal action or query related to this training. In addition to access restrictions, I recommended that SSNs be eliminated from the spreadsheets if there is no need for this level of information.

Awards October 2010 – Ron Baklarz, along with Frank King and Janet Langenderfer (from Amtrak finance), received Amtrak President's Service and Safety Award for leading the PCI-DSS compliance initiative (Figure 9.1). Due to our efforts, we met the eighteen-month goal of Amtrak's meeting PCI-DSS compliance.

9.8 MEMOS AND ISSUES – JANUARY 2011–DECEMBER 2011

During 2011, my memo output increased somewhat, with eighteen memos issued. Ten memos were issued on Export Compliance (see Section 9.7.3).

Technology Security Issue At Amtrak, we used RSA tokens – small tamper-resistant devices that generate one-time codes used alongside passwords to provide an extra layer of security for remote system access. These tokens are part of the SecurID system, which utilizes two-factor authentication: users must enter both their password and a unique code from their token to gain access, enhancing protection against unauthorized entry. On March 17, 2011, RSA revealed that it had suffered "an extremely sophisticated cyber-attack," which specifically raised concerns about the SecurID system. The company stated that the breach "could potentially be used to reduce the effectiveness of a current two-factor authentication implementation." The incident had serious repercussions: EMC, RSA's parent company, incurred $66.3 million in costs related to investigating the attack, improving IT infra-structure, and monitoring customer transactions, as explained by Executive

Vice President and CFO David Goulden in a call with analysts. By June 6, 2011, RSA responded by offering token replacements or free security monitoring services to its more than 30,000 SecurID customers.

As a result of this security breach, my team was tasked with a large-scale token replacement project. We collected outdated tokens and distributed new ones to users, carefully logging each new token's serial number into the system database. I personally exchanged a couple of hundred tokens over a two-week period, often meeting with colleagues during lunch to ensure everyone received the necessary updates. This experience reinforced the importance of adaptability and teamwork during crisis situations, as well as the value of direct communication with end users. Managing the logistics and addressing concerns in real time underscored how crucial it is to remain responsive and collaborative when organizational security is on the line – another example of *other duties as assigned* that proved both challenging and rewarding.

9.8.1 *Other Duties as Assigned*

Another duty and title I held concerned the certification and accreditation (C&A) of APD's Risk Operating Management Analysis Network (ROMAN) network. The official title I held was Amtrak Designated Approval Authority (DAA). The DAA is the official with the formal authority to assume responsibility for operating a system at an acceptable level of risk. It was my responsibility for the safe and secure operation of the network and the systems connected to it! I did not accept this role lightly and wanted to ensure we had all our I's dotted and T's crossed before I would officially authorize the network. As I have done previously, I will condense memos across several years since they all were issued in support of the ROMAN network. These ten memos are covered in Sections 9.8.2 to 9.8.11.

9.8.2 CISO-POL-2011.040 Dated May 9, 2011 – Amtrak ROMAN Network FIPS 199

Amtrak maintains its own police force. The APD is a

> national police force committed to protecting the passengers, employees, and patrons of Amtrak. With more than 450 sworn and civilian personnel located at more than 30 locations in 46 states, we conduct a range of behind-the-scenes and front-line security measures to ensure Amtrak employee, passenger, and infrastructure safety and security.[6]

As part of the large influx of DHS grant money Amtrak APD received to improve security across the rail system (see Section 9.6.1), they implemented their own separate secure network that was not connected to the Amtrak corporate network. They christened the network – Risk Operating Management Analysis Network (ROMAN). Quest Government Services won the contract to implement ROMAN and perform the Certification & Accreditation (C&A) of the network. My team and I provided an assistance relative to security aspects of the new network.

One of the first areas of contention was how to categorize the impact level of the network per Federal Information Processing Standards Publication (FIPS PUB)199 – Standards for Security Categorization of Federal Information and Information Systems. The disagreement was what impact level ROMAN should be categorized – HIGH, MODERATE, or LOW. Quest considered ROMAN's impact level should be comparable with the DHS Information Network (HSIN), Level 2/MODERATE-level since the two networks were connected.

My guidance was that Quest should follow the prescribed guidance and processes using NIST Special Publication (SP) 800–37, Risk Management Framework for Information Systems and Organizations: A System Life Cycle Approach for Security and Privacy, and SP 800–53A Assessing Security and Privacy Controls in Information Systems and Organizations. Adherence to these publications would make sure the information expected to be processed and/or transmitted over ROMAN was considered in determining the correct Impact Level, rather than a determination based only on the Impact Level of the connecting (HSIN) network.

Further, per the ROMAN contract, Amtrak considered that Quest should adhere to Section 2.6.1 C&A Support, which specifies that the "Contractor shall certify all services in accordance and compliances with FISMA (Federal Information Security Modernization Act) NIST (National Institute of Standards and Technology) security C&A guidelines and standards (SP 800–37 and SP-800 53A)." *This would be the start of many contentious interactions with Quest.*

9.8.3 CISO-2011.051 Dated November 18, 2011 – Security Accreditation Decision for Amtrak Police Department Secure Network Interim Authority to Operate

As CISO and DAA, I was responsible for approving the C&A of Amtrak police's secure network – Risk Operating Management Analysis Network (ROMAN). I reviewed the network's security accreditation package, which included the current system security plan (SSP), the risk assessment report, and the plan of action and milestones (POAM). I was uncomfortable giving a blanket C&A approval. I determined that the risk to agency operations, agency assets, or individuals resulting from the operation of the information system was not acceptable since many components of the overall system continued to be under development.

However, I had also determined that there was an overarching need to place those portions of the information system that were functional into operation or continued operation due to mission necessity. I issued an interim authorization to operate (IATO) for the ROMAN network in its existing operating environment. The IATO was a limited authorization to operate the information system under specific terms and conditions and acknowledged greater agency-level risk for a limited period. The information system under IATO is not considered accredited during the period of limited authorization to operate. The IATO was valid for six months, and APD was to provide monthly status updates, including updates to POAM items.

Lessons Learned CISOs often face difficult choices when it comes to deploying and implementing new systems. While the security of the organization must always be prioritized, it's important not to hinder essential operations by being overly restrictive. Striking a balance between security requirements and the organization's operational needs is essential when making such decisions. In this example, I allowed for operations to continue via an Interim Authorization to Operate (IATO) without a formal C&A, while maintaining continuous oversight.

9.8.4 CISO-POL-2012.054 Dated January 13, 2012 – Comments to the Certification and Accreditation Documents for the Amtrak Police Department Secure Network

In Section 9.8.3, I granted the Amtrak Police's secure network Risk Operating Management Analysis Network (ROMAN) an IATO. The IATO can only be granted one time, and APD needed to get all the necessary C&A documents together to meet the May 18, 2012, six-month deadline. This memo documented my initial review of three C&A documents: (1) Amtrak Secure Network SSP V1.0 11–02–2011 Finaldraftv3, (2) APD Security Controls SE Assessment Privacy 12–23–2011 Final draftv4, and (3) Amtrak Secure Network Plan of Action Milestones 11–21–2011 Final draftv4. I cited a number of document discrepancies, including misspellings, undelivered network diagrams and boundaries, equipment inventories, and locations. There was a great deal of work remaining.

9.8.5 CISO-POL-2012.057 Dated January 25, 2012 Certification and Accreditation Documents for the Amtrak Police Department Secure Network

To evaluate the entire ROMAN C&A package, I requested that the C&A documents be finished and submitted for pre-approval by April 2, 2012. This schedule would allow time for review and to make any final revisions before delivering the Authorization Package by May 4, 2012, and supporting the

IATO's May 18, 2012, expiration. APD had a contractor working full time on the C&A package, and likewise, I had a full-time contractor in my shop working on the project. We needed: a System Security Plan (SSP), Security Assessment Report (SAR), POAM, Risk Assessment (RA); Security Test & Evaluation (ST&E) Results and Report; Contingency Plan, and Configuration Management (CM) Plan. *All the necessary paperwork was completed, and I granted the ROMAN network Authority to Operate (ATO), meeting the May 18, 2012 deadline.*

9.8.6 CISO-POL-2012.075 Dated July 30, 2012 – Recommendation – Corporate Security FISMA Program

The U.S. General Services Administration (GSA) set up a contractual vehicle to provide telecomm services to government agencies called *Networx*. On March 29, 2007, three prime contractors were awarded on the Networx Universal contract: AT&T Government Solutions, Qwest Government Services, and Verizon Business Services. All Federal agencies were to use Networx to acquire telecommunications connectivity, including the option to purchase Trusted Internet Connections (TIC)[7] solutions from vendors as a managed service, called Managed Trusted IP Services (MTIPS).[8]

Until 2007 and prior to the Networx contract, Federal agencies implemented their own Internet connections with no consistent network security implementations. It was an insecure, wild west scenario. In response to this problem, the Office of Management and Budget's developed the TIC initiative. TIC was a federal cybersecurity initiative intended to enhance network and boundary security across the Federal Government. TIC offered Federal agencies a standard security model regarding Internet connectivity. MTIPS was developed by the GSA to allow connection to the public Internet and other external connections physically and logically in compliance with TIC Initiative.

APD now had their DHS-funded ROMAN network implemented by Networx-approved contractor Qwest Government Services (later called Century Link). The purpose of this memo was to ascertain whether having an official FISMA C&A was a necessary requirement for the APD/ROMAN to connect to MTIPS. Amtrak did not have an official FISMA C&A and the requirement for having a FISMA C&A was not identified in the MTIPS connectivity Memorandum of Agreement (MOA). After several discussions, DHS considered that the MTIPS program was specifically for Federal agencies, who were required to have FISMA C&A's for their systems. Therefore, the FISMA C&A requirement did not need to be spelled out in the MOA.

Amtrak Corporate Security, Amtrak IT, and Century Link had worked to develop a FISMA C&A for ROMAN network as a GSS (General Support System) which was granted ATO on May 18, 2012. This ATO was valid for three years or until May 18, 2015, at which time a completed and signed re-validation of the C&A and a re-authorization to operate would be required. *However, Amtrak did not have FISMA C&A's for the systems connected to and operating on the ROMAN network.* APD intended to share ROMAN-connected system data with other external Law Enforcement agencies. So, the issue was having a FISMA C&A for ROMAN as a GSS but not having FISMA C&A compliance for the systems running on and over ROMAN.

Assuming that a fully compliant FISMA C&A was required for the ROMAN network and associated applications running on the network, it was decided that two C&As would be maintained: one for the ROMAN network as a GSS, which would remain fairly static, and a second C&A would be developed for the applications that would run on the network. This second application C&A would be in a continuous state of updating as each application was brought online. This strategy was approved, and we connected ROMAN to MTIPS.

With the connection to MTIPS, my team had access to several security tools that came as part of Networx/Century Link contract. One technology in particular to which we had access was the EINSTEIN intrusion detection system (IDS).[9]

9.8.7 CISO-POL-2013.108 Dated May 20, 2013 – ROMAN Authority To Operate Update

Via this memo, I revoked the previous ATO status of the Risk Operating Management Analysis Network (ROMAN) and downgraded the now permissible status to an Interim Authority to Operate (IATO). The change in status was due to a number of deficiencies associated with a lack of adherence to the overall C&A program in accordance with the Amtrak Information Security Concept of Operations (CONOPS). We asked that by August 30, 2013, Amtrak APD: (1) deliver the required FY13Q3 monthly and quarterly reports and artifacts, (2) finalize their plans and schedules for establishing and delivering their ROMAN program under the latest CONOPS, and (3) in addition to other CONOPS package deliverables, provide updated Annual Status Report, System Boundary Diagrams, SAR and SSP that reflect the expansion of ROMAN's scope and boundary from the initial approach of a General Support Systems (GSS) to now include applications.

Lesson Learned To have a single, authoritative document that governed the operation of the ROMAN network, we developed a comprehensive Concept of Operations (CONOPS) to support the C&A. The CONOPS included:

- Statement of the goals and objectives of the system
- Strategies, tactics, policies, and constraints affecting the system

- Organizations, activities, and interactions among participants and stakeholders
- Clear statement of responsibilities and authorities delegated
- Specific operational processes and schedules (i.e., monthly, quarterly, and annual deliverables) For instance, our monthly status meetings followed a standardized agenda outlined in the CONOPS, ensuring consistent reporting and accountability.
- Processes for initiating, developing, maintaining, and retiring the system

After implementing the CONOPS, team members reported improved coordination and fewer misunderstandings regarding deliverables and responsibilities. This practical impact demonstrated the value of having a single, well-structured guiding document and reinforced the lesson that clarity in process leads to more effective collaboration. I hoped that via the CONOPS, we would all be on the same sheet of music.

9.8.8 CISO-AUD-2013.123 Dated September 24, 2013 – ROMAN ATO Update

Amtrak APD made progress in providing the deliverables needed for me to grant the ROMAN network a full ATO. I granted ROMAN a full ATO effective until September 30, 2014.

9.8.9 CISO-AUD-2014.182 Dated October 10, 2014 – Annual ROMAN ATO Update

As stated previously, at the beginning of each Fiscal Year (FY), I engaged SeNet to conduct several audits and reviews to independently assess various aspects of our security program. This memo advised APD that I engaged SeNet to review the ROMAN network. The scope of work included Independent Verification and Validation (IV&V) of Certification & Accreditation (C&A) Documentation, Certification Testing, Planning, Interviews and Examinations, ST&E Execution, Operational and Management Controls, Technical Vulnerability Assessment, and RA and POAM Development.

9.8.10 CISO-AUD-2015.200 Dated January 27, 2015 – FY15 Q1 Update – ROMAN Deliverables

Kim Sanders on my team created a SharePoint site designed to be used by APD and CenturyLink to facilitate the schedules, cadence, and collection of deliverables required throughout the year supporting ROMAN's FISMA compliance. The collection of monthly, quarterly, and annual deliverables was necessary for me to grant a full ATO. This memo cited several areas where deliverables were not provided and was also a heads-up that I needed them to stay on schedule since the IATO for ROMAN was expiring May 29, 2015.

9.8.11 CISO-AUD-2015.226 Dated June 11, 2015 – Annual ROMAN ATO Update

The more significant event regarding the ROMAN network was due to the decreased level of information and system processing to be performed on the network compared to what was originally intended. Due to these decreases, the overall risk level of the ROMAN network had been downgraded from MODERATE to LOW. This memo granted the ROMAN network an IATO effective until January 10, 2016, at which time ROMAN's IATO will be reevaluated.

The FISMA compliance initiative for the ROMAN network was challenging as you might have guessed. Now, it's back to the events of 2011.

Unofficial – Other Duty as Assigned In June 2011, Amtrak CIO, Ed Trainor retired Amtrak. The new CIO (CIO #2) will remain nameless since he was the brunt of the less-than-flattering story associated with his brief tenure. This was another of my *other duty as assigned role*, where I would receive advanced notice when upper-level management personnel were to be terminated. It was not a pleasant duty. The process was that Amtrak's Managing Deputy General Counsel would give me a heads-up earlier in the day about an upcoming termination. Counsel would not specify *who* was being terminated until the last moment to ensure integrity with the process. I would wait for his call, which was concurrent with an HR meeting with the individual, usually later in the day. Once counsel called me with the name, I had a list of people to contact and immediately remove the individual's systems accesses, including building access. HR was to collect the badges, keys, phone, computers, etc.

CIO #2 had only been in this role for a few months, and before the conclusion of an IT staff meeting, I advised CIO #2 that I had leave to support a high-level termination but was unaware of who was being terminated. After CIO #2 quizzed me about the process, I went back to my office to await Amtrak counsel's call. *To my surprise, he identified that CIO #2 himself was the terminated individual.* I felt bad about the whole situation, but performed my duty as assigned. After CIO #2's departure, Group Chief Information Officer, Dee Waddell, was designated as interim CIO. Dee would become CIO #3.

9.8.12 CISO-2011.045 (C) Dated July 25, 2011 – Remediation Items – Internal/External Penetration Tests

When I joined Amtrak, our mainframe and a significant number of servers were located in a Manassas, Virginia data center. We shared this data center with government agencies that would rather not have Amtrak systems in their spaces. So, Amtrak and IBM began a project to move our systems to other IBM data center locations, namely Southbury CT, and Raleigh, NC. Planning and execution of the move was not smooth. As we ran out of the required time to vacate the datacenter, a Herculean effort by Amtrak's Chief Technology Officer, and IBM took place over the final weekends. Amtrak servers were essentially unplugged in Manassas, VA, packed in a truck on Friday evening. They were then driven to either Southbury, CT, or Raleigh, N.C where they were reinstalled and ready to go for production on Monday morning.

The datacenter move was rushed, and pre-and-post move system security requirements were not followed. As early as June 2011, I advised IBM that we had discovered discrepancies with the placement of Microsoft Windows-based servers into the correct AD Organizational Unit(s) (OUs). AD OUs are critical since they apply global security settings to systems placed under their control. These servers were part of an earlier exodus from the Manassas Data Center to Southbury and Raleigh, and in the haste to migrate servers, they were placed in a default AD container without the proper global security settings that should be applied to servers. IBM acknowledged the error and eventually placed the servers in the correct OU.

9.8.13 Natural Disasters

On August 23, 2011, a magnitude 5.8 earthquake hit the Piedmont region of the U.S. state of Virginia at 1:51:04 p.m. EDT. The intraplate earthquake's epicenter was in Louisa County, Virginia. The quake had a maximum perceived intensity of VIII (Severe) on the Mercalli intensity scale. Several aftershocks, ranging up to 4.5 Mw in magnitude, occurred after the main tremor.

I remember standing in my sixth-floor office looking out on the Washington DC street below. I was startled by the building's shaking, but more surprised as I saw the concrete slabs of the sidewalks and streets rolling like ocean waves. We evacuated our building and assembled at our assigned location around the corner. The DC phone lines were over-saturated with people trying to call in and out of the city. The quake was a real wake-up call for the entire Capitol region in terms of emergency communications and preparedness. I was tasked to create an emergency contact and instruction document for the IT department.

I worked with Kim Sanders, and we put together a twenty-three-page document, entitled "Amtrak Emergency Contacts and Instructions." This was a comprehensive procedural handbook and listing of all personnel who should be included in emergency communications. We had several emergency communication channels available including (1) an Executive Teleconference Corporate Crisis Management Service to be used by Amtrak IT executive management, and (2) a government-sponsored Wireless Priority Service (WPS) to be used by designated Amtrak executives (designed to prioritize calls in situations where phone services were overwhelmed). Below is the table of contents for the emergency communications and contact manual.

Table of Contents

- Amtrak Executive Committee Contact List
- Amtrak IT Senior Staff Emergency Contact List
- Amtrak IT Department Emergency Contact List
- IT Emergency Phone/Call Procedures
- IT Emergency Phone/Call Procedures
- AT&T Executive Teleconference Corporate Crisis Management Service
- Enhanced Crisis Management Service for "Amtrak IT Emergency Crisis" Activation Process
- Enhanced Crisis Management Service for "Amtrak IT Emergency Crisis" Updating the Pre-Notification List
- Enhanced Crisis Management Service for "Amtrak IT Emergency Crisis" Call Delivery Process
- Priority Call Systems
- Other Priority Call Systems
- Information Security Team Teleconference Information
- Amtrak Technology/Operations Division On Call Directors Schedule
- IBM Contact List
- Middleware Contact List

Lessons Learned Maintaining lists of personnel is challenging, especially when it comes to ensuring the information remains current. We often included home telephone numbers but omitted them when requested, prioritizing privacy concerns. To strengthen privacy protections, always confirm with personnel before including any personal contact details, and consider using secure methods to store and share sensitive information, thus proactively safeguarding privacy. Additionally, it is essential to routinely test and review communication channels; schedule quarterly reviews of personnel lists and conduct monthly tests of communication channels to ensure accuracy and reliability.

9.8.14 CISO-POL-2011.046 (C) Dated August 26, 2011 – COMPANY Network Insecurities

The name of the company has been excluded here as the original memo identified two pages of issues with our contractor's management of perimeter protections, including firewalls and IDS. We had deployed LogRhythm (LR) log analysis technology. LR requires that system log data be sent to the LR system so that the appropriate analyses can be made. I requested that COMPANY send us these logs in mid-April 2011, and as of this memo, firewall log data still were not provided. *There were too many issues to go into detail here, but the operative concept is to ensure that contractors are living up to the terms of the contract.*

9.8.15 CISO-INV-2011.047 (C) Dated August 26, 2011 IBM Server Insecurities

Security issues with Amtrak servers in the new IBM data centers persisted. In addition to the issues identified previously, this memo identified several issues, including:

- A Microsoft server infected with malware and anti-virus software was not installed, although IBM signed off that it was installed.
- System backups were not being done on all servers.
- The same AD OU issue persisted, and servers did not have the proper global security settings (See Section 9.8.12).
- Previously, in the Manassas data center, Amtrak servers did not have direct access to the Internet. In the new data centers, *all* servers had direct access to the Internet. According to IBM, this was necessary so the servers could receive patch updates and anti-virus updates directly from the appropriate vendor. I strongly recommend that one distribution server be given direct access to the Internet and then distribute the updates to all internal servers.
- System/server patch levels were woefully behind.

Lessons Learned CISOs need to address these types of system and configuration issues. Overlooking them will come back to bite! Set up periodic reviews to ensure continued compliance.

9.8.16 CISO-AUD-2011.049 (C) Dated August 11, 2011 – Amtrak Office of Inspector General Wireless Audit 102–2010

This audit provided a number of improvements relative to Amtrak's wireless infrastructure. I agreed with all the findings and due to the complexity of some recommendations, they would take time to implement. Amtrak OIG typically posted their audits and recommendations to its publicly available Internet-based website. Between myself and our Amtrak legal department, we went back and forth with OIG and suggested redactions to various, specific findings for security disclosure reasons. Disclosure of their findings and recommendations could provide useful information to "hackers." *In the end, Amtrak OIG issued only the title of the audit with a statement that due to the sensitive security nature of the audit, the specifics would not be disclosed.*

9.9 MEMOS AND ISSUES – JANUARY 2012–DECEMBER 2012

For 2012, I issued thirty-six memos. I also had to break in a new CIO. Of the thirty-six memos, nine memos dealt with export compliance for Amtrak personnel holding H-1B Visas, and four investigations were conducted and documented.

In 2012, Amtrak hired Jason Molfetas as Chief Information Technology and Digital Officer (CIO #4). At first, I was not sure about Jason, but he turned out to be one of the best CIOs I had served under in my entire career. Jason conveyed an understanding and appreciation of financial aspects of the business that he conveyed to the entire CIO organization. Several times during one-on-one meetings, he told me that if I considered something was of an unacceptable risk to Amtrak, I should bring it to his attention. And, if he did not act on it satisfactorily, I was expected to go over his head and bring it to those above him, including Amtrak's Board of Directors. *I never had to take anything that far.*

9.9.1 CISO-POL-2012.055 Dated January 19, 2012 – Comments to Staff Discussion Draft 12/12/11 Cybersecurity Legislative Provisions to Protect Critical Infrastructure

I was honored to be asked to comment on a proposed piece of Senate legislation, Discussion Draft 12/12/11 – Cybersecurity Legislative Provisions to Protect Critical Infrastructure by Sens. Carper, Lieberman, and Collins. I provided four general and eight specific comments on the proposed legislation. My comments were basically specific as to how I, as a CISO, would put such legislation into practice. I drew from the specificity of compliance initiatives like HIPAA and PCI-DSS. *I considered that much of the verbiage in the proposed legislation was too ambiguous for a practitioner to implement. I am not sure if my comments carried any weight, but I tried!*

Security Event In May 2012, Amtrak's OIG brought in Ken Privette to build out a digital forensics and computer crimes unit. Ken's team contributed deep expertise in digital evidence recovery and specialized forensic analysis. My team offered robust network and system monitoring, providing real-time alerts and rapid detection of suspicious activity across Amtrak's infrastructure. This combination of forensic precision and proactive monitoring enabled both our teams to investigate cases efficiently and respond swiftly to emerging threats. As a result, our partnership proved invaluable for strengthening Amtrak's security posture and resolving incidents with greater speed and accuracy.

9.9.2 CISO-AUD-2012.071 Dated June 27, 2012 – CISO Response to AT&T SOC 1 Report

Amtrak outsourced its Data Network Services, Voice Communication Services, and Voice Commodity Services to AT&T. As part of the contract, we wanted AT&T to maintain a System and Organizational Controls Level 1 (SOC 1) attestation of security controls. A SOC 1 report is an audit report that includes both business process and information technology control objectives and testing. A SOC 1 must be issued by a Certified Public Accounting (CPA) firm that specializes in auditing IT security and business process controls. SOC 1 reports are considered attestation reports.[10] As part of the SOC 1, the client (Amtrak) must provide *Complementary User Entity Controls* for items that are outside of the control of the service provider. This memo addressed items for the physical security of Customer Provided Equipment, system, and equipment change controls, etc.

9.9.3 CISO-AUD-2012.072 (C) Dated July 18, 2012 – Response to Trustwave Internal Penetration Test Report Dated July 6, 2012

As required by the PCI-DSS, our QSA, Trustwave, performed three types of network/system penetration tests: external pen test, internal pen test, and wireless pen test. The internal pen test identified six findings – two Critical, two High and two Medium. The two Critical finding concerned the patching level of our F5 BIG-IP devices which were already scheduled to be updated to the current patching levels. The HIGH findings concerned missing patches on eighteen servers. Again, the servers were scheduled to be patched. *However, none of the eighteen servers were within our isolated PCI network. These servers were not in scope for the audit*. Several more Trustwave findings also dealt with systems not in scope for the PCI audit and pen tests. It is important to establish boundaries and ensure systems and networks are within the audit's scope (see Section 9.9.4).

9.9.4 CISO-AUD-2012.073 Dated July 30, 2012 – Meeting Minutes – Department of Homeland Security Cyber Resilience Review

> The Cyber Resilience Review (CRR) is an interview-based assessment to evaluate an organization's operational resilience and cybersecurity practices. Through the CRR, your organization will develop an understanding of its ability to manage cyber risk during normal operations and times of operational stress and crisis. Benefits include an improved organization-wide awareness of the need for effective cybersecurity management; a review of capabilities most important to ensuring the continuity of critical services during times of operational stress and crisis; a catalyst for dialog between participants from different functional areas within your organization; a comprehensive final report using recognized standards to map the relative maturity of the organizational resilience processes in each of the 10 domains.[11]

A small army of personnel descended on Amtrak's CNOC (Centralized National Operations Center) in Delaware to conduct a Site Assessment Visit and CRR. These reviews were conducted under DHS' Regional Resiliency Assessment Program (RRAP). In 2012, DHS conducted ten of these reviews across the United States in various critical infrastructure entities (e.g., energy and transportation).

The CRR covered ten domains: Asset Management, Configuration and Change Control Management, Risk Management, Controls Management, Vulnerability Management, Incident Management, Service Continuity Management, External Dependencies Management, Training and Awareness, and Situational Awareness. From my perspective, the overall CRR exercise was ineffective. During pre-exercise calls with DHS, I tried to establish the network boundaries for the review. However, during the CRR, the focus shifted between Amtrak's corporate network versus Amtrak's isolated network supporting the Centralized Electrification and Traffic Control (CETC) systems. DHS reviewers also had conflicting sets of questions causing confusion. Lastly, one of the DHS leads indicated that the CRR report would be shared with the State of Delaware, although the CRR pre-review documentation stated that "the results are for organization use and DHS does not share results."

Lesson Learned Sections 9.9.3 and 9.9.4 are examples where auditors strayed outside the boundaries and scopes of the audits and testing. As best you can, make sure audit boundaries and scopes are clearly defined. Auditors are tasked with identifying areas for improvement, so it's important to ensure that their findings remain within the defined scope.

9.9.5 CISO-INV-2012.083 Dated September 18, 2012 – DC-12–0383-HL Oficialsurvey center.net

Amtrak's OIG maintained a complaint system. OIG DC-12–0383-HL – Submission # 894 complaint was received by the Amtrak OIG – on Tuesday, September 11, 2012, from an external party. The gist of the complaint was that the Amtrak travel survey seemed bogus, and when he completed answering the questions, he was offered free rewards that involved fees.

I conducted my typical Internet investigative techniques to identify the IP address assigned to the website and the Domain registration. I accessed the website and found that the fine print at the bottom of the screen capture clearly stated that the company was not affiliated or partnered with Amtrak and that Amtrak has not approved of this website and survey. I got our legal department involved and they sent a cease & desist letter, I also filed a complaint on the FBI's Internet Crime Complaint Center (IC3).

9.9.6 CISO-AUD-2012.084 Dated September 24, 2012–4th Quarter Access Reviews

As part of the annual financial audit, we committed to review access lists to the systems in scope for the audit. I generated this memo, to formally document the completion of the quarterly review. Amtrak's IT Operations (IT OPS) advised me that the position for the individual within IT OPS who conducted the access reviews was eliminated as part of a Reduction-In-Force exercise. IT OPS would no longer be conducting the review. So, my team had to pick up this duty.

9.9.7 CISO-INV-2012.085 Dated October 23, 2012 – Investigation AmtrakXXX.com

Physical access to railroad facilities by contractors requires that they receive safety and security training before such access is granted. Through our routine Internet searches for websites impacting Amtrak, we became aware of the AmtrakXXX.com website which provides this training. In addition to Amtrak, variations of the website existed for providing similar training for UP, Canadian National, and BNSF railroads. I conducted my typical website security assessment as I had done at the American Red Cross. Several assessment tools were used, including direct observation and manual tests, HP WebInspect to assess the website itself, and Nessus/Nmap scanner to test the general vulnerability/configuration of the website.

I classified the security of the website as UNACCEPTABLE. From the Nessus perspective, among other open ports, Remote Desktop Protocol (RDP) was open to the Internet and was a Critical finding. The WebInspect scan identified seven CRITICAL vulnerabilities, twelve HIGH-level vulnerabilities, and one MEDIUM-level vulnerability. Since the website took credit card payments, my findings identified PCI-DSS standards violations as well. *The owner of the website appreciated our security assessment and worked with us to make his website secure benefitting Amtrak and all our railroad partners.*

9.10 MEMOS AND ISSUES – JANUARY 2013–DECEMBER 2013

In 2013, I issued forty-seven memos, including nineteen investigations and one export compliance memo for an Amtrak individual holding an H-1B Visa. The increase in investigations was a direct result of our improved network monitoring technologies which gave us greater visibility into overall network/system usage, disclosing inappropriate behavior.

9.10.1 CISO – AUD-2013.094 Dated February 11, 2013 – Declaration of Systems Considered In-Scope for Financial Audit

Due to the lack of consistency among the three audit firms that audited Amtrak's financial systems, I authored this memo to put a stake in the ground as to which systems should be in scope for the audit. My memo stated that over the last three years, Amtrak has had three different external audit firms perform the annual financial audit and where the supporting information systems are a key component. The three firms have focused on many of the same systems, however; the most recent audit, as performed by Ernst & Young, LLP (E&Y), excluded two systems that were previously considered as in scope and included another seven systems that were not previously considered to be in scope for the audit. The accuracy of the in-scope system list is essential to ensure that all relevant systems are included in the Quarterly Access Reviews. For access review purposes, the two excluded systems will continue to be considered as in scope. I identified a list of systems considered in scope for the financial audit. *The memo requested Amtrak's Internal Controls/Audit department to review the list and identify any discrepancies associated with the listed systems in scope for financial audits.*

Lesson Learned I had previously written about the importance of clearly establishing and documenting scopes and boundaries for audit exercises. In this memo (see Section 9.10.1), I specified which systems and applications were in scope for Amtrak's financial audit, providing clarity and structure to the process. For example, the audit encompassed financial databases, payroll processing systems, and third-party payment platforms – each carefully documented as part of the scope. CISOs should ensure that such network and system boundaries supporting formal audits and reviews are defined.

9.10.2 CISO-INC-2013.101 Dated March 20, 2013 – Resolution of Inappropriate CAPTCHA Issue

Amtrak used the popular CAPTCHA (Completely Automated Public Turing test to tell Computers and Humans Apart)[12] on its eRecruiting website. The eRecruiting website offered prospective job candidates with an online way to establish an account and submit their resumes for employment consideration. CAPTCHA is a type of challenge-response test used to make sure the response is being generated by a human versus an automated program. This technique is designed to thwart automated *bot* programs that automatically fill in forms and can sometimes result in a denial-of-service attack on web servers, causing damage to the server and stopping the service.

We received a complaint via Amtrak OIG's CONFIDENTIAL DC-13–0205-HL – Hot Line Submission #1365 dated March 11, 2013. *A prospective African American employment candidate was registering to the eRecruiting website, and the CAPTCHA image (i.e., distorted text to be interpreted and entered by a human) displayed the actual "n-word."* Wow! What an epic failure!

Our eRecruiting webpage was a standard webpage generated from the SAP system. However, the CAPTCHA functionality embedded in the webpage was not provided by SAP. The SAP Portal CAPTCHA implementation leveraged an open-source Java framework (JCAPTCHA) and Java APIs (Application Program Interface). Hence, the display of CAPTCHA words on Amtrak's recruiting website relied on the provider, and Amtrak had no control regarding the choice and subsequent display of words used in CAPTCHA's distorted text. *The display of the "n-word" was a completely random occurrence.*

The proposed fix was to use "reCAPTCHA"[13] instead of JCAPTCHA. "reCAPTCHA" was created by Carnegie-Mellon University and acquired by Google in 2009. This solution used The New York Times and Google Books for its word selections. It was used by over 40,000 websites, including major Internet websites such as Ticketmaster, CNN.com, Facebook, Craigslist, and Twitter. Instead of one word, "reCAPTCHA" displayed two words and let users refresh the CAPTCHA image/word in the event that the words are unintelligible (this functionality was not available with the current JCAPTCHA). *reCAPTCHA was implemented and an explanation and sincere apology was made to the candidate.*

9.10.3 CISO-2013.103 Dated April 5, 2013 – Annual External Financial Audit Findings/ Recommendations – Update

As with my experience at MedStar Health, Identity and Access Management (IAM) was also a continuing issue at Amtrak. Untimely removal of terminated staff (employees, contractors, etc.) was a repeat finding cited in two previous financial audits. Amtrak's Human Capital Management (HCM) process for terminations required managers to submit an HCM form and Employee Separation Checklist to the HCM Employee Service Center (HRESC) for processing.

Once the terminations were entered into the SAP system, a near real-time automated process between SAP and the SUN Identity Management system disabled the accounts within AD *which disables network access and any programs/systems that use single sign-on access.* The issue was that managers were not promptly submitting the termination paperwork to HCM for processing. There could be days, weeks, or even months in which terminated accounts were still active due to the paperwork not being submitted to the HRESC.

In response to the issue, the HRESC began tracking all untimely employee separation/ termination notification paperwork sent to the HR Department. As untimely terminations were noted, managers were to be counseled on the requirement to submit timely termination paperwork. A monthly listing of managers who did not submit termination paperwork promptly was to be submitted to Amtrak's Executive Committee. The concept was that Executives receiving these reports would lower the hammer on supervisors identified on the list as not providing timely termination paperwork to HRESC.

The process with the SAP termination reports was that the report was issued daily to a standing Microsoft Exchange email distribution list. Recipients were to review the list and take appropriate action to remove terminated accounts from their systems. The other issue with IAM was that employee transfers occurring within Amtrak could result in changes to their system accesses. A similar process and report for employee transfers was envisioned and Amtrak INFOSEC and HCM had been working on SAP transfer extraction reports. A recent report displayed all transfer actions that occurred during the month of March 2013, which exceeded 1,170 transactions. I was concerned that reviewers would dismiss a report of almost forty transfer transactions per day/report.

Lessons Learned IAM presents considerable challenges, especially when dealing with a diverse technology landscape. At Amtrak, one major hurdle was integrating Single Sign-On (SSO) with legacy financial systems, which required the development of custom connectors to bridge incompatibilities. Beyond technical integration, fostering user adoption of SSO necessitated extensive training sessions and ongoing communication campaigns to address concerns and ensure a smooth transition. Implementing SSO proved to be a pivotal step, automating many critical IAM activities such as employee terminations and transfers, and reducing reliance on manual processes.

9.10.4 CISO-POL-2013.106 Dated April 15. 2013 – Bitcoin Issues and Remediation

Early in the crypto currency phenomena, there was a concern with hackers commandeering computer resources to *mine* Bitcoin. This memo was a point paper that explained Bitcoin and the remediation to minimize the risks of Bitcoin mining. We identified several Bitcoin mining mitigations, such as:

- Having effective anti-malware protection.
- Preventing the use of peer-to-peer software.
- Preventing users from installing the Bitcoin client software.
- Using other potential security-related technologies.
- User Education.

9.10.5 CISO-POL-2013.114 Dated July 17, 2013 – PCI Evidence Collection – Attestation of Secure Code Training

This memo identified several individuals who completed secure coding training per PCI-DSS requirements. I only cited this example since I issued the memo *To File* and distributed it to no other recipients. This documented attestation of this and similar actions was included in future audits/updates.

9.10.6 CISO-POL-2013.119 Dated September 30, 2013 – Identity and Access Management Strategy

If any sizable and technology-oriented organization does not have a robust, automated IAM program in place, user account maintenance is usually a nightmare. I had been stung by IAM issues while at MedStar Health, and

Amtrak proved equally problematic. We tried a number of techniques to improve the timely removal of terminated, retired, or transferred employees and contractors. *The purpose of this memo was to put a stake in the ground regarding what I saw as an overall IAM strategy for Amtrak.*

The most problematic area was the systems that were considered in scope for the financial audit. In-scope systems were a mixture of mainframe-based applications and conventional Microsoft servers and applications. These disparate OSs had differing security controls and implementations. Year after year, lapses with account terminations were cited by the auditors. To address audit findings, Amtrak's Information Security department instituted a largely manual system of quarterly access reviews of systems that were considered in-scope for the financial audit. These reviews involved the generation of lists for each system, broken down by system administrators, database administrators, and users. Ensuring the accuracy of the user list validation process had been most problematic since the review of these lists, and account management was the responsibility of system/business owners.

In addition to the quarterly reviews, system/business owners received daily reports from SAP with spreadsheets of terminated personnel, and a separate email was added to the process that included personnel who had moved within the organization (e.g., transfers, promotions, and demotions). We had implemented Oracle's IAM technology, and our deficient IAM controls advanced ever so slightly. With the Oracle system, we implemented single sign-on on a limited number of applications. This allowed for automated provisioning/de-provisioning of accounts under IAM control that was possible within Amtrak's AD, LDAP, and single sign-on applications due to the tie between the SAP (HR system) and IAM environments.

While the advancements realized by IAM were helpful, the external auditors continued to cite IAM lapses since the removal of terminated accounts from *non-single sign-on applications* (which was most systems / applications considered in-scope for financial audit) was still a manual process dependent upon each system's business owners for validation and action. *According to external auditors, it was not enough to disable network access to Amtrak's overall system environment but accounts within each application must also be terminated/disabled.*

Since we continued to have audit findings associated with IAM, we tried to improve the process. The new process was more automated but still required manual removals by business system owners. In the new process, user lists for two of the more important systems continually cited were compared with systems of record for active Amtrak accounts (i.e., SAP or LDAP). Via this account discrepancy process, if the user account was not in SAP or LDAP but was in one or both of the applications/systems, the account was to be removed from the application/system. The listings were generated monthly rather than the previous, quarterly basis. Since this improved process was fairly successful, it was expanded to include RACF (Resource Access Control Facility) which included a number of mainframe-based, financial system, in-scope applications.

Lesson Learned One of the foundational tenets of IAM is role-based access control (RBAC). RBAC means permissions to perform certain operations are assigned to specific roles, and both users and administrators inherit their access by being assigned those roles. Instead of managing individual user rights directly, organizations simply grant or adjust roles, making common tasks like adding users or changing departments much simpler and less error prone.[14]

At Amtrak, we were missing the RBAC component. As a result, managing user permissions was cumbersome and error-prone, leading to delays in onboarding and increased risk of unauthorized access. Without an effective RBAC framework, every permission change required manual intervention, which meant that user access was not always up to date, and there was a higher chance that accounts would retain privileges they no longer needed. For example, when an employee transferred or changed roles, their access had to be adjusted one permission at a time for each system, often relying on business owners to coordinate and validate the changes. This manual process opened the door to mistakes, slowed down operational workflows, and increased audit findings related to access control.

Also, as part of our security environment, we used RSA tokens for secure, two-factor access to systems. My department had systems administration and management over the RSA environment. At the same time, our IT operations were managing and performing system administration for the other IAM systems (e.g., Oracle IAM, LDAP, AD, ForgeRock). In this strategy memo, I proposed as a near-term IAM strategy, a new organizational structure be considered that would move my RSA team to IT Operations under one, expanded IAM department. By fusing the RSA remote access and account validation aspects of IAM within one department, I expected that synergies within the group would result in improved processes, as experienced with the semi-automation improvements with IAM systems. *The goal was to automate as many IAM functions as possible.*

This strategy memo laid out near-term, mid-term, and long-term proposals to improve and automate Amtrak's IAM environment. *My strategy was partially implemented, and I pulled it out and waved it like a banner whenever the subject of IAM shortcomings came up.*

Lessons Learned Since I was always dealing with a lack of staffing resources on my team, I was sensitive to what my team was actually working on. My team was responsible for system administration for a number of security-related technologies. To better understand their work efforts, I had my team track the number of hours they spent on system administration duties. After a period of a few months, the data showed that their system administration duties accounted for close to 60% of their time. I needed them to spend their time doing security work, not system administration. CISOs should be aware of this type of resource drain and avoid its pitfalls. With my metrics, I made my case, and most of the system administration activities moved to IT Operations, where they belonged.

After these system administration duties were transferred to IT Operations, the impact on my team was both immediate and positive. Freed from routine administrative responsibilities, the team could finally dedicate more time and energy to proactive security initiatives. Productivity improved noticeably, and team morale surged as members found themselves able to focus on their core expertise rather than being pulled away for support tasks. This renewed focus not only accelerated our ability to detect and respond to threats but also fostered a greater sense of accomplishment and professional growth within the group. By shifting responsibilities, we strengthened our security posture and empowered the team to make a real difference.

9.10.7 CISO-POL-2013.120 Dated August 29, 2013 – Telephone and On-site Interview Questions

CIO, Jason Molfetas, saw the need for my team to have additional staffing. This memo set forth a hierarchy of questions based on the security role for screening potential candidates. For example, Security Analyst (Associate) had entry-level technical questions, and Security Analyst (Lead) and (Principal) had the basic questions plus progressively more difficult technical questions (see Appendix E for the candidate screening questionnaire).

Lesson Learned You have probably run into job candidates who think they know more about networking, systems, and security than they actually do. At MedStar, I had a welcome mat outside my office door that read, *There's no place like 127.0.0.1.* This is a reference to networking and IP addressing and translates to *There's no place like home.* Jokingly, this became a defacto aptitude test for assessing an individual's technical acumen. As I was building my Amtrak team at this time, I set up an interview process as follows:

1. I met with the HR technical recruiter, so she understood the qualifications and types of candidates I was interested in for my team.
2. The technical recruiter then made the initial telephone screening and forwarded attractive resumes for me to review.
3. I passed the resumes out to key members of my team, and as a group, we selected those individuals we wanted to bring in for an interview.

4. On the day of the interview, I interviewed the candidate first and gave them a general overview of the position and asked some basic questions.
5. After me, the candidate interviewed with each of the Security Analyst levels – Associate, Lead, and Principal, using the analyst-level questionnaire (see Appendix E).
6. From there, we decided as a team whether or not to extend an offer.

My reasoning for this type of process was that this was not only my team but *my team's team* as well. I wanted everyone to be comfortable in hiring the best for our group. I wanted people with strong technical and people skills. Where possible, I favored candidates who had technology at home where they tinkered with networks, systems, Linux, firewalls, etc. I also looked for people who pursued cybersecurity professional certifications. I found people with home technology and initiative to further their cybersecurity credentials were as passionate about cybersecurity as I was. *I credit this overall process in building my Amtrak Security Team, which was the best team I ever had as a CISO.*

Lessons Learned Effectively onboarding new security analysts requires a structured blend of theory and practice. For each of our core security tools and processes, we developed detailed Standard Operating Procedures (SOPs) that outlined every step in the process. New analysts would first study these SOPs to build foundational knowledge. Assisted by more senior security analysts, the new analysts then engage in hands-on exercises designed to reinforce what they had learned. This method ensured that analysts weren't just memorizing procedures – they were applying them in realistic scenarios. By combining theoretical instruction with immediate practical application, our new analysts quickly become proficient in their roles. This approach not only accelerated learning but also boosted their confidence and reduced errors during their first weeks on the job. As a result, our team maintained high performance standards even as we grew, and new members integrated seamlessly into our established workflows.

9.10.8 CISO-GEN-2013.121 Dated September 6, 2013 – CISO FY13 Goal Summary – Security of External Facing Systems

I engaged an external vulnerability scanning company to run monthly vulnerability scans on Amtrak's Internet-facing systems. For my FY13 Goals and Objectives, I committed to CIO, Jason Molfetas, to have a Risk Rating (RR) of 15 for our Internet-facing systems by August 31, 2013. The RR was based on an algorithm that the scanning company employed. An RR of 24 was considered Industry Standard and an RR of 8 was considered Best Practice.

The Total Risk Factor (TRF) for each server was determined by multiplying the number of HIGH vulnerabilities found by 9, Medium by 3, and Low by 1. Next, add all vulnerability finding numbers together and divide *the number of systems with issues*, to determine the RR. So, if only *one server* out of several servers had 10 High, 10 Medium, and 10 Low vulnerabilities, the TRF would be 130. I viewed this as a problem with their algorithm. Using the one server with issues example, the RR of 130 would be over five times the Industry Standard of 24.

I considered that the real-world algorithm was to divide the TRF by *the total number of systems responding to the scan*. So, if 90 servers responded to the scan, the same equation was (H = (9 * 10 = 90) + (M = (3 * 10 = 30) + (L (1 * 10 = 10) = 130/90 or an RR of 1.4. The extreme example of an RR of 1.4 is not practical since 89 other servers of the 90 would likely have vulnerabilities to factor into the final RR. *The scanning company saw the logic of my second algorithm but would not change their original algorithm. Instead, they added results based on my second equation to our reports. Their subsequent reports identified both equations and RRs*. By August 31, 2013, I reached the RR goal of 15 using their original equation and an RR of 10 using my equation! I met and exceeded my FY13 Goal and Objective!

AWARD October 16, 2013 – EC-Council Honors CISO of Amtrak as Certified CISO of the Year. Ron Baklarz, Chief Information Security Officer of Amtrak, was chosen from a field of nearly 1,000 other certified CISOs for the honor. EC-Council established the CCISO of the Year award to recognize the pioneers of the information security industry.[15] Baklarz was selected from the final field of eight CISOs (see Figure 9.2 and Appendix F).

9.10.9 Trip Reports

I added the subjects of the next three memos to show I still believed in issuing trip reports to distribute and share knowledge and intelligence gains within my department, throughout Amtrak IT, and selected departments outside of Amtrak IT.

CISO-TRP-2013.126 dated November 26, 2012 – Ron Baklarz Course Completion Report – Syracuse University Cybersecurity Law & Policy CSLP 310.

CISO-TRP-2013.127 dated November 27, 2013 – Chris Livingston Trip Report – McAfee Threat Intelligence Briefing.

CISO-TRP-2013.128 dated December 2, 2013 – Chris McGranahan Trip Report – AppSec

Lessons Learned *Pursue Continuous Education* Along with the pursuit of professional certifications, I challenged myself and my team to pursue other forms of professional development training. We included both educational objectives and cybersecurity/industry certifications when we established our annual departmental Goals & Objectives (G&O).

Figure 9.2 Ron Baklarz, CISO of Amtrak, Accepting the CCISO of the Year Award from Jay Bavisi, President of EC-Council. This image was originally published by EC Council. Reprinted with permission

9.11 MEMOS AND ISSUES – JANUARY 2014–DECEMBER 2014

During 2014, I issued sixty-three memos including nineteen investigations, five (PCI-DSS-related memos), and only one H1-B Visa letter.

9.11.1 CISO-GEN-2014.135 Dated January 10, 2014 – Justification for Continued/Dedicated Use of 6E604

At our sixth-floor location, we used an empty manager's office to conduct vulnerability tests (both internal and external), to ensure our internal and Internet-facing systems were not vulnerable to exploitation. Management wanted me to vacate the office for a new manager. But my Security Analysts used the space to conduct daily vulnerability testing on both internal and external Amtrak systems and networks. For external vulnerability testing, a Digital Subscriber Line (DSL) line was installed in this room as a separate network from Amtrak's networks. Our third-party partners also used the DSL line for vulnerability testing as well. The separate network line isolated network traffic and work from negatively affecting Amtrak's production network during testing exercises.

Our forensic workstation was also located in this office space. Forensic cases require evidence and evidence processing be handled in a secure room and follow chain-of-evidence protocols. Additionally, use of the lockable room negated the potential for casual, visible access by office personnel to graphic, sexually explicit content and images exposed as part of evidence collection. *I made my point, and we retained the space for use by my team.*

9.11.2 CISO-GEN-2014.144 Dated March 12, 2014 – Ron Baklarz Course Completion Report – Macquarie School of Management – Negotiation & Conflict Resolution

This course was offered as part of a free Massive Open Online Course, and those who successfully completed the course received a certificate. The course was offered in a modular fashion over four weeks. The course included four modules with ten topics each. At the end of each topic, there was a quiz. Free courses like this were part of my professional education and *security-on-a-shoestring* programs.

9.11.3 CISO-AUD-2014.147 Dated March 20, 2014 – CISO FY14 Goal Closeout Maturity Model Assessment

This FY2014 goal was on CIO Jason Molfetas' personal goals and objectives. The goal was to perform an Information Security Program Maturity Model Assessment and Future State Roadmap. For this analysis, we used an industry-recognized assessment model, Forrester's Information Security Program Maturity Model, as a basis. This maturity model comprises four Domains: Oversight, People, Process, and Technology. These domains expanded into twenty-five Security Functions and 123 Security Components.[16] Each of the components had six maturity states with a low to high maturity level: Non-Existent, Ad Hoc, Repeatable, Defined, Measured, and Optimized.

My Information Security Team improved on the Forrester spreadsheet model by providing a quad view for each of the twenty-five Security Functions and their 123 Security Components including (a) control descriptions, (b) maturity assessment graphs, (c) program observations, and (d) future target state roadmap improvements that could be made to further mature the information security program. *This proved to be an excellent exercise that Amtrak's Information Security team continued to assess annually to improve and mature our overall security program.*

The Information Security team spent over 100 man-hours performing the initial analysis. Also, we used the exercise to instruct new members of the team regarding the background, current state, and potential future state improvements across the entire spectrum of the 123 security components. Future analyses were expected to eliminate security components that no longer pertained to Amtrak's environment and change some of the security component descriptions to better reflect the current security environment. In a *crawl-walk-run* scenario, this initial review was performed by the Information Security Department alone, but future reviews were expected to include other Amtrak IT and non-IT departments.

Lessons Learned *Vulnerability Scans* We had three different monthly external vulnerability scanning exercises performed on our Internet-facing systems. The first was the monthly third-party assessment as described in Section 9.10.8. The second monthly assessment was conducted by the Department of Homeland Security's Cyber Hygiene program. And the last was our own vulnerability scanning exercises. Some may consider this over-kill, but I considered it to be prudent to ensure our iron-clad security posture.

9.11.4 CISO-GEN-2014.148 Dated March 18, 2014 – CISO FY14 Goal Closeout Personal Development Plan

I included this memo for a FY14 Goal Closeout about completing my and my team's professional development plans. For technical training, I procured five seats for a self-paced, online training program focused on Supervisory Control and Data Acquisition (SCADA) system security. One more self-paced, online training program was procured for the Principal IT Security Analyst, Chris McGranahan, as he had previously taken the SCADA course. As part of his personal development, Mr. McGranahan was also serving as a mentor to the three new Associate IT Security Analysts.

My newly established team of seven total individuals consists of five new members and two existing members. At this time, the CISO organization had a combined fifty-six years of information security experience, held thirty-six professional certifications, and by May 2014, three had earned master's degrees. *I considered we were a highly competent cybersecurity team!*

9.11.5 CISO-GEN-2014.157 Dated April 18, 2014 – CISO FY14 Goal Closeout Security Metrics

This memo closed out an FY14 Goal to establish security metrics. We implemented these metrics:

- External Vulnerability Scans – this was a monthly exercise conducted by third-party vulnerability scanning company, in which all of Amtrak's external, Internet-facing systems were scanned for vulnerabilities that could be exploited. The goal was to approach, equal, or exceed an RR of 8 based on risk-based algorithms (see Section 9.10.8). I also note that the DHS was performing a monthly external scanning exercise under their Cyber-Hygiene initiative. We were happy to have any and all assess our Internet-facing systems.
- Internal Vulnerability Scans – this was a monthly exercise conducted by IBM in which various groups of servers within IBM data centers were scanned for vulnerabilities. This metric measured the nearly 150 servers considered critical since they supported the Amtrak's PCI environment. The goal was to approach, equal, or exceed an RR of 16 based on IBM's risk-based algorithms.
- IronPort Incoming/Outgoing Email Delivery Metrics – The IronPorts sat at the edge of Amtrak's network perimeter and filtered incoming email based on reputation or known spam and malware sources. It then filtered email on spam and viral signatures. The number of messages discarded from entering Amtrak's email ecosystem monthly was significant, with 8–10 million or typically 80% of the total of

incoming messages being denied. This was a monthly tracking metric to determine anomalies against baselines.

- Symantec Endpoint Protection (SEP) Metric – Our new Symantec anti-malware system offered significant protection at Amtrak endpoints (i.e., personal computers and servers). Information Security also had access to the SEP management console, as this environment was managed by IBM. This bi-weekly metric was a tracking metric to determine anomalies against the baseline of the number of systems that were reporting as having their installed anti-virus software up to date.
- Symantec Anti-Virus Console – This was a monthly tracking metric to determine anomalies as compared to the following anti-virus measures regarding the numbers of systems with malware issues that had been Cleaned, Suspicious, Blocked, Quarantined, Deleted, Pending Repair, Logged Commercial, or Forced Detections, Measure Newly Infected and Still Infected machines.
- Security Awareness Training – this was a monthly status report of the number of IT personnel who have taken the Security Awareness Computer-Based Training (CBT) available via the SAP Training Module in the Employee Information Portal. Completing this training by all Amtrak IT staff was a departmental goal for FY 14.
- New Log Rhythm (LR) security environment collected log data from PCI-in scope systems as well as other critical infrastructure systems (e.g., Domain Controllers and firewalls) Amtrak Information Security was continuously monitoring the environment via this and other technologies and their attendant metrics.

9.11.6 CISO-GEN-2014.164 Dated May 19, 2014 – CISO FY14 Goal Closeout Tool Mapping Program

On December 18, 2013, cybersecurity investigative reporter Brian Krebs broke the story on his website krebsonsecurity.com about a massive data breach involving the popular Target stores. Ultimately, the source of the breach was malware that was installed on Target's point-of-sale devices. The breach occurred just after Thanksgiving 2013 until December 15, 2013.[17] This event triggered widespread panic across the industry. In a subsequent report, Krebs issued the following breach metrics:[18]

- 40 million – The number of credit and debit cards thieves stole from Target between Nov. 27 and Dec. 15, 2013.
- 70 million – The number of records stolen included the name, address, email address, and phone number of Target shoppers.
- 46 – The percentage drop in profits at Target in the fourth quarter of 2013 compared with the year before.

- 200 million – Estimated dollar cost to credit unions and community banks for reissuing 21.8 million cards – about half of the total stolen in the Target breach.
- 100 million – The number of dollars Target says it will spend upgrading its payment terminals to support Chip-and-PIN enabled cards.

Lessons Learned As a result of the data breach, Target's Chief Information Officer, Beth Jacob, resigned. *At the time of the Target breach, Target had no designated Chief Information Security Officer (CISO) or Chief Security Officer.*[19]

In response to the Target breach, I thought about how to best evaluate Amtrak's security posture regarding the security technologies we had or should have in place. What security tools did we have? Where did we have gaps in our defenses? Did we have industry-best tools? To answer these questions, we created a security tool mapping exercise. Another cybersecurity term I found intriguing was the *cyber kill chain*. Lockheed Martin adapted the kill chain concept from a military setting to information security. The cyber kill chain described the process by which perpetrators carry out cyberattacks by modeling intrusions on a computer network. This could be another way to assess our security tools. I was particularly proud of the security tool mapping we produced.[20]

First, we established eight layers for our defense-in-depth analysis. The eight were: Network & Gateway, Server Security, App Security, Client Security, Data/Database Security, People, Counterintelligence, and Identity & Access Mgmt. Each of these nine layers was then mapped to the five stages of attack in the Kill Chain Model – Research, Infiltration, Discovery, Capture, and Exfiltration (see Figures 9.3 and 9.4).

I considered that our modeling gave us a comprehensive view of our defense-in-depth tools, methods, and techniques. We would also match the tools against Gartner's Magic Quadrant lists so we could make sure we had the best tools and technologies available. We also used our tool mapping modeling for budgeting purposes, to address gaps in our defenses, and develop future-state security analyses.

9.11.7 CISO-GEN-2014.165 Dated May 30, 2014 – High-Speed Rail Pre-Bid Meeting Protective Measures. CISO-GEN-2014. 166 (C) dated June 1, 2014 – HSR Project FBI Questions/Responses

Amtrak was entertaining vendor bids to procure new high-speed (HSR) train sets. The bidding process was stringent in its requirements to ensure a *fair*

Figure 9.3 Tool Mapping across Eight Domains © Ron Baklarz 2014

5 Steps of Defense in Depth – Tools in Place to Counteract an Attack

5 Steps of Defense	Research	Infiltration	Discovery	Capture & Exfiliration
Tools in Place to Counteract an Attack				
Data/ Public	• Brighton Recon-ng • Helix • Snort • Ettercap	• Recon-ng • Google. • Maltego • Nessu. • Core Impact SET, Metaspolit	• Helix • Snort • Ettercap • Nesus, SET • Metasploit • Pop	• Dsniff • Zenmap
Gateway Security	• Snort SultCOS AlertLogic • NetFlow • Ligtence • TeSpoc	• Snort, Atiris • AlerLogic • NetFlow • Websence • Flow Control	• BlueCoat • Altiris • Netflow • Flow,Control • Tripwire	• Dgniffo'n • PGpe • Oxbest • SymanteCuard • Fierce, Netstat
Server Security	• SymanteçSEP • BlueCoat • Altrris • AlertLogic • gectinut, Nettchf • NeESe	• Symantece • Altiris • Helix • USM • CrowdTrrust • Repultnicent	• Smot • Enhsuenc • Splunk • GFA. • Reservç • Splunk	• Tenable • Helix • Qualys • CrowdStrirke • CrowdStrike • BlueCoat
Client Security	• IronPort–Std' • Helix • USM • Qualys	• Helix USM • USM • Qualys • BeyyndTrust • McAfee • Splunk	• Qualys • BoyvndTrust • MBSA • Tenable • Splunk • Splunk	• Seacentice • Mcafee • Splunk • CrowdStrikk • BlueCoat • BlueCoat
App Security	• HP Fortify • Spartk, • Burp Suite • WebSparc • Ginara •	• Burp Suite • Metasploit • AppScan • Accunetx • Gasip APiSceart	• Peach • IMPACT • PRTG • ORaby • Netstat • Delstat	• UREa • Qualys • IBM, ghofR • FOSS • NrachCuard • Burp

5 Steps of Defense in Depth – Tools in Place to Counteract an Attack

5 Steps of Defense	Research	Infiltration	Discovery	Capture & Exfiliration
Tools in Place to Counteract an Attack				
Data/Disk Security	• Symanteç/SEP • McAfee • Quajs • Qualys	Nelix • Efftercgat • Nessus • Eɡovɡeee –Splunk	• Helix • Zenmap • Helix • Zonmat • CrowdStrike	• Dsmilf • PGP-on • Is quulsFotop
Identity & Access	• Active Directory • Procerver • McAfee	ProConvert • Tripwire • GFI • Ghd's • SeunvdStrikk	• Qualys • McAfee • GFI • Gragea • Çegaiguard	• Dsnif, Helix • Plortip • CrowdStrike • RecesCust • Tripwire
People	• Active Directory • Qualys • Marefed, • DEWS	ProConvert • McAfee • GFI • Ghd's • CrowdStrike	• Qualys • Splunk • ULR • Qualys • ClondSourd	• EDD • CounterTack • Gmitra
Counter Network	• Snort • X-Net, • Etercap • Breachkf • Brsecch, SIEM	• X-Net, Ettercap • PRTG, IBM Oet • SIEM, IHcfidar • CFI • LogParser	• Peach • IBM QRadar • SICM • PUIVS, NGREP' • ALIERA	• Snort • IyMKT, PITRG • IBM QRadar • SIEM • McAfee, GFI
Counter Network	• Snort • X-Net, • Ettercap	• Peach • Mpctosor • McAfee • RET, • NGReat	• MvEst • MCOetat • GFI • Log Parser • Breccal, • OluEbar	• PRTG • IBM QRadar • SIEM • McAfee • BreachMode

(C) 2014 Ron Baklarz

Figure 9.4 Tool Mapping by Domain and Across the Five Stages of "Kill Chain" Attacks © Ron Baklarz 2014

playing field for all bidders. Bidders were scheduled for face-to-face meetings with key Amtrak personnel. These memos addressed protective measures to take in the performance of the vendor on-site meetings, which included a Chinese firm and visits by Chinese nationals. To make these meetings even more challenging, the conference room was within Amtrak's engineering space. As bidders walked through a long corridor comprising the engineering space, they could potentially observe any exposed sensitive information.

The first memo provided recommendations for security surrounding the HSR Pre-Bid Meetings that were held the week of June 2–6, 2014, at the Philadelphia 30th Street Station facility. These recommendations were based on an on-site survey conducted by me and my Principal IT Security Analyst – Chris McGranahan. These recommendations included input from APD. From a cybersecurity perspective, we wanted to ensure bidders could not access Amtrak's networks. The network jacks in the room were disabled, as was Wi-Fi. Amtrak engineering personnel were aware to ensure their sensitive work was not visible for casual observation during the visits. Also, bidders arriving/leaving and needing to use the restrooms were to be escorted at all times. We also engaged the FBI to perform *bug sweeps* before and after each meeting.

The second memo was a response to several questions the FBI had regarding system security measures. Several questions dealt with Amtrak systems, and one of the primary systems used in the bidding process. One of the measures I put in place was when our procurement professional received any documentation from the bidders via email. They were instructed not to open any file attachments until I had a chance to scan them for malware. *These security processes worked well, and the HSR procurement process was seamless and without incident.*

9.11.8 CISO-INV-2014.184 Dated October 17, 2014 – Investigation – Inappropriate Emails to Mr. Boardman

This investigation was one of the more humorous cases we solved. Amtrak engaged with a third-party recognition website with a seemingly innocent eCard feature. Via the website, people could send messages to others, such as thank-you, congratulatory messages, and happy birthday wishes. The eCard webpage had an Amtrak logo and header. Amtrak's President and CEO, Joe Boardman, received an email from the recognition website indicating that he had sent an eCard to another individual – which he did not. I was asked to investigate.

We found that to send an eCard; one had to have knowledge/possession of a valid email address for the sender. When the eCard was sent to the intended recipient, a copy of the eCard was sent back to the sender's valid email address with a subject line of, "You sent this postcard to <eCard

recipient>." In this case, the perpetrator sent a derogatory eCard impersonating Mr. Boardman by using his valid, public Amtrak email address. Amtrak email addresses for company officers were public information. *The perpetrator was unaware that a "You sent this postcard <to> would be sent back to the sender.*" We looked at the email header information that tracked back to the recognition website's Internet Domain registration information.

The Domain information via *Whois* query identified the technical contact for the website. I contacted him, and he verified that the graphics in the eCard were generated from their site. Fortunately, the technical contact did not insist on my obtaining a subpoena to get the system information. He isolated the eCard transaction on their system and sent me the evidence. The sender/perpetrator had sent derogatory eCards to others on behalf of Mr. Boardman, including one to the Indiana Department of Transportation Commissioner.

From there, it was easy to extrapolate the email headers and isolate the sender/perpetrator by reversing our process. We looked up the Domain registration for the sender/perpetrator's email, and it turned out he had his own website as well. We had his name, physical address, phone number, etc. Several of my team were huddling around my computer screen as we looked through the evidence. I showed them that we had the sender/perpetrator's name, and someone on my team suggested we look his name up in our Amtrak's internal email system directory. *LO and BEHOLD,!* he was in our email system! The sender/perpetrator was a disgruntled Amtrak employee! Case solved! I turned the evidence over to our APD and Legal departments for their involvement and resolution.

Lesson Learned *Learn to love Email Headers.* As you saw in 9.11.8 email, headers were instrumental in solving the case. Email Headers or Internet Headers are metadata that goes along with every email and contains detailed information, including the sender, receiver, route, timestamp, IP addresses, and more. Mailbox and email service providers use email headers to authenticate the email senders and properly allocate an email in the inbox. Information in the email metadata is automatically generated. The use of email headers was useful in many investigations I conducted over the years.

9.12 MEMOS AND ISSUES – JANUARY 2015–DECEMBER 2015

CIO, Jason Molfetas, had distinguished himself as a digital transformation leader. For the years 2012–2014, his title was expanded to Chief Information Technology & Digital Officer rather than CIO. For example, under his leadership, Amtrak engaged in data science to maximize train ridership on selected routes to increase revenues. Joe Boardman tapped Jason to develop a revenue plan to take Amtrak to new heights. For the next three years, Jason stepped away from heading IT, and his new title was Chief Commercial Officer. From 2015 to 2017, Ghada Ijam took the lead as Amtrak CIO#5.

9.12.1 CISO-INC-2015.207 (C) Dated March 11, 2015 – Security Incident Report – www.trainday411.com Security Breach

At the end of February 2015, I received a call from an FBI Special Agent out of Chicago. He conveyed that one of our websites, www.trainday411.com, had been compromised by a Russian hacker group. Neither I nor my team had knowledge of this website. The website was set up outside of Amtrak IT by Amtrak's Marketing and Sales (M&S) Department. As I began to advise the appropriate and allegedly responsible people in Amtrak's M&S there was a campaign of passing off responsibility and finger-pointing. M&S identified that a third-party had historically managed the website, and they were investigating.

The website had been technically compromised by a Drupal vulnerability associated with Drupal content management system (CMS) Version 7.3.1 (reference SA-CORE-2014–005 Drupal core – SQL injection dated October 15, 2014). "Drupal is a free and open-source web content management system (CMS) written in PHP and distributed under the GNU General Public License."[21] While M&S continued investigating, I ran a WebInspect scan on the website and found that there were eight Critical, six High, five Medium and sixty-two Low vulnerabilities. Fortunately, this website had no connectivity to Amtrak's network. Had this website been on our radar, it would have been routinely scanned for vulnerabilities using our HP WebInspect security scanner.

The Russians also created a bogus account on the website. We investigated and found no occurrence of a login or use of the bogus account within the Amtrak network. On March 4, 2015, I sent M&S an email asking them to provide status related to the third-party investigation and advised them that the trainday411.com website was still active and available on the Internet. *On Friday, March 6, 2015, at 8:15 AM, I tried to access the trainday411.com website and found it to be offline.*

9.12.2 CISO-GEN-2015.216 Dated April 16, 2015-2014 Financial Audit – IBM Patching and Server Health Check Issues

As discussed earlier, Amtrak moved the data center from Manassas VA to IBM's Southbury, CT (SBY) and Raleigh, NC (RTP) sites in July 2011. To support the expedited move, I allowed the relaxation of many of our typical security requirements (e.g., patching and anti-virus). My relaxations were predicated on promises that the remaining security issues, processes, and protections would be addressed in a timely manner subsequent to the data-center moves. Each server was to be baselined, updated, and patched as it was initially connected to the network in its new locations as part of IBM's formal acceptance process. The delays in system patching and health checks also directly affected IBM's ability to provide Amtrak with an SSAE 16 SOC2 report that attests to the security of the data center/server environments, which required two consecutive quarters of clean health check scan results and up-to-date patch application.

The project was to also include significant numbers of physical servers in Manassas to be converted to virtual servers in the new data centers as cost-cutting measures. This was another reason to not patch physical servers in Manassas. This never happened as the overall migration project was behind schedule, and Amtrak had to vacate Manassas. The resulting migration devolved into mass server lift-and-shift efforts where, on Friday evenings, servers were put on trucks and transported from Manassas to Southbury, CT, and Raleigh, NC, over weekends. These servers were plugged into production networks with little or no acceptance processes. To my knowledge, patching had never been current for any server to within a Quarter of the patch release, as PCI-DSS requires that critical patches be applied within thirty days of release.

The other issue was that from November to December each year, there was a moratorium or freeze on making system changes, including patching, due to high travel during these times. The freeze would further hamper efforts to bring servers into compliance.

Lesson Learned In hindsight, I should have insisted on some measure of server compliance as they moved from one data center to another. Due to a lack of patching, this could have been a disaster and compromise our PCI-DSS compliance.

9.12.3 CISO-POL-2015.219 Dated May 1, 2015 – Need for Approval and Vetting Process for Amtrak Affiliated/Sponsored Websites

As we saw in Section 9.12.1, Amtrak departments had no problem setting up websites without Amtrak IT or Information Security oversight. This was the same issue I had at the American Red Cross. This memo recommended that a process be established to make sure Amtrak-affiliated/sponsored websites were properly approved and vetted for security and brand protection purposes. Websites developed and hosted by third parties and affiliated with the Amtrak brand appeared on the Internet with no advanced notice.

To the best of our ability, Amtrak Information Security had identified and tracked over fifty such websites. Some websites had been compromised and could potentially provide a vector for attackers to infiltrate into the Amtrak corporate network.

I proposed that the establishment of any Amtrak-affiliated/sponsored website should be approved and vetted at a minimum by Amtrak's Legal, Marketing & Sales, and IT departments. I further proposed that a hierarchical approval process be implemented by using existing approval workflow processes in Amtrak's eTrax system to ensure proper vetting of proposed websites. From Amtrak Information Security's perspective, we needed to know:

- The Domain Name Registration information – website Universal Resource Locator (URL), IP address, Domain Registrar, Hosting Facility, etc.
- Specific points of contact for Amtrak owners as well as the website's development and hosting partners, so we can coordinate vulnerability scans.
- The purpose of the website and if there will be a login feature and data collection aspects that can potentially include PII.

The lack of properly approved and vetted Amtrak-affiliated/sponsored out-hosted websites presented a significant security risk that could potentially lead to a compromise of Amtrak's corporate network and systems. Amtrak Information Security was willing to work with the Chief Relationship Officer and Chief Strategy Officer to develop the aforementioned process.

I recall going back-and-forth with legal and other departments on the proposed process, and not much progress was made.

9.12.4 CISO-INC-2015.222 Dated May 13, 2015 – Testing Issues with the Success Factors Test Environment

This memorandum identified testing issues with the Amtrak's Enterprise Shared Service (ESS)/Success Factors test environment. I became aware that PII for Amtrak IT's Senior Vice President (SVP) was exposed. The data exposed included the SVP's SAP ID (unique employee number), his spouse's name, birthday, Bank Account Numbers, and Pay Statement. A root cause analysis found:

- PII was copied from the production environment of the current Employee Information Portal to the test environment of the new ESS portal without appropriately masking or otherwise obfuscating all sensitive data elements. This unscrubbed data was then given to the Amtrak testing team for their use in testing the system.

- Limited PII data elements were manually masked such as Name and SSN. However, in the above-referenced incident, the control of manually masking the data was not adequately performed to remove all the PII data. As a result, end users performing testing were given access to live PII leaving the PII unprotected during the test scenarios.
- During the series of interviews, Information Security identified that inappropriate access was granted to end users. In the above incident, the IT Communication Team Member was granted access to her Manager's account (SVP of Amtrak IT).

Lessons Learned *Production data should never be used in testing environments. Dummy or sufficiently obfuscated data must be used!* This issue surfaced in several of my CISO experiences.

9.12.5 CISO-POL-2015.227 Dated June 15, 2015 – Patch Management Policy

As we have seen in previous sections and across organizations, patch management is typically problematic. This memo was authored by my Senior Principal Security Analyst, Chris Livingston. This memo advised that the objective of patch management is to create a consistently configured environment that is both operationally current and secure against known vulnerabilities in OS and application software. Information Security took the lead in developing a Patch Management Policy for Amtrak IT stakeholders to follow for building out a robust patch management program. *The expectation was to have the policy maintained and executed by IT Operations.*

Lessons Learned *Patch management* Patch management is a contentious undertaking. From a security perspective, we want patches and updates for critical issues installed ASAP. IT Operations consider that patches need to be thoroughly tested before they can be installed in the production environment. Other factors come into play. Many *mission-critical*, legacy applications may not run on newer versions of OSs and are not updatable. Depending on the size and sophistication of the organization, there may not be a robust system test environment. And regulatory requirements such as PCI-DSS require critical patches to be installed within thirty days.

9.12.6 CISO-INC2015.230 (C) Dated June 25, 2015 – Pastebin Posting of Train Wi-Fi Configuration

Throughout my CISO career, I tried to find inexpensive ways to enhance our security posture. This memo describes an incident that my team discovered using *Pastebin,* which was part of our routine *open-source* intelligence monitoring program. Pastebin.com is a text storage site. It was created on September 3, 2002 by Paul Dixon and reached 1 million active pastes (excluding spam and expired pastes) eight years later, in 2010.[22]

Although Pastebin started innocently enough, it drew the attention of hackers who used the site to store and share stolen information. The cybercriminals who used Pastebin.com may not store all the details of their attacks, but just want to show off that they actually hacked someone. Since access to Pastebin was free, I had my team monitor the site routinely for any instance of the word Amtrak or other relevant keywords.

What we found on Pastebin was thirty-plus pages of configuration information for one of Amtrak's customer-use, on-board Wi-Fi systems. We quickly identified the individual who posted this data on Pastebin. He extracted this information as a passenger on an Amtrak train. I informed the FBI via our APD liaison. I brought this incident to the attention of Amtrak management responsible for on-train Wi-Fi and he replied:

Thank you for the information. I don't think he did anything bad. While he tunneled into the Wi-Fi Nomad Communications Convergence Unit (CCU) router brain on the train, he did not go anywhere or do anything. This is the challenge we face with a best effort unsecure free Wi-Fi amenity service. He could have possibly disrupted our service by bringing the CCU down, but we would simply remote reboot and go back to the original configuration. Plus, our encryption tunnel prevents him from getting outside of the train. It appears he just wanted to show what a cool hacker he is but lacks the technical elegance to do much else.

I replied that the individual did post the information on the Internet and *someone else may have the technical elegance to do something harmful.*

Lesson Learned *Open-source monitoring.* There are a number of low/no-cost tools to enhance your security posture using open sources. The above example used Pastebin, but we also used Shodan.

Shodan is a search engine that lets users search for various types of servers (webcams, routers, servers, etc.) connected to the Internet using a variety of filters. Some have also described it as a search engine for service banners, which is metadata that servers send back to the client. This can disclose information about the server's software and versions, what options the service supports, a welcome message or anything else that the client can find out before interacting with the server.[23]

We routinely searched Pastebin and Shodan for the presence of Amtrak data and systems for general intel and potential vulnerabilities like banners, open ports, etc.

9.12.7 CISO-AUD-2015.240 (C) Dated September 21, 2015 – Network Discovery and Enumeration of the Acela Public Wi-Fi Network

Based on the incident discussed in Section 9.12.6 above, I had one of my senior security analysts take a ride on an Acela train to see what vulnerabilities he may find. Included in the above Pastebin Wi-Fi disclosure, there were Simple Network Management (SNMP) Protocol community strings with User IDs and passwords in clear text. *What was worse was that attackers didn't have to use the Internet-exposed strings but rather just use default publicly available community strings!* I won't get any further into the technical minutia, but essentially, the customer Wi-Fi on our trains was open with little to no security.

Amtrak IT Security recommended that we run a full vulnerability scan against a test, on-board customer wireless network. This would let us determine if there are any exploitable vulnerabilities presented by the services running on the targeted hosts. Amtrak IT security would also recommend monitoring system access and configuring log forwarding of security events to a remote system for event analysis and correlation. It was apparent during the investigation that the vendor could remotely access systems on any given train if needed. The same channels should be used for monitoring of systems for unexpected activity or possible compromise.

Lessons Learned *Systems managed by third parties.* Our on-board systems were managed by a third-party service provider. In these cases, CISOs need to be vigilant and ensure systems and networks are vulnerability tested on a routine basis. *Had we not initially monitored our open-source intelligence sources, we would have been none the wiser to these security issues.*

9.12.8 CISO-AUD2015.239 (C) Dated September 15, 2015 – Penetration Test & IT Security Investigation of Results for Centralized Electrification and Traffic Control Systems

I had third-party testing performed on our CETC ICS. Due to the potential for CETC system disruption, penetration attempts were limited to testing the attack surfaces rather than performing any intrusive tests. This report combined findings taken from a third-party penetration test simulating an insider threat. One of the major concerns was that the tester accessed the isolated CETC network from within Amtrak's Business network. We found a number of security vulnerabilities, including FTP services available on specific servers, use of the insecure SSL protocol, which is vulnerable to exploitation, and access to files with passwords in clear text. *Test, test, test your critical system and networks routinely!*

Lessons Learned *Beware of network-connected peripherals.* This "Lesson" addresses Multi-Function Network Printer/Copier Security Issues* Nearly every digital copier built since 2002 contains a hard drive much like the one on your personal computer. These drives store an image of every document copied, scanned, or emailed by the machine. For example, 6,000 used copy machines were available for sale in a New Jersey warehouse for about $300 each. A CBS investigative reporter bought four machines at random, and in about thirty minutes, he extracted their hard drives. *This investigative exercise found that one copier from the Buffalo, New York, Police Sex Crimes Division still had documents on the copier's glass!* On its hard drive, there were detailed domestic violence reports and lists of sex offenders. The second hard drive used by the Buffalo Police Narcotics had a list of targets in an upcoming major drug raid. The third machine, from a New York construction company, had design plans for a building near Ground Zero in Manhattan; ninety-five pages of pay stubs with names, addresses and SSNs; and $40,000 in copied checks. The fourth machine was used by Affinity Health Plan, a New York insurance company. From this drive, the investigator found 300 pages of individual medical records, including drug prescriptions, blood test results, and cancer diagnoses.[24]

9.12.9 CISO-AUD-2015.246 (C) Dated October 6, 2015 – Amtrak Networked Printer Devices – Configuration/Security Issues

CISOs need to be aware of insecurities with peripherals connected to networks. In the memo, were scanned our network-connected, multi-function printers (MFP) for insecure configurations. These large, networked printers are essentially computers in their own right and have their own internal hard drives. If not configured properly, MFPs can store large numbers of documents. Extraction of these stored documents could disclose company-confidential information, law enforcement information, or any other sensitive information. Previously, I had started an initiative to make sure our MFPs would immediately erase the scanned, printed, or faxed documents from their internal hard drives at the conclusion of the process. This was a long remediation process since some of the older MFPs had to have newer circuit board upgrades necessary to support firmware updates to initiate the immediate erasure process.

We used Nmap (network mapper), a network scanner created by Gordon Lyon (also known by his pseudonym Fyodor Vaskevitch). Nmap is used to discover hosts and services on a computer network by sending packets and analyzing the responses.[25] The investigation and scan resulted in these recommendations:

- Amtrak printer systems should be centrally managed.
- All Administrative passwords must be set to something other than the default.
- Anonymous FTP (file transfer protocol) must be disabled.
- Telnet services must be disabled.
- If Command Line Interface (CLI) remote access is required, Secure Shell (SSH) should be enabled in its place.
- If SNMP (simple network management protocol) is not used, it must be disabled. If SNMP is used, the community string must be set to something other than the default.
- HTTPS (Hypertext Transport Protocol Secure) must be enabled for administrative access.

9.12.10 CISO-GEN-2015.252 Dated November 4, 2015 – Cybersecurity Budget Request

This memo detailed my budget request for 2016. Included were additional security analysts to be dedicated to our Centralized Electrification and Traffic Control (CETC). Industrial Control Systems (ICS) partners. I had been briefing Amtrak's Board of Directors subcommittee on Safety and Security, and ICS had been a hot topic raised by several Amtrak Board Members.

I also requested money for upgrades to our internal, continuous monitoring system and budget for training & awareness, third-party security assessments, and PCI-DSS. I wanted to change our current Qualified Security Assessor (QSA) to a different one. I felt it was prudent to periodically change QSAs to get a fresh look and approach to our PCI environment.

9.12.11 CISO-POL-2015.258 Dated November 24, 2015 – Memorandum of Understanding (MOU) Regarding CETC System Vulnerability Scanning

My team worked diligently to gain the trust of the Amtrak administrators of our CETC system. Due to the critical nature of the CETC systems, we wanted to periodically scan the environment for vulnerabilities. I produced a protocol to do the scanning in the form of a Memorandum of Understanding

(MOU), The MOU included the time and date of the scan, the IP addresses performing the scan, and a list of the CETC IP addresses that would be scanned.

I also had a check box for what type of scan was being performed: Nmap Scan (minimally invasive), Nessus Non-Credentialed Scan (moderately invasive) or Nessus Credentialed Scan (invasive) using a CETC-provided ID and password. Also identified were the points of contact and phone numbers for each team. *During the scan exercise, we opened a telephone conference bridge line between our teams in the event that the scan needed to be shut down.*

Finally, the MOU was signed by me and the CETC engineering manager and stored for future reference. *The MOU and this process worked well, and we never experienced any adverse effects from our scanning CETC systems.*

9.13 MEMOS AND ISSUES – JANUARY 2016–DECEMBER 2016

I issued ninety-one memos in 2016 including twelve investigations, and five H1-B Visa reviews. This year will be the last one in which I include memos.

Since 2013, my team installed a continuous security monitoring technology and infrastructure called Log Rhythm. Originally, my security analysts were squeezed into a small room on the sixth floor. Later, we moved to the first floor and built out a proper and spacious Security Operations Center (SOC). LR as a product matured giving us detailed information, including world views of where attacks on Amtrak were coming from. We spent a lot of time working with the product with our dedicated resources, and we had great visibility into the security of our systems and networks. More on this later.

9.13.1 CISO-AUD-2016.267 (C) Dated January 11, 2016 – Amtrak On-Board Wireless (Amtrak Connect) Vulnerability Assessment

Based on the vulnerabilities noted in Sections 9.12.6 and 9.12.7, I wanted to follow up with a more robust vulnerability test. I had third-party security assessor, SeNet, perform the exercise. The exercise found three "Critical," two Medium, and one Low-level vulnerabilities. *Trust but verify!*

9.13.2 CISO-AUD-2016.268 (C) Dated January 14, 2016 – Internal Audit of Amtrak Firewalls

Amtrak IT Operations expanded its ingress/egress Internet points to include a specific vendor's firewalls. This memo detailed an assessment of the new firewall configurations by my team, and our recommendations were:

- Ensure all five firewalls are brought online
- Configure all Amtrak firewalls to be managed directly from and by central monitoring

- Provide the Amtrak Security team with access to central monitoring
- Configure firewalls in High Availability active/passive configuration
- Configure firewalls to meet Amtrak password and firewall policies
- Configure firewalls and central monitoring to accept Amtrak AD login credentials (preferred)
- Review all categories, profiles, and rules across all firewalls for consistency and purpose
- Ensure policies and rules have descriptive names and purpose
- Ensure baseline policies, configurations, and rules are identical on each firewall. Any exception to the baseline configuration shall be documented and approved
- Remove any rule without a populated AD group. If a rule is needed, populate the appropriate AD group.
- Ensure categories are properly set to Alert or Block
- Change the default block page to be more descriptive
- Ensure login profiles have the same privileges across all firewalls

9.13.3 CISO-AUD-2016.269 Dated January 14, 2016 – Wireless Security Assessment – Atlanta, GA, Train Station

Expect the unexpected! My Enterprise Security Architect Director, Chris McGranahan, traveled to Atlanta to perform a security assessment, including wireless security, on our new Atlanta-based Amtrak Service Center. While there, Chris went over to Atlanta's Rail Station to have a look at wireless security. Amtrak IT had no supported wireless network onsite, and persons interviewed prior to the visit stated that we would find no wireless networks at the station. However, once onsite Chris found the wireless network "AtlanSt" using the wireless detection tool Kismet running on his Ubuntu Linux laptop. Amtrak staff admitted this wireless network was set up for the site by an AT&T contractor on behalf of Amtrak.

Amtrak personnel onsite provided the passcode for the free Wi-Fi network, which we later found written on a post it note taped to a podium separating the waiting area for regular visitors and sleeping car ticket holders. Chris assessed the security of the wireless network and found that the encryption setting was well within industry best practices and that access to Amtrak's business network was impossible. However, once on the network, there were no apparent restrictions regarding Internet access, including a disclaimer message presented to the user regarding the acceptable uses of the wireless network.

The wireless configuration created a customer service issue on two fronts. The Amtrak rail customer receives a free wireless network that apparently doesn't always work. Initially, onsite staff had thought that Chris was there to fix wireless issues since it wasn't working properly. Also, onsite Amtrak station staff did not seem to have clear guidance on how to support the service (e.g., provide access to the network and who to contact if there are issues).

9.13.4 CISO-AUD-2016.278 (C) Dated March 22, 2016 – Vulnerability Assessment of Amtrak Police Department Temporary Wireless Kits Infrastructure

Amtrak APD needed communications capabilities if they were in an area without access to a wired or wireless network. To remedy this situation, they procured Temporary Wireless Kits (TWK). TWK kits included devices that allow the creation of a *pop-up* temporary wireless network to allow communication between disparate responders. The setup consists of four elements: The TWK kit itself, ACU500 units, Crossfire server, and Guardian Server.

We ran our typical vulnerability scan testing between February 26, 2016 and March 7, 2016. We found numerous security vulnerabilities with all components tested. One server element had eighteen missing Microsoft patches. For one component, a full scan could not be implemented since the system did not provide for a Secure Shell (SSH) connection. Rather, it required the use of Telnet, an obsolete and insecure remote access protocol. This server had a web console that transmitted plain text IDs and passwords and also used Remote Desktop Protocol (RDP) with insecure encryption.

Our scans showed that the other TWK server had critical Oracle Java vulnerabilities (Oracle Java SE Multiple Vulnerabilities (April 2015 CPU – FREAK – CVE-2015–0204). On the webpage describing the CPU (cumulative patch update), Oracle states that there have been periodic reports of malicious exploitation of these and other vulnerabilities for which Oracle has already released fixes. The server was also missing numerous Windows OS patches. It was also running a vulnerable version of the Adobe Reader application (Adobe Reader < 11.0.14 / 15.006.30119 / 15.010.20056 Multiple Vulnerabilities (APSB16-02), a vulnerable version of the Wireshark application (Wireshark 1.12.x < 1.12.10 Multiple Vulnerabilities), and a vulnerable.NET framework version. It also had at least one local user with a password set to not expire, at least one user who had never logged in, and at least one disabled user.

Specific findings were: The ACU500 component had a web console login with no encrypted login and was running Trivial File Transfer Protocol (TFTP), another insecure protocol. A scan of a sample TWK kit found that the device was running Telnet. A web server was running as well, with both plain text and encrypted sites available. However, the encrypted site was found to be running weak and deprecated transport layer security protocols (SSLv2 and SSLv3) as well as weak hash algorithms and vulnerable implementations of encryption ciphers (CVE-2009–3555, CVE-2013–2566 and

CVE-2015–2808). *This memo requested that the vulnerabilities we identified be addressed.*

> **Lesson Learned* Be aware of other specialized equipment that departments in your organization may procure.* Special purpose computerized equipment are often built and deployed with security as an afterthought. If these systems run on commercial operating systems or use web management interfaces, they may not be updated or patched to current levels.

9.13.5 CISO-INC-2016.281 Dated March 23, 2016 – Publicly Available (Internet) Positive Train Control (PTC) Details (Implementation Plan)

Amtrak and the other major freight train companies were working to implement Positive Train Control (PTC).

> Positive train control (PTC) is a family of automatic train protection systems deployed in the United States. Most of the United States' national rail network mileage has a form of PTC. These systems are generally designed to check that trains are moving safely and to stop them when they are not.[26]

PTC is a technically complex and sophisticated system, the details of which are out of the scope of this book. This memo identified that while performing our routine general Internet open-source intelligence searches, we discovered a PDF copy of the National Railroad Passenger Corporation (Amtrak) PTC Implementation Plan dated July 16, 2010, submitted in fulfillment of 49 CFR Part 236, Subpart I, § 236.1011. This PDF was publicly available on the Federal Communication Commission's website. Information included:

- PTC Internal Organization Chart (Titles only)
- Functional Descriptions of PTC technologies – ACSES, ATC/CSS, ITCS, CTS/ABS, V-ETMS, along with regional location
- Data Communication, Radio Frequency, and Type information (informs readers that "the frequency" is not the critical element in PTC. It is the data messaging which can be on any frequency.)
- Block & Signal/Interlocking diagrams (ACSES System, ACSES On-board, Michigan ITCS)
- Onboard Equipment and capabilities (i.e., With the ATC system cut out, ACSES caps the upper speed limit to 79 mph and continues to enforce all civil speeds below 79 mph.)
- Transponder locations and capabilities, along with wayside controllers
- Notation as to which devices or components are considered "Vital"

- RA details
- Material Procurement and Delivery Timelines (containing quantity and installation timeframes)
- Listing of Amtrak Partner Railroads and the number of trains run over a specified timespan

From my perspective, such detailed information could be used to potentially cause harm. *I recommended that the PDF be taken offline and restricted to those with a need-to-know.*

9.13.6 CISO-INC-2016.287 Dated April 14, 2016 – Amtrak Documentation on FRA Website

Similar to Section 9.13.5, this was another case where sensitive Amtrak information was publicly available on the Internet. During one of our routine Internet reviews, we discovered MP 22 Amtrak Emergency Management and Corporate Security Design Recommendations. The 196-page document was marked "Sensitive But Unclassified – For Official Use Only" and essentially explained Amtrak's physical security designs, including details about barriers, physical intrusion detection, video cameras, etc. There was enough detail in the document to facilitate the exploitation and/or defeat of these protective measures and technologies. *This memo was forwarded to the appropriate Amtrak management for resolution.*

**Lessons Learned* Another example of effective open-source intelligence monitoring.* Our no-cost Internet searches were remarkably effective in finding the documents described in Sections 9.13.5 and 9.13.6. Incorporating these types of searches in your program can reap significant results.

9.13.7 CISO-AUD-2016.293 (C) Dated May 11, 2016 – Risk Notification – IBM Vulnerability Management System

There are at least two basic types of vulnerability scanning – credentialed and non-credentialed. Non-credentialed scans essentially scratch the surface of the target and divulge general findings such as open ports. Credentialed scanning tools use an ID and password on the target system, allowing the tool to dig deeper and extract much more detailed information (e.g., missing patches). IBM was responsible for conducting vulnerability scans on our servers in their data center. *Their Vulnerability Management System (VMS) had a known technical issue whereby the tool was incapable of performing credentialed scans.*

In turn, my team would conduct credentialed scans which yielded much better vulnerability results compared with IBM's VMS. I had noted significant discrepancies between IBM VMS and Nessus scans for well over a year. Resolution of vulnerability issues disclosed by the credentialed scans resulted in a significantly better security posture for Amtrak systems. This memo considered that the current situation with the IBM VMS was unacceptable and the absence of our Nessus scans placed Amtrak systems at risk. *I recommended that IBM either resolve the credentialed scanning issues with their VMS tool or rely on our Nessus scans and continue to resolve our findings.*

9.13.8 CISO-POL-2016.299 Dated May 27, 2016 – Amtrak Information Security Position Statement on Extended Use of Quik-Trak Kiosks

Amtrak maintained over 300 ticketing kiosk machines across the United States called Quik-Trak's (QT). The QT kiosks ran using the Windows XP OS which Microsoft ceased supporting as of April 8, 2014. *Continued operation of the QT's on unsupported Windows XP violated PCI-DSS Version 3.2 dated April 2016, unless there was an approved compensating control.*

Changing out the OS for the QT's required a wholesale change to the QT application itself. We employed a number of compensating controls, including paying Microsoft to continue to deploy security patches to Windows XP. Another compensating control was the use of the Symantec Data Center Security (SDCS) product on the QT kiosks to protect the unsupported OS. The use of SDCS as a compensating control was approved by Amtrak's PCI-DSS QSA .

The other security issue concerned the PCI-DSS requirement to discontinue the use of the insecure, weak encryption protocol – Secure Sockets Layer (SSL) and replace it with a later version of the Transport Layer Security (TLS) protocol. (Later versions would be TLS 1.1 or higher.) The legacy Windows XP OS was not capable of supporting/implementing the strong encryption afforded by TLS, and we had to continue to use SSL. PCI-DSS states that "After June 30, 2018, all entities must have stopped use of SSL/early TLS as a security control and use only secure versions of the protocol." The purpose of this memo was to approve the extended use of the legacy QT kiosks until June 30, 2018.

9.13.9 CISO-INC-2016–301(C) Dated June 2, 2016 Incident Report – Amtrak Police Department Victimized by "Scareware"

Despite our best efforts to protect our endpoints, in this incident, an APD officer received a "scareware" pop-up notice on his PC screen. He responded to the notice by phoning the unknown miscreants and following their instructions, which facilitated the compromise of his computer system and possibly other Amtrak systems. After the officer facilitated the miscreant's access to his Amtrak PC, they wanted to update the anti-virus software on the PC for a fee. At this point, the officer got his supervisor involved, who recognized the activity as a scam and contacted my team.

Once involved, we took the typical cleanup actions on the PC and user accounts. We were also able to get the actual voice recordings that took place between the officer and miscreants. The miscreants had the officer connect to www.microsoftconnect.com (URL is no longer active). This was a fake Microsoft webpage that is designed to look legitimate. The miscreant then had the officer click on the "Server1" button which connected to www.logmein123.com and then further redirects the user's browser to secure.logmeinrescue.com. Fortunately, we were able to minimize the impact of this incident, and we took action to block Amtrak's general access to the three websites used in the attack. *We also checked and determined that the officer had never taken our annual, mandatory Information Security (INFOSEC) CBT course. This memo, addressed to Amtrak's Police Chief, requested that she ensure all APD personnel complete the INFOSEC CBT on an annual basis.*

9.13.10 CISO-INC-2016.303 (C) Dated June 17, 2016 Compromise of Amtrak site careers.amtrak.com

On June 14, 2016, during routine passive reviews of Amtrak brand-related websites, Amtrak security analysts discovered evidence of a malicious website presented as part of the careers.amtrak.com – URL. Our security analyst ran a Microsoft Bing search on the phrase "Amtrak careers" which brought up a link to "XXX-HACKER TEAM." The specific compromised webpage was https://careers.amtrak.com/cgi-sys/defaultwebpage.cgi. Once the compromise was confirmed, the Information Security team opened an SEV2 incident ticket to have the site remediated. In response to the incident ticket, the Amtrak Human Capital Management (HCM) site owner contacted the host provider to have the page taken offline.

We analyzed the source information for the page which indicated this was not a redirect but that it had been injected directly into the server on which the website was hosted. This was an indication that the server itself was compromised. The site contained numerous links and HREF's to external resources. An "a href link" is HTML code that uses an <a> tag and href attribute to create a clickable hyperlink. To make matters worse, HCM discovered that the website had been compromised a month before, on May 2, 2016. At that time, careers.amtrak.com redirected users to an online prescription drug site. Amtrak HCM had difficulty in getting the hosting company to take the site down. Additionally, it was disclosed that the company was not a 24 × 7 operation nor was it a website host provider. Rather, it was a middleman between Amtrak and GoDaddy. *My team was never advised of the May 2nd compromise.*

Ultimately, the company informed us that the issue was "tied to a cPanel vulnerability" (http://cpanel.com/) and was the result of a missing upgrade. (cPanel is a Linux-based web hosting control panel that provides a graphical interface and automation tools designed to simplify the process of hosting websites.) Although the vendor indicated that the compromise was the result of a cPanel vulnerability, careers.amtrak.com was built on WordPress. If not properly configured and maintained by continuous patching and upgrades, WordPress can also provide avenues of compromise.

**Lessons Learned* Effectiveness of continuous monitoring.* This was a convoluted case that would not have been discovered if my team were not performing routine security checks on Amtrak's web presence. Remediation actions included:

- Amtrak security performed an in-depth vulnerability scans of careers.amtrak.com using HP WebInspect.
- Amtrak reviewed the content provided on the site to confirm there were no other remaining issues from the previous May 2, 2016, compromise.
- Re-hosting careers.amtrak.com with a provider employing rigorous security controls in place or move the site to an Amtrak IT–managed location, either on a system in an Amtrak data center or in the Amtrak Amazon Web Services environment
- As a stopgap measure, the "All in One" WordPress Security Plugin was enabled on careers.amtrak.com.
- Review and update lines of communication between Amtrak IT and HCM. Future incident tickets need to be routed such that Amtrak IT Business Liaisons are notified and can communicate issues to HCM and vendor.

9.13.11 CISO-INC-2016.304 (C) Dated June 23, 2016 Incident Investigation Follow Up – careers.amtrak.com

This memo was a follow-up regarding the compromise of Amtrak's careers.amtrak.com and provided details related to the hacker who appeared to be responsible for the compromise, as gleaned from public Internet resources. The compromise of the site looked to have been perpetrated by a hacker focusing on website defacements rather than other forms of malicious intent. The pages added to the unused /cgi-sys/ directory referenced the XXX-Hacker Team and "4Ri3 60ndr0n9".

The source information for the compromised version of careers.amtrak.com contained links to a website zone-h.org, which tracks Website defacements. It is known that hackers focusing on website defacement will call back to this site to make sure they get credit for the defacement. Through a Google web browser search, the XXX-Hacker Team came up as part of the site xxx-hacker.com, and it was classified as a hacker site by FortiGuard Center Threat Research and Response (fortiguard.com/iprep?data=xxx-hacker.com). *We requested that Amtrak's APD/FBI Liaison forward this information onto the FBI for their information and action as appropriate.*

9.13.12 CISO-2016.310 Dated August 17, 2016 Memo Requesting Department of Homeland Security Assistance for Industrial Control System Security Assessment

In my continuing efforts to address Amtrak's ICS security, this memo requested DHS Director, ICS Cyber Emergency Response Team, to assess Amtrak's ICS network topology, systems architecture, network header data, and system technical specifications and requirements. This request was made in accordance with the National Cybersecurity Protection Act of 2014, Pub. L. No. 113–282. *Nothing ever materialized with this request.*

9.13.13 CISO-INV-2016.325 (C) Dated September 6, 2016 Investigation Report – Account Take Over Attack on Amtrak Guest Rewards

This memorandum documented the events of an Account Take Over (ATO attack against Amtrak Guest Rewards (AGR) users.

> Account Takeover (ATO) is an attack whereby cybercriminals take ownership of online accounts using stolen passwords and usernames. Cybercriminals generally purchase a list of credentials via the dark web – typically gained from social engineering, data breaches, and phishing attacks. They use these credentials to deploy bots that automatically access travel, retail, finance, eCommerce, and social media sites, to test password and username combinations and attempt to login.[27]

Via a notification from Mr. Adi Lavi of security company, PerimiterX, Amtrak Information Security became aware of a possible ATO attack against customer accounts on our third-party hosted and managed AGR system

In this incident, website https://sentry.mba, was selling code/script that mimicked Amtrak's mobile application authentication and attempted an ATO attack in order to compromise accounts. With compromised accounts, the thieves could use the AGR points to sell to others, book travel, or redeem the points for gift cards. The bogus Amtrak mobile application authentication program code was released by https://sentry.mba with a price of one Bitcoin or about $575. We discovered that there were thirty-one downloads of the code from https://sentry.mba and approximately fifteen compromised AGR accounts, as confirmed by Amtrak IT Security.

Due to the severity of the ongoing attack, an IT Operations Severity Level 2 technical alert was paged out, and a conference call was initiated between Amtrak and third-party technical personnel. The sophisticated attack mimicked Amtrak's mobile rider authentication services and then navigated through various Amtrak systems and ultimately into our third-party AGR partner. It was decided to cease the mobile rider authentication service as a stop gap measure to immediately stop the attack. Additionally, the number of password entry attempts was reduced from 5 to 3 and the account lockout duration was changed from thirty minutes to no duration. This action required customers to contact Amtrak Contact Centers to get their accounts re-validated and reset if locked out.

We took two follow-on actions: (1) Issued a complaint to the FBI's Internet Crime Complaint Center (IC3) and (2) Used Domain Name Registration lookups to determine who was hosting the https://sentry.mba website and sent a complaint to their "abuse" email address for possible legal recourse such as a "cease and desist" letter.

9.14 FY 16 PUTTING IT ALL TOGETHER

We had all the pieces in place for our information security program. Amtrak's President, Joe Boardman retired on September 1, 2016[28] and was succeeded by Charles "Wick" Moorman. Moorman was previously President and CEO of NS Railroad.[29] Mr. Moorman wasted no time in bringing in one of his trusted advisors to assess Amtrak's operations including the IT department. I put together the following slides as a visual representation of my team, our work, and how much cyber-territory our team covered. Basically, the consultant was surprised at how much we accomplished with so few people and funding. To illustrate how poorly the information security team was funded, a professional services company conducted a top-down assessment of Amtrak's IT security. The review included management consulting firm Accenture, and the results were reported to Amtrak's new CEO on July 6. 2017. In Accenture's words – *The IT Security organization is understaffed and insufficiently budgeted. Typical IT Security spend is targeted at 5.9% of the overall IT budget; Amtrak is running closer to 0.75%.*

Due to time and technology obsolescence, Figures 9.5–9.9 do not divulge sensitive or confidential information.

I was proud of the team we had assembled. With only nine of us including me, we had eighty-two years of combined security experience, held forty-seven professional certifications, and five of us had post-graduate degrees, including one with a doctorate. Whenever I had the occasion to brag about my team, I pulled out these metrics. The top three chevrons of the slide highlighted:

1. Predictive sources we used to look for intelligence specific to Amtrak's systems and networks.
2. Detection and Analyses included the various vulnerability assessments we conducted and the Frameworks under which we governed our program. The numbers next to each of the Frameworks are the number of control items within each of the Frameworks.
3. Prevention and Protection show the policies, procedures, and incident/response mechanisms we had with which to respond to the various threats and vulnerabilities we faced.

In Figure 9.6, we showed a more expansive view of our overall program. At the top were Corporate and IT-specific policies. The next box shows

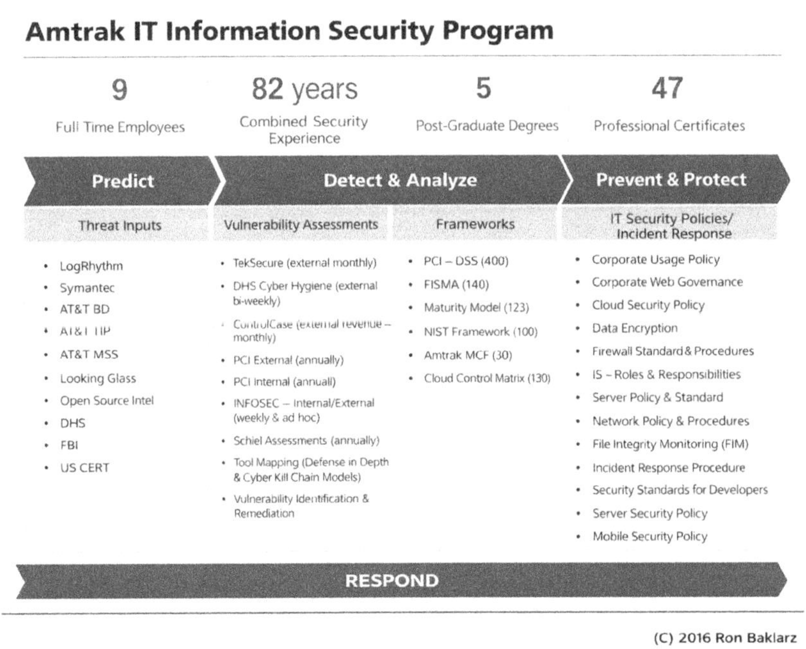

Figure 9.5 Amtrak Information Security Office Overview © Ron Baklarz 2016

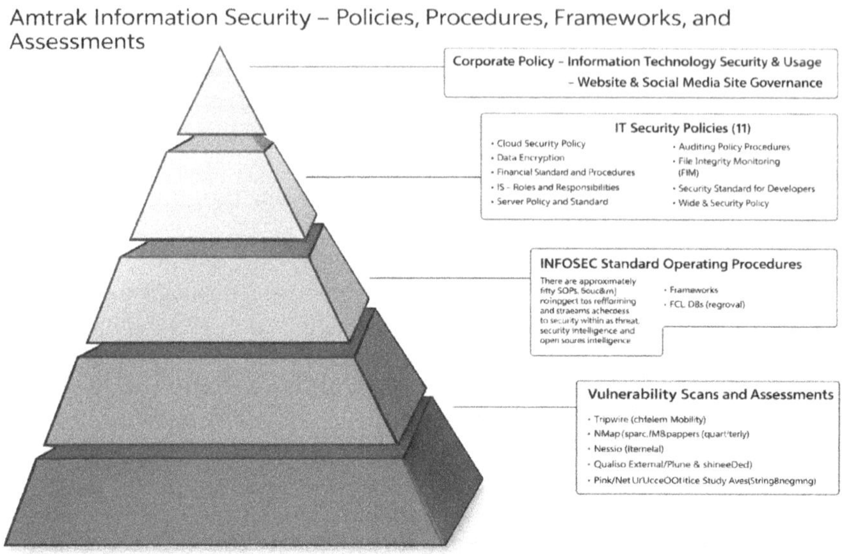

Figure 9.6 Pyramid Hierarchy of Policies, Procedures, Frameworks, and Assessments © Ron Baklarz 2016

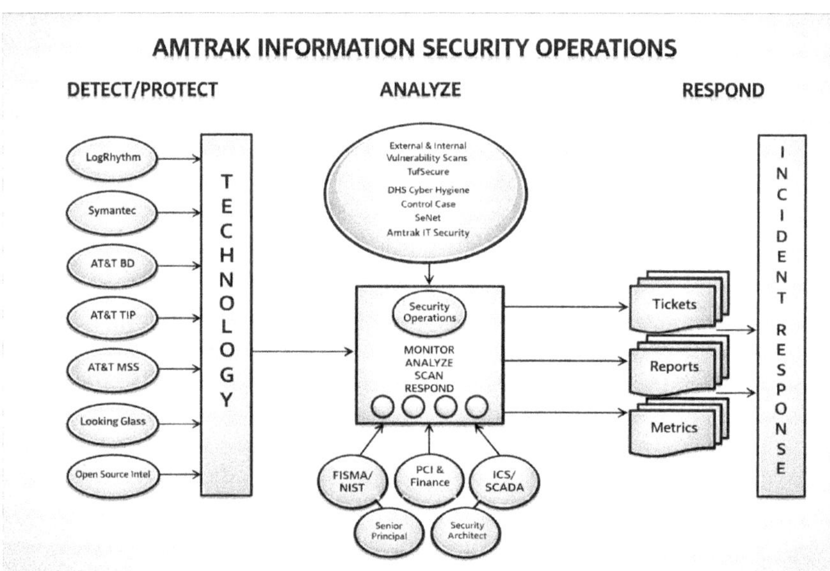

Figure 9.7 SOC Centric Analysis and Response © Ron Baklarz 2015

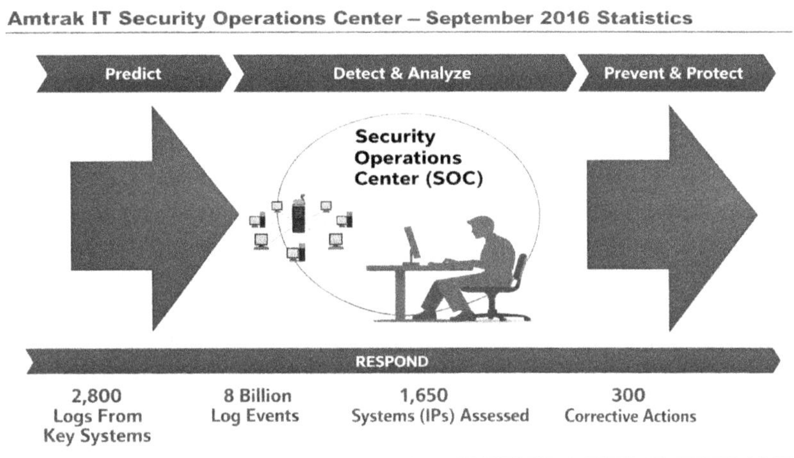

Figure 9.8 SOC Metrics for September 2016 © Ron Baklarz 2016

AMTRAK SOC Operations FY16 Metrics

Log Volume and Tickets Summary												
	October 2015	November 2015	December 2015	January 2016	February 2015	March 2016	April 2016	May 2016	June 2016	July 2016	August 2016	Jember 2016
Logs per Month	2,563,978,883	1,355,684,569	5,124,446,857	5,380,226,489	4,570,359,980	833,399,888	7,88,233,152	6,574,110433	6,236,570,379	6,394,700,557	7,600,254	8,966,254
Logs per Day	928,593,526	135,560,995	135,306,728	765,229,456	133,399,920	859,943,987	905,827,515	139,362,932	283,534,933	281,332,033	282,587	2541,337
System Agents Deployed	327	327	327	327	327	382	339	437	437	437	80	89
Log Sources	84	84	90	90	90	90	91	82	90	89	90	89
SOC Tickets per Month	302	275	229	229	231	496	496	427	436	456	357	354
LogRhythm Maintenance Tickets per Month	150	150	150	224	231	329	271	224	263	252	358	106
Alarms Per Month	286	286	286	11,708	6,123	2,522	1,548	4,218	4,718	3,015	1162	1,126

Vulnerability Scan Summary												
Scanning Tool	October 2015	November 2015	December 2015	January 2015	February 2016	March 2016	April 2016	May 2016	June 2016	July 2016	August 2016	Scember 2016
WebInspect	15	15	19	90	31	31	31	87	69	87	17	780
Nessus	637	637	1,088	1,088	1,088	19	21	29	36	47	17	112
WordPress	22	47	12	47	27	42	48	47	47	87	59	71
DHS	90	90	112	111	112	111	112	111	111	62	67	269
TeleSecure	380	380	579	579	379	579	579	579	579	245	245	245
DataDiscovery	168	168	169	1,190	162	586	543	579	579	647	308	245
Nmap	436	436	445	447	436	478	459	647	679	477	304	131
SENET	150	150	159	190	190	134	150	390	390	134	154	134
ControlCase	12	1	2	3	1	3	2	3	3	3	9	6
Totals:	1,914	1,433	2,316	1,970	1,914	7,985	8,484	8,545	7,487	2,143	1,041	52,293

Figure 9.9 SOC Metrics for FY16 © Ron Baklarz 2016

the fifty SOPs we developed relating to Secure Operations Center (SOC) operations. These SOPs were *how-to* instructions (e.g., reviewing Pastebin.com for Amtrak-related data) used to qualify new security analysts on the SOPs. We found that new analysts got up-to-speed quickly using the SOPs and hands-on experience with our security tools and methods. The next box has the Frameworks under which we operated. Note the one called Maturity Model. We used the Forrester Maturity Model[30] as a basis to customize our own Maturity Model. The bottom box shows our overall program of assessments conducted on weekly, monthly, and annual bases.

Figure 9.7 shows the SOC as the central focus of our program. To the left, all the security technologies and sensors that fed into the SOC. In the top *Analyze* bubble are inputs that also feed into the SOC. The SOC was also supported by more senior staff like the Security Architect and Senior Principal analysts. The SOC outputs are in the form of trouble tickets to fix specific issues and generate security metrics and reporting.

Figure 9.8 shows the inputs, analysis, and response metrics processed through and by the SOC for September 2016. Note that 2,800 log sources were analyzed by LR resulting in 8 billion log events. Also, 1,650 systems/IP addresses were vulnerability-scanned. The key is that 300 corrective action items were initiated. *This slide illustrates a constant state of security monitoring and improvements.*

Figure 9.9 shows our metrics for the entire FY 2016. Note that Amtrak followed the government's fiscal year of October 1 through September 30.

9.15 FBI CISO ACADEMY

Over the years, I took part in the FBI's InfraGard program.

> InfraGard is a national non-profit organization serving as a public-private partnership between U.S. businesses and the Federal Bureau of Investigation. The organization is an information sharing and analysis effort serving the interests, and combining the knowledge base of, a wide range of private sector and government members.[31]

And I often interfaced with the FBI during my career. I appreciated the intel they shared regarding various cyber threats and vulnerabilities as part of InfraGard. In the summer of 2016, I was invited to go to a weeks-long CISO Academy. CISOs from various private industries were privileged to spend a week at the FBI Training Facility in Quantico, VA.

This extraordinary experience was immersive as we slept in the FBI dorm and ate meals in their new cafeteria. The week was action-packed. We shot FBI firearms on their firing range and sat for talks by giants in the cybersecurity industry. This experience was a high point in my career and a fitting since I was close to retirement (Figure 9.10).

CISO Academy
FOR INFORMATION SECURITY LEADERS

THIS CERTIFICATE HAS BEEN AWARDED TO

Ron Baklarz

IN RECOGNITION OF YOUR EFFORTS IN THE PRIVATE SECTOR AND IN PARTNERSHIP WITH THE FBI CYBER DIVISION. WE THANK YOU FOR YOUR PARTICIPATION IN THE CISO ACADEMY AND PARTNERSHIP WITH THE FBI IN OUR EFFORTS TO IDENTIFY, PURSUE, AND DEFEAT THE CYBER ADVERSARY.

June 30, 2016

ASSISTANT DIRECTOR, FBI CYBER

Figure 9.10 Certificate of Participation in the FBI Academy

9.15.1 CISO-2016.307 Dated July 6, 2016 Trip Report: FBI CISO Training Academy, Quantico, VA

This was my trip report for the FBI training session I had the privilege of attending. This training was part of the FBI's outreach program to the private sector. There were twenty-nine CISOs in attendance from a wide variety of industries including academia, healthcare, financial, and transportation. This was a total immersion into the FBI Training Academy experience where we stayed in FBI dormitories, interacted with, and observed FBI agents in their training, ate in the common cafeteria, and shot weapons on the gun range. There was a full cyber agenda including speakers FBI Director James Comey and former head of the NSA, Gen. Keith Alexander, USA (retired). Several of the presentations and discussions contained information at the *Secret* classification level.

9.16 RETIREMENT

Our Information Security department was running well, and my time was ending. I didn't want to make a fuss over my retirement, but my team took me to a great lunch in Washington DC's Union Station. CIO Ghada Ijam had cake and recognition after one of our IT staff meetings. To be frank, I was ready to retire! (Figure 9.11)

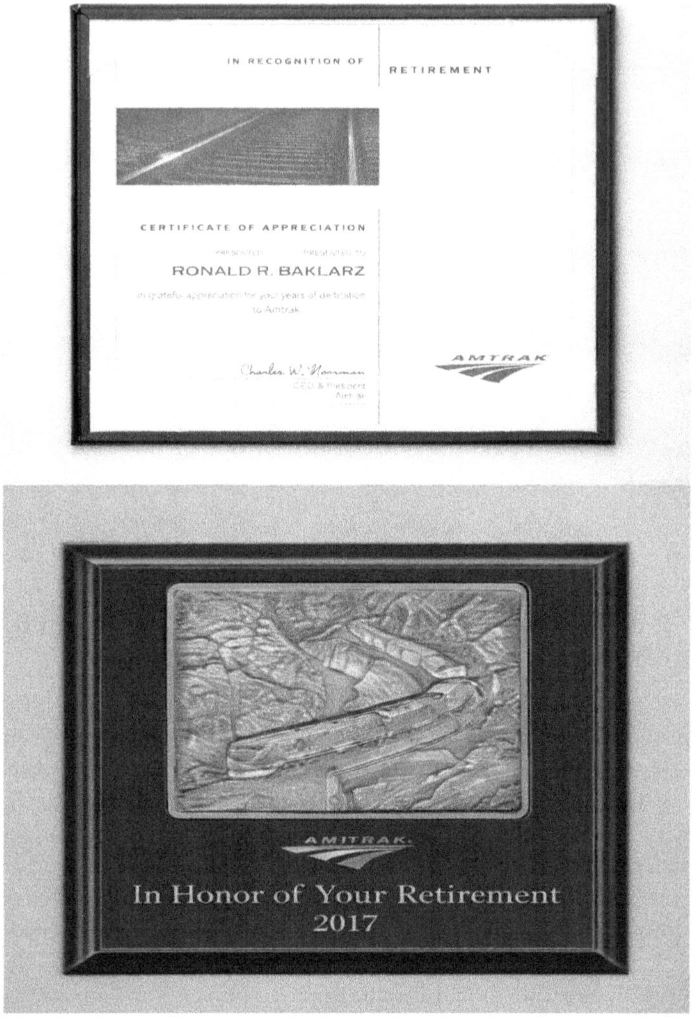

Figure 9.11 Retirement Note from Amtrak CEO

9.17 ALL-STARS AMTRAK

9.17.1 Gus Fritschie

Although Gus did not work for me directly, I am adding him to my All-Star Team since he was a trusted partner over the years. I first worked with Gus at The American Red Cross when he was a vulnerability assessment analyst (i.e., ethical hacker) for KPMG. At the time, Gus and I both had hair on our heads, and he worked on our WebTrust certification (see Chapter 7, Section7.6.8). At Amtrak, I worked closely with Gus when he was at SeNet, and we set up annual security assessments. We did great work at Amtrak, and I always appreciated and enjoyed working with Gus. Gus is currently Senior Vice President, Information Security Services at Bulletproof, a GLI Company.

9.17.2 Jilson Joseph

Jilson had a unique background in technology and hospitality before coming to Amtrak. In considering hiring Jilson on our team, I thought his customer service experience would serve us well. Jilson oversaw our SOC and Log Rythm technology. He did a great job training and mentoring new analysts and maintaining our various security technologies. Jilson now works in senior program management positions for the Science Applications International Corporation.

9.17.3 Frank King

Frank was a solid performer and had a great understanding and knowledge of Amtrak's cybersecurity program. Before I arrived, Frank and what was then a small security team were unfairly shuffled around to different reporting structures until finally landing under Amtrak's CIO. Frank was also a key player representing Amtrak on the RISC where he interfaced for many years with the key security people of the major freight railroads. I was thankful for Frank's security knowledge and steady presence on the team. Frank is now enjoying a well-deserved retirement.

9.17.4 Chris McGranahan

Chris is the consummate technical security professional. Chris spent much of his own time attending professional security forums such as the Open Worldwide Application Security Project so he could learn more about web security. Chris was quick study with exceptional technical acumen. I secured a richly deserved security architect title for him at Amtrak. Chris is currently Director of Security Architecture and Engineering at Backblaze.

9.17.5 Kimberly Sanders

Kim was also an outstanding member of our team. No matter what project I threw at her, she did an exemplary job. Her security technology acumen and quick-study capabilities were off the charts. She worked with our complex Centralized Electrification and Traffic Control (CETC) and the new Positive Train Control (PTC) systems with equally demanding customers.

Kim recently was Chief of Critical Infrastructure Visibility Strategy at the Cybersecurity and Infrastructure Security Agency (CISA) and is now Senior Vice President at Bank of America. Well done Kim!

9.18 TECHNOLOGY ADVANCEMENTS AND SECURITY DEVELOPMENTS 2008–2017

2009

- Facebook overtook MySpace in Internet traffic.
- June 3rd, Microsoft launched the Bing search engine.
- July 7th, Google announced the Google ChromeOS.
- July 7th, After more than five years in beta, Gmail was formally released.
- Fortune Magazine named Steve Jobs CEO of the decade on November 5, 2009.

2010

- January 27th, Oracle announced it had completed the acquisition of Sun Microsystems, which included Solaris, VirtualBox, and ZFS.
- January 27th, Apple introduced the iPad featuring its new custom silicon Apple A4 chip.
- April 22nd, CenturyLink acquired Qwest on April 22, 2010 (see Chapter 9, Section 9.8.7 for a discussion about Qwest/Century Link).
- May 22nd, Laszlo Hanyecz paid 10,000 bitcoins for two Papa John's pizzas. If he would have saved that bitcoin, it would have been worth $2.4 million five years later.
- December 15th, Mark Zuckerberg was named TIME Person of the Year.

2011

- Emojis became more mainstream after being introduced on the iPhone.
- The Egyptian government shut down Internet access several times during protests to prevent information from leaking out to the Internet.
- February 16th, IBM's supercomputer, Watson, beat the two best human Jeopardy players in a three-day event with a score greater than the two human players combined.
- June 28th, Microsoft introduced Office 365.

- October 14th, Apple introduced the iPhone 4 which included FaceTime.

2012

- American Cryptocurrency Exchange, Coinbase, was founded by Brian Armstrong and Fred Ehrsam.
- October 4th, Facebook officially crossed the 1 billion active users mark.
- October 15th, YouTube broke an Internet record as over 8 million concurrent live viewers watched Felix Baumgartner jump from the edge of space (128,100 feet).

2013

- February 1st, Microsoft announced it would be discontinuing the Hotmail brand and began moving over 300 million users to the new Outlook.com e-mail service.
- March 29th, One of the largest cyberattacks in Internet history occurred when a massive DDoS (Distributed Denial of Service) attack targeted The Spamhaus Project.
- June, Edward Snowden flew to Hong Kong and disclosed classified NSA (National Security Agency) documents to journalists Glenn Greenwald, Laura Poitras, Barton Gellman, and Ewen MacAskill. Disclosures included numerous global NSA and Five Eyes surveillance programs prompting discussions about national security and individual privacy.

2014

- October 1st, a Japanese man was the first person to be sentenced to two years in prison for manufacturing 3D-printed guns.
- October 20th, Apple introduced the Apple Pay and Force Touch features for its devices.

2015

- Microsoft replaced Internet Explorer with Microsoft Edge.
- Amazon.com held its first Amazon Prime Day.
- Starlink, a satellite-based Internet network developed by Elon Musk's aerospace company SpaceX, was first announced.
- February 6th, RadioShack filed for bankruptcy.
- Apple officially released the Apple Watch on April 24, 2015.

- December 10th, OpenAI was founded.

2016

- February, the FBI requested Apple to create an iOS version to bypass the iPhone 5C security to investigate a 2015 holiday party massacre.
- February 2nd, Google parent Alphabet passed Apple's market cap to become the world's most valuable public company.
- May 7th, Joshua Brown became the first person to die in a Tesla Model S self-driving car accident.
- June 13th, Microsoft announced it had agreed to acquire LinkedIn for $26.2 billion.
- September 26th, Yahoo confirmed that hackers stole account information of around 500 million users in a 2014 network breach.
- October 20th, Otto and Budweiser completed the world's first shipment by a self-driving truck.

2017

- Microsoft introduced Microsoft Teams.
- August 1st, The first block of Bitcoin Cash was created and anyone who owns bitcoin automatically received an equal amount of bitcoin cash.
- September 7th, Equifax announced that it had a security breach in July and that up to 145 million American accounts were stolen. The stolen information included SSNs, credit card information, and other personal information.

NOTES

1 Amtrak. (n.d.). *Amtrak. Wikipedia.* https://en.wikipedia.org/wiki/Amtrak
2 Association of American Railroads. (n.d.). *Association of American Railroads. Wikipedia.* https://en.wikipedia.org/wiki/Association_of_American_Railroads
3 Malkin, M. (2015, January 14). *Hey, how's America's rail security doing? RealClearPolitics.* https://www.realclearpolitics.com/articles/2015/01/14/hey_hows_americas_rail_security_doing_125247.html
4 Federal Railroad Administration. (n.d.). *Automated Track Inspection Program (ATIP).* U.S. Department of Transportation. https://railroads.dot.gov/railroad-safety/divisions/track/atip-overview
5 U.S. Department of Labor. (n.d.). *H-1B visa program.* https://www.dol.gov/agencies/whd/immigration/h1b
6 Amtrak Police Department. (n.d.). *About us.* https://police.amtrak.com/about-us.html
7 Trusted Internet Connection. (n.d.). *Wikipedia.* https://en.wikipedia.org/wiki/Trusted_Internet_Connection

8 Managed Trusted Internet Protocol Service. (n.d.). *Wikipedia*. https://en.wikipedia.org/wiki/Managed_Trusted_Internet_Protocol_Service
9 Einstein (US-CERT program). (n.d.). *Wikipedia*. https://en.wikipedia.org/wiki/Einstein_(US-CERT_program)
10 System and Organization Controls. (n.d.). *Wikipedia*. https://en.wikipedia.org/wiki/System_and_Organization_Controls
11 Cybersecurity and Infrastructure Security Agency. (n.d.). *Cyber Resilience Review (CRR)*. https://www.cisa.gov/resources-tools/services/cyber-resilience-review-crr
12 CAPTCHA. (n.d.). *Wikipedia*. https://en.wikipedia.org/wiki/CAPTCHA reCAPTCHA. (n.d.). *Wikipedia*. https://en.wikipedia.org/wiki/ReCAPTCHA
13 Role-Based Access Control. (n.d.). *Wikipedia*. https://en.wikipedia.org/wiki/Role-based_access_control
14 EC-Council. (n.d.). *EC-Council honors CISO of Amtrak as certified CISO of the year*. https://foundation.eccouncil.org/ec-council-honors-ciso-of-amtrak-as-certified-ciso-of-the-year/
15 Forrester Research. (2010). *The Forrester information security maturity model*. https://www.forrester.com/blogs/10-07-27-the_forrester_information_security_maturity_model/
16 Krebs, B. (2013, December 18). *Sources: Target investigating data breach. Krebs on Security*. https://krebsonsecurity.com/2013/12/sources-target-investigating-data-breach/
17 Krebs, B. (2014, May 6). *The target breach by the numbers. Krebs on security*. https://krebsonsecurity.com/2014/05/the-target-breach-by-the-numbers/
18 Streitfeld, D. (2014, March 6). *Target's chief information officer resigns. The New York Times*. https://www.nytimes.com/2014/03/06/business/targets-chief-information-officer-resigns.html
19 Cyber Kill Chain. (n.d.). *Wikipedia*. https://en.wikipedia.org/wiki/Cyber_kill_chain
20 Drupal. (n.d.). *Wikipedia*. https://en.wikipedia.org/wiki/Drupal
21 Pastebin. (n.d.). *Wikipedia*. https://en.wikipedia.org/wiki/Pastebin.com
22 Shodan. (n.d.). *Wikipedia*. https://en.wikipedia.org/wiki/Shodan_(website)
23 Digital Photocopiers Loaded WITH Secrets. (2010). *CBS News*. https://www.cbsnews.com/news/digital-photocopiers-loaded-with-secrets/
24 Nmap. (n.d.). *Wikipedia*. https://en.wikipedia.org/wiki/Nmap
25 Positive Train Control. (n.d.). *Wikipedia*. https://en.wikipedia.org/wiki/Positive_train_control
26 Imperva. (n.d.). *Account takeover (ATO)*. https://www.imperva.com/learn/application-security/account-takeover-ato/
27 Boardman, J. H. (n.d.). *Joseph H. Boardman. Wikipedia*. https://en.wikipedia.org/wiki/Joseph_H._Boardman
28 Moorman, C. (n.d.). *Charles Moorman. Wikipedia*. https://en.wikipedia.org/wiki/Charles_Moorman
29 Forrester Research. (n.d.). *The Forrester information security maturity model. CSO Online*. https://www.csoonline.com/article/542917/the-forrester-information-security-maturity-model.html
30 InfraGard. (n.d.). *Wikipedia*. https://en.wikipedia.org/wiki/InfraGard

Chapter 10

CISO: Evolution of a Vocation

Per the Wikipedia definition,

> A chief information security officer (CISO) is the senior-level executive within an organization responsible for establishing and maintaining the enterprise vision, strategy, and program to ensure information assets and technologies are adequately protected. The CISO directs staff in identifying, developing, implementing, and maintaining processes across the enterprise to reduce information and information technology (IT) risks. They respond to incidents, establish appropriate standards and controls, manage security technologies, and direct the establishment and implementation of policies and procedures.[1]

10.1 THE EARLY YEARS (1950–1970)

During these decades, you can follow the advancements in system and networking technologies that closely align with the evolution of the cybersecurity vocation. When ARPANET[2]—the precursor to the Internet—became operational in 1971, it introduced a new era of interconnected systems, which brought about emerging security challenges that had not previously existed. Technical staff, who served as forerunners to the CISO role, began to encounter challenges such as securing remote access, protecting data transmitted across networks, and addressing vulnerabilities related to unauthorized system use. Their security responsibilities were often added to their primary job duties, or "other duties as assigned," including managing user access controls, monitoring system activity for anomalies, and responding to early cyber threats. These practices laid the groundwork for the evolution of dedicated information security roles in the years that followed.

Before 1960, first-generation computers were massive systems that relied on vacuum tubes as their logic circuitry. For example, by the end of its operation in 1956, ENIAC contained 18,000 vacuum tubes, 7,200 crystal diodes, 1,500 relays, 70,000 resistors, 10,000 capacitors, and approximately

DOI: 10.1201/9781003650645-13

5,000,000 hand-soldered joints. Tubes failed at a rate of one every two days, and it took fifteen minutes to locate the failed tube. These limitations paved the way for significant innovations in computer design, prompting engineers to seek more reliable and efficient technologies. By 1960, transistorized computers came online, introducing lower costs, higher speeds, and reduced power consumption. This transition not only made computers more accessible to businesses and institutions but also set the stage for the rapid development of modern computing, fundamentally changing how organizations operated and paving the way for the digital revolution that would soon follow.

Circa 1966, Bob Taylor served as director of the Information Processing Techniques Office at the Advanced Research Projects Agency in the Pentagon. In his office at the Pentagon, he managed three separate terminals, each directly connected to separate mainframe systems at MIT, UC Berkeley, and another at a California mainframe supporting the Strategic Air Command. At that time, each mainframe operated in relative isolation, with no means for the systems to communicate or collaborate, making data sharing between institutions a slow and cumbersome process. Taylor's frustration with having to individually log into each system to access information highlighted the technical limitations of the era and inspired him to propose a unified network. This proposal led to the creation of ARPANET, the first network to implement packet switching, which became the foundation for the Internet as we know it today.

Mainframe and mid-range computer usage was expensive and early corporate mainframe applications primarily supported the Chief Financial Officer's (CFO) accounting and financial functions. So, those with data security responsibilities often reported to the CFO, as did the organization's technology function, since there was no official Chief Information Officer (CIO) role either.

> The role of chief information officer was first defined in 1981 by William R. Synnott, former senior vice president of the Bank of Boston, and William H. Gruber, a former professor at the Massachusetts Institute of Technology Sloan School of Management.[3]

Networking was a nascent technology. These were the days without the Internet as we know it today, Wi-Fi, or broadband. Early networking was built on IBM's Systems Network Architecture.

> Systems Network Architecture (SNA), a proprietary networking architecture, created in 1974. It is a complete protocol stack for interconnecting computers and their resources. SNA describes formats and protocols but, in itself, is not a piece of software. The implementation of SNA took the form of various communications packages, most notably Virtual Telecommunications Access Method (VTAM), the mainframe software package for SNA communications.[4]

> SNA was designed in the era when the computer industry had not fully adopted the concept of layered communications. *Applications, databases, and communication functions were mingled into the same protocol or product, which made it difficult to maintain and manage.*[5]

As computer systems became more prolific and interconnected, the need for a security role became apparent. The person responsible for managing security was known as the data security officer. The data security officer granted and revoked user access to computing resources and data, reset passwords, and ensured the physical security of the data center itself. Logical controls included implementing password policies, user authentication protocols, and regularly updating access permissions. Additionally, data security officers managed backup and recovery procedures, such as performing daily tape backups of critical data and storing these tapes in secure offsite locations to protect against data loss from disasters or equipment failures. By overseeing these various aspects, data security officers helped ensure the integrity and availability of organizational data.

10.2 MIDDLE YEARS (1970–2000)

With the advent of the microprocessor, microcomputers began to emerge beginning in 1975. Computing was getting personal as computers moved from isolated, standalone workstations to the user's desktop. As the Internet and local area networking matured, security positions were largely relegated to subordinate roles within programming or networking groups. Office automation continued to mature, including the proliferation of personal computers in the workplace, client-server computing, and relational databases. Concurrent with computing technology advancements, organizational changes advanced as well. Cybersecurity at this point was still not mainstream and was technically oriented versus business focused. The criticism leveled at the security function was that corporate requests for new computing capabilities and services were usually met with an emphatic "no." The security staff did not understand the business and the business did not understand technology and its associated security implications. But this was about to change as well.

In the context of evolving corporate reliance on technology, we need to consider advent of the CIO role. CIO responsibilities for technology and data management are closely aligned with the Chief Information Security Officer (CISO), who oversees information security within the organization. CIOs play a critical role in businesses use of technology and data since they are the primary interface between the business needs, user needs, and the information and communication technology used in the business. However, since technology investments commanded significant expenditures, early CIOs were often in the background and reported to CFO rather than Chief

Executive Officers (CEOs). The organizational structure necessary to support the growing importance of computers to the success of the organization was evolving and the need for a formal security role and function would soon follow.

The Internet continued to evolve with the adoption of Vint Cerf and Bob Kahn's Transmission Control Protocol/Internet Protocol (TCP/IP). TCP/IP became operative on January 1, 1983. Without TCP/IP, the Internet we know today would not exist. By 1986, 28,000 nodes chattered across ARPANET, causing congestion with speeds dropping from 32 Kbps to 40 bps across relatively small distances.[6]

In 1988, the infamous Morris worm was distributed via the nascent Internet and was the first to gain significant mainstream media attention. Robert Tappan Morris, a graduate student at Cornell, was the first in the United States to be convicted of a felony under the 1986 Computer Fraud and Abuse Act. Morris launched the worm on 8:30 PM November 2, 1988, from the Massachusetts Institute of Technology network.[7] As the result of a disjointed response to the Morris worm, the Computer Emergency Response Team/Coordination Center (CERT/CC) was created in Pittsburgh in November 1988 at the direction of the Defense Advanced Research Projects Agency. The CERT/CC Program partnered with government, industry, law enforcement, and academia to develop advanced methods and technologies to counter large-scale, sophisticated cyber threats.[8]

Another incident that brought nationwide focus to computer security was chronicled in the 1989 book *The Cuckoo's Egg* by Clifford Stoll. The story began in 1986, when Dr. Stoll, managing computers at Lawrence Berkeley National Laboratory in California, was asked by his supervisor to investigate a seemingly minor seventy-five-cent discrepancy in computer usage accounts—a reflection of how valuable computing cycles were at the time. What started as a routine audit quickly turned into a complex, three-year investigation that tested Stoll's persistence and ingenuity.

Stoll soon found himself tracking the elusive German hacker Markus Hess, facing numerous challenges and setbacks along the way. His relentless pursuit involved collaboration with the Federal Bureau of Investigation (FBI), the Central Intelligence Agency, the National Security Agency, and the United States Air Force Office of Special Investigations. Ultimately, his efforts led to Hess's capture and prosecution in 1989, marking one of the first well-documented cases of a computer break-in. This groundbreaking case not only demonstrated the far-reaching implications of cyber intrusions—especially with Hess selling sensitive information to the Soviet Union's KGB—but also raised public awareness about the vulnerabilities of computer systems. As a result, it spurred significant improvements in cybersecurity protocols across government and research institutions, making it a pivotal moment in the history of cybersecurity.

But *the hack that changed the world* for the CISO role occurred in 1994 when Russian hackers stole over $10 million from Citibank. In the mid-1990s, Citibank was one of the largest banking providers in the US and arguably the world. It's size and prestige made it a target, while its extensive use of connected IT created a significant risk factor. One that an opportunistic criminal took full advantage of in 1994.

> From a computer terminal in his apartment in St. Petersburg, Russia, Russian software engineer Vladimir Levin broke into a Citibank computer system in New York and, with support from several accomplices, stole $10.7 million by transferring the funds to accounts around the world. The incident came to underscore the vulnerability of banks and financial institutions at the time, as they increasingly relied on electronic transactions but lacked knowledge and countermeasures to protect these new systems.[9]

The first CISO in the world was Steve Katz, who served as the CISO for Citigroup from 1995 to 2003 and is known for his pioneering work in the cybersecurity industry. Katz had no idea what the CISO job was when he accepted it in 1995. Neither did Citicorp. "They said you've got a blank cheque, build something great — whatever the heck it is," Katz recounted during the 2021 podcast. "The CEO said, 'The board has no idea, just go do something.'"[10]

Katz recognized early on the need for organizations to take cybersecurity seriously and put proactive measures into practice to protect Citigroup from cyber threats. Here are some interesting facts about Steve Katz and his role as the world's first CISO:

- Katz was responsible for starting a massive security overhaul at Citigroup, which included investing in cutting-edge security technology and hiring a team of security experts.
- Katz's experience at Citigroup earned him a reputation as a cybersecurity thought leader, and he advised other major corporations and governments on cybersecurity strategy.
- Katz's legacy as the world's first CISO lives on as organizations around the world continue to recognize the importance of cybersecurity and invest in measures to protect their valuable data and assets.
- Steve Katz's pioneering work as the first CISO in the world has had a profound impact on the cybersecurity industry, and his legacy continues to inspire new generations of cyber professionals to protect digital infrastructure from cyber threats.

It was precisely incidents like this that had brought both ISC2 and the CISSP certification into existence. The timing of the Citibank incident, along with the fact the story was made public

> due to attempts to extradite the accused, could not have been more appropriate. It underlined the need for highly educated and skilled cybersecurity leaders that could grasp and solve these challenges for banks and other major institutions, as well as government itself and its agencies.[11]

Beginning in the 1980s, the United States Department of Defense Computer Security Center began publishing the Rainbow Series or sometimes known as the Rainbow Books. These were a series of computer security standards and guidelines. I remember considering them as biblical references in executing my Computer Security Site Manager duties. The following is a partial list the Rainbow Series. Note that after 1985, the series was published by the National Computer Security Center.

In 1995, the first part of the BS 7799 standard was published by the British Standards Institute Group and included best practices for information security management. Also, in the mid-1990s, the US National Institute of Standards and Technology (NIST) established the Computer Security Resource Center to provide NIST resources on computer, cyber, and information security and privacy.

While there were advancements in security during this period, it was also marked by significant challenges. The era became a kind of "golden age" for hackers, many of whom were motivated by curiosity and a desire to understand how networks and connected systems functioned. The growing complexity of nationwide, computer-based telephone systems also attracted the attention of hacker groups seeking to explore and sometimes disrupt these networks. For example, on January 15, 1990, two members of the Masters of Deception—a well-known group of hackers from New York—managed to cause a major failure at AT&T. Their actions resulted in 75 million phone calls being blocked, demonstrating how individuals with technical skill could impact vital services and underscoring the urgent need for improved security measures.[12]

These high-profile events set the stage for a series of increasingly sophisticated cyber threats. The Morris Worm raised public awareness about the dangers of self-spreading malware, while the AT&T outage showed the real-world consequences of network vulnerabilities. Not long after, attackers began to target personal computers on a massive scale. For instance, on May 5, 2000, the "ILOVEYOU" virus was unleashed. This virus arrived as an email with the subject line "ILOVEYOU" and an attachment named "LOVE-LETTER-FOR-YOU.txt.vbs." When opened, it quickly spread to millions of Windows-based computers worldwide, causing widespread disruption and financial losses.[13]

Together, these incidents fueled what would become an "arms race" between cyber attackers and defenders. As hackers developed new methods to exploit weaknesses, security professionals and technology companies responded by creating innovative tools and strategies to protect systems.

This ongoing battle led to the emergence of antivirus software, intrusion detection systems, firewalls, and a wide range of cybersecurity services. Ultimately, this dynamic not only inspired rapid technological advancements but also gave rise to a booming cybersecurity industry dedicated to staying one step ahead of evolving threats – a cybersecurity industrial complex.

10.3 LATER YEARS (2000–PRESENT)

Steve Katz's hiring kicked off the first CISO era from 1995 to 2000. Todd Fitzgerald's podcast, CISO Stories, divided the changing CISO roles into a timeline of subsequent eras:[14]

2000–2004: Regulatory compliance CISOs
2004–2008: Risk-oriented CISOs
2008–2016: Threat-aware cybersecurity CISOs (social/mobile/cloud)
2016–2022: Privacy and data-aware CISOs
2022–2027+: The integrated, business-resilient CISO

From my early career at Ernst & Young, LLP through my time at the American Red Cross, I had consistently believed that a solid understanding of TCP/IP and Unix/Linux is essential for IT professionals. For instance, during my tenure at Ernst & Young, LLP, troubleshooting network issues required a deep understanding of TCP/IP protocols, while managing server infrastructure at the American Red Cross relied heavily on Unix/Linux expertise. These foundational technologies not only enable communication across networks but also form the backbone of most Internet systems, making them central to understanding both how systems work and where vulnerabilities may lie.

At this stage of my personal evolution, I considered that CISOs should be technically oriented rather than being "just a paper CISO." This technical foundation was echoed in industry best practices, where many leading organizations prioritized hands-on technical expertise when hiring CISOs. However, as organizations have grown more complex, the CISO role has expanded to require not only technical acumen but also strong leadership, communication, and risk management skills. Today, the most effective CISOs balance their deep technical knowledge with the ability to lead teams, communicate across departments, and manage organizational risk in an increasingly dynamic threat landscape.

But my view would change as the CISO role evolved and I needed to understand and focus on the businesses I was protecting. As I encountered increasingly complex business environments and saw firsthand how cyber risks affected organizational goals, I realized that understanding the business context was just as critical as technical expertise. This shift in perspective prompted me to broaden my approach, moving beyond purely technical considerations to include the strategic and operational needs of the organization. Recognizing these lessons in my own journey, I found similar patterns reflected in real-world incidents. But let's examine two significant data breaches where the company's CISO role was either nonexistent or the CISO's qualifications were questioned.

10.3.1 Home Depot Data Breach

Attackers had infiltrated Home Depot's network using a vendor's login credentials and deployed custom point-of-sale malware to skim payment card information between April 10, 2014 and September 13, 2014. They compromised a reported 56 million credit cards. As part of an agreement, *Home Depot agreed to employ a CISO who reports directly to the board of directors and senior executives* and provides security training to all workers with access to the company network or access to customer information. The agreement also required Home Depot to implement security safeguards regarding logging and monitoring, access controls, encryption, password management, two-factor authentication, file integrity monitoring, firewalls, penetration testing, risk assessments, and intrusion detection.[15] *In this case, Home Depot had NO CISO at all!*

10.3.2 Equifax Data Breach

In 2017, credit reference agency Equifax suffered a data breach that affected 147 million US citizens and 15 million Britons. Names, social security numbers, birth dates, addresses, and driver's licenses of over 10 million were exposed after attackers took advantage of a web security vulnerability to break into Equifax's systems. The breach also exposed the credit card data of a smaller group of 209,000 people.[16]

Immediately after the breach, Equifax's CIO and CISO resigned. Equifax did not name the departing executives in its initial press release, but the company's website indicated its chief information officer was David Webb, who joined the company in 2010 from Silicon Valley Bank. According to his biography on Equifax's site, he was also a vice president at Goldman Sachs and earned his bachelor's degree in Russian as well as a master's in business administration from Northwestern University.

Susan Mauldin previously held the position of chief security officer (CSO) at Equifax. According to her LinkedIn page, which had removed many of its public details since reports earlier in the day of the breach's disclosure indicated she *had earned degrees in music composition, raising eyebrows about her qualifications for the tech-focused job.*[17] A few days after the news of the data hacking broke, "Ms. Mauldin's LinkedIn page reappeared with a different website address and with the specific detail that her degrees were in Music Composition removed. Her surname Mauldin was also replaced with the initial letter M."[18]

> *Lessons Learned* *Don't judge a book by its cover.* It is essential to approach assessments of professional qualifications with fairness and neutrality. In the case of Ms. Mauldin and the Equifax data breach, I do not personally know her. So, I am unable to confirm or dispute her technical expertise or cybersecurity capabilities. My intention is simply to present the facts regarding the breach and the public discussion around her credentials, without casting judgment. It is worth noting that some individuals without formal technical or cybersecurity training have demonstrated significant aptitude and skill in these areas. This situation underscores the importance of evaluating individuals on the basis of their actual skills, experience, and performance, rather than relying solely on formal credentials or academic backgrounds. When considering candidates for critical roles, especially in cybersecurity, organizations should look beyond titles and degrees to assess true capability. Maintaining objectivity and fairness not only fosters a more inclusive professional environment but also helps ensure that the most qualified individuals are entrusted with important responsibilities.

As the CIO organizationally moved from under the CFO and reported directly to the CEO, the CISO followed and reported to the CIO. While the CISO role gained acceptance, many questions remained unanswered – Do we even need a CISO? What are the CISOs' responsibilities? To whom should the CISO report? Thus, CISOs went through an identity crisis as the role evolved, and organizations wrestled with what the role should be. There were other confusing organizational roles with the emergence of CSO and the Chief Risk Officer roles.

The FBI Cyber Division was created in 2002 to combat cyber-based terrorism, hostile foreign intelligence operations conducted over the Internet, and cybercrime by applying the highest level of technical capability and investigative expertise. I saw corporations hiring ex-FBI agents as corporate CSOs who were given information security responsibilities in addition to their physical security and enforcement duties. These former FBI agents, now corporate CSOs, were ill-equipped for the additional technology-related security duties. Especially in the late 1990s/early 2000s, as the FBI was just getting its feet wet in information security compared to today, where they have world-class expertise.

At this time, the information security field was gaining further acceptance and recognition with professional certifications such as Information System Security Certification Consortium's[2] Certified Information Systems Security

Professional and Information Systems Audit and Control Association's Certified Information Security Manager, and, more recently, EC-Council's Certifiedl CISO. Many companies now require that candidates for CISO jobs hold one or more of these professional certifications.

To compensate for the overemphasis on technical abilities and lack of business acumen, there was a move to hire CISOs with Master of Business Administration degrees. More than ever, today's CISOs must have a mix of technical and business acumen. They must be corporate cheerleaders and evangelize security to C-level executives and corporate boards of directors.

The threat landscape facing organizations was also evolving and the once curious hackers and virus writers weaponized their tools and techniques for criminal activities and nefarious nation-state mayhem. One significant threat is ransomware, a type of malicious software that takes control of a computer system and demands payment (a ransom) to restore access to important data. Millions of sensitive records and data have been pilfered from the US Government's Office of Management and Budget and consumer credit bureaus like the Equifax breach.

Besides the escalation in cyberattacks and massive data breaches, CISOs also face the challenge of securing their organizations' expanding use of technology. This includes the adoption of cloud computing (storing and accessing data and programs over the Internet instead of on local computers), mobile devices, web services, digital business platforms, and social media. As businesses rely more on these tools, CISOs must continuously adapt their security measures. The rising volume and variety of cyberattacks force CISOs to make difficult decisions about where to focus their resources, how to train staff, and which technologies to prioritize. Ultimately, the evolving threat landscape means that CISOs must stay alert, constantly update their strategies, and balance the need for innovation with the imperative of keeping information secure.

10.4 THE FUTURE – CYBERSECURITY AND THE CISO

I am excited about the future of computing and cybersecurity, but frankly, I am glad to have retired from this most challenging career and delighted to turn the torch over to the next generation of CISOs. Some of the future challenges include:

- *Specialization.* The best comparison I can make with regard to the evolution of cybersecurity is to compare it to the medical field. In the early days of medicine, there were primarily general practitioners, surgeons, and very few areas of specialization. Now, we have a proliferation of medical specializations for example, brain surgeons, cardiac specialists, orthopedic surgeons, geneticists, and allergists. While this comparison with cybersecurity may be an oversimplification, you get the idea that just as specialization has occurred in medicine and other complex professional disciplines, the same has and continues to occur within cybersecurity.

To make my point, Morey Haber, VP of technology at BeyondTrust, argues,

> It will also fall on CISOs of the future to bring in and manage specialist services to help them meet demands, outsourcing certain aspects of the operation to service providers who deliver on scale to multiple organizations. The shortage of security professionals will warrant using partners, MSSPs, consultants and other shared resources to accomplish goals versus bringing the entire expertise in-house. This means the CISO and his/her reports will be more like project managers, managing resources to accomplish goals versus reactive tactile responses.[19]

- *Regulations.* Regulations governing cybersecurity have generally exploded. As an example, on May 25, 2018, the General Data Protection Regulation (GDPR) became enforceable. GDPR is intended to strengthen and unify data protection for all individuals within the European Union (EU) and addresses the export of personal data outside the EU.[20] In my CISO roles, I worked under the Payment Card Industry – Data Security Standard (PCI-DSS) and Health Insurance Portability and Accountability Act of 1996 regulations. These regulations do not remain stagnant and are continuously updated. PCI-DSS itself went through several iterations, beginning with Version 1.0 in December 2004 and its current Version 4.0 of March 2022.[21] As future massive data breaches occur and other yet-to-be security failures occur, we will see more stringent regulations with "teeth," including fines and other punitive actions. CISOs themselves may become future targets for legal sanctions after security breaches.

  In 2024, significant new cybersecurity rules were enacted in major economies around the world, effectively transforming the global regulatory environment.

  > The regulations come as business leaders are increasingly open to enhanced cybersecurity rules. In fact, the World Economic Forum's latest Global Security Outlook found that 60% of executives believe proper cyber and privacy regulations effectively reduce risk – a major increase from the 21% in 2022.[22]

  Some of the new regulations include:
  - The EU – Network and Information Security Directive
  - The US National Cybersecurity Strategy
  - Singapore's Operational Technology Cybersecurity Masterplan
  - The European Cyber Resilience Act

- *Complexity.* In general, computing systems will continue to explode regarding technological complexity and the challenges to secure them. One way to look at complexity is to assess "Lines of Code (LoC)." In Robert N. Charette's article, "This Car Runs on Code" (IEEE Spectrum, 2009-02-01), he stated that "It takes dozens of microprocessors running 100 million lines of code to get a premium car out of the driveway, and this software is only going to get more complex." The following shows LoC complexity across various platforms, including the human genome:[23]
  - 0.4 million LoC — Space Shuttle
  - 2 million LoC — Hubble Space Telescope
  - 5 million LoC — Mars Curiosity Rover
  - 14 million LoC — Boeing 787 (total flight software)
  - 24 million LoC — F35 Fighter Jet (2013)
  - 100 million LoC — Automobile Software
  - 2 billion LoC — Google (all services)
  - 3,300 billion LoC — Human Genome

  Below are some of Windows' popular operating systems and their number of LoC:[24]
  - Windows 3.1 (1992) — 2.5 million LoC
  - Windows NT 4.0 (1996) — 16 million LoC
  - Windows 2000 (2000) — 29 million
  - Windows XP (2001) — 35 million
  - Windows Vista (2007) — 45 million
  - Windows 7 (2009) — 42 million
  - Windows 8 (2012) — 50 million
  - Windows 10 (2015) — 55 million
  - Windows 11 – there are no official LoC counts but estimates place it at between 60 and 100 million LoC.
- *Personal Liability.* "Personal liability for CISOs, in the context of cybersecurity incidents, refers to the potential for legal and financial repercussions landing directly on their shoulders, along with the implications these accusations have on their careers."[25]

> In late 2022, a federal jury handed down a guilty verdict to Joe Sullivan, Uber's former CSO on charges of "obstruction of the proceedings of the Federal Trade Commission and misprision of felony in connection with the attempted cover-up of a 2016 hack at Uber" according to a notice published by the Department of Justice (DOJ).[26]

It was found that "Sullivan affirmatively worked to hide the data breach from the Federal Trade Commission (FTC) and took steps to prevent the hackers from being caught."[27]

We can see that future cybersecurity-related business disruptions and data breaches costing millions of dollars in damages places a target on the back of CISOs for legal damages and sanctions. As the trend to hold CISOs personally responsible and possibly liable for system, network, and data compromises, there is a worry that CISOs may be leaving their positions. Jeff Pollard, VP and principal analyst at Forrester, is already seeing signs of top CISO talent opting out of the role.

> The CISO role was already thankless prior to these changes. And plenty of vendors exist out there that will gladly add a former operating CISO to their teams as an evangelist, thought leader, or even line of business leader. And those jobs are often better compensated than a traditional CISO role.

Pollard said. "More upside and far less downside makes shifting to vendorland an easy decision for most CISOs."[28]

So, what it may come down to is CISOs needing personal liability insurance.

> Morristown, N.J., November 11, 2024 – Crum & Forster (C&F) announces its new Professional Liability Insurance coverage for Chief Information Security Officers (CISOs). This groundbreaking new solution is designed to protect CISOs from personal liability in an increasingly challenging risk landscape. The policy offers crucial coverage for CISOs who, despite their pivotal role in defending organizations against complex cyber threats, often lack the same protections afforded to other senior executives designated as legal officers of the organization.[29]

- *Staffing.* Over my thirty years of cybersecurity experience, the annual complaint was an continues to be shortages of cybersecurity talent. I gave an example of our process for evaluating cybersecurity talent at Amtrak resulting in an effective and knowledgeable team. Despite uncertain economic conditions and impacts of AI, cybersecurity remains a high-demand field. The need for cybersecurity professionals is projected to grow, with a significant persistent global workforce gaps. Cybersecurity jobs are among the fastest-growing globally, with an estimated 3.5 million unfilled positions worldwide.
- *Artificial Intelligence (AI).* Obviously, AI is the 800 lb. gorilla in the room. AI will be used by hackers and nation-states to develop new and innovative methods to compromise networks and systems. Likewise, AI will be used to augment Secure Operations Centers to analyze millions of lines of data coming from those same network and system sensors. The end result will be an AI cybersecurity arms race and continuing game of whack-a-mole between criminal miscreants and CISOs. AI helped companies improve their efficiency, it also gave malicious actors new attack vectors. Below are a few examples:

- AI-optimized attacks. Generative AI and machine learning technologies can create more sophisticated malware, eliminate the typical indicators from a phishing email, or scale their attacks to more targets.

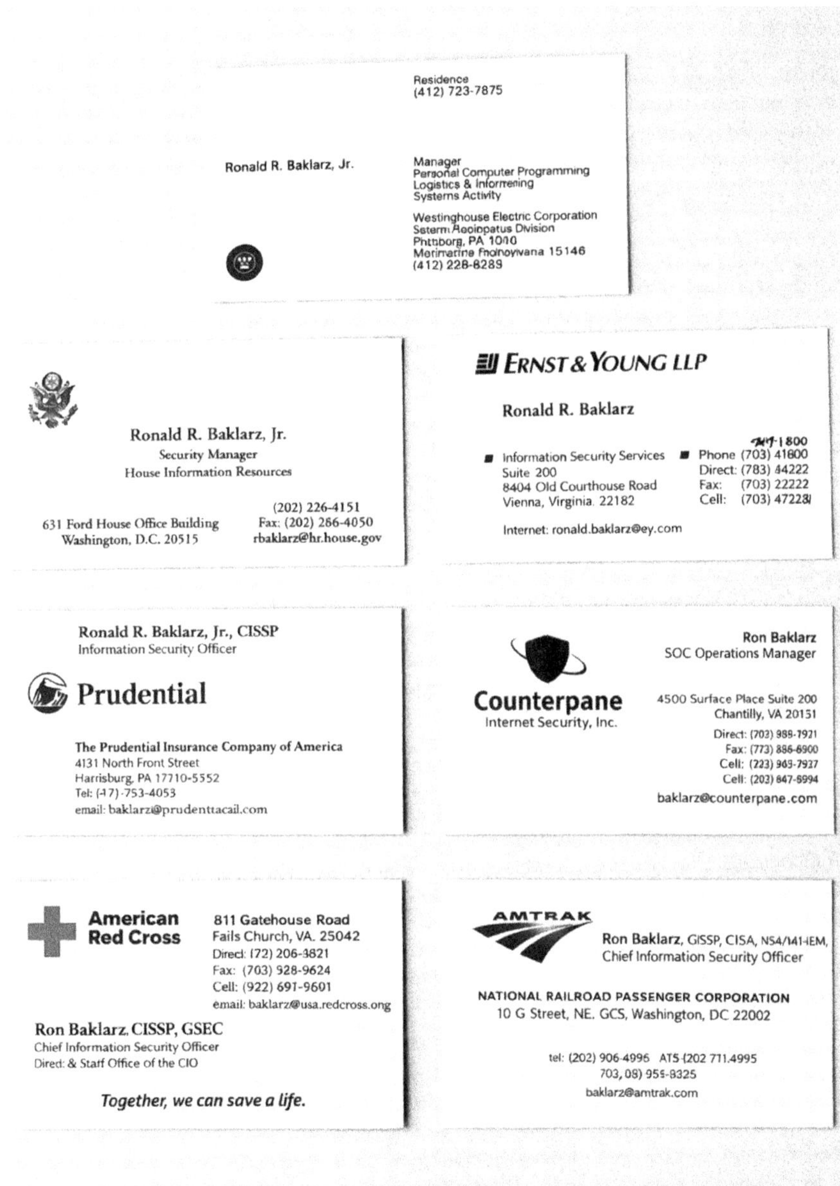

Figure 10.1 Ron Baklarz Business Cards through the Years.

- AI in deepfakes. AI can create fake realistic images, videos, and audio files that can be used to impersonate individuals or spread misinformation and malicious influence.
- Data poisoning. Malicious AI can inject false, biased, or corrupted data into AI training datasets causing inaccurate results and reducing performance.

Technology has and will continue to influence and enhance our lives. It is truly an exciting time in the history of mankind but future CISOs will be challenged more than ever to secure this vast and complex technological world. I will leave you with one last *Lessons Learned* item that sums up your responsibilities as CISOs.

Lesson Learned The last lesson I will leave you with is simple, and I tried to live up to it in each of my CISO positions. *Leave It Better Than You Found It* (Figure 10.1).

NOTES

1 Chief Information Security Officer (n.d.). *Wikipedia.* https://en.wikipedia.org/wiki/Chief_information_security_officer
2 ARPANET. (n.d.). *Wikipedia.* https://en.wikipedia.org/wiki/ARPANET
3 Chief Information Officer. (n.d.). *Wikipedia.* https://en.wikipedia.org/wiki/Chief_information_officer
4 Systems Network Architecture. (n.d.). *Wikipedia.* https://en.wikipedia.org/wiki/Systems_Network_Architecture
5 Systems Network Architecture. (n.d.). *Wikipedia.* https://en.wikipedia.org/wiki/Systems_Network_Architecture
6 Metz, C. (2013, January 3). *The internet turns 30. The Register.* https://www.theregister.com/2013/01/03/operational_internet_anniversary/
7 Morris worm. (n.d.). *Wikipedia.* https://en.wikipedia.org/wiki/Morris_worm
8 CERT Coordination Center. (n.d.). *Wikipedia.* https://en.wikipedia.org/wiki/CERT_Coordination_Center
9 ISC². (2024). *CISSP30: The Citibank cyber heist—30 years on.* https://www.isc2.org/Insights/2024/03/CISSP30-The-CitiBank-Cyber-Heist-30-Years-On
10 *30 years of the CISO role. CSO Online.* https://www.csoonline.com/article/1310847/30-years-of-the-ciso-role-how-things-have-changed-since-steve-katz.html
11 ISC². (2024). *CISSP30: The Citibank cyber heist—30 years on.* https://www.isc2.org/Insights/2024/03/CISSP30-The-CitiBank-Cyber-Heist-30-Years-On
12 Slatalla, M., & Quittner, J. (1995). *Masters of deception: The gang that ruled cyberspace.* HarperCollins.
13 ILOVEYOU. (n.d.). *Wikipedia.* https://en.wikipedia.org/wiki/ILOVEYOU
14 *30 years of the CISO role. CSO Online.* https://www.csoonline.com/article/1310847/30-years-of-the-ciso-role-how-things-have-changed-since-steve-katz.html

15 Home Depot Agrees to Pay $175 Million Multistate Settlement. (n.d.). *National Law Review*. https://natlawreview.com/article/home-depot-agrees-to-pay-175-million-multistate-settlement-following-2014-data
16 Taylor, M. (n.d.). *The biggest data breaches of the 21st century. CSO Online*. https://www.csoonline.com/article/534628/the-biggest-data-breaches-of-the-21st-century.html
17 Financial Times. (n.d.). https://www.ft.com/content/54de09fa-35a1–3c36-bab4-0ac13c997737
18 Equifax Chief Security Officer. (n.d.). *Hollywood LA News*. https://www.hollywoodlanews.com/equifax-chief-security-officer/
19 InfoSecurity Magazine. (n.d.). *The CISO of the future*. https://www.infosecurity-magazine.com/magazine-features/the-ciso-of-future-down-to-business/
20 General Data Protection Regulation. (n.d.). *Wikipedia*. https://en.wikipedia.org/wiki/General_Data_Protection_Regulation
21 Payment Card Industry Data Security Standard. (n.d.). *Wikipedia*. https://en.wikipedia.org/wiki/Payment_Card_Industry_Data_Security_Standard
22 World Economic Forum. (2024). *Cybersecurity regulation changes in the EU*. https://www.weforum.org/stories/2024/10/cybersecurity-regulation-changes-nis2-eu-2024/
23 McCandless, D. (n.d.). *Million lines of code. Information is Beautiful*. https://informationisbeautiful.net/visualizations/million-lines-of-code/
24 TechBloat. (n.d.). *How many lines of code in Windows 11*. https://www.techbloat.com/how-many-lines-of-code-in-windows-11.html
25 SAFE Security. (n.d.). *CISO personal liability*. https://safe.security/resources/blog/ciso-personal-liability/
26 Uber Breach Verdict Makes Personal Liability Real for CISOs. (n.d.). *CSO Online*. https://www.csoonline.com/article/573871/guilty-verdict-in-the-uber-breach-case-makes-personal-liability-real-for-cisos.html
27 Uber Breach Verdict Makes Personal Liability Real for CISOs. (n.d.). *CSO Online*. https://www.csoonline.com/article/573871/guilty-verdict-in-the-uber-breach-case-makes-personal-liability-real-for-cisos.html
28 Personal Liability Sours 70% of CISOs on Role. (n.d.). *CSO Online*. https://www.csoonline.com/article/3631759/personal-liability-sours-70-of-cisos-on-their-role.html
29 Crum & Forster. (n.d.). *Professional liability insurance for CISOs*. https://www.cfins.com/crum-forster-introduces-professional-liability-insurance-for-chief-information-security-officers/

Appendices

APPENDIX A – IS AUDIT AND CONTROL JOURNAL[1]

Figure A.1 Information Systems Audit and Control Association - IS Audit & Control Journal Volume III, 1998 Cover - This article was originally published in the ISACA® Journal. Reprinted with permission.

The Enemy Within — Y2K Issues Below the Application Level

By Ronald R. Baklarz, Jr.

Many people have mixed emotions regarding the upcoming change in millennium. Some view it as a mystical time in the course of human history while others will see it simply as an excuse to act as irrationally on New Year's Eve as usual. Activities will vary at the precise moment when the celestial odometer spins from 1999 to 2000. Some will be watching from the comfort of a living room while others will be anxious, wondering whether or not their businesses will be functioning properly. This uncertainty will be focused on the world's computer systems and no one will know for sure until that odometer has spun. Some experts believe that the events of the hours and days following the change may prove to be catastrophic.

What Is The Problem?

In the early stages of the computing phenomena, no one looked far enough into the future to worry about the change from the 20th to the 21st century. For efficiency's sake, programmers and system architects alike, truncated the first two digits of the *century* field which they knew would *always* be 19. This logic, or illogic as the case may be, was imbedded in literally millions of lines of software code throughout the decades. To make matters worse, this discrepancy was imbedded in hardware via all sorts of circuitry permutations that also neglect the need to recognize a new century.

Humans carry the chromosome of procrastination and have just recently begun to focus on this huge issue. After all, the Y2K problem was four years away, three years away, two years away... Now, hosts of consultants and systems analysts are scrambling to research and fix the major applications of banks, stock exchanges, military systems, etc. Software "boot camps" have been set up to train programmers how to find and fix the date field problems. Those who can work in *COBOL* are in demand as Y2K consultants. The Committee on Government Reform and Oversight's Subcommittee on Government Management, Information, and Technology conducted a *US Federal Government Year 2000 Survey* in the second quarter of 1996. In his statement dated 30 July, 1996, the subcommittee's chairman, the Honorable Stephen Horn, concluded that there was a "lack of awareness and preparedness" for Federal Agency systems to meet the challenges of the 21st century. As security professionals, some are deeply concerned that as part of the so called solution, *consultants* are sending mission critical software code off shore and round about outside organizations for Y2K maintenance.

Questions arise such as:

- Who will have access to the code?
- Who will check the bank's million lines of code upon its return to ensure that no computer virus or trojan horse has been added?
- While attempting to fix one problem, a number of other problems may have been aroused.

Problem Definition for Hardware

There are reasons to look at Y2K issues that lie below the obvious application level. The focus until now seems to have been with the software applications (i.e., code and interface) which is a HUGE issue. However, not much press has been given to the hardware aspects of the problem.

No one really knows how many non-compliant chips there are in service. In 1995, 3.5 billion microprocessors were sold. In 1996, that figure ballooned to sales of over 7 billion microprocessors. Greenwich Mean Time (GMT), a Y2K consultancy, found that 93 percent of PCs shipped before 1997 had Basic Input /Output System (BIOS) software installed that either did not roll over to 2000, or would encounter serious problems because the BIOS did not realize 2000 is also a leap year. For BIOS software installed in 1997, the failure figure declines to 47 percent — still too high a total, according to Karl Fielder, chief executive of GMT and an expert on the millennium issue. (web site at www.gmt-2000.com)

If the percentage of non-compliant chips is similar to the percentage of non-compliant lines of code in *COBOL* programs, then the standard estimate would allege that between five percent and ten percent of all chips are non-compliant. The only way to be absolutely certain that chips are compliant is to test them — TEST ALL CHIPS! One by one, system by system. This is not possible in the time remaining. The logistics of

Figure A.2 Information Systems Audit and Control Association - IS Audit & Control Journal Volume III, 1998 Page 1 - This article was originally published in the ISACA® Journal. Reprinted with permission.

testing is beyond the ability of most organizations. Let's assume that testing does take place and bad chips are identified. Bad chips must be either carefully removed and replaced or have some sort of software fix applied to the non-compliant system. Fixing the non-compliant chips and systems assumes that compliant chips or software fixes for each application are available from the manufacturer.

The Y2K hardware problem is as diverse as the number of available hardware architectures. In a PC, three components come into play with regard to date and time functions: (1) Complementary Metal Oxide Semiconductor (CMOS) Real Time Clock (hereon referred to as RTC) chip, (2) Basic Input /Output System (BIOS) software, and (3) the Disk Operating System (DOS) itself. Let us look at the role of each of these components in determining the system's ability to define dates.

The ***first*** date is maintained in the RTC chip — a hardware component that is normally found on the machine's motherboard. This date is kept current by the system's battery and in addition to being a clock is also a 100-year calendar. Going back in time, most will recall that the first PCs did not have a battery with which to keep the date current. Upon bootup, the user had to enter the current date each time the computer was energized. The user then had to enter the correct date and time. This situation was not acceptable and as the computer designs matured, so did their ability to store and record the accurate time and date.

The RTC chip stores seconds, minutes, hours, days of the month, months and years as two-digit values. This means that the RTC represents the year as a two-digit value (00-99) and remembers it. The component that contains the RTC also contains some battery-backed memory that is used for storing system configuration information. The BIOS uses some of this memory to store the century part of the year (e.g., 19, 20). Since the century byte is not a part of the RTC, it has to be set and maintained elsewhere. Many BIOS versions do this (which assure that the century piece of the year is remembered), as well as some operating systems.

BIOS is the software that handles the low-level input and output functions on PC hardware. BIOS provides the interface between the operating system and the PC hardware. It is sometimes called *firmware* because it is resident on the computer itself. It is typically stored in a re-programmable memory chip such as EPROM (Erasable Programmable Read Only Memory) or more recently Flash memory. This means that it can be updated during the life of the computer. Many BIOS versions have added a capability to handle the transition to the year 2000. This information is obtainable from the system vendor or manufacturer, the motherboard manufacturer, or the BIOS vendor to see whether the organization's BIOS version is capable of recognizing dates in the 21st century. If the user has an older BIOS version, there may be an updated version available from the BIOS provider.

Y2K problems are not restricted to PCs but impact less obvious, but critical components such as routers.

The ***second*** date is in the Disk Operating System (DOS and Windows) operating system software. This date is represented in a drastically different manner than is the case with the RTC/BIOS date. The RTC/BIOS date, which does include century date, is kept as century/two-digit-year/month/day a the DOS date is kept as the number of days-since-1980/01/ The DOS date (in days) is converted to four-digit-year/month/day when any application or program asks for i When DOS (or Windows) boots up, it normally initializes it current date by reading the date in the RTC and converting i to days-since-1980/01/01. DOS maintains the current date a long as the system is running; the RTC hardware maintains i date whether the system is running or not (via battery), but it does not maintain the century.

In most of the RTCs, year 99 overflows to 00 and the centu ry remains unchanged so the effective year becomes 1900; in DOS, year 1999 overflows to 2000. So until the system is rebooted there will appear to be no problem with the transition from year 1999 to 2000; but trouble lurks in the RTC date, which has become the year 1900. When the machine is re-booted, DOS will read 1900 as an out-of-range date from the RTC and the date conversion algorithm will calculate an erroneous 1980-01-04. That's what the DOS date will become after rebooting the system after the Year 2000 transition if the RTC exhibits the standard flaw.

Consider Components and Systems

The problem is not restricted to PCs, but impacts less obvious components that are just as critical. Most organizations are interconnected via networks. Most networks are interconnected for example, by components called routers. Routers also contain chips (i.e., hardware and firmware) that must be Y2K compliant. A visit to the web site of one of the major network component providers — Cisco (www.cisco.com) identifies an entire section on Y2K compliance. Cisco states that, "For those products which have separate hardware and software components, the product is only considered compliant if the hardware component is listed as compliant and the installed software is also compliant." Cisco's web site has a component-by-component list that identifies components, model numbers, software versions and a color code to identify the Y2K status of the component

There are numerous other systems based on hardware that should be considered including card swipe-based building entry systems, security systems, bar code systems, etc. The possibilities are endless.

More Bad News?

Not only will systems have to deal with the transition in centuries, but the Year 2000 is a leap year. Many systems will not recognize or account for this anomaly either. The common heuristic is that leap years occur every four years except in years divisible by 100. Unfortunately, an often forgotten exception is that there are also leap years in dates divisible by 400 (e.g. the year 2000). Not only will scores of programs lose a day in 2000, but some programs were also found to be calculating leap years based on only 2 digit years. In these

46 *IS Audit & Control Journal, Volume III, 199*

Figure A.3 Information Systems Audit and Control Association - IS Audit & Control Journal Volume III, 1998 Page 2- This article was originally published in the ISACA® Journal. Reprinted with permission.

cases, the number "1900" was being added before applying the algorithm.

Application Level Issues

According to a recent survey by Software Emancipation Technology (SET), 100 percent of the more than 20 organizations studied with complex C and C++ software programs suffer from undiscovered Year 2000 glitches. The study, issued on 25 March, 1997, was undertaken from late 1996 through early 1997 and is available at www.setech.com/press/pr970325.html. It included corporations across a range of industries, including financial services, telecommunications, healthcare and government, using C and C++ software primarily in mission-critical applications. These applications run on client/server and distributed systems platforms. The SET study cites statements from Ian Hayes, principal, Clarity Consulting. According to Mr. Hayes, "The false belief that Year 2000 issues are limited to mainframe COBOL applications has extremely damaging implications for many organizations. Little time and attention is devoted to critical software applications that run on non-mainframe platforms or use more recent languages."

SET's Year 2000 Business Manager Rajeev Arora categorized the most commonly found problems as follows:

Arithmetic Operations. Many programs commonly use the final two digits of years to determine time differences. Thus, 1996 is two years earlier than 1998 (98 - 96). But in 2000, a wide array of credit card, insurance claims processing and other systems will obtain unusable values when they subtract any year from "00."

"The false belief that Year 2000 issues are limited to mainframe COBOL applications has extremely damaging implications for many organizations."

Character Arrays: Programs sometimes use character arrays internally to store only the last 2 digits of a year. Such formats don't allow for the expansion of dates to four digits to properly handle the Year 2000 and beyond.

Screen Output - Hard coded "19s" are often appended to two-digit year fields in calls to screen print commands. For example, software systems often place the number "19" in front of the last two date digits in credit card systems (expiration dates), invoicing systems (due dates), etc. In the Year 2000, such dates become 1900. Some systems also print dates with hard coded 2 digit year fields, such as 3/15/97.

Use of Flags - End of century dates in a xx/xx/xx format are commonly used as flags for special conditions. For example, on one system 01/01/01 was used as a date initializer. On another system, 12/31/99 indicated the termination date of an event. In both cases, a date past the year 2000 would cause unexpected results.

What Can be Done?

The following are some simple testing procedures to perform to check applications for Y2K compliance:

1. Before attempting any of these tests make a backup of the entire system, in case a program failure corrupts the data.
2. If the application allows entry of four-digit-year dates, it is most likely Y2K compliant. Check anyway using both two and four digit years.
3. Enter the date "29/02/00" into any place on the screen where a date is required. If the program rejects the date, it is most likely *not* Y2K compliant. As stated earlier, the Year 2000 is a leap year, but the program may interpret the year as 1900, which was not a leap year.
4. Some financial programs may not allow entry of dates outside a current fiscal year. In that case, one may have to advance the year and period to Dec. 1999. *Never* conduct tests on "live" (i.e., production) data files; if possible, make a copy and use that instead.
5. Make some data entries for dates such as 31/12/99, 01/01/00 and 29/02/00. Run reports for Dec. '99 through to Feb. '00 and check that all of the test entries you entered appear in the expected date order. Missing transactions may indicate that the program assumed the 00 year was 1900.
6. If possible, check with the application's developers to guarantee that they have audited the software source code and database to determine potential date processing problems. This can be done by a combination of code and database scanning tools, and manual examination of source code algorithms (calculation methods) for correctness. The challenge here is keeping track of the interdependency of hundreds of files and programs.

Examinations and conversions of lines of code (LOC) take time and money. It is estimated that Y2K analysis costs about US $1 per LOC. Typically, organizations and companies have anywhere from hundreds of thousands to millions of lines of code in use. It is also estimated that it takes approximately ten hours per typical COBOL module (300 - 1000 LOC) to examine, correct, test, and document. Remember, Monday the 3rd of January 2000 is an ***absolute, fixed, deadline.***

PC Tests

Prior to testing PCs, ensure that the machine has not been set up to perform activities as a function of time such as a Y2K server that is used to authenticate users and thus requires the users to change their passwords every 60 days. At the conclusion of the test and depending on the application, *all* users may be forced to change their passwords since the system date has been altered.

1. Set the PC clock to 31/12/99 and time 23:59. Turn it off, wait more than a minute, and restart. If the date has reset to 1980, the BIOS is not Year 2000 compliant. Be careful of any unattended PCs (typically fax/file/print servers or machinery monitors) that will not roll over the date correctly when rebooted.
2. There are a number of utilities (e.g., DOSCHECK) that will automatically check a system for Y2K compliance. These are especially useful for testing a large number of machines throughout the organization.

Figure A.4 Information Systems Audit and Control Association - IS Audit & Control Journal Volume III, 1998 Page 3 - This article was originally published in the ISACA® Journal. Reprinted with permission.

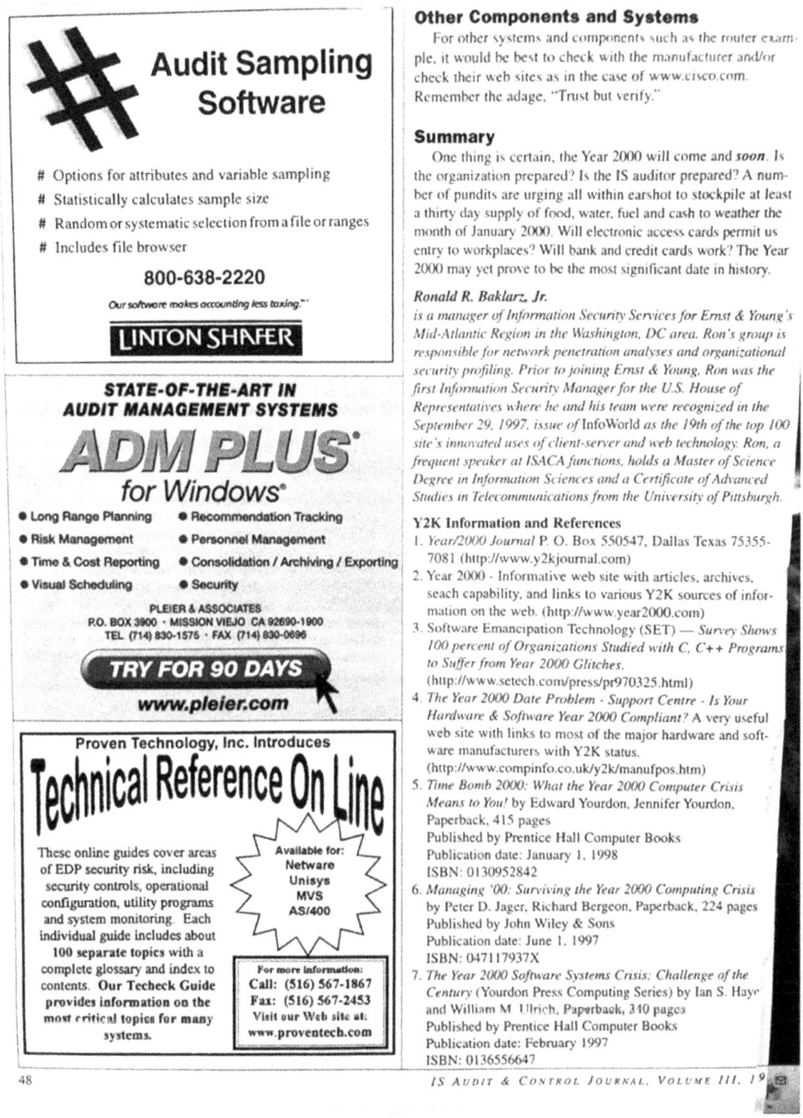

Other Components and Systems

For other systems and components such as the router example, it would be best to check with the manufacturer and/or check their web sites as in the case of www.cisco.com. Remember the adage, "Trust but verify."

Summary

One thing is certain, the Year 2000 will come and ***soon***. Is the organization prepared? Is the IS auditor prepared? A number of pundits are urging all within earshot to stockpile at least a thirty day supply of food, water, fuel and cash to weather the month of January 2000. Will electronic access cards permit us entry to workplaces? Will bank and credit cards work? The Year 2000 may yet prove to be the most significant date in history.

Ronald R. Baklarz, Jr.
is a manager of Information Security Services for Ernst & Young's Mid-Atlantic Region in the Washington, DC area. Ron's group is responsible for network penetration analyses and organizational security profiling. Prior to joining Ernst & Young, Ron was the first Information Security Manager for the U.S. House of Representatives where he and his team were recognized in the September 29, 1997, issue of InfoWorld *as the 19th of the top 100 site's innovated uses of client-server and web technology. Ron, a frequent speaker at ISACA functions, holds a Master of Science Degree in Information Sciences and a Certificate of Advanced Studies in Telecommunications from the University of Pittsburgh.*

Y2K Information and References

1. *Year/2000 Journal* P. O. Box 550547, Dallas Texas 75355-7081 (http://www.y2kjournal.com)
2. Year 2000 - Informative web site with articles, archives, seach capability, and links to various Y2K sources of information on the web. (http://www.year2000.com)
3. Software Emancipation Technology (SET) — *Survey Shows 100 percent of Organizations Studied with C, C++ Programs to Suffer from Year 2000 Glitches.* (http://www.setech.com/press/pr970325.html)
4. *The Year 2000 Date Problem - Support Centre - Is Your Hardware & Software Year 2000 Compliant?* A very useful web site with links to most of the major hardware and software manufacturers with Y2K status. (http://www.compinfo.co.uk/y2k/manufpos.htm)
5. *Time Bomb 2000: What the Year 2000 Computer Crisis Means to You!* by Edward Yourdon, Jennifer Yourdon, Paperback, 415 pages
   Published by Prentice Hall Computer Books
   Publication date: January 1, 1998
   ISBN: 0130952842
6. *Managing '00: Surviving the Year 2000 Computing Crisis* by Peter D. Jager, Richard Bergeon, Paperback, 224 pages
   Published by John Wiley & Sons
   Publication date: June 1, 1997
   ISBN: 047117937X
7. *The Year 2000 Software Systems Crisis: Challenge of the Century* (Yourdon Press Computing Series) by Ian S. Hayes and William M. Ulrich, Paperback, 340 pages
   Published by Prentice Hall Computer Books
   Publication date: February 1997
   ISBN: 0136556647

48 *IS Audit & Control Journal, Volume III, 19*

Figure A.5 Information Systems Audit and Control Association - IS Audit & Control Journal Volume III, 1998 Page 4 - This article was originally published in the ISACA® Journal. Reprinted with permission.

APPENDIX B – PRUDENTIAL'S FIRST QUARTER 1999 BUSINESS VALUE AWARD (BVA)[2]

Keeping *a watchful eye on* Prudential's networks and systems

Behind an ordinary office door in a somewhat secluded section of the ROS 3 Building in Roseland, NJ, is a room equipped with the latest technology helping to keep Prudential safe from hacker attacks.

The room, which is secured, monitored and accessible only to members of Prudential's Computer Emergency Response Team, is the site of the new Security Operations Control Center (SOCC), which implements technology that has never been used at Prudential—until now.

The Security Operations Control Center (SOCC) is where the Prudential Computer Emergency Response Team (PruCERT) monitors and tests the security of the company's critical network infrastructure and responds to hacker attacks.

"The SOCC is used enterprise-wide—it is the control center for incident handling, security software testing and intrusion detection monitoring," explains David Greenman, Senior Security Engineer. David was responsible for the selection of system software and hardware as well as the physical setup of the SOCC, which opened in February.

Inside the room are two side-by-side 37" monitors which rise above a row of four computers, all of which continually track what is happening throughout the company's critical systems networks.

The space is also equipped with Windows NT and UNIX workstations from which additional security testing and analysis is conducted. While the components and staff of the SOCC keep a watchful eye on Prudential's networks and systems, the SOCC facility is also being continuously monitored for security purposes, including the use of surveillance cameras.

"We needed a world-class facility from which to do this work and that's how the SOCC came into being," explains Ron Baklarz, Director of the Security Technology Group. "We use the latest and greatest in hacker tools to ensure our systems are secure from attack."

The two main tools used in the control center were licensed by Prudential from Internet Security Systems (ISS). The first is the ISS Scanner, which allows Prudential to scan large portions of the network at the same time, assessing security by identifying specific problems within systems.

The second is Real Secure, which acts as a burglar alarm for the network. Real Secure engines are preprogrammed to set off alarms when they sense an attack, such as hackers trying to get information through a firewall. If an attack is discovered by the Real Secure monitors, e-mail alerts and pager alerts are sent to PruCERT members so that other countermeasures can be initiated to negate or at least minimize the attack.

The SOCC also provides Prudential with computer forensic capabilities—procedures for analyzing and collecting evidence when an internal computer is linked to suspicious activity.

David and Ron recently received a First Quarter 1999 Business Value Award for developing and creating the SOCC. The facilities management area and Corporate Technology Services

Figure B.1 Page 1 of Article originally published in Prudential Insurance Company of America's July/August 1999 Operations & Systems Bulletin - Computer Hacker's Beware! Keeping a Watchful Eye on Prudential's networks and systems. Reprinted with permission of the Prudential Insurance Company of America

Ron Bubhox. above, is one of the iniiuiduals responsiole for deceloping and creuting the 3BCC—aud for aruning a inemoss liluo Award

nervrorking groups worked along with David and Reurie creice a more scauns informamor teclinolojy exvirortinent for Prupendal.

in addision to Ravid and Ron Tahor Inceaxns of the Prudcupial Hoiocsnon: Esmgeacr Respouse teams Insinde Hark Callrionc. Susioins Marager. Jar Lanovan: Acqortinatior of Patidenetls inexR: of Ritpover salbe um providcs. Vick Mather still a ferr fece jpoint for Intesr secoure ergegency response reams.

response reams. On a daily basis. the members of these glolial teams communicate with each other to. coordinate uicident prevention procedures, provide rapid response to incidents and share information.

For more information about the Security Operations Control Center, contact Ron Baklaru on linc or at 9?8-776-5283. If rou are suspicious of a possible comporer virss or atack. call the Company's tmno, hory tolem tne Compdny re al 800 634 1095

Figure B.2 Page 2 of Article originally published in Prudential Insurance Company of America's July/August 1999 Operations & Systems Bulletin - Computer Hacker's Beware! Keeping a Watchful Eye on Prudential's networks and systems. Reprinted with permission of the Prudential Insurance Company of America.

APPENDIX C – SAMPLE CUSTOMER SERVICE ADVISORY

Information Security Office
Customer/Field Service Advisory

CISO-2003.0012
Date: February 24, 2003
Re: W32/Lovgate@M

MEDIUM-LEVEL ADVISORY FROM RON BAKLARZ, CHIEF INFORMATION SECURITY OFFICER

Executive Summary

There are reports across the Internet regarding the propagation of several variants of the W32/Lovgate virus/worm. This malcode is particularly troublesome as it (1) engages aspects of social engineering techniques to entice victims to open the email and attachment, (2) is network-aware so it will spread using network shares, (3) has its own SMTP engine, and (4) drops a back door component to permit hackers to come back and infiltrate compromised systems.

For virus mitigation purposes, ARC quarantines attachments with .exe file extensions. The current 4248 DAT file will not detect/protect against the newer variants of the malcode. System administrators should distribute the 4249 DAT as soon as it becomes available.

TECHNICAL DETAILS

Mailing Component

The worm is capable of sending a reply to all messages found in the INBOX by using its own SMTP engine. This kind of propagation strategy would make this worm spread slower than classic mass-mailers, and this is reflected in "@M" suffix.

If, for example, you have a message in your INBOX from "???@wherever.com," the worm will reply to the message as follows:

Wherever.com account autoreply:

"I'll try to reply as soon as possible.

Take a look at the attachment and send me your opinion!"

>Get your Free wherever.com account now!<

Notice that the domain "wherever.com" has been used by the worm in its message body.

Worm Component

The worm has the capabilities of propagating through network shares. It searches for shared folders, including any subfolders, and copies itself using any of the following filenames:

- fun.exe
- images.exe
- news_doc.exe
- s3msong.exe
- pics.exe
- billgt.exe
- midsong.exe
- PsPGame.exe
- hamster.exe
- setup.exe
- tamagotxi.exe
- joke.exe
- docs.exe
- searchurl.exe
- card.exe
- pics.exe

Backdoor Component

The worm drops a Trojan component (77,824 bytes) with the following filenames: ILY.DLL, 1.DLL, REG.DLL, and TASK.DLL. The backdoor opens port 10168 on the computer and will send an email notification to the hacker that the computer has been compromised. Information about the infected machine is also sent to the hacker. This information may include the system password. Detection for the backdoor is in 4249 DATs.

APPENDIX D – AMTRAK NATIONAL NETWORK

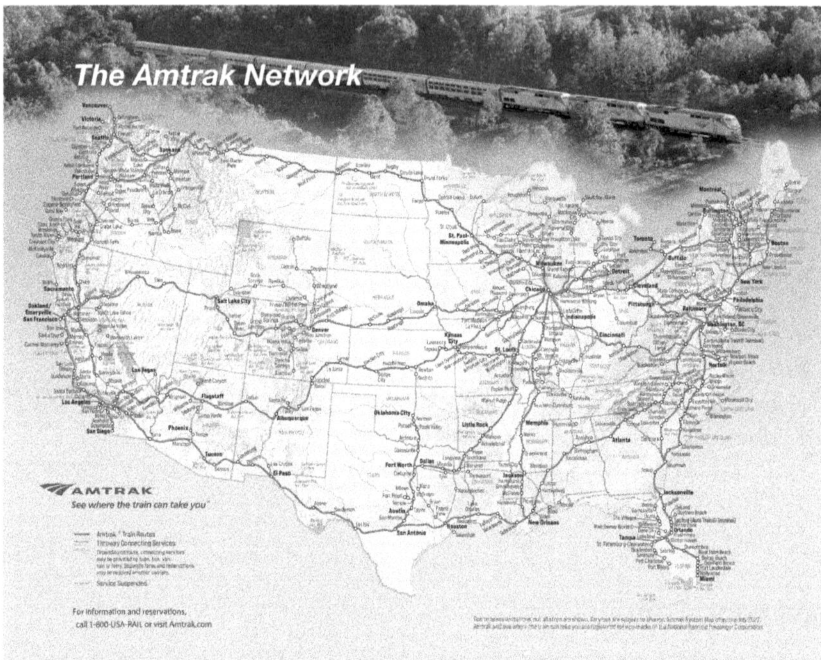

Figure D.1 Amtrak System Map Effective July 2022

APPENDIX E – PERSPECTIVE SECURITY ANALYST QUESTIONNAIRE

MEMO

CISO-2013.120

Date	August 29, 2013	From	Ron Baklarz Chief Information Security Officer
To	HR	Department	
cc		Subject	Interview Questions for Perspective Information Security Analysts

Candidate's Name ______________________
Date of Interview ______________________
Amtrak Interviewers ______________________
Position Applied: ______________________

(P, L, A) Please rate your proficiency with the following technology environments and security technologies using Novice (one year or less experience), Intermediate (three to five years of experience), Expert (over five years of experience) as a rating:

Table E.1

Phone Interview Questions

Role(s)	*Questions*	*Responses*
P, L, A	How many years of experience do you have in Information Security?	
P, L, A	What, if any, information security/technology-related certifications do you currently hold?	
P, L, A	What are your responsibilities in your current position?	
P, L, A	Describe in detail a security incident that you were involved in and what was your role in the response effort?	(Look for complete, thoughtful reply)
P, L, A	Describe any computer systems and networking that you have implemented in your home. What projects are you working on in your free time?	(Look for complete, thoughtful reply)
P, L, A	In what role do you see yourself in the next three, five, and ten years?	(Look for complete, thoughtful reply)

P, Principal; L, Lead; A, Associate

Table E.2

Technology	*Brand(s)*	*Experience (N, I, or E)*
Firewalls		
Intrusion detection/prevention systems		
Web content filtering		
Vulnerability scanners/ assessments		
PC forensic tools		
Encryption		
Operating Systems		
Anti-malware		
SIEM		
Application Security		
Mobile Application Security		

Table E.3

	On-Site Interview Questions	
Role(s)	*Questions – Cultural*	*Responses*
P,L,A	Please describe your daily work routine and what management style you prefer to work under (e.g., close, or hands-off management)	
P, L, A	Describe a team effort you were involved in that required collaboration.	
P, L, A	Describe a successful project you were involved with and what you learned from it.	
P, L, A	Describe an unsuccessful project you were involved with and what you learned from it.	
P, L, A	Who do you look up to within the field of Information Security? Why? *A standard question type. All we're looking for here is to see if they pay attention to the industry leaders, and to possibly glean some more insight into how they approach security. If they name a bunch of hackers/criminals that'll tell you one thing, and if they name a few of the pioneers that'll say another. If they don't know anyone in Security, we'll consider closely what position you're hiring them for. Hopefully it isn't a junior position.*	
P, L, A	Where do you get your security news? *We are looking to see how in tune they are with the security community. Answers such as Team Cymru, Reddit, and Twitter are good. The exact sources do not really matter. What does matter is that the candidate doesn't respond with, I go to the CNET website, or "I wait until someone tells me about events." It's these types of answers that will tell you is likely not on top of things.*	

P, Principal; L, Lead; A, Associate

Table E.4

On-Site Interview Questions		
Role(s)	*Questions – Corporate/Risk*	*Responses*
P, L, A	In your opinion, what is the goal of information security within an organization? *We are looking for one of two approaches; the first is the lockdown approach, i.e. to control access to information as much as possible. While admirable, this again shows a bit of immaturity. A much better answer in my view is something along the lines of, "To help the organization succeed." This type of response shows that the individual understands that business is there to make money, and that we are there to help them do that. It is this sort of perspective that I think represents the highest level of security understanding – a realization that security is there for the company and not the other way around.*	
P, L, A	What is the difference between a threat, vulnerability, and a risk?	
P, L, A	If you were to start a job as head engineer or CSO at a Fortune 500 company due to the previous guy being fired for incompetence, what would your priorities be? [Imagine you start on day one with no knowledge of the environment]. *We don't need a list here; we're looking for the basics such as: Where is the important data? Who interacts with it? Network diagrams. Visibility touch points. Ingress and egress filtering. Previous vulnerability assessments. What's being logged an audited? Etc. The key is to see that they can quickly prioritize, in just a few seconds, what would be the most important things to learn in an unknown situation.*	
P, L, A	As a corporate Information Security professional, what's more important to focus on: threats or vulnerabilities? *This one is opinion-based, and we all have opinions. Focus on the quality of the argument put forth rather than whether or not they chose the same as you, necessarily. My answer to this is that vulnerabilities should usually be the main focus since we in the corporate world usually have little control over the threats. Both are true, of course; the key is to hear what they have to say on the matter.*	(Look for complete, thoughtful reply)

P, Principal; L, Lead; A, Associate

Table E.5

	On-Site Interview Questions	
Role(s)	*Questions – Network Security*	*Responses*
P, L, A	Please explain the components of the OSI stack/model. (Physical, Link, Network, Transport, Session, Presentation, Application)	
P, L	What port does ping work over? *A trick question but an important one. If the candidate starts throwing out port numbers, you may want to immediately move to the next candidate. Hint: ICMP is a layer three protocol (it doesn't work over a port) A good variation of this question is to ask whether ping uses TCP or UDP. An answer of either is a fail, as those are layer four protocols.*	
P, L	How exactly does traceroute/tracert work at the protocol level? *This is a fairly technical question but an important concept to understand. It is not natively a security question really, but it shows you whether or not they like to understand how things work, which is crucial for an INFOSEC professional. If they get it right you can lighten up and offer extra credit for the difference between Linux and Windows versions.* *The key point people usually miss is that each packet that is sent out doesn't go to a different place. Many people think that it first sends a packet to the first hop, gets a time. Then it sends a packet to the second hop, gets a time, and keeps going until it gets done. That's incorrect. It actually keeps sending packets to the final destination; the only change is the TTL that is used. The extra credit is the fact that Windows uses ICMP by default while Linux uses UDP.*	
P, L	If you had to both encrypt and compress data during transmission, which would you do first, and why? *If they don't know the answer immediately it's ok. The key is how they react. Do they panic, or do they enjoy the challenge and think through it? If you encrypt first you will have nothing but random data to work with, which will destroy any potential benefit from compression.* *If they don't know the answer immediately it's ok. The key is how they react. Do they panic, or do they enjoy the challenge and think through it? If you encrypt first you will have nothing but random data to work with, which will destroy any potential benefit from compression.*	

P, Principal; L, Lead; A, Associate

Table E.6

On-Site Interview Questions		
Role(s)	*Questions – Application Security*	*Responses*
P, L, A	What's the difference between symmetric and public-key cryptography *Standard stuff here: single key vs. two keys, etc. In public-key cryptography you have a public and a private key, and you often perform both encryption and signing functions. Which key is used for which function?* *You encrypt with the other person's public key, and you sign with your own private. If they confuse the two, don't put them in charge of your PKI project.*	
P, L	What's the difference between HTTP and HTML? *Obviously the answer is that one is the networking/application protocol and the other is the markup language, but again, the main thing you're looking for is for him not to panic.*	
P, L	How does HTTP handle state? *It doesn't, of course. Not natively. Good answers are things like "cookies," but the best answer is that cookies are a hack to make up for the fact that HTTP doesn't do it itself.*	
P, L, A	What exactly is Cross Site Scripting? *We're looking for them to say anything regarding an attacker getting a victim to run script content (usually JavaScript) within their browser. Target = browser*	
P, L, A	What are the common defenses against XSS? *Input Validation/Output Sanitization, with focus on the latter. White/blacklisting may be provided as an option. This shows some understanding but we'd want to see the candidate indicate these solutions are incomplete at best (They may no longer be on the list of possible XSS solutions).*	
P, L, A	What is SQL injection? *We're looking for them to say anything regarding an attacker injecting SQL command code into a website in an effort to attack a database and exfiltrate data.* *Target = backend server*	
P, L	What is a NOP Sled? *Simply put, a NOP sled is a series of no operation commands meant to slide the computer processing unit's command execution stream to its final predetermined course.*	
P, L	Give three security issues you would want to see addressed in a corporate BYOD policy? BONUS – Are there any security benefits?	
P, L	What would you be looking for when running a wireless assessment of a location?	

P, Principal; L, Lead; A, Associate

Table E.7

On-Site Interview Questions		
Role(s)	*Questions – Miscellaneous Security*	*Responses*
P, L	Describe the last program or script that you wrote. What problem did it solve? *All we want to see here is if the color drains from the guy's face. If the candidate panics then we not only know he's not a programmer (not necessarily bad), but that he's afraid of programming (bad). Any high-level security guy needs some programming skills. They need to understand the concepts and at least be able to muddle through some scripting when required.*	
P, L	Do you have any security tools you use over and over again? ALTERNATE – What are your favorite open-source security tools?	
P, L	How would you set up an encryption key management solution to protect fields in a particular column on a table in a database? *Maybe too specific. What we are looking for here is that 3DES or AES encryption be mentioned and that encryption key management be recognized as the most important part of the solution. How will they be protected? The answer doesn't matter as much as the recognition of the need.*	
P, L	What would be your key requirements for a Mobile Device Management solution?	
P, L	Give three security issues you would want to see addressed in a corporate BYOD policy? BONUS – Are there any security benefits?	
P, L	How would you implement a secure login field on a high traffic website where performance is a consideration? *We're looking for a basic understanding of the issue of wanting to serve the front page in HTTP, while needing to present the login form via HTTPs, and how they'd recommend doing that. A key piece of the answer should center around avoidance of the MiTM threat posed by pure HTTP. Blank stares here mean that they've never seen or heard of this problem, which means they're not likely to be anything near pro level.*	

P, Principal; L, Lead; A, Associate

Candidate ________________________ Date ________________________

Handout to P, L, A for their input

What are some of the problems with this server scan result?

Port/Service/State	Comment
19/tcp open	__________
21/tcp open	__________
23/tcp open	__________
80/tcp open	__________
135/tcpopen	__________
139/tcp open	__________
443/tcp open	__________
445/tcp open	__________
3389/tcp open	__________
8080/tcp open	__________
9898/tcp open	__________
31337/tcp open	__________

APPENDIX F – EC COUNCIL PRESS RELEASE DATED OCTOBER 16, 2013 REPRINTED WITH PERMISSION OF EC COUNCIL[3]

What set Baklarz apart from the pool of applicants was the impressive number of firsts he's achieved in his career.

Atlanta, GA (PRWEB) October 16, 2013 – "It was an exciting day for all involved and we are very proud to have the opportunity to recognize such a trailblazing security professional," says Jay Bavisi, President of EC-Council, of the awards ceremony at the Global CISO Forum. Ron Baklarz, Chief Information Security Officer of Amtrak, was chosen from a field of nearly 1,000 other certified CISOs for the honor. EC-Council established the CCISO of the Year award to recognize the pioneers of the information security industry. According to Bavisi,

> It is important to honor the best and brightest of our immense pool of CCISO talent in order to shine a light on the tremendous growth and importance the CCISO has achieved in the less than 2 years it's been in existence. EC-Council is honored to count all of our CCISOs as our members.

Baklarz wasn't the only CCISO to be recognized by EC-Council, however. There were an impressive list of finalists as well, including Mauricio Angee, the CISO of Mercantil Commercebank; Frank Kai Fat Chow, a Senior Manager of Automated Systems (HK) Ltd.; Paul Horn, the CISO of DynCorp International LLC; Mike Loginov, the CISO of Ascot Barclay Cybersecurity Group; Ashish Chandra Mishra, the CISO of Tesco Hindustan Service Centre; Rakesh Radhakrishnan CSA of AMGEN; Paul Swarbrick, CISO of NATS, the National Air Traffic Service; and Silas Mohale, the CISO of ASTUTE FSE (PTY) LTD. Finalist traveled from around the world to attend the Forum and awards ceremony to participate in the keynotes, panels, and networking events taking place at the Global CISO Forum.

What set Baklarz apart from the pool of applicants was the impressive number of firsts he's achieved in his career. Currently, the CISO of Amtrak Baklarz oversees an impressive information security operation. Amtrak is America's Railroad®, the nation's intercity passenger rail service and its high-speed rail operator. A record 31.6 million passengers traveled on Amtrak in FY 2013 on more than 300 daily trains – at speeds up to 150 mph (241 kph) – that connect forty-six states, the District of Columbia, and three Canadian Provinces. During this period, Amtrak earned $2.1 billion in ticket revenue while employing more than 20,000 people.

The complexity and importance of this organization are staggering. Prior to his tenure with Amtrak, Baklarz's career includes an impressive series of firsts, including being one of the first information security managers in the Naval Nuclear Program, being the first Information security manager at the

US House of Representatives, building the first secure operations center at Prudential Insurance, being the first CISO at the American Red Cross, and the first CISO at Amtrak. His career in information security is unparalleled as he's served in CISO positions in military, government, healthcare, non-profit, private sector, and transportation organizations. He is truly a leader in information security and among the first-ever certified CISOs through EC-Council.

Index

Access Control List 124, 128, 196
Advanced Encryption Standard (AES) 104, 132
Advanced Interactive eXecutive proprietary UNIX OS (AIX) 104, 132
Advanced Research Projects Agency (ARPA) 8, 41, 259, 261
Amazon Web Services (AWS) 182, 244
American Red Cross 97–157
American Red Cross Computer Emergency Response Team (ARCcert) 104–105, 149
American Standard Code for Information Interchange (ASCII) 44, 78–79, 81
Armed Forces Emergency Services 98, 104, 128, 133
Artificial Intelligence (AI) 45, 270
Assistant NAVSEA Technical Representative (ANSTR) 16, 20, 28, 30, 35
COMSEC issues with local area network 25
Association of American Railroads 187, 256

Beginner's All-purpose Symbolic Instruction Code (BASIC) 7–8
Bettis Atomic Power Laboratory (BAPL) 15
Bird, Tina 89–90, 92
Board of directors 111, 207, 236, 265
Bolt Beranek and Newman (BBN) 7
Brady, Jerry 82
British Standards Institute Group 263
California Senate Bill Privacy Law (SB 1386) 115, 129
Callas, Jon 90
Canadian Institute of Chartered Accountants 136
Center for Internet Security 113, 124, 159
Center of Excellence 136, 138
Centralized Electrification and Traffic Control (CETC) 209, 234–237, 253
Centralized National Operations Center (CNOC) 209
Certification & Accreditation (C&A) 197–202
Certified Chief Information Security Officer (C|CISO) 153, 292–293
Certified Information Security Manager (CISM) 153, 267
Certified Information System Auditor (CISA) 105, 148, 153, 181
Certified Information System Security Professional (CISSP) 83–85, 88, 153, 181, 262
Chapman, Brent 90
Chief Information Officer (CIO) 97, 100, 135, 185, 203
Equifax CIO 265
origin of CIO role 225, 259–260
Chief Privacy Officer (CPO) 157, 174, 175
Chief Security Officer (CSO) 157, 181, 265–266, 269, 287
Chief Technology Officer (CTO) 83, 89–90, 93, 162, 204
Clinton, William J. 54, 63–64
Common Body of Knowledge 83–85

Common Business-Oriented Language (COBOL) 16
Communications Security (COMSEC) 13, 23, 31–32, 87, 147
Completely Automated Public Turing test to tell Computers and Humans Apart (CAPTCHA) 212–213, 257
Computer Emergency Response Team /Coordination Center (CERT/CC) 261, 272
Computer Fraud and Abuse Act 42–43, 261
Computer Security Site Manager (CSSM) 13–14, 20, 28, 32, 40
CSSM and DoD Rainbow Books 263
Concept of operations (CONOPS) 201–202
Configuration management (CM) 118, 147, 200
Control Objectives for Information and Related Technologies (COBIT) 105, 107, 124, 130, 135
ATLAS compliance review 146–147
Counterpane Internet Security 89–93
Credit card verification (cvv) 144
Cyber Resilience Review (CRR) 209

Darbyshire, Jon 76
Data Encryption Standard (DES) 9
Data loss prevention (DLP) 9, 162, 170, 178, 180
Data Processing Management Association (DPMA) 83
Defense Information Services Agency (DISA) 128, 154
Defense Messaging System (DMS) 128
Demilitarized zone (DMZ) 108–109, 130
Department of Defense (DoD) 13, 15, 47, 63, 128
Department of Energy (DoE) 25–26, 28, 31–32, 40, 154
clearances 14–15
DoE Orders 20–21
Department of Homeland Security (DHS) 134–136, 149, 190, 200
information network (HSIN) 197–198
cyber-hygiene reviews 223
industrial control system security assessment 245
Designated Approval Authority (DAA) 184, 197–198
Digital subscriber line (DSL) 221
Distributed denial of service (DDOS) 93, 155, 255
Domain name system (DNS) 106, 109, 141

Ehlers, Vernon 66
EINSTEIN 201, 257
Electronic blood donor record (eBDR) 104, 111–118, 129, 131
Elliott Company 4–6
Emission security (EMSEC) 23
EnCase 104, 117–118, 133, 168, 193
Encrypting file system (EFS) 115–116
EPIC Metals 2–4
Ernst & Young Limited Liability Corporation (E&Y, LLC) 59, 75–81, 83, 93, 264
Amtrak financial system audits 211
European Union (EU) 268
Extended Binary Coded Decimal Interchange Code (EBCDIC) 79
Extensible authentication protocol (EAP) 115

Farmer, Dan 45, 65–66
Federal Bureau of Investigation (FBI) 45, 53, 66, 127, 135
Cyber Division 152, 266
FOBI Training Academy Quantico, VA 250–251
NCFTA 151–152
pastbin disclosure 233
Sober worm 154
trainday411.com website compromise 229
Federal Communications Commission (FCC) 22–23. 46
Federal Food and Drug Administration (FDA) 99, 101
Federal Information Security Modernization Act (FISMA) 198, 200–201, 203
Federal Information Systems Security Educators' Association (FISSEA) 130, 141, 149
Federal Railroad Administration 192–193, 241
Federal Telecommunications System (FTS) 34–36, 38, 46
File transfer protocol (ftp) 42, 44, 60, 109, 112

InstantDX security breach 161
multi-function printers 235–236
server vulnerabilities 125
temporary wirless kits 239
Formula Translator or Formula Translation (FORTRAN) 7, 10, 16
Forum of Incident Response and Security Teams (FIRST) 127, 135, 149, 156
ARCcert 104–105
PruCert 85
US-HCERT 65–66
Frame relay 125
Franz, Ken 76
Frequency hopping spread spectrum 115
Fritchie, Gus 106, 189, 252

General Data Protection Regulation (GDPR) 189, 223, 268
General support system 14, 235
Georgetown University Hospital 14, 187, 192
GFI LANguard 177
Government Forum of Incident Response and Security Teams (G-FIRST) 14
Gramm–Leach–Bliley Act 188
Gross, Andrew 89
Gula, Ron 93

Health Insurance Portability and Accountability Act (HIPAA) 167, 175, 182–182, 188–189, 187
patient health record access violation 177–178
requirement for CSO and CPO positions 157
requirement for unique IDs 174
Healthcare Information and Management Systems Society (HIMSS) 14, 190
Hewlett-Packard (HP) 14
High-speed rail 14, 230, 264
High-Tech Crime Investigators Association (HTCIA) 14, 97
House Information Resources 14, 74, 78, 93–94
Human Capital Management (HCM) 14, 249, 283
Hurricane Katrina 122, 178–182
Hypertext markup language (HTML) 43, 71, 106, 243, 289
Identity and access management (IAM) 157, 158, 160, 164
Azyxxi access management issues 167–170, 173–174
challenges 213–216
MedStar 180–181
Independent verification and validation (IV&V) 202
Industrial control systems (ICS) 190, 234, 236 ,245
Information Assurance Technical Framework (IATF) 127
Information System Audit and Control Association (ISACA) 105, 148, 153
INFOSEC Assessment Methodology (IAM) 144
INFOSEC Evaluation Methodology (IEM) 144
InfraGard 127, 135, 159, 250, 257
Institute of Electrical and Electronics Engineers (IEEE) 73, 164, 156, 269
International Business Machines Corporation (IBM) 6–8, 10, 40–43
IBM vs. Apple 26–27, 40–43
personal computers 4, 10, 19, 22–23
selectric typewriters 18–19
International Information System Security Certification Consortium (ISC2) 83–85, 262
International Organization for Standardization 135
Internet Crime Complaint Center (IC3) 151–152, 210, 246
Internet of things (IoT) 44
Internet relay chat (IRC) 125
Internet Security Systems (ISS) 59, 74, 83
Internet service provider (ISP) 8, 98, 126

Kaplan, Steve 76–77
Katz, Steve 262, 264
Key performance indicators (KPI) 105, 139
Knolls Atomic Power Laboratory (KAPL) 15–16, 26, 36, 38
Klynveld, Peat, Marwick, Goerdeler (KPMG) 105–106, 109, 136–137, 192, 252
Kurtz, George 76

Lainhart IV, John W. 47, 49, 55, 72, 105
U.S. House of Representative network audit 59–60
U.S. Hose of Representative policies 62
INFOWorld article 69, 72, 105
Lawrence Berkeley National Laboratory (LBNL) 261
Lightweight directory access protocol (LDAP) 168, 215–216
Lines of code (LoC) 269, 273
Local area network (LAN) 13, 25, 27–29, 31–33, 41
Longstaff, Tom 32

Machinery Apparatus Organization (MAO) 15–16, 26, 36, 38
MailSweeper 108
Managed security monitoring 89, 92–93
Managed security service provider (MSSP) 140–141
Managed Trusted Internet Protocol Services (MTIPS) 200–201
Massive Open Online Course (MOOC) 221
Master of Science (MS) 17, 39
Masters of Deception (MoD) 263
MedStar Health 157–181
Memorandum of understanding (MOU) 236–237
Miller, Ken 47, 50, 57, 62, 71–72
Multipurpose internet mail extensions (MIME) 44, 146

National Biomedical Computer System (NBCS) 101, 132
National Computer Security Center (NCSC) 263
National Cyber-Forensics & Training Alliance (NCFTA) 151–152
National Cybersecurity Division 134, 149
National Donor Deferral Registry (NDDR) 101, 132
National Infrastructure Protection Center (NIPC) 127
National Institute of Standards and Technology (NIST) 198, 263
National Railroad Passenger Corporation (Amtrak) 184–252
Navy Ships Parts Control Center (SPCC) 16, 32, 36
Nessus 106, 109, 141, 144, 147
vulnerability scanning 166, 211, 237, 242
Network Solutions, Inc (NSI) 109–110
Network-Attached Storage (NAS) 194
Network-Based Application Recognition (NBAR) 118–119
New Technologies, Inc (NTI) 84–85, 103
Nikto 132, 141–142, 166
Nmap 106, 105, 132, 141–142, 166
vulnerability testing 211, 236–237, 257
Non-Secure Internet Protocol Router NETwork (NIPRNET) 128–129
NT file system (NTFS) 114

Office automation (OA) 7, 33, 40, 59, 260
early office automation 18–20
Lotus Notes issues 158
OA server compromise 124–125
personal computer impacts 26–27
technology advancements 41
Office of Security Strategy and Special Operations (OSSSO) 190–191
Office of the Chief Information Security Officer (OCISO) 139–143, 145–149
Office of the Inspector General (OIG) 189, 194, 207–208, 210
Online Donation System (ODS) 136–137, 144, 145
Open Worldwide Application Security (OWASP) 94, 253
ORACLE 114, 132, 153, 215–216, 239
acquisiton of SUN microsystems 254
Organizational Unit (OU) 204, 206

Paller, Alan 85. 151
Payment Card Industry–Data Security Standard (PCI-DSS) 147, 184, 188, 192, 268
Personally identifiable information (PII) 57, 112, 129, 131, 148
data classification policy 188
disclosure 231–232
Pittsburgh Naval Reactors (PNR) 20–21, 25, 28, 39
Plan of action and milestones (POAM) 198–200, 202

Point-of-sale (POS) 224, 265
Positive train control (PTC) 240, 253
Poulsen, Kevin 161, 183
Pretty Good Privacy (PGP) 65, 90
Price Waterhouse 47, 59, 76
PricewaterhouseCoopers (PwC) 105, 107, 119, 124, 130
Primary domain controller (PDC) 112
Protected health information (PHI) 161–162
Prudential Computer Emergency Response Team (PruCert) 85
Prudential Insurance Company of America 82–86

Qualified Security Assessor (QSA) 186, 208, 236, 242
Quality Circle (QC) 26–27
Quik-Trak 26–27

Radio frequency identification (RFID) 8, 174
Rail Industry Security Committee (RISC) 187, 253
Ranum, Marcus 58
Reconnex 169–171, 176, 178–180
Red Hat Linux 45, 106, 109, 111, 125, 141
Regional Resiliency Assessment Program (RRAP) 209
Remote authentication dial-in user service (RADIUS) 115
Remote desktop protocol (RDP) 211, 239
Report on Compliance (ROC) 186
Republic of Egypt Information Center (PAIC) 67
Resource access control facility (RACF) 215
Risk Operating Management Analysis Network (ROMAN) 197–199, 201–203
Role-based access control (RBAC) 168, 174, 216, 257
Rowley, Tom 89–90

Sachs, Marcus 151
Santos, Ray 91
Schneier, Bruce 89
Schultz, Eugene 32
Secure Remote Area Network (SECRAN) 32, 34–36
Secure shell (SSH) 236
Secure sockets layer (SSL) 123, 125–126, 137, 235, 242
Security access manager (SAM) 114
Security Administrator Tool for Analyzing Networks (SATAN) 45, 65–66, 74
Security Assessment Report (SAR) 200–201
Security Operations Center (SOC) 89, 165, 208, 237
Counterpane 91–93
SBC outsource review 140–141
Amtrak SOC 248–250, 253
Security Operations Control Center (SOCC) 83, 85–86, 89
Service level agreement (SLA) 140, 168
Service set identifier (SSID) 114
Shimomura, Tsutomu 66–67, 89
simple mmail transfer protocol (SMTP) 119, 161, 282
simple network management protocol (SNMP) 43, 234, 236
Single sign-on (SSO) 213–215
Special Interest Group (SIG) 104
SSLDigger 166
Standard operating procedure (SOP) 218, 250
Stoll, Clifford 261
Structured query language (SQL) 8, 124, 154, 161, 229
Supervisory control and data acquisition (SCADA) 182, 186–188, 190–191, 193, 223
Symantec Endpoint Protection (SEP) 224
SysAdmin, Audit, Network, and Security Institute (SANS) 85, 135, 150–151
System security plan (SSP) 198–201
Systems network architecture (SNA) 7, 8, 259–260, 272

TEMPEST 22–24, 28, 46
Temporal key integrity protocol (TKIP) 115
Tivoli Directory Integrator (TDI) 158
Tivoli Directory Server (TDS) 158
ToneLoc 77–78, 81
Transaction processing facility (TPF) 191–192

Transmission control protocol (TCP) 7–9, 288, 291
Transmission control protocol/ internet protocol (TCP/IP) 7, 9, 41, 58, 264
Transport layer security (TLS) 87, 239, 242
Trivial file transfer protocol (TFTP) 239
Trusted Internet Connection (TIC) 200. 256

United States Government Accountability Office (US GAO) 76–77
United States – House Computer Emergency Response Team (US-HCERT) 65
United States House of Representatives 47–72
email investigation 55–56
United States Agency for International Development (US-AID) 67
Universal Resource Locator (URL) 120, 138, 145, 231, 243
Universal serial bus (USB) 178, 182

Venema, Weitse 45, 65
Veteran's Administration (VA) 76–79
Virtual private network (VPN) 125, 139, 178–179
Virtual telecommunications access method (VTAM) 259
Vulnerability management system (VMS) 241–242

Web Ferret 123
Westinghouse Plant Apparatus Division (WPAD) 6, 11, 13–41, 50, 97
Wide area network (WAN) 13, 33–36, 38–40
Wi-Fi Protected Access (WPA) 154
Windows 3.1 269
Windows NT 44, 86, 94, 114, 120
InfoWorld article 71
vulnerability testing 80
Hurricane Katrina 110, 114, 120, 269
lines of code 269
Windows XP 117, 154–155, 159–160, 242, 269
Wired equivalent privacy (WEP) 114–115
Wireless networking (Wi-Fi) 7, 114, 233–234, 238
Wireless Priority Service (WPS) 205
Woolley, Dan 75–76
WordPerfect 23–24, 41, 46
World Health Organization (WHO) 43

Year 2000 (Y2K) 7, 71, 74, 80, 83
Prudential response 85–87
Yoran, Amit 93–94, 134

Zenith Data Systems (ZDS) 23
Zwicky, Elizabeth 89–90, 92

For Product Safety Concerns and Information please contact our EU representative GPSR@taylorandfrancis.com
Taylor & Francis Verlag GmbH, Kaufingerstraße 24, 80331 München, Germany

www.ingramcontent.com/pod-product-compliance
Ingram Content Group UK Ltd.
Pitfield, Milton Keynes, MK11 3LW, UK
UKHW022216190926
475702UK00003B/394
9781041095460